TEAM PERFORMANCE IN HEALTH CARE

Issues in the Practice of Psychology

SERIES EDITOR:

George Stricker, *Derner Institute of Advanced Psychological Studies,
Adelphi University, Garden City, New York*

CLINICAL PERSPECTIVES ON ELDERLY SEXUALITY
Jennifer L. Hillman

TEAM PERFORMANCE IN HEALTH CARE:
ASSESSMENT AND DEVELOPMENT
Edited by Gloria D. Heinemann and Antonette M. Zeiss

HANDBOOK OF QUALITY MANAGEMENT IN BEHAVIORAL HEALTH
Edited by George Stricker, Warwick G. Troy, and Sharon A. Shueman

PSYCHOTHERAPY AND BUDDHISM: Toward an Integration
Jeffrey B. Rubin

A Continuation Order Plan is available for this series. A continuation order will bring delivery of each new volume immediately upon publication. Volumes are billed only upon actual shipment. For further information please contact the publisher.

TEAM PERFORMANCE IN HEALTH CARE
Assessment and Development

Edited by

Gloria D. Heinemann
Veteran's Affairs Western New York Healthcare System
Buffalo, New York

and

Antonette M. Zeiss
Veteran's Affairs Palo Alto Healthcare System
Palo Alto, California

Kluwer Academic / Plenum Publishers
New York, Boston, Dordrecht, London, Moscow

Library of Congress Cataloging-in-Publication Data

Team performance in health care: assessment and development/edited by Gloria D. Heinemann, Antonette M. Zeiss.
    p. cm. — (Issues in the practice of psychology)
  Includes bibliographical references and index.
  ISBN 0-306-46707-0
    1. Medical care—Miscellanea. 2. Teams in the workplace—Evaluation. 3. Medicine—Miscellanea. 4. Public health—Miscellanea. I. Heinemann, Gloria D. II. Zeiss, Antonette M., 1944– III. Series.

RA394 .T43 2002
362.1'068—dc21

2001038934

ISBN: 0-306-46707-0

©2002 Kluwer Academic / Plenum Publishers
233 Spring Street, New York, New York 10013

http://www.wkap.nl/

10 9 8 7 6 5 4 3 2 1

A C.I.P. record for this book is available from the Library of Congress

All rights reserved

No part of this book may be reproduced, stored in a retrieval system, or transmitted in any form or by any means, electronic, mechanical, photocopying, microfilming, recording, or otherwise, without written permission from the Publisher.

Printed in the United States of America

This volume is dedicated to Jan Hart Feazell, R.N., M.P.H., who initiated, advocated for, and provided resources to the Interprofessional Team Training and Development (ITT&D) Program within the Veterans Affairs (VA) system during her tenure as Deputy Dirctor, Office of Academic Affairs, VA Headquarters, Washington, DC. She was an unfailing source of inspiration and support for us and encouraged us in our efforts to develop, train, and improve health care teams.

FOREWORD

The idea of teamwork in health care emerged at several times during the 20th century as the result of shifts in the nature and demands of health care and societal needs. Examples include medical and surgical teams serving the military in World War II, primary care teams staffing Community Health Centers created by President Johnson's War On Poverty, and geriatric care teams established to serve the rapidly growing number of aging citizens. Collaborative teamwork surfaced as a rational solution to health care needs, but political and economic consensus to support widespread implementation was lacking. The increasing complexity of providing health care seemed best served by the skills and efforts of interdisciplinary teams, but such care was viewed as expensive so evaluation of its effectiveness became essential.

There were major problems in conducting such evaluation, however. First, no clear theory guided the concept and practice of teamwork. Early attempts to employ theoretical constructs explaining the behavioral and organizational phenomena of teamwork borrowed from theories of group dynamics, communication, organizational development, and general systems. Further, few reliable, validated instruments existed to evaluate team process, function, or effectiveness. The best early efforts at research and evaluation came from academic centers funded by the Office of Interdisciplinary Programs of the Bureau of Health Professions (1975-78) and from the Veterans Affairs' Interprofessional Team Training & Development Program. These programs emphasized training health professionals to function effectively as teams, and the goals and measures of assessment emphasized training rather than patient outcomes. Nor was cost a major consideration; these early interdisciplinary teams were mandated to provide services to the underserved and were not held to detailed evaluation of the process.

Hopefully, this brief introduction to past problems serves to highlight the enormous and long overdue accomplishments of the authors of "Team Performance in Health Care: Assessment and Development." At last we have a resource that defines a clear and detailed model of team performance and, equally important, provides a framework for critiquing and evaluating current and future performance assessment tools. The editors and authors perform the uniquely valuable service of defining the current state of the art in assessment of team performance, as well as suggesting directions for the future. As we enter a period of renewed interest in and use of health care teams, this careful and thorough analysis is both timely and necessary.

>DeWitt C. Baldwin Jr., MD
>Senior Fellow, Institute for Ethics and
>Scholar-in-Residence, American Medical Association
>*Chicago, IL*

This book appears at a propitious time for teamwork in health care. Recent reports from the Pew Health Professions Commission, the Institute of Medicine, and the President's Advisory Committee on Consumer Protection and Quality in the Health Care Industry focus attention on the importance of an interdisciplinary team approach in health care and the need to prepare health professionals to work together to improve the quality of health care. Other initiatives also suggest unparalleled interest in interdisciplinary practice and education, such as interdisciplinary training funded by the Kellogg, Hartford, and Robert Wood Johnson Foundations and reorganization of the Health Resources and Services Administration Bureau of Health Manpower to create a Division of Interdisciplinary Community-Based Programs.

Many health care factors converged to heighten interest in teams, including morbidity problems related to aging and lifestyle issues, interest in health promotion, models in which physicians are employees and part of a total system of care, and shortages of personnel in some disciplines requiring development of new relationships to preserve quality of care and control costs. The introduction of business models into health care, the quality/cost crisis, and the marriage between managed care and quality improvement have been critical factors as well. The interest in interdisciplinary practice is premised on the belief that such collaboration can improve the quality and cost of care, but there is scant, though developing, knowledge to support this belief. Lack of knowledge has been related to research and evaluation efforts that were short-term at best and often non-existent. To sustain commitment to interdisciplinary practice in an evidence-based environment, professional self-monitoring, systematic evaluation, and research are needed to establish the outcomes of interdisciplinary team care and the processes of care delivery. A lack of adequate instruments for team assessment has limited a stronger knowledge base; this limitation is addressed directly in this volume.

This book is a welcome, much needed contribution to methodology for self-monitoring, education, evaluation, and research in this important area at just the right time. The writers, Directors of the Veterans Affairs' Interprofessional Team Training & Development Program, pioneered interdisciplinary training for students and practitioners both in the VA system and the private sector, and they struggled with the limited instruments available to conduct their own research and program evaluations. We are grateful to them for their commitment to making future work a bit easier by compiling instruments to evaluate team process and performance and providing descriptions, critical evaluations, and a framework within which to organize them.

Madeline H. Schmitt, Ph.D., R.N., FAAN
Professor and Interdependence Chair in
Nursing and Interprofessional Education
University of Rochester
Rochester, NY

PREFACE

While we, as editors, took the lead on this book, it resulted from a collaborative effort of the 12 Directors of the Veterans Affairs' (VA's) Interprofessional Team Training and Development (ITT&D) Program. All of us work with teams because we value the collaboration and interdependence necessary for health professionals to provide quality treatment and care to patients with complex and/or chronic problems. Working together on this project provided an opportunity to pool our knowledge, skills, and experience. Not all ITT&D Directors could commit the same level of time and energy, but all were united in supporting and contributing to the project.

ITT&D is a clinically based educational program for VA employees and future health professionals/student trainees. Through didactic and experiential instruction, as well as clinical supervision and role modeling, the program fosters collaboration and interactive problem solving among professionals from diverse disciplines and promotes understanding of the roles and contributions all disciplines make in delivering care and services to patients. It also emphasizes evaluating quality of accomplishments and patients' responses to them.

A VA Headquarters initiative, the program began as the Interdisciplinary Team Training in Geriatrics (ITTG) Program to develop and improve teamwork in geriatrics. Programs opened between 1979 and 1983 in 12 VA medical centers–Birmingham, AL; Buffalo, NY; Coatesville, PA; Little Rock, AR; Madison, WI; Memphis, TN; Palo Alto, CA; Portland, OR; Salt Lake City, UT; Sepulveda, CA; Tampa, FL; and Tucson, AZ. Over the years, the name was changed to the Interdisciplinary Team Training Program (ITTP) to reflect a broader mission of serving all types of health care teams. The name changed a third time to the ITT&D Program to reflect more accurately the program's emphases on (a) collaboration among health professionals and (b) team development, consultation, education, assessment, and evaluation as well as training.

Through 1999, each host site had a Program Director and funding support for educational activities from the VA Office of Academic Affiliations. The program is a resource for team development, maintenance, and improvement at each host site, throughout the VA system, and in the private sector. It has provided leadership in interprofessional/interdisciplinary education and team development throughout the country.

Our purpose in writing this book is threefold. First, we saw a need for a conceptual model of team performance. Second, we saw a need for a compendium of multidimensional instruments measuring team performance. Third, we believed that present "best measures" should be identified, along with the issues related to measuring team performance in the future. In this volume, we address clinical heath care teams, natural work groups, quality improvement teams, committees, and task forces made up of employees in health care settings.

We are grateful to Fortune Kennedy, R.N., Ed.D., Office of Academic Affiliations, Veterans Affairs Headquarters, Washington, DC, who became our program liaison after the retirement of Jan H. Feazell. Fortune provided much needed encouragement and resources for face-to-face working sessions as the project developed. The ITT&D Program Directors took time from busy schedules to collect, review, and evaluate instruments measuring team performance. We shared our experiences developing and adapting instruments for use with health care teams and using them in education, consultation, and research settings. Small groups of Directors met to brainstorm about the conceptual dimensions of team performance and provided feedback on our team performance model.

We want to thank Dean Clyde Willis and his staff at Bowling Green State University, Toledo, Ohio, for providing conference room space prior to the annual interdisciplinary health care team conferences for our meetings and discussions regarding this project and for presentation time on the formal program of this conference.

Finally, we owe a debt of gratitude to ITT&D trainees and consultants who assisted us on this project. Four individuals deserve special thanks. First, we are deeply indebted to Sara A. Brallier, Ph.D., who assisted us on almost every facet of this project during the time she was an ITT&D consultant, VA Western New York Healthcare System, and graduate student in the Department of Sociology, University at Buffalo, SUNY. We also appreciate the editing of Kenneth Olson, M.A., Education Specialist at the VA Medical Center, Portland, OR, and the helpful insights of Renata Szczepanski, Ph.D., former psychology intern and ITT&D trainee at the VA Palo Alto Health Care System. Melanie Fox, undergraduate student at Coastal Carolina University, assisted us with the indexing and references.

Gloria D. Heinemann, Ph.D.
Buffalo, NY

Antonette M. Zeiss, Ph.D.
Palo Alto, CA

EDITORS

Gloria D. Heinemann, Ph.D. is Director of the Interprofessional Team Training and Development (ITT&D) Program and the Primary Care Education (PRIME) Program at the VA Western New York Healthcare System, Buffalo, NY. She is a clinical faculty member in the School of Medicine, University at Buffalo, State University of New York (SUNY). A sociologist and social gerontologist, Dr. Heinemann received her Ph.D. from the University of Illinois in Chicago. She is President, Past Treasurer, and a Charter Fellow of the Association for Gerontology in Higher Education; she serves as a member of The Gerontological Society of America's Executive Committee and the North American Editorial Board of the *Journal of Interprofessional Care*. She also is a Past-President and Past-Treasurer of the State Society on Aging of New York. Her research, scholarly interests, and publications are in the areas of interdisciplinary health care teams, aging and health, widowhood and coping with loss of spouse, and support systems of older persons.

Antonette M. Zeiss, Ph.D. is Clinical Coordinator and Director of Training in the Psychology Service at the VA Palo Alto Health Care System, Palo Alto, CA. She was Director of the ITT&D Program there from 1983 to the summer of 1998. Dr. Zeiss received her Ph.D. in clinical psychology from the University of Oregon. She is a clinical faculty member at the Stanford University School of Medicine, a Fellow of Division 12 (Clinical Psychology) of the American Psychological Association (APA), and a Charter Fellow of the American Psychological Society. She is Past-President of the Association for Advancement of Behavior Therapy, Past-President of the Section on Clinical Geropsychology (Section II, Division 12) of the APA, and a member of the North American Editorial Board of the *Journal of Interprofessional Care*. Her research, scholarly interests, and publications are in the areas of treatment of depression in the elderly, sexual function and treatment of dysfunction, and processes in interprofessional teamwork.

LIST OF CONTRIBUTORS

Sara A. Brallier, Ph.D., Assistant Professor, Department of Sociology, Coastal Carolina University, Conway, SC.

Charles P. Broderick, Ph.D., Crenshaw Street, Visalia, CA.

Glenda F. Brown, N.P., Ed.D., Chief, Interprofessional Education, VA Central Arkansas Healthcare System, Little Rock.

Carla Corral, Ph.D., Postdoctoral Fellow, Stanford Center for Research in Disease Prevention, Stanford University School of Medicine.

Alice M. DeFriese, Ph.D., R.N.C., Associate Chief of Staff for Education, VA Northern California Health Care System–Sacramento, Mather, CA.

Theresa J.K. Drinka, Ed.D. President, River's Edge Consulting, Waupaca, WI.

Patricia L. Evans, M.S., Professor, Division of Social Sciences, Department of Human Services, Niagara County Community College, Sanborn, NY.

D. Erik Everhart, Ph.D., Assistant Professor, Department of Psychology, East Carolina University, Greenville, NC.

Elizabeth Fox, M.S.N., Director (retired), ITT&D Program, VA Medical Center, Birmingham, AL.

Terry Fulmer, R.N., Ph.D., F.A.A.N., Professor/Director of The Muriel and Virginia Pless Center for Nursing Research, New York University, School of Education, Division of Nursing, NYC.

Stephen K. Harmon, Ph.D., Director, ITT&D Program, VA Medical Center, Salt Lake City, UT.

Gloria D. Heinemann, Ph.D., Director, ITT&D/PRIME Programs, VA Western New York Healthcare System, Buffalo, NY.

Carrie L. Hill, M.A., Psychology Intern, VA Western New York Healthcare System, Buffalo, NY.

Stephanie B. Hoffman, Ph.D., Director, ITT&D/PRIME Programs, James A. Haley VA Medical Center, Tampa, FL.

Kathryn Hyer, Dr.P.A., M.P.P., Director, Aging Training Academy, Florida Policy Exchange Center on Aging, University of South Florida, Tampa, FL.

Kimberly D. Kalish, M.A., Applied Behavioral Sciences Specialist, Continuing Developmental Services, Fairport, NY.

Julia Kasl-Godley, Ph.D., Postdoctoral Fellow, VA Palo Alto Health Care System, Palo Alto, CA.

Steven Lovett, Ph.D., Director, ITT&D Program, VA Palo Alto Health Care System, Palo Alto, CA.

Evelyn P. Mahairas, Ph.D., Director, ITT&D Program, VA Medical Center, Coatesville, PA.

Charlotte C. Malone, M.A., Speech Writer, Navy Recruiting Command, Millington, TN.

Thomas F. Miller, Ph.D., Director, Quality Management, Wm. S. Middleton VA Medical Center, Madison, WI.

Carole Morrell, R.N., M.S., Staff Development Coordinator, VA Northern California Health Care System–Sacramento, Mather, CA.

Linda O. Nichols, Ph.D., Director, ITT&D Program, VA Medical Center, Memphis, TN.

Amy L. Noe, Ph.D., Psychology Resident, Buffalo General Hospital, Buffalo, NY.

Ruth Ann Tsukuda, M.P.H., Associate Director, Parkinson's Disease Research Education and Clinical Center, VA Medical Center, Portland, OR.

Martha S. Waite, M.S.W., Director, ITT&D Program, VA Greater LA Healthcare System, Ambulatory Care Center & Nursing Home, Sepulveda, CA.

Antonette M. Zeiss, Ph.D., Clinical Coordinator and Director of Training, Psychology Service, VA Palo Alto Health Care System, Palo Alto, CA.

TABLE OF CONTENTS

Part I: Conceptualizing Model and Measurement

Chapter 1 Teams in Health Care Settings
Gloria D. Heinemann 3

Chapter 2 Measuring Team Performance in Health Care Settings
Antonette M. Zeiss 19

Chapter 3 A Model of Team Performance
Gloria D. Heinemann and Antonette M. Zeiss 29

Chapter 4 Organizational and Team Structure
Sara A. Brallier and Ruth Ann Tsukuda 43

Chapter 5 Organizational and Team Context
Stephen K. Harmon, Sara A. Brallier, and Glenda F. Brown 57

Chapter 6 Team Process
Linda O. Nichols, Alice M. DeFriese, and Charlotte C. Malone 71

Chapter 7 Team Productivity
Martha S. Waite and Stephanie B. Hoffman 89

Part II: Reviewing and Evaluating Team Performance Instruments

Chapter 8   Critiquing and Summarizing Instruments
Sara A. Brallier, Steven Lovett, and Thomas F. Miller 115

Chapter 9   Focused Instruments
Ruth Ann Tsukuda 123

Chapter 10   Middle-Range Instruments
Stephanie B. Hoffman 169

Chapter 11   Broad-Spectrum Instruments
Martha S. Waite and Linda O. Nichols 209

Chapter 12   Full-Spectrum Instruments
Glenda F. Brown and Evelyn P. Mahairas 299

Chapter 13   Instruments for Health Care Teams
Glenda F. Brown and Martha S. Waite 359

Chapter 14   Assessment and Development: Now and in the Future
Steven Lovett, Antonette M. Zeiss, and Gloria D. Heinemann 385

Index 401

LIST OF TABLES

1.1 The Four Developmental Stages and Off-Diagonal Group Conditions 9

1.2 Stages of Group/Team Development and Leadership Styles 11

1.3 Stages of Group/Team Development and Informal Roles 12

3.1 Team Performance: Domains, Dimensions, and Elements 32

9.1 Summary of Focused Instruments 126

10.1 Summary of Middle-Range Instruments 172

11.1 Summary of Broad-Spectrum Instruments 212

12.1 Summary of Full-Spectrum Instruments 302

13.1 Instruments Developed for Health Care Teams 361

13.2 Instruments Adapted for Health Care Teams 362

13.3 Generic Instruments Used in Health Care Settings 364

13.4 Supplemental Instruments with Potential for Adaptation 365

14.1 State-of-the-Art Instruments 388

14.2 Honorable Mention Instruments 391

14.3 Team Performance Instruments by Dimensions Measured 396

TEAM PERFORMANCE
IN HEALTH CARE

PART I
CONCEPTUALIZING MODEL AND MEASUREMENT

CHAPTER 1
TEAMS IN HEALTH CARE SETTINGS

Gloria D. Heinemann, Ph.D.
VA Western New York Healthcare System, Buffalo, NY, VISN 2

The delivery of health care and services via a team approach occurred throughout the twentieth century. As medical specialties developed in the early 1900s, physicians viewed the team approach as a mechanism for coordinating the medical specialties and for keeping lines of communication open between specialists and general practitioners. In the 1930s, nurses began to advocate for the team approach in hospital settings as a means of coordinating the efforts of growing numbers of health professionals and health workers employed there. By the mid 1900s, teams were providing care to chronically ill patients in such areas as home care, mental health, and rehabilitation. President Johnson's Great Society and War on Poverty Programs of the 1960s gave impetus to teamwork delivered in community-based, primary care settings to poor and under-served, urban populations.

Personnel shortages, especially among highly trained health professionals, resulted in federal funding for training students in the interdisciplinary team approach to care in the 1970s. In the late 1970s and early 1980s, the Department of Veterans Affairs (VA) launched its Interdisciplinary Team Training in Geriatrics (ITTG) Program. The scope of ITTG eventually expanded beyond geriatrics, and later it was renamed, accordingly, the Interprofessional Team Training and Development (ITT&D) Program. Also during the 1980s, the Bureau of Health Professions began awarding Geriatric Education Center and Rural Health initiative grants to schools and consortia of health sciences programs in universities throughout the country. The purpose of these grants is to teach collaboration and teamwork to medical and health professionals working in geriatrics and to students serving rural populations, respectively. The Joint Commission on the Accreditation of Healthcare Organizations (JCAHO, 1998, 1999) also requires that patients' care plans, especially those for older patients be interdisciplinary in nature (i.e., show how health professionals collaborate and utilize a team approach in delivering treatment and care to patients).

Beginning in the 1990s, primary care teams, primary care geriatric teams, and managed care teams proliferated as health care became focused more and more on healthy lifestyles, disease prevention, and care based in ambulatory rather than inpatient settings. Both federal and private sector funds have provided training in the team approach to health care for medical and health professional students [e.g., the VA's Primary Care Education (PRIME) Program, the Hartford Foundation-funded Geriatric Interdisciplinary Team Training (GITT) Program, and the Robert Wood Johnson-funded Collaborative Interprofessional Team Education (CITE) Initiative]. Also as a result of cost-cutting and cost-saving pressures and JCAHO standards, many health care organizations began implementing performance improvement [often referred to as continuous quality improvement (CQI) or total quality improvement (TQI)] teams to improve the organization and delivery of health care. A more detailed history of health care teams is documented in the literature (see Baldwin, Jr., 1996; Nagi, 1975; Schmitt, 1982; Tsukuda, 1998).

As we move into the twenty-first century, the team approach to health care is continuing to enjoy favor as a result of the reorganization of health care and restructuring of health care organizations analogous to businesses. In today's hospitals, the team approach is evident not only in clinical settings, but also throughout all levels of the organization (e.g., care lines, management teams, natural work groups, and performance improvement teams). JCAHO standards, requiring that hospitals have a performance improvement process in place (i.e., a CQI/TQI program), ensure the use of these types of teams on a continuing basis in health care settings.

Health care teams of today and tomorrow must learn to adapt to new expectations, new technologies, and increasing demands for quality performance. Documentation of team performance and outcomes of team care are becoming more data driven and much more of an expectation within the health care organization's culture. The proliferation of various types of teams functioning simultaneously throughout a hospital, coupled with the downsizing of health care employees, presents hospital managers with the challenge of balancing the time employees spend serving on different types of teams. That is, employees' day-to-day job responsibilities in their respective clinical teams or natural work groups should not suffer because they are serving on several other task forces, committees, or problem solving teams as part of collateral duty assignments.

In this chapter, we describe the types of teams currently functioning in health care settings and the components of a well performing team. We also provide a rationale for the team approach, discuss when its use is appropriate, identify levels of team functioning, and differentiate between poorly and well functioning teams. Finally, we explore ways to assess, monitor, and improve performance in teams. At the end of the chapter, we explain the organization of this volume.

HEALTH CARE TEAMS

A variety of different types of teams exist within health care settings. Interprofessional clinical teams provide care and services to patients in both acute and chronic care settings; management teams set policy and provide organizational leadership; natural work groups are responsible for one or more specific functions within a health care organization. Additionally, short-term quality improvement teams, committees, and task forces are organized around specific issues, needs, and problems requiring attention from major system inefficiencies and breakdown to planning recognition and rewards ceremonies for employees.

Interprofessional Clinical Teams

The Department of Veterans Affairs has been a leader in the use of the team approach in health care. Within the VA health care system, the clinical team is made up of a core team that includes members from nursing, medicine, and social work plus a variety of extended team members, determined by the needs of the client or patient population the team is serving. For example, audiologists, chaplains, dentists, dietitians, occupational/physical therapists, optometrists, pharmacists, podiatrists, psychologists, recreation/music therapists, and speech pathologists often serve as members of teams, either full-time, part-time, or in a consultant capacity. Some teams include various types of support personnel (e.g., technicians, aides, clerical staff) and volunteers. At times, the patient and his or her family caregiver also may be included as members of the team.

In summary, the clinical team is made up of medical and health professionals from at least three different disciplines or professions, who share a common purpose and work together collaboratively and interdependently to serve a specific patient/client population and achieve the team's and the organization's goals and objectives. When this type of team functions well, team experts refer to it as an "interdisciplinary" or "interprofessional" team.

Naturally Occurring Work Groups

Apart from the clinical teams, collaboration and interdependence are requirements among other work groups in health care organizations. Naturally occurring work groups can be found at many levels of the organization from management to front-line employees. Management or leadership teams include employees in upper level management [e.g., the Chief Executive Officer (CEO), care line managers or chiefs of departments/services within the organization] and coordinators of special functions (e.g., public relations, education, research). Section leaders and supervisors within care lines also may be included at times.

Other naturally occurring work groups include employees responsible for the operation of a specific inpatient unit (e.g., nurse manager, nursing staff, and volunteers) or a specific function within the organization. For example, the naturally occurring work group in "acquisitions and materials management" might include: (a) employees who serve as purchasing agents and technicians, materials handlers, accounting technicians, and voucher auditors and (b) employees who process, stock, and decontaminate equipment or work in receiving, storage, and distribution. The group usually includes one or more immediate supervisors as well. Other examples of naturally occurring work groups in many large hospitals are engineering, environmental management, fiscal, food service, and medical records.

Members of well functioning work groups cooperate and work together efficiently with minimal direction from an outside supervisor. The group is self-managed; the employees in a particular group take responsibility for the group's scheduling, assignments, work, and outcomes. Managers and supervisors serve as coaches and mentors in facilitating further growth and development of these employees and the work group as a whole.

Performance Improvement Teams

Performance improvement teams (e.g., CQI or TQI teams, also referred to as design teams, assessment teams, organizational improvement teams, and process-action teams) include employees convened around organizational processes or systems problems. Such teams might address how to improve work processes or how to change processes associated with the organization's culture or infrastructure. Some teams assess how well an organization or a specific process is functioning. Performance improvement teams within a hospital also might address the design and implementation of a primary care program, integration of several health care facilities into one facility, patients' access to and timeliness receiving specialty care, patients' satisfaction with care and treatment, and improving services to patients.

Employees–professional, paraprofessional, and nonprofessional–from any level of the organization might serve together on a performance improvement team if they are experiencing the problem in question, are involved in the related process, or have ideas, skills, or expertise that would help improve the process or resolve the problem. Research findings indicate that these teams need clearly focused goals and deliverables for which they are held accountable. The work they accomplish should be treated as part of team members' core jobs (Mohrman, Cohen, & Mohrman, 1995). In order to maximize success, their charter should specify to whom they report and include a clear statement of the task and the authority delegated to them to implement changes. These teams use a multi-phase approach. First, members attempt to understand the process or problem in question; next they identify causes by analyzing the process or problem via data collection and customer feedback, and finally they make recommendations for improvement through an implementation plan. These teams are time-limited and usually disband once they implement a plan of action, determine its effectiveness, and refine it as necessary (Scholtes, 1988; U.S. Department of Veteran Affairs, 1996).

Rationale for the Team Approach

The team approach to health care is most useful when issues, needs, and problems are complex, chronic, and overlapping, and their resolution requires input from a variety of diverse perspectives. Input from several health professionals with different knowledge bases, skill levels, and value systems may be required for a satisfactory outcome. For example, consider a patient needing medication, but unable to afford the cost of filling the prescription. In a problem solving discussion around this issue, the pharmacist might recommend a less expensive, generic alternative be prescribed. The physician might provide the patient with a month's supply of samples he or she obtained from a pharmaceutical company, or the social worker might identify a new funding source for medications for which the patient is eligible. When employees depend upon one another to accomplish a task or resolve a problem, teamwork is essential. Under these circumstances, the team approach increases efficiency as a result of less duplication and fragmentation of effort, increases cost-effectiveness, and improves quality of care and services to customers (e.g., patients/clients and their caregivers). A major assumption underlying the rationale for the team approach is that the team itself is well functioning.

Team Development and Functioning

The most commonly used framework for understanding team functioning or performance is stages of small group or team development (Bennis & Shepard, 1956; Bion, 1961; Farrell, Heinemann, & Schmitt, 1986; Gibb, 1964; Jones, 1973; Jones & Bearley, 1994; Kormanski, 1985; Kormanski & Mozenter, 1987; Schutz, 1982; Tuckman, 1965; Tuckman & Jenson, 1977; Wheelan,

1993; Yalom, 1970). According to this framework, teams move through at least four sequential stages: (a) testing and dependency or "forming;" (b) conflict or "storming;" (c) cohesion and consensus or "norming;" and (d) functional role relatedness or "performing." Teams designed to address and resolve short-term issues (e.g., CQI/TQI teams) also go through a fifth stage, termination, disengagement, or "adjourning" (Tuckman, 1965; Tuckman & Jenson, 1977; Wheelan, 1993).

Movement through the stages of development is not always a linear progression. Kormanski (1990) found three patterns of development among freshman academic teams: (a) progression–increasing development or maturation; (b) regression or decline in maturation; and (c) a varied pattern of increasing and decreasing maturation. In health care, teams frequently experience the latter pattern, often labeled the "roller coaster" development of teams as both external and internal factors impact them and affect their maturation and performance levels. Jones and Bearley (1993, 1994) developed a four-by-four table depicting the predictable stages of development that result from the interaction of two behavioral dimensions, task behaviors (i.e., orientation, organization, open data flow, and problem solving) and process behaviors (i.e., dependency, conflict, cohesion, and interdependence). Teams that move through these two dimensions at approximately the same pace develop along the four diagonals or through the four stages of development identified in the previous paragraph from immature group to effective, synergistic team. Teams whose task and process behaviors do not progress at the same pace are characterized as "off diagonal." For example, a team at the conflict level of process behaviors and the interdependence level of task behaviors is characterized as "issue-oriented polarization." A team exhibiting interdependent process behavior with open data flow (task behavior) is characterized as "supportive with good communication," although it may not problem solve well and, therefore, might have questionable outcomes (see Table 1.1).

Multidisciplinary Versus Interdisciplinary Teams

Too often the terms, multidisciplinary and interdisciplinary, are used interchangeably to describe teams. In reality, multidisciplinary teams are less well developed than interdisciplinary teams. Schmitt (1982) characterized members of a multidisciplinary team as working in a parallel or sequential manner; that is, members tend to wear discipline-specific blinders and work in isolation from one another. They often communicate, but rarely collaborate. In contrast, a well functioning team in the fourth stage of development is interdisciplinary in that all members participate in the team's activities, share leadership, and rely on one another to accomplish goals. They attend to both task-oriented goals (i.e., goals related to their mission and purpose) and process goals (i.e., goals related to interpersonal relationships among team members, group processes, and improving team functioning). Members of interdisciplinary teams achieve their goals through "a complex integration or synthesis of various ... perspectives" (Schmitt, 1982, p. 183).

Table 1.1. The Four Developmental Stages and Off-Diagonal Group Conditions

Process Behaviors	Orientation	Organization	Open Data Flow	Problem Solving
Interdependence	"Flying Circus" Free Expression of Feelings	Flexibility Negotiating	Supportive Good Communication	**Stage IV** Effective Team
Cohesion	Tightly Knit Trust "We-ness"	Harmony Cooperation	**Stage III** Sharing Group	Ownership Safety
Conflict	Resistance Leadership Struggle Disagreement	**Stage II** Fractionated Group	Encounter Task-Oriented Confrontation	Issue-Oriented Polarization
Dependency	**Stage I** Immature Group	Inefficiency Search for Procedures	Telling-Asking One-Way Communication	Experting Leader-Centered Decision-Making

Task Behaviors

SOURCE: From *Group Development Assessment* ©1993 John E. Jones, Ph.D., & William L. Bearley, Ed.D. Reproduced with the permission of Organization Design and Development, Inc., King of Prussia, PA.

Leadership in Teams

In most clinical health care teams, leadership comes from within the team, or in matrix models, team members are accountable to leadership within the team and a supervisor within their respective professions outside the team. In many natural work groups, leadership comes from a supervisor outside the group unless the employees have been trained and are expected to function as self-directed or self-managed work teams. CQI/TQI team leaders usually comes from within the team; they can be either appointed by management or selected by team members.

Positions of leadership can be either formal or informal. Some team programs have officially or formally designated leadership positions that come as part of the team package. In other teams, leadership is informal in that a team member may designate him/herself as leader or team members come to an agreement about which member will serve as leader. Newly developing teams (stages one or two) often have only one or sometimes two leaders. Better performing teams (stages three or four) share leadership among members based upon the need for specific kinds of expertise needed at a given point in time.

Leadership can be both task-oriented and socioemotional or relationship-oriented. According to Bennis and Nanus (1985), teams benefit from both types of leadership. The task-oriented leader employs skills required to accomplish the team's goals and objectives and to move the team through each stage of development (i.e., the leader facilitates improving team performance); the relationship-oriented leader influences and inspires individual team members to work up to their potential at each stage of development.[1]

Several team experts have noted that the stages of development produce and/or require different styles of leadership. Kormanski (1985) and Kormanski and Mozenter (1987) linked the development of team leaders with the development of teams themselves. According to their model, the team, as it moves through the stages of development, requires a different leadership style from the leader in order to maximize performance at each stage (see Table 1.2). The appropriate leadership style at any particular stage of development depends upon members' readiness level. For example, in a newly developing team (stage one), members are inexperienced and hesitant to become involved (i.e., a low level of readiness). Such a situation requires a directive or "telling" leadership style, characterized by high task and low relationship behavior on the part of the leader. In contrast, a team in the performing or fourth stage of development requires a "delegating" leadership style in which the leader exhibits low task and low relationship behavior since its members are experienced and willing (i.e., a high level of readiness).

In similar fashion, Jones and Bearley (1994) state that leadership demands differ across the four developmental stages. In the immature group, the leader must provide structure and help members establish norms. This requires the leader to clarify tasks to the group, provide members with the proper perspective, and be sensitive to their dependency needs. In contrast, at the optimal stage of development, the leader's role should shift to one of participant, consultant, and inspirer by providing the team with vision, challenging it toward excellence, and providing the support it needs to maximize its functioning.

---

[1] These definitions of task-oriented and relationship-oriented leadership parallel yet differ from the definitions of task-oriented goals and process goals in the previous section. In the previous section, facilitating a team's progress through the stages of development is considered a process function rather than a task function. And the definition of process goals is broader than the one for relationship-oriented leadership given by Bennis and Nanus.

Farrell, Heinemann, and Schmitt (1986) also linked leadership styles with stages of team development. Through content analysis of videotapes of weekly team meetings, they identified informal roles assumed by leaders that are specific to the early stages of development. For example, in a newly developing team, the leader might take the role of Wonder Woman or Superman, a leader who is task-oriented, extremely competent in his/her professional role, and very

Table 1.2. Stages of Group/Team Development and Leadership Styles

Stage of Group Development	Group/Team Development Theme	Situational Leadership Style	Group/Team Leader's Behavior	Followers' Readiness Behavior
Stage 1. Forming	Awareness	Telling	High task, low relationship	Inexperienced and hesitant
Stage 2. Storming	Conflict	Selling	High task, high relationship	Inexperienced and willing
Stage 3. Norming	Cooperation	Participating	Low task, high relationship	Experienced and hesitant or lacking confidence
Stage 4. Performing	Productivity	Delegating	Low task, low relationship	Experienced and willing
Stage 5. Adjourning	Separation	Participating	Low task, high relationship	Experienced and hesitant

SOURCE: From Kormanski, C., & Mozenter, A. A new model of team building: A technology for today and tomorrow (p. 262). In J.W. Pfeiffer (Ed.), *The 1987 annual: Developing human resources.* San Diego, CA: University Associates ©1987. Reprinted by permission of Jossey-Bass, Inc., a subsidiary of John Wiley & Sons, Inc.

enthusiastic. This particular style is beneficial to the team short-term, but if it persists too long, team members never "buy in" and become committed to the team. This is due to the intimidating leadership style of Wonder Woman or Superman. Additionally, the leader in this informal role often does not have the patience to allow enough time for others to "buy in" and comfortably assume responsibility. The Wonder Woman or Superman, reluctant to give up power, shoulders most of the team's responsibilities and eventually burns out. In contrast, as team members become more participatory and the team moves into the later stages of development, leadership is shared among team members, and they become characterized as a coalition of colleagues (see Table 1.3).

Table 1.3. Stages of Group/Team Development and Informal Roles

Stage of Development	Atmosphere	Structure	Informal Roles
Stage 1: Testing & Dependency (Forming)	Tense due to uncertainty & lack of mission/role clarity; members unwilling to take responsibility; commitment low	One leader & followers	Superman Wonder Woman Tyrant Reluctant Candidate Party Host Leader's Helper Wise Old Sage
Stage 2: Conflict (Storming)	High tension & hostility; negative feelings among members; majority remains unwilling to take responsibility	Traditional leader challenged by new leader; polarization of members around two leaders	Mom & Pop Hatchetman Clown Scapegoat Caring Ear
Stage 3: Cohesion & Consensus (Norming)	Heightened sense of solidarity & trust; team identity or "we" feeling develops among members; democracy & equal participation are emphasized	Coalition of colleagues	None
Stage 4: Functional Role Relatedness (Performing)	Members become interdependent & utilize one another on basis of leadership & professional skills/abilities; coordination & efficiency are stressed; open, honest problem solving	Coalition of colleagues	None

SOURCES: Farrell, M.P., Heinemann, G.D., & Schmitt, M.H. (1986). Informal roles, rituals, and styles of humor in interdisciplinary health care teams: Their relationship to stages of group development. *International Journal of Small Group Research, 2,* 143-162.

Heinemann, G.D. (1991). Informal roles as indicators of team development and functioning. In D. Farzan, D. Hanlon, P.A. Burns, S.S. Ditmar, & M.P. Stanton (Eds.), *Traumatic brain injury conference: Companion monograph for rehabilitation nurses* (pp. 91-100). Buffalo: University at Buffalo, SUNY.

Components of Effective Teamwork

Some authors have attempted to delineate the components of well performing teams. Heinemann and Garner (see Heinemann, 1994) identified 12 components of effective teamwork from communication, cooperation, cohesiveness, commitment, and collaboration among members to confronting problems directly, coordinating efforts, managing conflict, and making decisions via consensus, which at times requires some compromise. Other components include being consistent with and caring about one another and the customers served by the team. The final component is the feeling among members that they and the team itself are making a contribution. Larson and LaFasto (1989) acknowledged the importance of administrative support, regular team meetings, clear and realistic goals, competent team members, standards of excellence, leadership, a collaborative climate, a results-driven structure, continuing evaluation, and rewards and recognition. We expanded upon these components in developing a broad, multidimensional model of team performance, presented in Chapter 3.

The well performing team functions as a feedback system. Members of clinical teams assess the patients, identify their needs and problems, develop and implement individualized plans of care, conduct follow-up reviews to determine patients' outcomes, and modify the plans as needed (Ducanis & Golin, 1979). Nonclinical teams go through a similar series of activities as they identify and assess a problem, create an action plan, and review and refine it after an implementation period. The well functioning team carries out these activities for both task-oriented and process goals. Authors provide additional examples of this feedback system in Chapter 7 under "strategies for productivity."

Barriers to Quality Team Performance

Noise can disrupt this feedback system of the team due to barriers to quality performance. Barriers can be identified at any of three levels–the organization in which the team works, the team itself, or individual team members. For example, at the organizational level, managers might not understand the team approach and, as a result, might not provide appropriate resources to the team. At the team level, members might not clarify their roles vis-à-vis one another or might neglect to develop rules and procedures for operating. At the level of the individual, some team members might compete with others and become involved in "turf" battles rather than cooperating and working together. If teams are to minimize and/or eliminate barriers to their effective functioning, their members must be able to identify what kind of barrier is limiting them. One of the most effective ways to overcome these barriers is to develop strategies for continuously assessing and monitoring team functioning or performance.

ASSESSING TEAM PERFORMANCE

Assessing team performance is important in health care since it directly and indirectly impacts both the quality of care provided to patients and the resulting patients' responses to care. Outcomes of health care teams often are more complex and diverse than outcomes of teams in business or other settings, in part, because people rather than products are the focus of effort. For example, some outcomes of clinical teams involve the patients' health status (e.g., cure, improvement, maintenance, slowed decline, and death with dignity). These outcomes are emotionally charged for both care providers and patients since they strongly impact quality of life and life, itself. This emotional investment leads to another set of team outcomes, satisfaction of customers (e.g., patients, their family members, team members, members of other teams, and other employees). These outcomes also serve as an indirect measure of the quality of care and services provided to both patients and their informal care providers (e.g., family members). Assessing performance in health care teams also is unique given the interprofessional nature of clinical teams. Having highly educated professionals–some whose professions have more status than others in teams–has special implications for the quality of certain team processes (e.g., leadership, power, cooperation, and conflict) and the quality of team functioning. Therefore, the assessment of team performance becomes critical.

Education and data collection are key elements in assessing team performance. Team members must learn how to "step outside the team" and evaluate its performance objectively. In educational workshops, this can be accomplished by gradually building participants into teams through experiential exercises and having them evaluate their processes and outcomes. Critiquing participants in role playing exercises, having them identify strengths and weaknesses in pictures or cartoons of teams, and having them draw pictures of well functioning teams also facilitate the development of assessment skills. Quantitative instruments measuring team performance can be introduced in educational workshops to evaluate participants' experiential work together. Once team members feel comfortable critiquing the team as a working unit, they can begin to assess their own and one another's strengths and weaknesses as members of the team. Initially, an objective consultant should be present to help set ground rules for personal critiquing.

MONITORING AND IMPROVING TEAM PERFORMANCE

Team performance can be monitored and improved using either or both qualitative and quantitative strategies. Some teams schedule monthly or quarterly meetings in which members identify the team's strengths and weaknesses and discuss ways to improve performance. Consultants' observation of and feedback about team meetings, rounds, space, care plans, and general work patterns can be beneficial to teams. The consultant can facilitate a discussion about what the team does well and where and how it can improve.

Teams also use quantitative instruments (i.e., structured questionnaires that convert answers to numeric symbols for analysis) to monitor quality of functioning. Instruments used to measure health care team performance should take into account the unique culture of health care and the unique subcultures within health care organizations. Members can choose to collect information on overall team performance or focus more specifically on areas in which the team is experiencing problems. Usually they collect baseline data to compare to data collected at intervals over time. Here, too, discussion of findings and interventions facilitate improved performance. Findings provide consultants, team members, and upper level management with objective data about a team's effectiveness and improvement in its performance over time. Such data serve to inform managers when to reward teams for their accomplishments and when a team would benefit from additional consultation and education to improve its effectiveness. This volume focuses on quantitative instruments designed to assess team performance.

ORGANIZATION OF THE VOLUME

We have organized this volume into two parts. Part One is conceptual and theoretical. In Chapter 1, we described the team approach to health care, the types of teams found in health care settings, the characteristics of effective teams, and strategies for monitoring and assessing team performance. Measuring team performance is the focus of Chapter 2; it includes a rationale for such measurement, our rationale for focusing on multidimensional instruments in this volume, inclusion criteria for the instruments, and general measurement issues. In Chapter 3, we describe our model of team performance as it relates to recent changes in the health care system. It includes an overview of the four domains of performance–structure, context, process, and productivity. Also included are the eight dimensions within the four domains: (a) organizational structure and team structure; (b) organizational context and team context; (c) interdependence and growth and development; and (d) strategies for productivity and actual accomplishments. In Chapters 4 through 7, we present the elements within each dimension of team performance. The elements of structure are the focus of Chapter 4. Chapters 5 and 6 address the elements of context and process, respectively. Chapter 7 focuses on the elements of productivity.

Part Two of the book is methodological, and in it we discuss and critique the multidimensional measures of team performance that met our inclusion criteria for this volume. We also discuss measurement issues, developing and adapting instruments for use with health care teams, "best measures," and future directions for measuring team performance. In Chapter 8, we present an overview of the types of instruments in this volume, the guidelines and criteria for critiquing them, and how we have summarized them. In Chapter 9, we present the focused instruments, those measuring one to three dimensions of team performance. In Chapter 10, we present the middle-range instruments, those measuring four dimensions of performance, and in Chapter 11, we present the broad-spectrum instruments, those measuring five to six dimensions of performance. Chapter 12 includes the full-spectrum instruments; these instruments measure seven to eight performance dimensions. Each of these four chapters begins with an overview of the respective group of instruments followed by a summary table and the critiques.

In Chapter 13, we address the instruments developed or adapted for use in health care settings, generic instruments frequently used in health care settings, and instruments that can be used in conjunction with team performance measures or that have potential for adaptation as team performance measures. Finally, in Chapter 14, we identify the "best measures" of team performance along with the criteria and rationale for their selection. We also address future measurement of team performance as health care organizations, teams, and technologies change. Finally, we discuss how our model of team performance can be used to enhance education and consultation with teams and help them improve their own self-monitoring and evaluation.

REFERENCES

Baldwin, Jr., D.C. (1996). Some historical notes on interdisciplinary and interprofessional education and practice in health care in the U.S. *Journal of Interprofessional Care, 10*, 2, 175-187.

Bennis, W.G., & Nanus, B. (1985). *Leaders: The strategies for taking charge.* New York: Harper & Row.

Bennis, W.G., & Shepard, H.A. (1956). A theory of group development. *Human Relations, 9*, 415-437.

Bion, W.R. (1961). *Experiences in groups.* New York: Basic Books.

Ducanis, A.J., & Golin, A.K. (1979). *The interdisciplinary health care team: A handbook.* Germantown, MD: Aspen Publications.

Farrell, M.P., Heinemann, G.D., & Schmitt, M.H. (1986). Informal roles, rituals and styles of humor in interdisciplinary health care teams: Their relationship to stages of group development. *International Journal of Small Group Research, 2*, 143-162.

Gibb, J.R. (1964). Climate for trust. In L.P. Bradford, J.R. Gibb, & K.D. Benne (Eds.), *T-group theory and laboratory method: Innovations in re-education.* New York: John Wiley.

Heinemann, G.D. (1991). Informal roles as indicators of team development and functioning. In D. Farzan, D. Hanlon, P.A. Burns, S.S. Dittmar, & M.P. Stanton (Eds.), *Traumatic brain injury conference: Companion monograph for rehabilitation nurses* (pp. 91-100). Buffalo, NY: State University of New York.

Heinemann, G.D. (1994). Geriatric and primary care: Models for interdisciplinary team training. In E.M. Bobby (Ed.), *Making the team work: Proceedings of the 2nd congress of health professions educators* (pp. 81-92). Washington, DC: Association of Academic Health Centers.

Joint Commission on Accreditation of Healthcare Organizations. (1998). *Comprehensive accreditation manual for long-term care.* Oakbrook Terrace, IL: Author.

Joint Commission on Accreditation of Healthcare Organizations. (1999). *Comprehensive accreditation manual hospitals.* Oakbrook Terrace, IL: Author.

Jones, J.E. (1973). A model of group development. In J.E. Jones & J.W. Pfeiffer (Eds.), *The 1973 annual handbook for group facilitators* (pp. 127-129). San Diego, CA: University Associates.

Jones, J.E., & Bearley, W.L. (1993). *Group Development Assessment.* King of Prussia, PA: Organization Design and Development, Inc.

Jones, J.E., & Bearley, W.L. (1994). *Group Development Assessment: Facilitator guide.* King of Prussia, PA: Organization Design and Development, Inc.

Kormanski, C. (1985). A situational leadership approach to groups using the Tuckman model of group development. In L.D. Goodstein & J.W. Pfeiffer (Eds.), *The 1985 annual: Developing human resources* (pp. 217-226). San Diego, CA: University Associates.

Kormanski, C. (1990). Team building patterns of academic groups. *The Journal for Specialists in Group Work, 15,* 206-214.

Kormanski, C., & Mozenter, A. (1987). A new model of team building: A technology for today and tomorrow. In J.W. Pfeiffer (Ed.), *The 1987 annual: Developing human resources* (pp. 255-268). San Diego, CA: University Associates.

Larson, C.E., & LaFasto, F.M. (1989). *Teamwork: What must go right/What can go wrong.* Newbury Park, CA: Sage Publications, Inc.

Mohrman, S.A., Cohen, S.G., & Mohrman, A.M. (1995). *Designing team-based organizations: New forms for knowledge work.* San Francisco: Jossey-Bass.

Nagi, S.Z. (1975). Teamwork in health care in the U.S.: A sociological perspective. *The Milbank Memorial Fund Quarterly, 53* (Winter), 75-91.

Schmitt, M.H. (1982). Working together in health care teams. In E.H. Janosik & L.B. Phipps (Eds.), *Life cycle group work in nursing* (pp.179-198). Monterey, CA: Wadsworth Health Sciences Division, A Division of Wadsworth, Inc.

Scholtes, P.R. (1988). *The team handbook: How to use teams to improve quality.* Madison, WI: Joiner Associates, Inc.

Schutz, W.D. (1982). *The Schutz measures: An integrated system for assessing elements of awareness.* San Diego, CA: University Associates.

Tsukuda, R.A. (1998). A perspective on health care teams and team training. In E.G. Siegler, K. Hyer, T. Fulmer, & M. Mezey (Eds.), *Geriatric interdisciplinary team training* (pp. 21-37). New York, NY: Springer Publishing Company.

Tuckman, B.W. (1965). Developmental sequences in small groups. *Psychological Bulletin, 63,* 384-399.

Tuckman, B.W., & Jensen, M.A.C. (1977). Stages of small group development revisited. *Group and Organizational Studies, 2,* 419-427.

Wheelan, S.A. (1993). *The Group Development Questionnaire: A manual for professionals.* Philadelphia, PA: GDQ Associates.

Yalom, I.D. (1970). *Team development manual.* New York: John Wiley & Sons.

U.S. Department of Veterans Affairs. (1996). *Team skills training guide: Total quality improvement.* Prepared under contract between the American Productivity and Quality Center (APQC) and the Veterans Health Administration. Houston, TX/St. Louis, MO: APQC/VA St. Louis Employee Education Center.

CHAPTER 2
MEASURING TEAM PERFORMANCE IN HEALTH CARE SETTINGS

Antonette M. Zeiss, Ph.D.
VA Palo Alto Health Care System, Palo Alto, CA, VISN 21

With the restructuring of the health care system and increased emphasis on performance improvement, health care teams are experiencing new demands as expectations for them change and evolve. Managers in health care organizations expect teams to utilize new technologies to communicate and document their activities (i.e., to be accountable for their levels of productivity and their outcomes). At the same time, they look to clinical teams to manage a greater number of patients with more diverse needs and increasingly complex health problems, and they expect members of natural work groups to collaborate more and depend less on outside supervision. Additionally, teams need to employ systems thinking and link their activities with other teams, units, and programs within the health care organization if the organization is to achieve its goals. Quality interactions across teams, as well as within teams, have become essential.

OBSTACLES TO MEASURING TEAM PERFORMANCE

In addition to the growing pressures on teams, management increasingly expects them to demonstrate that they are functioning efficiently and cost-effectively. In this environment, having tested and proven methodologies for assessing and evaluating team performance has become essential. A plethora of instruments is available, but numerous obstacles reduce the usefulness of many of them. First, many are proprietary, available only at considerable cost through consulting companies. In some cases, these companies require a broader consulting contract for training in the use of the instrument or having the company score, analyze, interpret, and present results. Second, the development of instruments has not been consistently reported in any standardized way. The non-proprietary approaches to assessment often have been passed along from team to team through informal personal contacts as a cottage industry. Finding the original source or the source of a revised version of an instrument can be difficult in some instances and impossible in others. Additionally, psychometric testing, conducted on an original instrument, may no longer be relevant to the version a team currently uses. Third, many of the instruments were developed for use in business or industry with limited application to health care settings. The instrument may be based on a relevant conceptual framework, but include items worded such that health care team members cannot respond to them meaningfully. Finally, the information that does exist about the development of instruments is scattered across numerous fields and disciplines in both published and unpublished literatures. Thus, for many instruments, it becomes arduous and time consuming to obtain information about their respective rationales for development, theoretical underpinnings, scoring instructions and templates, and data supporting reliability and validity.

The result of this state of instrument development is that teams confront numerous obstacles attempting to locate a well-established measure to assess and evaluate their performance or effectiveness. Team members or leaders must choose between instruments for purchase from proprietary consulting firms and those that have been informally modified over time and available through the grapevine. In either instance, little information about the instrument's quality and soundness is available to them, and they are unable to do any "comparative shopping" for the instrument that best serves their purposes.

We designed this volume to remedy some of these problems by compiling team performance instruments, which have specific or potential relevance to health care settings. We have critiqued these instruments and reviewed relevant data on their reliability, validity, and utility. Organizational managers, team members, and team consultants will be able to use this volume to select the most relevant measure for their purposes. In addition, we have attempted to expose gaps in the current literature and in the instruments themselves regarding the measurement of team performance. Researchers interested in team functioning and students of research methodology will see many possibilities for fruitful work to enhance the current state-of-the-art in developing and scaling team performance instruments.

CRITERIA FOR INCLUDING INSTRUMENTS

We decided to focus on multidimensional measures of team performance. With one exception, all of the instruments in this volume include at least two of the eight dimensions in our team performance model described in Chapter

3. We omitted instruments that measure only one facet of teamwork such as communication, leadership, interpersonal styles, or conflict and its management. Such measures may have particular utility for teams in the early stages of development or when a team is attempting to improve a specific aspect of its performance. We excluded these types of instruments because we are concerned with the need, in health care system of today and tomorrow, to assess comprehensively how well the members of a team are working together, how well the team is working within the organization, and how effective the team's outcomes are. We did include instruments that are measures of collaboration and meeting effectiveness. Collaboration includes numerous facets of working together and is a requisite for successful interdisciplinary teams. Conducting effective meetings is a very important accomplishment for teams and can influence the quality of other outcomes as well as productivity of the team. We also included two instruments that measure skills of team members and/or trainees since few instruments address this element within the dimension of growth and development. Thus, our focus is on instruments that attempt a comprehensive assessment of team performance per se or of some of its dimensions.

Limiting our focus did not result in a paucity of relevant measures. We identified 65 multidimensional instruments and one unidimensional one (i.e., measuring only one dimension of our model of team performance, described in Chapter 3). Some instruments were developed specifically for teams in health care settings. Others have been used with health care teams, either as originally developed or after some adaptation, and still others have potential for use with such teams.

Because there is no overarching conceptual/theoretical framework clearly specifying core dimensions of team performance, what the instruments actually measure varies considerably. Some reflect the idiosyncratic view of their respective developer(s), and few are truly comprehensive in addressing all the aspects of this concept. Most measures have particular areas of strength. Some cover the concept of performance in considerable breadth, while others address fewer aspects of performance, but cover them in greater depth. We return to a consideration of the comprehensiveness issue in the last chapter of this volume after providing a careful review and evaluation of each instrument.

FACTORS AFFECTING MEASUREMENT ISSUES

A number of factors are important in considering the potential value of team performance instruments and the resulting data, especially in health care settings. These include the nature of the assessment process itself, the level at which data are collected, and the standards and issues related to determining reliability and validity. Each of these factors is explored in more detail in the following sections.

Nature of the Assessment Process

The assessment process includes such issues as determining the eligibility of respondents (i.e., who should participate), using an appropriate data collection instrument, and establishing rapport with and the cooperation of respondents, which often requires ensuring confidentiality (Schutt, 1999).

Prior to data collection, the team's boundaries should be ascertained. When relevant team members are excluded from participating or refuse to participate, the ability to accurately measure team performance is compromised. Determining who should participate in the assessment of team performance is potentially challenging. Low status members of a team, such as nursing aides or clerical staff, may feel left out if not invited to participate. A decision to include such members should be based upon both their perceptions of themselves and other team members' perceptions of them as team members. If they are not an integral part of the team and its activities, their responses about the team's performance will be meaningless and will bias the data. In contrast, high status team members, such as physicians, sometimes decline to participate due to their busy schedules or their lack of understanding of the importance of the assessment. The payoff for the extra effort spent drawing them into the process is better quality data.

Including team members with different educational backgrounds raises issues about the complexity of the material in the instrument and its response format. The more education team members have, the higher their likely reading level, familiarity and comfort with test taking, and flexibility in using a variety of test formats. When less educated team members are included, it is especially important to check the reading level of the instrument and the complexity of the response format in order for them to respond meaningfully.

Establishing rapport with and gaining the cooperation of all team members are important antecedents to quality data collection (i.e., gaining an accurate picture of the team's performance). Team members should understand why they are engaging in an assessment of their team's performance. They also should have an investment in the resulting information. When team members actively participate in the decisions about what should be assessed and how the information will be used, they are more likely to cooperate and provide accurate information.

Too often management perceives a serious problem related to a team and brings in a consultant to deal with it. The consultant typically is an outsider who may be linked to a powerful manager embroiled in the problem. In this type of situation, defensive responses and lack of cooperation are not surprising. Management should not force members of a team to complete an assessment instrument; in such circumstances, they tend to provide the answers that they believe management wants to hear.

The assurance of confidentiality is another important issue in establishing rapport with and gaining the cooperation of team members. Members are often concerned about being identified and linked to the information they provide. For self-administered instruments, relevant issues include whether a name or Social Security number is requested on the instrument, who collects the completed instruments, and who has access to the information provided. Similarly, with observational instruments, team members often are concerned about whether their specific behaviors and statements are identifiable and whether their supervisors will have access to the information. The issue of confidentiality is especially relevant to teams in health care settings, given the downsizing of employees in health care organizations and, thus, the concern among employees about their job security.

All of these issues need to be considered and addressed in order to identify the eligible respondents or team members, establish rapport with them to gain their trust and cooperation; achieve an acceptable response rate, especially when using self-administered instruments; and maximize the quality of data collected.

Levels of Data Collection

The most comprehensive assessment of team performance would include information from multiple perspectives, including the self-reports of team members regarding their perceptions and experiences, observation of team members' interactions, and reports from others who are influenced by the team (e.g., patients, managers, supervisors, trainees). The goal is to obtain an overall understanding of the team's functioning or performance level. In reality, most instruments are self-administered (i.e., designed to be completed anonymously by individual team members). Often developers design instruments to collect team members' perceptions of their own experience on the team, their perceptions of other members, and/or the effectiveness of the team's efforts. Combining data collected from all team members provides these summary measures; however, such measures also can obscure important information about variability in the team. A few developers of instruments have recognized this and offer ways to report variability of team perceptions along with central tendencies. Even when developers do not offer such options, they can be employed when using the instruments, and in many of our critiques, we include suggestions for accomplishing this.

The use of self-administered instruments has developed as the dominant approach to the assessment of team performance. Until the last decade, the emphasis in team assessment was education rather than research. Teams usually were assessed as part of development and training programs. The purpose of assessment was to hold a mirror up to the team and identify areas in needed of change. In this context, team members' experiences were the most appropriate source of data. As we discussed at the beginning of this chapter, however, the purposes of team assessment have broadened. Now, teams need to provide evidence that they are functioning well and cost-effectively within a health care organization or large health care system that insists on accountability. In response, other approaches to measurement increasingly are needed.

As suggested above, underutilized approaches to measuring team performance are observing interactions and behaviors within the team and obtaining information about the team's impact on patients, colleagues and coworkers, and the overall health care organization within which it functions. We return to these issues in the critiques of the instruments and in Chapters 8 and 14.

Psychometric Testing

A basic expectation for instruments is that they show evidence of some reliability and validity. Reliability statistics reflect how well the items of an instrument, scale, or subscale contribute toward the measurement of a concept or phenomenon and how well an instrument measures the same concept or phenomenon repeatedly. Validity statistics address whether an instrument accurately measures the concept or phenomenon it was designed to measure and whether its data show expected relationships to data from other instruments measuring similar or related phenomena (Carmines & Zeller, 1979). Some developers of team performance instruments make sweeping claims regarding their ability to capture crucial information about a team's performance without any evidence that their instruments are reliable or valid. We argue that these basic expectations about the development of a useful assessment instrument should be met and that instruments demonstrating adequate psychometric properties are superior to those that do not. At the same time, standard procedures for determining reliability and validity must be interpreted in the context of understanding how they apply to the measurement of team performance.

While the general principles of psychometric testing apply to team performance instruments used in health care settings, guidelines for use and interpretation of such tests in these settings are necessary as well. We discuss three types of reliability–internal consistency, test-retest, and inter-rater; we also examine numerous types of validity as well as issues related to both kinds of psychometric testing.

Internal Consistency

Internal consistency refers to the relationship among items and the extent to which they contribute together to measure a larger concept. Internal consistency analysis is appropriate for instruments where multiple items are used as part of a scale or subscale measuring a particular content area. Such analysis facilitates the development of conceptually rigorous measures. For example, consider an instrument that measures the level of morale in a team. The developer may have included items such as perception of individual worth, degree of work-related stress, level of commitment, and satisfaction with interpersonal relationships among members. Testing for internal consistency would clarify whether these various items all belong in a single scale measuring morale or whether they should be organized in some other, more internally coherent way.

Assessing internal consistency is not appropriate for instruments measuring multiple facets of team performance using only one item per facet and an item analysis to understand results. One would not necessarily expect high internal consistency across all items of such a measure since each item measures a conceptually different aspect of performance. For example, the level of managerial support to a team, the quality of team members' communication, and the team members' care planning skills can be unrelated to each other.

Test-Retest Reliability

A high test-retest coefficient demonstrates that an instrument is stable over time (i.e., it measures the same thing each time it is completed by members of a team). However, the time between data collection periods needs to be relatively short (e.g., approximately four to eight weeks) when assessing health care teams because they are not static entities. Membership on the team can change; resources become available or are withdrawn, and trainees enter and exit the team. It is important to consider what changes have occurred in the team's environment before interpreting a test-retest coefficient to avoid measuring real changes in team performance.

Inter-Rater Reliability

Inter-rater reliability is a measure of the extent to which independent observations or administrations of an instrument by more than one consultant or interviewer yield similar results. For example, an instrument should be designed and standardized such that two consultants observing the same team at the same time have similar ratings of performance. This type of reliability is appropriate when persons outside the team observe the team or interview team members. It has no relevance for the many team performance instruments that are designed for self-administration. However, a small number of instruments do involve having outside observers rate the team's performance during actual team meetings or problem solving discussions. For such measures, demonstration of inter-rater reliability (i.e., that each rater agrees with the others about what they observed) is important.

Types of Validity

The types of validity most often tested in these instruments are content, concurrent, construct, predictive, and discriminant. Content or face validity refers to the immediately obvious connection between an instrument's items and the phenomenon they attempt to measure. For a team performance instrument, content validity can be determined by having experienced team consultants or experts rate its items for relevance both to team performance generally and in terms of measuring specific dimensions or elements of performance. Multiple experts in this area should agree that relevant items have been included and important items have not been excluded.

Concurrent validity refers to the relationship between one measure of a particular concept and another previously validated measure of the same concept. If we had a "gold standard" measure of team performance, then any new measure would need to show that it was related to the "gold standard." Additionally, it would need to make some substantial improvement over the "gold standard" [e.g., be shorter, easier to administer, or more inclusive of the underlying concept(s) being measured].

Construct validity refers to whether a concept relates to other concepts as theoretically anticipated. For example, a measure of communication skills among team members ought to be related to a measure of quality of relations with other teams in the hospital since good communication would be relevant to the latter situation as well as to the way team members relate to one another.

Predictive and discriminant validity are less frequently assessed for these instruments. Predictive validity refers to a measure's ability to predict future events or performance. For example, the level of support that management provides to the team at the present time can be an indicator of how the team will function in the future. Or a measure of the team's current performance in terms of flexibility and openness to growth and development might predict how well the team will handle later challenges such as staffing changes or increased responsibility. With regard to discriminant validity, a measure should be unrelated to measures from which it should be distinct (e.g., team members' positive reports of their team should be unrelated or only marginally related to the tendency to respond in a socially desirable manner).

Issues Related to Validity Testing

Testing for validity in health care settings does present some challenges, in part, because team experts lack consensus regarding the concept of team performance (i.e., its components and how to measure them). Thus, no "gold standard" measure of this phenomenon exists, and this adds to the challenge of obtaining concurrent validity data for the instruments. Psychometric data that do exist address content, concurrent, and construct validity most often.

Predictive validity presents some special challenges. It can be difficult to assess in health care settings for two reasons. First, teams are dynamic; they develop, mature, and sometimes regress. Under normal circumstances, forces beyond the team's control (e.g., relocation of an inpatient team and its patients, turnover of members and trainees) can influence its level of functioning. Second, current restructuring and reorganization of the U.S. health care system create additional external forces that can negatively affect the team's performance (e.g., withdrawal of resources, extensive collateral duties assigned to team members, time required to refocus in new directions). These external forces can interfere with the predictive ability of team performance data apart from problems with the instrument itself. Developers have used discriminant validity most often to show that differences in perceptions of team functioning among members is not based on their demographic characteristics such as age or gender.

In Chapter 14, we suggest guidelines for future efforts to establish the psychometric properties of present and future team performance instruments.

REFERENCES

Carmines, E.G., & Zeller, R.A. (1979). *Reliability and validity assessment.* Newbury Park, CA: Sage Publications, Inc.

Schutt, R. (1999). *Investigating the social world: The process and practice of research* (2nd ed.). Thousand Oaks, CA: Pine Forge Press.

CHAPTER 3
A MODEL OF TEAM PERFORMANCE

Gloria D. Heinemann, Ph.D.
VA Western New York Healthcare System, Buffalo, NY, VISN 2

Antonette M. Zeiss, Ph.D.
VA Palo Alto Health Care System, Palo Alto, CA, VISN 21

Team performance is a multifaceted concept; therefore, it is essential to delineate a comprehensive model capturing all of its facets. In reviewing literature on teams and teamwork, we were unable to find a model that identifies the major components of performance and the relationships among them. In this chapter, we describe our process of developing such a model and present an overview of the domains and dimensions of the model as they relate to the current changes in the health care system and the growth and evolution of teams. The elements of each dimension of the model are delineated in Chapters 4 through 7.

We relied heavily on two broad theoretical frameworks related to team performance, the stages of small group development (Tuckman, 1965; Tuckman & Jensen, 1977) and the team embedded within a larger organization (Anderson, 1987; McClane, 1992; McGregor, Bennis, & McGregor, 1967; Parry, 1987; Reagan, 1996). The first framework facilitates an understanding of the development of teams over time and the various levels of functioning through which they move as they mature and become better functioning. The second framework delineates factors outside the team that can benefit or create barriers to its functioning; this framework acknowledges the team as a functional unit of a complex organization. It must be integrated into the organization and network with other parts of it in order to achieve both the team's and the organization's goals. Both frameworks identify some of the characteristics of well performing teams, but neither of them provides an overall model of high quality performance. From the literature about teams, discussions among the Directors of the Veterans Affairs' (VA's) Interprofessional Team Training and Development (ITT&D) Program, and facets of team performance measured in the multidimensional instruments included in this volume, we developed a conceptual model that identifies the components of team performance.

DEVELOPING A MODEL OF TEAM PERFORMANCE

Many of our ideas came from familiarity with the literature about teams and teamwork and our experiences with consulting, educating, and training health care teams throughout the VA system and in the private sector. Brainstorming sessions among the ITT&D Program Directors provided a deductive beginning for the development of a model of team performance. Simultaneously, we began an inductive investigation of the instruments we had collected to identify what is measured currently under the rubric of team effectiveness and performance. Next, we attempted to merge and organize this information into a theoretical model. As an additional step, we presented earlier versions of the model at professional meetings and refined it based on the feedback we received.

Our methodology involved specifying the elements of effective team functioning and the relationships among them. This mandated the development of a hierarchical model, delineating some overarching concepts, and expanding each concept by defining facets within it. Ultimately, we developed a three-tiered model. At the highest conceptual level, we identified four "domains" of team performance, discussed extensively in diverse literatures, but not integrated into a multifaceted examination of teams. At the middle hierarchical level, each of the four domains has two "dimensions," and finally, each dimension has multiple "elements" that specify, more concretely, the specific behaviors and experiences that make up the dimension.

A MODEL OF TEAM PERFORMANCE

Domains, then, refer to broad conceptual groupings identifying the essential overarching components of team performance. Our model includes four such domains–structure, context, process, and productivity. At the next level, dimensions refer to the essential components of the domains. Each of our four domains has two dimensions for a total of eight–organizational and team structure, organizational and team context, interdependence and growth and development within the process domain, and strategies for productivity and team accomplishments within the productivity domain. The elements refer to specific components of the dimensions (i.e., the day-to-day, concrete realities at a level closer to the actual experience of team members). Our model includes a total of 86 elements or element groupings (see Table 3.1).

Structure

Two types of structure are important with regard to team performance–the structure of the organization in which the team is working and the structure of the team itself. By structure we refer to what the organization (e.g., the hospital, nursing home, or other health care facility) and the team or work group "look like." What are the various parts of each, and how are they linked to make up the whole (i.e., the framework and belief system)? And finally, how do they relate to one another? That is, how does the team fit, or what is its role, within the organization?

Organizational Structure

The structure of an organization can benefit or create barriers to a team's or work group's ability to function. Some health care organizations have structures that support the team approach and others do not. In a supportive structure, the team approach is understood, appreciated, and utilized throughout various levels of the organization, and management supports teams with resources and rewards for effectiveness and productivity. Where the team approach is not well understood or supported, teams have to fight for resources; only individuals are rewarded, and team members often become demoralized and "burned out."

Recently, the traditional organizational structure of hospitals and health care organizations has given way to a more integrative care line structure. The traditional structure was a hierarchical ordering from top management down to nonprofessional, front-line employees. These employees were hired, supervised, evaluated, and rewarded through a profession-specific or discipline-specific service or department (e.g., Nursing Service, Medical Service, Social Work Service, Engineering Service), each of which was headed by a Service Chief and was geographically separated from the others. The new, more horizontal structure utilizes care lines and their respective sub-care lines across professional/departmental boundaries. Thus, the organization tries to define natural groupings of employees who serve the same patients or carry out a specific set of functions within the health care organization such as providing primary care, mental health services, or a variety of support services (e.g., laundry, housekeeping, other environmental management).

At its best, this new structure utilizes a team approach for setting and accomplishing goals, involves more collaboration among employees, and requires less dependence on top management and supervision external to its teams and natural work groups. In fact, in many of the teams and work groups, self-management is a goal. In the new structure, employees are hired,

Table 3.1 Team Performance: Domains, Dimensions, and Elements

TEAM PERFORMANCE:			
Structure		Context	
Organizational	Team	Organizational	Team
Mission, goals & direction Performance standards Norms, values & expectations Regulations, procedures, planning Team fit within organization Allocation of authority/ responsibility to teams Availability & adequacy of resources Assignment of competent employees & leaders Provision of education & training Mechanisms for communication & decision-making Reporting system/ channels of accountability Appraisal/reward system Objective recognition & rewards for teamwork and to teams	Mission, purpose & direction Goals, objectives & priorities Fit between organizational, team & individual goals Consistency between purpose/goals & processes/activities Roles & responsibilities Norm, values, expectations & standards Order, rules & procedures Boundaries & permeability Organization of space	Managerial modeling of & support for the team approach Career development & employee assistance Change, flexibility & innovation Issues about time & cost constraints Trust, confidence, respect & value Commitment, cohesion & loyalty Motivation & morale Relations across teams & stakeholders Team's reputation within organization Satisfaction/security with job & working relationships Organizational impact on field/marketplace	Attitudes toward teams & teamwork Cautious, tentative, overly polite climate Being oneself & getting to know others Congenial, sociable climate Caring, warm, accepting climate Trust, confidence, respect & value Relaxed, comfortable vs. tense, hostile climate Climate permits free expression Feeling pressure & stress Support & encouragement Commitment to team, members & teamwork Cohesion, unity & team identity Team spirit, morale, energy & enthusiasm Work viewed as interesting, challenging & important Satisfaction with colleagues, team & teamwork

DOMAINS, DIMENSIONS, & ELEMENTS

Process		Productivity	
Interdependence	Growth/Development	Strategies	Accomplishments
Utilization of resources & team members Participation & workload sharing Communication Giving & receiving feedback Collaboration Cooperation, coordination & efficiency Power & leadership sharing Utilization of leadership skills Decision-making Problem solving Conflict management Utilization of appropriate team processes Task orientation & effective task implementation Balance between task & process activities	Skills mastery, maintenance & application Informal learning & improving Utilization of feedback/ learning from mistakes Preventing insulation Role bending & cross-training Flexibility Creativity, uniqueness, innovation & risk-taking	Action plans Patient care plans Individual development plans Use of technology Information management Marketing Time management Self-monitoring & evaluation Education, training & consultation Incentives, rewards, & celebrations	Achievement of goals/ successful completion of tasks Effective meetings Effective leadership/ self management Effective team functioning Effective customer relations Positive outcomes related to patients & trainees Impact on organization

supervised, evaluated, and rewarded within the care lines with input from executive professionals in their respective professions, disciplines, or skill areas. Additionally, teams as well as employees are evaluated and rewarded.

Of course, the success of this new infrastructure is heavily influenced by how well it facilitates the actual day-to-day treatment, care, and service delivery within the organization. The new structure does not necessarily imply an escape from hierarchical thinking; the hierarchy is simply redefined according to the new organizational units. It is flattened to be more inclusive of a wider array of employees than the traditional structure.

While the horizontal organizational structure inherently has more potential to support quality team performance, it does not always do so, nor is the traditional structure always a barrier to good teamwork. Employees working within a hierarchical structure must learn to balance loyalty to their respective discipline-specific departments or services and loyalty to their teams. At the same time, involvement with like-minded professionals and coworkers, in a specific department or service, helps employees stay up-to-date professionally and represent their respective professions or disciplines appropriately within the team. In both types of structures, management must support the clinical teams and natural work groups if they are to perform well.

In addition to the restructuring within health care organizations, many hospitals in both the VA system and the private sector are undergoing two additional structural changes, integration and consolidation at a regional or network level. Where two to three hospitals exist in relatively close geographic proximity, they are being merged into one large facility with one administrative structure as a cost-saving measure. In the VA system, 22 Veterans' Integrated Service Networks (VISNs) are the result of consolidating a number of hospitals into large, geographic regional systems of care in which care lines are or will become network-wide rather than merely facility-wide (i.e., a network-wide administrative structure is in place). A network or VISN is analogous to a large HMO with numerous access points (i.e., the various hospitals within a particular network). Communication occurs via e-mail, video-conferencing, and occasional face-to-face meetings and retreats. Each hospital in the network offers some unique type of care or service to avoid duplication of effort.

This integration and regional structuring has increased the number of "virtual" teams and work groups operating in health care. They require the use of new technologies for members to meet and communicate effectively with one another. Thus, changes in organizational structure can place new demands on and create new challenges for teams. Members of teams must find new ways of communicating and working together and learn new technologies for doing so. These structural changes have implications for team performance and its measurement.

Not all teams or work groups are influenced equally by organizational structure. Most natural work groups in hospitals (e.g., employees working in fiscal service, food service, laundry, housekeeping) are enmeshed in and dependent upon the organizational structure. These employees' work activities have to do with the day-to-day functioning of the organization itself. In contrast, clinical teams can be differentially affected by this structure depending upon their location in and relationship to it. For example, a team serving only inpatients is highly dependent upon the organizational structure for many of its operational policies, resources, and rewards. In contrast, home care and adult day care teams, often based in the hospital, function on its periphery because they serve outpatient populations, provide considerable support to the patients' own caregivers, and in the case of home care, provide care in the patients' homes. Such teams are less dependent on the hospital's organizational structure. Some of these teams may have their offices and work areas at some distance from the main hospital building, which further dilutes the impact of organizational structure on them. Finally, a freestanding, community hospice team may be accountable only to a team leader or program director and a board of directors.

Team Structure

The structure within a team or work group also influences how well it performs. A team is unable to function well if: (a) its mission is not clear to all members; (b) members' roles and responsibilities are not well defined and understood; and (c) its culture (i.e., norms and values, rules and procedures for operating) is not well developed. Team structure is related to the stage of a team's development (Farrell, Heinemann, & Schmitt, 1986; Wheelan, 1993). In newly developing teams, lack of mission and role clarity results in hesitancy on the part of members to become actively engaged in the team's tasks, and they become overly reliant on the team leader to accomplish them. Under these conditions, structure is best described as a leader with many followers. In the conflict stage of development, another team member often vies with the traditional leader for power and authority in the team. The team becomes polarized around these two leaders, each with his or her own set of followers. As the team continues to develop over time, members come to have a shared understanding of the team's mission, goals, and objectives, and they participate more equally in the team's tasks. The team's structure begins to resemble a "coalition of colleagues" (Farrell, Heinemann, & Schmitt, 1986). Initially the members rigidly take turns trying on new roles and responsibilities; later they assume the roles that coincide with their respective interests and expertise. The team develops a culture that includes shared norms, values, and expectations of one another, as well as rules and procedures for accomplishing its tasks (e.g., the conduct of team meetings, interdisciplinary rounds) more efficiently.

The structure of naturally occurring work groups often extends outside the group itself since leadership is vested in a supervisor who does not function as part of the group. As members work together over time and the group becomes better functioning, they tend to rely more on themselves for self-management and less on the supervisor. Responsibility and power are shared among members who communicate and collaborate with one another. Where supervisors persist outside the work group, their relationship to employees changes in that they become coaches, mentors, and role models rather than directive supervisors.

Management also influences team structure when organizational policy designates official leadership positions in clinical team programs. The time frame for the emergence of a mature team structure, in these situations, tends to vary from team to team. It depends upon leadership skills and the tone or climate set by the leader(s), commitment and participation of team members, and the quality of interpersonal relationships among members. The proximity or access of members to one another also is an important element of team structure. Team members in close proximity tend to develop a shared purpose, goals, and culture earlier than do those whose offices are scattered throughout the hospital. The close proximity of members also facilitates the development of a positive team climate, interdependent team processes, and maturation of team members and the team itself.

Context

Context refers to how it "feels" to work in a particular place. Context is the atmosphere, climate, milieu, or environmental affect in which employees are embedded. Like structure, it occurs at both the organizational and team levels. It, too, can create benefits or barriers to team functioning. Context is strongly influenced by leadership style and the quality of interpersonal relationships among employees and team members.

Organizational Context

Organizational management can provide general support for the efforts of teams and individual team members, or it can create barriers that impede the work of the team. For example, organizations that are flexible and offer opportunities for employees' career and personal development will be experienced very differently than those that are concerned only about time and cost constraints and that insist on rigid adherence to established performance guidelines. Managers can set a climate for collaboration; respect among employees; and feelings of empowerment, enthusiasm, and pride and satisfaction with one's job. Conversely the climate set can be one of mistrust, constraint due to micro-management, apathy, low morale, and feelings of under-appreciation. Obviously, the former climate creates a more positive context and permits the manager to model the values essential for effective team process and performance.

When teams work in supportive organizational contexts, they are better able to focus on the tasks specific to their role, carry out work effectively, and be innovative and flexible in dealing with new challenges. When the organizational context is not supportive, much of employees' energies are spent worrying or being frustrated and angry. In such situations, it becomes difficult to focus the team on task-oriented goals, and its members have less energy available for working productively. Additionally, it becomes more difficult to mesh team members' goals with those of the organization.

As with structure, teams and work groups are differentially affected by organizational context depending upon their location within the organization (i.e., inpatient or within the hospital, on the periphery, or freestanding in the community).

Team Context

The context within the team refers to the affect and climate among team members–their perceptions and feelings regarding the socioemotional atmosphere in which they work. Team context is influenced by the stage of a team's development, the styles of relating among team members, and the interpersonal skills of the leader(s) (Dimock, 1987; Farrell, Heinemann, & Schmitt, 1986). In the newly developing team, the atmosphere is often tense due to uncertainty about the team's mission and goals, expectations and roles of team members, and authority. As a result, members are hesitant to accept responsibility, and commitment is low. In the second or conflict stage, tension is high and can be accompanied by hostility. Negative feelings exist among some team members, and commitment and participation remain low. In the third stage, team members become more cohesive and develop a sense of solidarity and unity. They begin to work together more democratically and participate in the team's tasks more equally. In the fourth stage, the atmosphere in the team is characterized by high trust; this permits members to communicate and disagree openly with one another without fear of negative repercussions. Members build upon one another's strengths more effectively, complete tasks efficiently, and develop a sense of pride and satisfaction with teamwork.

Team leaders can do much to help set the tone or climate in the team. A leader who is warm and caring as well as task-oriented and who attempts to be democratic with team members will help set a positive, comfortable team climate in which members share and participate eagerly. In contrast, a leader who is impatient, overly task-oriented, and authoritative in dealing with team members is likely to find him/herself working in an atmosphere of tension, fear, and low commitment on the part of others.

Process

Process refers to a series of progressive and increasingly integrative activities used by teams to accomplish their tasks and achieve their goals. Team process has two dimensions: (a) activities of members demonstrating increased interdependence and (b) growth and development of both members and the team itself as skills, abilities, and team functioning improve.

Interdependence

Interdependence is key to interprofessional and interdisciplinary teamwork. Making effective use of the team's resources and team members' skills and abilities, communicating and problem solving effectively, and working together to accomplish tasks and share the workload are major components of this concept. In well functioning teams, members learn to work interdependently with one another, and the team itself learns to work interdependently with other teams, work groups, and units within or across the organization.

Interdependence does not come naturally to members of teams. Teams in the early stages of development often are characterized much like young children in parallel play who are in conflict frequently because they are unwilling to share. As the team matures, members learn from one another and become better able to take the role or perspective of the other. They understand where their professional roles are unique and where they legitimately overlap. Communication and collaboration across professions and disciplines become more natural. Often education and training programs or consultations with experts in teamwork are necessary for team members to achieve interdependence. While interdependence is necessary for a team to perform well, an additional challenge for the increasing number of primary care teams is learning to distinguish patients who require an interdependent approach from those whose needs can be met by one professional on the team.

When quality team processes are in place and team members depend upon one another to accomplish tasks and goals, productivity increases. The team is likely to have positive outcomes and a positive impact on the organization.

Growth and Development

The ability to grow and mature applies to both team members and the team itself. Organizational management can influence this growth and development based on its willingness to provide education and training for teams and team members. In newly developing teams, the leader is influential in creating conditions that support continued growth and development among members. The more open and democratic the leadership, the greater the ability of the team and its members to grow and improve over time. As trust, cohesion, and a sense of unity develop among members, they, individually and jointly, are more comfortable being flexible, trying new ways of doing things, and taking risks. They not only share their perceptions of one another and the team, but also utilize this feedback to improve individual and team performance. For a team to be high performing, members must take advantage of education, training, and consultation. As a result, employees learn to be better clinicians/health care providers and more highly skilled employees, as well as better members of their respective teams. As employees become better team members, teams mature and improve their functioning (i.e., they mature to higher performing stages of development).

Productivity

Productivity includes both the strategies teams use to be productive and their actual accomplishments. Today's teams and their members are being held accountable to high productivity standards. In the past, their performance was based almost entirely on improvements with regard to the elements of process (e.g., quality communication, consensus decision-making, and ability to manage conflict). In contrast, teams now and in the future must document not only process improvements, but also accomplishment of goals, levels of productivity, quality outcomes, and impact on the organization itself. In addition, teams are being held accountable for using a variety of strategies to ensure productivity. Monitoring the strategies used and their impact on facets of productivity also requires documentation by teams.

Strategies

In this new era of accountability, it is useful to consider how teams become productive (i.e., the strategies they use to produce results) along with their actual accomplishments. Teams must devise and use new strategies to document results, such as action plans, patient care plans, and individual development plans. They must collect, store, manage, analyze, and present information documenting their productivity and accomplishments. They must market their programs and target them to the appropriate customers, and they must learn to manage their time efficiently. More mature teams accept responsibility for monitoring and evaluating their own performance and request or make use of education and training programs to enhance their knowledge bases, skills, and abilities. Incentives, celebrations, and rewards within the team also can be beneficial with regard to energizing and motivating team members.

Accomplishments

Achievement of both task-oriented and process goals is necessary if the team is to perform well. As explained in Chapter 1, task-oriented goals are related to the team's mission and purpose; process goals are related to how effectively members work together to accomplish tasks. Review and analysis of action plans, patient care plans, and individual development plans provide data for determining the team's ability to achieve its goals. Achieving task-oriented goals can result in the expansion of the team's mission, and the potential accomplishments of the team become more numerous as its mission expands. For example, some clinical teams, once they become well functioning and have an appropriate patient population under their care, may choose to add to their mission the education of medical and health professions trainees. This becomes an additional area of productivity that must be monitored and accomplished successfully. Successful achievement of process goals results in a stronger interdisciplinary effort on the part of team members. They become more collaborative and interdependent, and the team becomes a mature, well performing work unit that is better integrated with other parts of the health care organization. The increased efficiency that comes with being a better functioning team also permits the team to expand its mission.

Effective team meetings and effective relationships with other teams in the organization and with customers are important accomplishments of the well performing team. Understanding when meetings are necessary and conducting well planned and profitable meetings are key components of meeting effectiveness. Good working relationships across teams throughout the organization help enhance quality treatment, care, and customer service, all of which improve satisfaction among its customers, including employees. Marketing, time management, and communicating via new technologies are useful strategies for these accomplishments. Good relationships with management help ensure that teams' outcomes are recognized, rewarded, and implemented throughout the organization.

Positive outcomes with regard to patients' health status are major accomplishments of clinical teams. Examples include (a) patient and family education that results in healthier lifestyles, disease prevention, and compliance with the team's plan of care and (b) treatment and care that result in cure, maintenance, or a slowed decline in health status. Additional positive outcomes are maintaining quality of life, ensuring death with dignity, and supporting the family throughout the duration of a patient's involvement with the team. The team needs to collect, analyze, and document its outcomes carefully. Teams able to show positive outcomes should continue to receive support and resources from management. Additionally, such documentation is the basis for rewards to teams and their members.

APPLICATION OF THE MODEL

We use the model of team performance in the second part of this volume to guide our examination of the measurement instruments. In the critiques of the instruments, we identify the number of domains and dimensions of the model that each instrument measures. We categorize and present the critiques of the instruments on the basis of the number of dimensions of team performance addressed in the second part of the book (see Chapters 9 through 12). Additionally, we use the model to develop some of the criteria for the "best measures," and we refer to it in discussing the facets of team performance omitted in current instruments and require inclusion in future instruments (Chapter 14). Finally, in Chapter 14, we discuss how the model can be used in educational programs and consultations with teams to help members identify their respective team's strengths and weaknesses and improve their ability to monitor performance.

REFERENCES

Anderson, W. (1987). The Individual-Team Organization (ITO) Survey. In J.W. Pfeiffer (Ed.), *The 1987 annual: Developing human resources* (pp. 135-148). San Diego, CA: Pfeiffer & Company.

Dimock, H.G. (1987). *Groups: Leadership and group development.* San Diego, CA: University Associates, Inc.

Farrell, M.P., Heinemann, G.D., & Schmitt, M.H. (1986). Informal roles, rituals and styles of humor in interdisciplinary health care teams: Their relationship to stages of group development. *International Journal of Small Group Research, 2,* 143-162.

McClane, W.E. (1992). Evaluation and accountability. In American Congress of Rehabilitation Medicine, *Guide to interdisciplinary practice in rehabilitation settings* (pp. 158-172). Skokie, IL: Author.

McGregor, D., Bennis, W.G., & McGregor, C. (1967). *The professional manager.* New York: McGraw-Hill.

Parry, S.B. (1987). How effective is your team? In M. Silberman (Ed.), *Team and organization development sourcebook* (pp. 127-135). New York: McGraw-Hill.

Reagan, G. (1996). U.S. Style Teams (USST) Inventory. In J.W. Pfeiffer (Ed.), *The 1996 annual: Volume 2, consulting* (pp. 141-151). San Diego, CA: Pfeiffer & Company.

Tuckman, B.W. (1965). Developmental sequences in small groups. *Psychological Bulletin, 63,* 384-399.

Tuckman, B.W., & Jensen, M.A.C. (1977). Stages of small group development revisited. *Group and Organizational Studies, 2,* 419-427.

Wheelan, S.A. (1993). *The Group Development Questionnaire: A manual for professionals.* Philadelphia, PA: GDQ Associates.

CHAPTER 4
ORGANIZATIONAL AND TEAM STRUCTURE

Sara A. Brallier, Ph.D.
Coastal Carolina University, Conway, SC

Ruth Ann Tsukuda, M.P.H.
VA Medical Center, Portland, OR, VISN 20

The structure of an organization or a team refers to its organizing framework or how its various parts fit together and are expected to function. The structure of an organization creates the foundation for the system in which its teams and work groups are embedded. A team's structure creates the foundation for the system in which specific employees or team members are embedded. Team performance is affected by the structures of both the organization and the team (Gomberg & Sinesi, 1994; Hackman, 1987; Lenkman & Gribbins, 1994; Moos & Billings, 1991; Shortell, Rousseau, Gilles, Devers, & Simons, 1991). These structures can either benefit or create barriers to team functioning and effectiveness.

ORGANIZATIONAL STRUCTURE

A supportive organizational structure is vital to optimal team performance (Anderson et al., 1994; Ducanis & Golin, 1979; Larson & LaFasto, 1989; McGregor, 1960; Parker, 1990; Rowe, 1996; Shortell et al., 1994; Teague, Drake, & Ackerson, 1995). The management or leadership team of a health care organization is responsible for developing the organization's structure. Teams, however, can influence management to ensure that this structure benefits them. Such influence can take the form of appeals and proposals from teams' leadership or high productivity levels and quality accomplishments of teams that come to the attention of management. Teams not supported by the organization are at risk of losing sight of and commitment to their own and the organization's mission and goals. In some cases, inadequate investment in a team results in its failure and possibly its demise (Rennecker, 1996).

The organization's structural elements that affect teams begin with its mission, goals, direction, and values and extend to its performance standards, regulations, and allocation of resources, including employees and team leaders and their education and training. Additionally, mechanisms for communication and decision-making, accountability, appraisal, and rewards are a part of this structure. We address these elements in the following sections with regard to how they affect team performance.

Mission, Goals, and Direction

The organization's mission, goals, and direction set the parameters for employee and teamwork activities. Management should articulate them clearly to all employees and teams. Employees invest more effort in their work when they understand how it contributes to the mission and goals of the organization (Hackman, 1987). When the direction of the organization changes, management should communicate these changes, in a timely manner, to employees, teams, and work groups along with a rationale for the changes and an explanation of ramifications these changes have for mission statements, position descriptions, and work activities.

Performance Standards, Norms, Values, and Expectations

Management and supervisory staff set performance standards for employees. These should be disseminated to all employees and teams. Such standards and competencies should address the individual as an employee, as a professional, and as a team member. In order for employees to take performance standards seriously, mechanisms should be in place to assess competencies and performance in relation to the standards. In addition, ethical guidelines should be available that delineate expectations for the behavior of employees, teams members, and teams themselves (Anderson, 1987; Ducanis & Golin, 1979; Given & Simmons, 1977).

Employees are more likely to accept the norms and values of the organization when management makes their importance evident. For example, when management values the team approach, expects collaboration and interdependence within and across teams and work groups, and communicates these expectations clearly, employees become committed to teamwork and work up to management's expectations (Anderson, 1987; Husting, 1996; Lenkman & Gribbins, 1994; Parker, 1990; Ramos & Ratliff, 1997). The team approach, then, becomes the norm or agreed upon standard within the organization; teamwork becomes the approach employees use to deliver care and services, to get work done, and to solve problems.

Regulations, Procedures, and Planning

Management and supervisors develop, with input from employees, the regulations, policies, and procedures that enable employees and teams to prioritize and standardize their work activities across the organization. For example, employees need clear guidelines about expected work schedules and leave policies. If policies state that all employees on a team will have a common work schedule, or that the schedule will ensure round-the-clock coverage for inpatient settings, team members can turn their attention to working out more important elements of planning and coordinating their work activities. Such policies need to be revisited and updated on a regular basis to ensure rapid response to change within the organization. If the mission changes from providing outpatient services on week days to providing outpatient services plus home visits as needed, management needs to work out new policies with team members to ensure that they coincide with clinical needs and workload capabilities. Teams need the clarity and structure that these broad guidelines provide; they also require flexibility to take advantage of unforeseen opportunities and unexpected events (Forrester & Drexler, 1999). If employees work overtime to prepare for a Joint Commission on the Accreditation of Healthcare Organizations (JCAHO) accreditation visit, providing flexible schedules and/or additional leave time may be in the best interest of the team and the organization. Thus, regulations and procedures should not be overly rigid or controlling.

In order for organizational planning to be useful to employees, they should be included in the planning process. Quality planning at the organizational level should facilitate planning at the level of teams and work groups and prevent employees from operating in a crisis mode except in unusual circumstances.

Team Fit within Organization/Allocation of Authority to Teams

For teams to be successful, employees must understand their respective team's position and role within the organization and how their team's work contributes to the mission of the organization. The organization's strategic plan should outline the expectations of teams with regard to their roles and activities within the organization, such as the quality of care, treatment, and services they provide (Ramos & Ratliff, 1997; Rennecker, 1996). Employees also need to understand the resources and constraints within which their respective teams operate as well as their team's role vis-à-vis other teams and organizational units. Team members should have an opportunity to learn how their work affects and is affected by other teams and work groups. The more they understand about how their team or work group is integrated with other parts of the organization, the greater the potential for synergy within and across teams and the less likelihood for duplication of efforts.

If teams are to be effective within organizations, managers and supervisors must give them the authority and responsibility to work effectively and to be productive. When teams have authority consistent with their responsibilities, their members can make important decisions related to their work more effectively and the organization functions more efficiently. For example, when management allocates space to its teams, it also should give them the authority to organize that space to maximize functioning and effectiveness. The team that must appeal to the organization's Space Committee every time it wants to relocate offices or redirect its patient flow will not only become frustrated as a result of lack of autonomy, but also will function inefficiently.

Allocation of Appropriate Resources to Teams

Teams need resources to function effectively (Anderson, 1987; Hackman, 1987; Parker, 1990; Ramos & Ratliff, 1997). For teams in health care settings, these resources include such things as supplies; equipment; a budget line; space in which to work; and competent, skilled personnel. Lack of adequate resources is commonly cited as a cause of poor team performance or inability to make meaningful contributions to the organization (Barczak, 1996; Rennecker, 1996). The resources of space and employees, including those in leadership positions, hired and assigned to teams play key roles in making teams effective and productive.

Space (e.g., office space, conference and examination rooms, patient care and family areas) is an important resource to teams, and space allocation to teams is indicative of managerial support to them (Moos & Billings, 1991). Teams benefit from their members working in close proximity (Ducanis & Golin, 1979), and managers who understand team dynamics recognize that working near one another encourages informal interaction, consultation, collaboration, and interdependence among members, all of which contribute to team productivity (Ducanis & Golin, 1979; Given & Simmons, 1977).

Hiring new employees should reflect the organization's commitment to the team approach (Parker, 1990). Managers should design interview questions and conduct reference checks to identify applicants who have experience working in teams or who have the potential to become strong team members. Careful assignment of existing staff to teams should bring together complementary knowledge, skill, and expertise (Ducanis & Golin, 1979; Given & Simmons, 1977; Hackman, 1987; Rennecker, 1996; Seago, 1996). Positive attitudes toward teamwork and good interpersonal skills are as important as technical or clinical knowledge and should be taken into consideration when hiring employees and assigning them to teams (Hastings, Bixby, & Chaudhry-Lawton, 1986). Finally, management should consider involving team members in decisions about hiring or assigning employees to their respective teams. This can be controversial, especially in clinical teams where members may be unable to evaluate the clinical competencies of other professionals. This problem can be overcome if managers from a specific profession select a set of qualified applicants, and then the team is involved in interviewing them and making recommendations regarding which applicant would best fit into the team.

In addition to selecting competent, "team friendly" employees, managers also need to consider the number and skill mix of employees necessary on any particular team. In teams that are too small, members often have too many assignments to complete their work in a timely manner (Dyer, 1984). Too small a clinical team also may not have the appropriate skill mix to meet the needs of its patient population. Conversely, if a team or work group is too large, coordinating members' activities becomes difficult, and efficiency suffers (Hackman, 1987). Teams are more effective and produce better outcomes when the size and skill mix of members coincides with the amount and type of work the team must accomplish (Hackman, 1987; Shortell et al., 1994).

Management often assigns leaders to teams (Ducanis & Golin, 1979), and effective leadership is vital to quality team performance (Kormanski & Mozenter, 1987; Shortell et al., 1991). Team leaders link the team to the larger organization and facilitate its completion of tasks and achievement of goals. They are responsible for keeping the team focused on organizational goals and ensuring that members receive information from management that is relevant to their work. Additionally, they serve as team advocates to management and keep managers informed regarding the team's productivity and accomplishments. Managers must be familiar with the skills of effective team leadership in order to select employees with these qualities. Perhaps most importantly for a well functioning interdisciplinary or interprofessional team is a leader's willingness to share power and encourage leadership skills and the leadership function in other team members in order to enhance collegiality and interdependence and to utilize all of the expertise present among members of the team.

Provision of Education and Training

Providing education and training to teams, their members, and their leaders is a major element of a supportive organizational structure (Anderson et al., 1994; Forté, 1997; Given & Simmons, 1977; Hackman, 1987; Lenkman & Gribbins, 1994; Rowe, 1996). Teams and their members require education and training in several areas, such as updating professional and technical skills, becoming more knowledgeable about their respective patient populations, and acquiring interpersonal and teamwork skills. Leadership training, too, should be available to team members as well as formal team leaders.

In addition to the financial investments, managers can support education and training by maximizing learning readiness among employees. They can ensure that all team members have the opportunity to attend scheduled training by having other teams or other employees "cover" for them while they are away from the work site. The timing of an educational program and the need for the skills in the work place must coincide; any special equipment should be in the work place and ready for use prior to training employees to use it.

Finally, managers should be committed to the continued growth and development of teams. This requires that teams have access to training and/or consultation as they mature over time. Providing education and training to teams results in skilled team members who are more effective in carrying out their respective team's tasks. Well-trained team members also report higher levels of job satisfaction (Campion, Medsker, & Higgs, 1993; Hackman, 1987; Teague, Drake, & Ackerson, 1995).

Mechanisms for Communication and Decision-Making

In most health care organizations, multiple teams work to achieve organizational goals (e.g., delivery of quality patient care, being an employer of choice, ordering and distributing supplies). These various teams and work groups need to have efficient ways to communicate with one another and with management. This becomes increasingly important the larger and more complex the organization becomes (e.g., an organization that includes several merged facilities or is spread over a large geographic region). To facilitate communication throughout the organization, management must ensure that all employees understand the organizational structure and the roles of other teams and units located within it. Teams unaware of the functions of other units or work groups often fail to share useful and appropriate information with them (Brett & Rognes, 1986; Fitzsimmons & White, 1997) or fail to make use of their skills and abilities.

Flow of communication between management and teams should be reciprocal. Teams need ready access to management when questions or problems arise that cannot be answered and resolved within the teams. Managers, too, should establish mechanisms permitting team members to have input into organizational planning and policy setting (Moos & Billings, 1991). Teams and employees excluded from participating in such decision-making processes often lack motivation and commitment to the organization and its goals (Moos & Billings, 1991). Managers, too, need to know how teams and their members are performing in order to recognize and reward those who contribute significantly to accomplishing the organization's mission and achieving its goals.

Given modern technology, mechanisms for communication can take various forms, including such diverse options as face-to-face meetings; written memos, proposals, and consult requests; teleconferences; conference phone calls; voice mail; and e-mail (see Chapter 7, uses of technology). The challenge to managers, supervisors, and team leaders is to select the most efficient and effective mechanisms and standardize some of them, along with the rules and procedures for their use, across the organization. When mechanisms for communication are in place, employees and/or teams receive all of the relevant information they need to make decisions. In turn, decisions are made at the appropriate levels of the organization. The results are better decisions, increased perceptions of fairness, and higher job satisfaction among employees.

Reporting System, Accountability, and Reward System

Once management has established effective mechanisms for communication, they can be used as part of the reporting system and channels of accountability. A clear reporting system helps employees and teams understand to whom they are accountable. They should know who reviews their progress reports, who provides them with feedback and direction, and who evaluates them and their work.

If employees and team members are to feel satisfied with their jobs, they must understand the appraisal and rewards system and perceive it as fair and equitable. Incentives and rewards based on team effectiveness facilitate loyalty to teams and increase efforts to improve their functioning (Husting, 1996). Conversely, health professionals, who are supervised, evaluated, and rewarded only through their respective disciplines or departments, focus their loyalties and efforts there (Ducanis & Golin, 1979). The inclusion of teamwork in the appraisal and rewards system is a crucial component of organizational support to teams (Parker, 1990).

Recognition and Rewards for Teamwork and to Teams

Recognizing and rewarding employees for their contributions to teams is one of the most effective ways organizations can promote teams and teamwork (Hackman, 1987; Larson & LaFasto, 1989; Parker, 1990). Rewards need not always be "cash in hand." Acknowledgments in organizational newsletters, commendations at employee gatherings, visibly displayed plaques and certificates, or an expense paid trip to an educational seminar or conference are other ways of recognizing teams' accomplishments (Parker, 1990).

Employees, rewarded by management for their contributions to the team, report more positive attitudes toward the team and higher commitment to the team's tasks. Additionally, when teams are rewarded, the clarity of their goals and roles improves, and members establish better work norms (Dyer, 1984; Gladstein, 1984; Hackman, 1987; Larson & LaFasto, 1989).

TEAM STRUCTURE

Just as organizations need structure, so do teams. The structure of the team influences how its members interact with one another and implement and complete tasks (Barczak, 1996). Teams rarely rely on organizational charts to display their structure; a documented purpose and related goals and objectives may be the only formal indicators of it. The teams mission, goals, and priorities provide the underpinnings for the other elements of structure. These include the roles and responsibilities of members; the team's norms, values, expectations, and standards; and its rules and procedures. Additionally, the team's purpose and goals should drive its processes and activities. Other structural elements include the team's boundaries and their permeability and the organization of space allocated to the team.

Mission, Purpose, and Direction

A team cannot be effective if its members do not understand its mission and purpose (Parker, 1990). In well functioning teams, members spend considerable time developing a mission statement (i.e., why the team exists and what it expects to accomplish). This statement is based upon organizational goals and the role of the team as defined by the organization (Anderson, 1993; Husting, 1996; Keating, 1997; Parker, 1990) and by the expertise embodied in the team. A team's mission statement should be broad and inclusive. For example, a clinical team's mission would certainly include providing quality care to its population of patients and involving patients' families and informal caregivers in developing and implementing plans of care. Other aspects of its mission might include marketing the team's program to increase the number of patients it serves, continuously monitoring the level of functioning of both the team and its members to facilitate improvement, conducting research, and providing a clinical site for training future health and medical professionals. Understanding and commitment to the mission are central to team performance (Katzenbach & Smith, 1993; Swezey & Salas, 1992). The mission statement should be accompanied by action planning that includes specific goals and objectives (Anderson, 1993).

Goals, Objectives, and Priorities

A team's goals and objectives flow from its mission statement and help facilitate the planning process (Parker, 1994). Goals help focus the team to get results. They should be worthwhile, measurable, and attainable (Barczak, 1996; Larson & LaFasto, 1989). Additionally, they should be clearly stated since clear goals can reduce the potential for negative conflicts within the team (Parker, 1994). A team without clear goals may lose sight of its direction (Forrester & Drexler, 1999), and experience failure (Barczak, 1996). Specific and clearly stated objectives help the team define its work, focus its efforts, and set priorities to achieve its goals (Katzenbach & Smith, 1993).

Consistency between Purpose/Goals and Processes/Activities

When members contribute to the development of the team's purpose and goals, they are more likely to use processes and perform activities that coincide with them and increase the likelihood that the team achieves them. Effective teams revisit their mission and goals periodically to ensure that their actions appropriately support them (Parker, 1990; Swezey & Salas, 1992).

Fit between Organizational, Team, and Individual Goals

Effective teams use the organizational mission statement to guide members in setting priorities and ensuring their efforts are in line with the organization's goals (Rennecker, 1996). Poor functioning and high levels of conflict often occur in teams that "exist outside the rules of the organization" (Seago, 1996). However, teams need some latitude in setting goals. Effectiveness is maximized when teams have autonomy to set their own priorities and decide how to carry out their tasks (Luft, 1984).

Members need to understand their own personal relationship to the team's goals (Kormanski & Mozenter, 1987). Team effectiveness is jeopardized when individual team members have personal goals that differ from or are in conflict with those of the team (Parker, 1990). In well functioning teams, achieving the team's goals also results in members achieving some of their own professional and personal goals.

Roles and Responsibilities

Health professionals and other employees come to their respective teams or work groups with different perspectives, values, and goals; often they do not know how to integrate the skills of others with their own (Given & Simmons, 1977). They do not understand what is unique about their respective roles and where they legitimately overlap with those of other team members. They do not realize that they are working under different assumptions and value systems. As a result, they inappropriately evaluate one another using their own disciplinary perspectives. For example, the team physician might become frustrated with the time it takes professionals in the psychosocial disciplines to complete assessments of patients because medical assessments often can be made on the basis of quickly completed lab tests. The physician might inappropriately label the psychologist or social worker as "lazy" and "inefficient" without understanding that testing for cognitive functioning and family role functioning must be conducted more than once, sometimes with more than one person, and sometimes at different times of the day.

Unclear and rigid roles can result in "turf battles" among team members. For example, both the nurse and the dietitian might define their role as including education of the diabetic patient regarding a diet appropriate to maintain normal blood sugar levels. Such battles are characterized by tensions and conflict, unrealistic expectations of one another, overstepping role boundaries, duplication of efforts, and inefficiency (Givens & Simmons, 1977; Hackman, 1987). When cooperation should be paramount, team members often are competing with one another. In such situations, they become frustrated, stressed, and dissatisfied. Under these circumstances, turnover of membership can be high and productivity low (Parker, 1990).

Poorly defined and unclear roles often lead to duplication of effort among team members. Such duplication can have negative consequences for patients (Brooks, 1996; Evers, 1981). For example, when too many team members converge on a patient to collect information, the patient can become overwhelmed and overly tired, and as a result, he or she can lose confidence in the team. One team member using a multi-purpose assessment form can improve efficiency and create less stress for the patient (Brooks, 1996; Lenkman & Gribbins, 1994).

To collaborate effectively, team members must have a clear understanding of their own and other members' roles (Barczak, 1996; Given & Simmons, 1977). Role clarity facilitates the ability of team members to use one another's strengths and skills effectively and enhances team functioning and productivity (Barczak, 1996, Parker, 1990). The team cannot be effective if its members are confused about their roles and responsibilities (Parker, 1990).

Norms, Values, Expectations, and Standards

The development of positive norms and values, along with clear roles and responsibilities, helps team members know what to expect from one another and facilitates collaboration. Norms are agreed upon standards of behavior that regulate behavior within a group or team (Hackman, 1987). Examples of group norms include open communication and shared leadership, which encourage a cooperative work environment and participation among team members (Barczak, 1996; Parker, 1990). If a team gives early explicit attention to the kinds of behaviors and attitudes that will be valued, the team functions better. Effective teamwork occurs when members share and enact a set of core values (Schermerhorn, Hunt, & Osborn, 1994). When the values of the team and the organization coincide, they serve as a bond connecting the team to the larger organization (Forrester & Drexler, 1999).

Order, Rules, and Procedures

Rules and procedures, developed by the team, impose an order for team members' interactions and the completion of tasks. For example, to ensure that patient care plans are developed and updated, team members might decide to institute a rule that all new patients' care plans must be completed within a week of admission to the team program and must be reviewed at least quarterly thereafter. Through its rules and procedures, the team can ensure a structure that is "results driven." That is, its rules and procedures focus team members on achieving specified results and outcomes.

Boundaries and Permeability

In order for members to get to know one another's skills and abilities, develop shared values and procedures, and become collaborative and interdependent, the team's boundaries must be clearly defined and relatively stable over time. Members become frustrated and performance suffers when there is high turnover within the team or when there is ambiguity regarding team membership (Hackman, 1987). When a team's boundaries are overly permeable, members tend to be influenced more by their respective identities and organizational groups outside the team. This often leads to conflict among members and poor team functioning (Lichtenstein, Alexander, Jinnett, & Ullman, 1997). While boundaries need to be clearly defined, a team's boundaries should not be so rigid as to insulate members from consultants and experts outside the team. Some permeability facilitates the use of consultant members of the team, interactions with other teams and work units within the organization, and experts outside the organization.

Organization of Space

Space is one of the team's most valued resources. Once management has allocated space to the team, members should decide how to organize and utilize it to maximize efficiency and effectiveness. Offices in close geographic proximity encourage team members' collaboration and joint problem solving. The team needs a conference room for meetings and for dialogue among members. A break or coffee room also can provide an informal meeting area where team members get to know one another and explore ideas and issues. If the team program is a clinical training site, office space should be set aside for the health and medical trainees.

For clinical team programs, patients' waiting areas should be located near the entrance to the program and its scheduling and intake areas. Examination and treatment areas should expedite the flow of patients. Availability of privacy rooms facilitates interviewing and counseling patients or their family.

SUMMARY

Supportive organizational and team structures increase the likelihood of effective team processes and performance. In well-structured organizations, management clearly communicates the organizational mission and goals to employees and teams. Employees and teams understand their roles in the organization and organizational expectations, policies, procedures, and channels of accountability. Management provides the resources employees and teams need to function effectively and rewards high performance and accomplishments appropriately. Additionally, management creates a structure that is responsive to changing needs and includes employees and teams in decision-making and planning processes. In well-structured teams, the team's mission and goals are clearly stated and understood by all members. Members understand the team's boundaries, their own and others' roles and responsibilities in the team, what is expected of them as team members, the resources allocated to the team, and their rules and procedures for operating.

REFERENCES

Anderson, L. (1993). Teams: Group processes, success, and barriers. *Journal of Nursing Administration, 23,* 15-19.

Anderson, L.A., Persky, N.W., Whall, A.L., Campbell, R., Algase, D.L., Gillis, G.L., & Halter, J.B. (1994). Interdisciplinary team training in geriatrics: Reaching out to small and medium sized communities. *The Gerontologist, 34,* 833-838.

Anderson, W. (1987). The Individual-Team-Organization (ITO) Survey: Conscious change for the organization. In J.W. Pfeiffer (Ed.), *The 1987 annual: Developing human resources* (pp. 135-148). San Diego, CA: Pfeiffer & Company.

Barczak, N. (1996). How to lead effective teams. *Critical Care Nursing Quarterly, 19,* 73-82.

Brett, J.M., & Rognes, J.K. (1986). Intergroup relations in organizations. In P.S. Goodman (Ed.), *Designing effective workgroups* (pp. 202-235). San Francisco: Jossey-Bass Publishers.

Brooks, I. (1996). Using ritual to reduce barriers between sub-cultures. *Journal of Management in Medicine, 10,* 23-30.

Campion, M.A., Medsker, G.J., & Higgs, A.C. (1993). Relations between work group characteristics and effectiveness: Implications for designing effective work groups. *Personnel Psychology, 46,* 823-850.

Ducanis, A.J., & Golin, A.K. (1979). *The interdisciplinary health care team.* Germantown, MD: Aspen Systems Corporation.

Dyer, J. (1984). Team research and team training: A state-of-the-art review. In F.A. Muckler, (Ed.), *Human factors review* (pp. 285-323). Santa Monica, CA: Human Factors Society.

Evers, H.K. (1981). Multidisciplinary teams in geriatric wards: Myth or reality? *Journal of Advanced Nursing, 6,* 205-214.

Fitzsimmons, P., & White, T. (1997). Crossing boundaries: Communication between professional groups. *Journal of Management in Medicine, 11,* 96-101.

Forrester, R., & Drexler, A.B. (1999). A model for team-based organization performance. *Academy of Management Executive, 13,* 36-49.

Forté, R. (1997). The high cost of conflict. *Nursing Economics, 15,* 119-123.

Gladstein, D.L. (1984). Groups in context: A model of task group effectiveness. *Administrative Science Quarterly, 29,* 499-517.

Given, B., & Simmons, S. (1977). The interdisciplinary health-care team: Fact of fiction? *Nursing Form, 16,* 165-185.

Gomberg, S., & Sinesi, L. (1994). A collaborative interaction model and the implementation of shared governance. *Holistic Nursing Practice, 8,* 12-21.

Hackman, J.R. (1987). The design of work teams. In J.W. Lorsch (Ed.), *Handbook of organizational behavior* (pp. 315-342). Englewood Cliffs, NJ: Prentice-Hall, Inc.

Hastings, C., Bixby, P., & Chaudhry-Lawton, R. (1986). *The superteam solution*. Aldershot, England: Gower Publishing Company Limited.

Husting, P.M. (1996). Leading work teams and improving performance. *Nursing Management, 27*, 35-38.

Katzenbach, J.R., & Smith, D.K. (1993). *The wisdom of teams: Creating the high-performance organization*. Boston, MA: Harvard University Press.

Keating, D.J. (1997). Rehab center develops unique caregiving model. *Healthcare Benchmarks, 4*, 27-29.

Kormanski, C., & Mozenter, A. (1987). A new model of team building: A technology for today and tomorrow. In J.W. Pfeiffer (Ed.), *The 1987 annual: Developing human resources* (pp. 255-268). San Diego, CA: Pfeiffer & Company.

Larson, C.E., & LaFasto, F.M. (1989). *Team work: What must go right/What can go wrong*. Newbury Park, CA: Sage Publications, Inc.

Lenkman, S., & Gribbins, R. (1994). Multidisciplinary teams in the acute care setting. *Holistic Nursing Practice, 8*, 81-87.

Lichtenstein, R., Alexander, J.A., Jinnett, K., & Ullman, E. (1997). Embedded intergroup relations in interdisciplinary teams: Effects on perceptions of level of team integration. *Journal of Applied Behavioral Science, 33*, 413-434.

Luft, J. (1984). *Group processes: An introduction to group dynamics*. Mountain View, CA: Mayfield Publishing Company.

McGregor, D. (1960). *The human side of enterprise*. New York: McGraw-Hill, Inc.

Moos, R.H., & Billings, A.G. (1991). Understanding and improving work climates. In J.W. Jones, B.D. Steffy, & D.W. Bray (Eds.), *Applying psychology in business: The handbook for managers and human resource professionals* (pp. 552-562). Lexington, MA: D.C. Heath.

Parker, G.M. (1990). *Team players and teamwork: The new competitive business strategy*. San Francisco: Jossey-Bass Publishers.

Parker, G.M. (1994). *Cross-functional teams: Working with allies, enemies, and other strangers*. San Francisco: Jossey-Bass Publishers.

Ramos, M.C., & Ratliff, C. (1997). The development and implementation of an integrated multidisciplinary clinical pathway. *Journal of Wound, Ostomy, and Continence Nurses, 24*, 66-71.

Rennecker, J.A. (1996). Team building for continuous quality improvement. *Seminars in Perioperative Nursing, 5*, 40-46.

Rowe, H. (1996). Multidisciplinary teamwork–myth or reality? *Journal of Nursing Management, 4*, 93-101.

Schermerhorn, J.R., Hunt, J.G., & Osborn, R.N. (1994). *Managing organizational behavior* (5th ed.). New York: John Wiley & Sons.

Seago, J.A. (1996). Culture of troubled work groups. *Journal of Nursing Administration, 26*, 41-46.

Shortell, S.M., Rousseau, D.M., Gilles, R.R., Devers, K.J., & Simons, T.L. (1991). Organizational assessment in intensive care units (ICUs): Construct development, reliability, and validity of the ICU Nurse-Physician Questionnaire. *Medical Care, 29*, 709-726.

Shortell, S.M., Zimmerman, J.E., Rousseau, D.M., Gillies, R.R., Wagner, D.P., Draper, E.A., Knaus, W.A., & Duffy, J. (1994). The performance of intensive care units: Does good management make a difference? *Medical Care, 32*, 508-525.

Swezey, R.W., & Salas, E. (Eds.). (1992). *Teams: Their training and performance*. Greenwich, CT: Ablex.

Teague, G.T., Drake, R.E., & Ackerson, T.H. (1995). Evaluating use of continuous treatment teams for persons with mental illness and substance abuse. *Psychiatric Services, 46*, 689-695.

CHAPTER 5
ORGANIZATIONAL AND TEAM CONTEXT

Stephen K. Harmon, Ph.D.
VA Medical Center, Salt Lake City, UT, VISN 19

Sara A. Brallier, Ph.D.
Coastal Carolina University, Conway, SC

Glenda F. Brown, Ed.D.
VA Central Arkansas Health Care System, Little Rock, AR, VISN 16

Context is the social-psychological atmosphere, environment, milieu, or climate of the organization and the team. Context is important because it directly influences the quality of processes and tasks carried out in the organization and the team. When the context is perceived positively, employees and teams are more likely to thrive and be productive. When it is perceived negatively, frustration, dissatisfaction, and low productivity result. This chapter examines elements within the organizational and team context that can maximize or inhibit team performance.

ORGANIZATIONAL CONTEXT

Organizational context refers to the emotional climate in which teams and natural work groups are embedded and carry out their work activities. Managers and supervisors influence this climate through the various leadership styles they adopt and the level of resources and support they provide to employees. Managers can foster a positive organizational context by modeling the team approach and providing employees with programs that meet their needs. A positive organizational context also is one in which managers foster commitment and loyalty to the organization by empowering employees, making them feel part of the organization, and developing a sense of mutual trust and confidence with them. Employees expect management to set the tone for a positive work environment. While managers do influence employees' feelings and experiences, they also react to employees' behaviors. When employees respond positively to managers, trust and empowerment result; when employees ignore or respond negatively to the efforts of managers, they jeopardize the positive feedback cycle.

Supportive managers also promote positive interpersonal relationships among employees and across teams; are flexible and open to change, creativity, and innovation; and attempt to minimize excessive time and cost constraints, while permitting appropriate time for team processes. A positive context helps in the recruitment and retention of competent employees (Moos & Billings, 1991). In such a context, employees develop high levels of motivation, morale, commitment to, and pride in the organization. They also are more likely to be satisfied with their jobs and have high levels of productivity.

Managerial Modeling and Support for the Team Approach

One of the strongest indicators of support for the team approach is its direct use by organizational leaders and managers. Utilizing teams at all levels of the organization communicates to employees that management understands the value of teamwork in accomplishing the organization's mission. When upper level managers themselves function effectively as a team, they are better able to empathize with and anticipate the needs of other teams in the organization. Additionally, they often become effective role models, coaches, and mentors for middle level managers, supervisors, and team leaders throughout the organization. Finally, management's use of the team approach establishes teamwork as an organizational expectation or norm (Parker, 1990).

Given the impact managers have on employees' regard for and acceptance of teamwork, they must be both knowledgeable about the characteristics of high performance teams and when to utilize the team approach (Barczak, 1996). They should affirm publicly the organization's commitment to teamwork and the value the organization places on employees as team members. For example, managers can acknowledge and reinforce the importance of teamwork during organizational meetings and in publications such as newsletters and annual reports (Parker, 1990).

Career Development and Employee Assistance

Many employees expect their work will provide the opportunity for both professional, work-related growth and personal growth (Moos & Billings, 1991). Nonprofessional and paraprofessional employees often are interested in furthering their education toward a professional career, and professionals often desire to expand both their career goals or pursue a second career. For these employees, degree programs sponsored by the organization, tuition support, tutorial computer courses, satellite broadcasted programs, and evening and weekend programs are attractive. Other career development initiatives include travel expenses for professional meetings and conferences and rewards for presentations, publications, and innovative ideas/discoveries. Sponsorship of employee assistance programs demonstrates organizational commitment to the well-being and personal development of its employees. Such programs as psychological counseling, substance abuse, weight loss, and smoking cessation offer benefits to employees that become benefits to the organization as well.

Employees faced with personal problems have difficulty focusing on work assignments and being productive on the job. They often make excessive use of sick leave and experience low morale and job dissatisfaction. Conversely, employees, who have employee assistance resources available, feel supported and valued. High levels of loyalty, morale, and job satisfaction and low levels of employee turnover are outcomes often found in organizations with employee assistance programs (Shortell et al., 1994).

While these programs affect all employees, whether they work in teams or not, the need for such programs may be even greater for members of teams. Team members must learn to balance their own personal and professional goals with the goals of their respective teams and the goals of the organization; counseling programs can be beneficial in this regard. Employees who work on high stress teams such as those in critical care areas (e.g., surgery, intensive care, and the emergency room) may require stress management training. Members of hospice teams may need to learn how to handle grief and loss. Employees who work on teams in a prolonged conflict stage of development may need help dealing with anger and frustration in their interpersonal relationships, low energy levels, and low productivity. Counseling also can be an important resource for difficult or problematic team members (e.g., those who have serious personal or interpersonal problems) as well as employees who must work with them on a regular basis.

As organizations strive to be "equal opportunity employers," they must meet the special needs of their employees. For example, employees with disabilities can be incorporated into the organization's workforce through the provision of specialized equipment, workload sharing agreements, sign language specialists, and other strategies that capitalize on the strengths and capabilities of these individuals. Likewise, day care programs and flexible work schedules provide tangible benefits to employees who have young children or frail elderly parents.

Change, Flexibility, and Innovation

Perhaps the greatest challenge facing health care organizations today is change (Pritchett & Pound, 1993). In order to survive and thrive in this period of health care restructuring and reorganization, hospitals, nursing homes, and other health care facilities must be flexible and innovative. Not only the high costs of health care, but also the availability of new technologies and advances in the fields of biology and medicine increase the likelihood of change in health care settings. Organizations must be able to shift their attention, resources, and values to take advantage of these new technologies and therapeutic interventions. For example, a hospital may close a number of its expensive inpatient units and establish a primary care program that provides care and treatment to patients via outpatient services. Patients' records may be transferred from hard copy to electronic form; communication options expand, and continuing education becomes increasingly important to keep employees abreast of advances in their respective fields and ensure that they can effectively operate new equipment and machinery.

While many of these responses to change benefit employees and teams, employees undergoing change often feel vulnerable and powerless. Especially during periods of transition, they must work long hours, meet expectations to produce or do more, and get by on flat line budgets and/or fewer resources than might be optimal. Pritchett and Pound (1993) emphasize the importance of managers using "psychological paychecks" to employees and teams during these times. This involves keeping employees informed about changes and the reasons for them and ensuring that they continue to feel important to the organization. If managers are not willing to listen to employees' ideas about ways to improve the quality of their work environments or their productivity, morale can be seriously compromised (Dyer, 1977). Likewise, if managers are too controlling, they can impede employees' personal growth and create tension in the work environment (Moos & Billings, 1991).

Issues and Concerns about Time/Cost Constraints

Teams perform more efficiently and effectively in organizations where management emphasizes the production of quality work rather than merely accounting for time and cost (Porter-O'Grady & Wilson, 1998). Organizations, known for high productivity and quality products and/or services, recognize the importance of realistic expectations related to employees' workloads. Presenting employees with unrealistic assignments and/or conflicting priorities does not result in cost savings; rather, it frequently leads to frustration due to an inability to meet excessive demands.

Leaders and upper level managers should balance their high expectations of timelines and cost-effectiveness with appropriate support, resources, and recognition.

Issues related to time and cost constraints are especially relevant to team performance. Misguided attempts at cost-saving, on the part of managers and supervisors, often result in denying teams the time required to meet, plan, and coordinate their work efforts and attempt to improve their processes. The essence of teamwork in health care is interdependence and collaboration, which require time for interaction among members rather than an insistence on time being spent only on production and outcomes.

Trust, Confidence, Respect, Value/Motivation and Morale

Management demonstrates its trust and confidence in employees by empowering them and making them feel that they, their ideas, and their work are valued. Employees also have a responsibility to work up to the expectations of managers and supervisors to earn this trust and respect. Employees, who work in an atmosphere of mutual trust, tend to be motivated, have high levels of commitment to the organization and its mission, and utilize their full potential in carrying out their tasks. Conversely, when employees do not experience strong backing and support from management, they become less interested and involved in the organization and are less willing and able to accomplish their work tasks effectively. Managers also need to demonstrate trust, confidence, respect, and value for teams as well as individual employees since trust building positively affects them and the motivation and morale of their members. When employees and team members feel included as important parts of the organization, they tend to have high motivation and morale, high levels of productivity, and high levels of job satisfaction (Furnham & Goodstein, 1997; Lichtenberg, Strzepek, & Zeiss, 1990).

Commitment, Cohesion, and Loyalty

Employees become committed to and identify with the organization when they perceive administrative practices, interdepartmental coordination and communication, and the effectiveness of managers, leaders, and supervisors positively and are satisfied (Baehr, 1999). When organizational managers encourage employees' involvement in the planning and decision-making processes that affect their jobs and their teams or work groups, they become committed and motivated to follow through and complete their work assignments. With continued support from management, they develop a sense of belonging, loyalty, and identification with their jobs, their teams, and the organization. Under these circumstances, they develop high levels of productivity and job satisfaction (Parker, 1990).

Relations across Teams and the Team's Reputation

Frequently teams depend upon information and resources from other teams and organizational units. Employees should spend time developing positive relationships with colleagues and coworkers in other parts of the organization to ensure that their teams mutually benefit one another and their team-to-team relationships are cooperative, not competitive. Clinical team members who communicate and collaborate effectively with colleagues in other parts of the organization tend to improve the quality of their work, and their patients receive more efficient, integrated, and continuous care. When rapport and quality working relationships exist across the organization, job satisfaction also improves.

Conversely, when teams and organizational units have low opinions of one another or employees perceive some teams as unqualified to meet their work requirements, working relationships and quality of care and services suffer. For example, in order to shield themselves from the negative perceptions of others, members of a particular team might become overly cohesive and insulate themselves from other parts of the organization. Such behavior negatively affects their ability to receive or respond to relevant and important information, and poor decision-making results (Janis, 1972; Janis & Mann, 1977).

Job Satisfaction/Security and Perceptions of the Organization

A supportive work environment contributes to employees' self-esteem, personal and team identities, and sense of job satisfaction and security. Conversely, a work environment that lacks support and compassion for employees and teams fosters feelings of isolation, frustration, stress, and dissatisfaction (Moos & Billings, 1991).

The perception employees have of their organization influences their commitment to it, their morale and motivation, and ultimately their productivity. Health care professionals and workers, who believe their place of employment provides high quality care and services to patients and is a leader in the health care delivery arena, are proud of it. Such employees are likely to have high commitment to organizational and team goals and high job satisfaction.

TEAM CONTEXT

Team context refers to the climate within the team. It influences and is influenced by attitudes toward teams, how well members know one another, how comfortable they feel being themselves in the team, and the quality of their relationships with one another. Team context also includes the social psychological climate of the team (e.g., relaxed and comfortable, tentative, tense, or hostile). Additionally, the development of enthusiasm, commitment to the team, team spirit, and identity are a part of team context. Finally, viewing the team's work as challenging and worthwhile and feeling a sense of pride in and satisfaction with the team also fall under this rubric.

Attitudes toward Teams and Teamwork

Optimally, team members believe that teamwork enhances group dynamics and group processes among professionals from different disciplines and ultimately results in more efficient and effective outcomes. Other less positive attitudes also exist among members of teams. Some prefer to work alone or perceive teamwork as a waste of time; still others are threatened by the equal status among team members or by working closely with individuals from other health professions or disciplines. Team leaders, through their leadership styles and relationships with members, can reinforce either positive or negative attitudes toward teams held by members. When team members have positive attitudes toward teams, the team tends to function well. Members have less confusion about mission and role clarity, better communication, higher levels of cohesion, and better relationships with other teams and units within the organization (Heinemann, Schmitt, Farrell, & Brallier, 1999).

Cautious, Tentative, Overly Polite Climate

A cautious, tentative, overly polite climate is evident in most newly developing teams and teams that have not matured beyond the first stage of development (Farrell, Heinemann, & Schmitt, 1986; Tuckman, 1965; Wheelan, 1993). Team members often are reserved and hesitant to express thoughts, ideas, and feelings. They are unclear about the team's purpose and what is expected of them in terms of roles, responsibilities, and accomplishing the team's goals and objectives. They do not know one another well enough to challenge opinions, approach problems creatively, or openly disagree. They tend to support the majority view or concur prematurely on issues requiring a more thorough discussion and group interaction. In such a climate, team members are inhibited, and the processes of creative problem solving, decision-making, and synergy are diminished significantly.

Being Oneself and Getting to Know Other Team Members

As the team develops and begins to overcome the reserved style typical of early stage team interactions, members become more familiar with one another, both professionally and personally. Trust and confidence develop among them, and the support and encouragement they give each other further increases openness and sharing. In well functioning teams, members are comfortable being themselves. Their working relationships become more collaborative as they utilize one another's skills appropriately, build on each other's strengths, and compensate for any weaknesses (Mechanic, 1962). In well performing teams, members also learn to balance personal sharing and support with task-oriented activities.

Congenial, Caring, and Accepting Climate

One way team members learn about one another is through socializing together. Taking coffee breaks, eating lunch, and participating in other social activities together provide team members with opportunities to interact and become friendly in less restrictive environments. As they find shared interests and commonalties, they develop a more caring and accepting atmosphere in which to work. Gradually members gain confidence in themselves and in one another. They become better able to empathize with and support one another. Such a congenial climate enhances group cohesion, and, over time, members develop a sense of unity and team identity.

Trust, Confidence, Respect, and Value

In well functioning teams, members trust and have confidence in one another and the team's leadership (Phillips & Elledge, 1989; Porter-O'Grady & Wilson, 1998). Team members feel they can count on each other and have confidence in their collective ability to perform well even under stressful circumstances. Members respect one another as professionals or technical experts, value each other, and feel valued and appropriately utilized in the team. While it takes time and energy to develop trust among team members, a high level of trust has positive payoffs. Communication becomes more open and honest as trust increases. Members are less reserved and more willing to express their own ideas and opinions to one another and become better able to disagree with one another (Chartier, 1991). When trust is high in the team, members' behaviors are more open and interdependent. A high trust level in the team also is related to personal growth of members and team productivity (Gibb, 1977).

Relaxed, Comfortable Versus Tense, Hostile Climate

In teams where members know each other well and come to trust, value, and respect one another, the climate is relaxed and comfortable, and the quality of communication is enhanced. Group discussions, decision-making, and problem solving are more pleasant and productive. Members are able to bring divergent views out in the open for discussion and express their feelings, both positive and negative. They are less likely to take things personally or become angry over disagreements. A climate that permits free expression reduces the likelihood of conflict or morale problems and permits the team to function more efficiently and effectively (Hall, 1969; Shockley-Zalabak, 1981; Zeiss & Steffen, 1996).

Conversely, when trust, value, and respect among team members do not develop, the team often becomes "stuck" in the conflict stage of development where hostility, anger, and frustration prevent the open airing of feelings and the use of disagreement to make better decisions. Energies that should be directed into productivity and team accomplishments are often used to fuel conflict and dysfunctional competition among team members (Farrell, Heinemann, & Schmitt, 1986).

Feelings of Pressure and Stress

If the team is not functioning efficiently (e.g., members duplicate efforts and do not use their time well), or if its workload is unrealistic due to overzealous cost cutting on the part of management, members experience high levels of work-related stress, frustration, and low morale. Additionally, caring for critically ill, chronically ill, or dying patients can be stressful to team members. Excessive stress and feelings of frustration among members can compromise their physical and emotional health and, ultimately, reduce the quality of care and services they deliver to patients (Moos & Schaefer, 1987). Team leadership should encourage mechanisms for members to reduce excessive stress such as keeping lines of communication open within the team and with management. Also helpful are discussions about loss of patients and participation in exercise, stress management, or other employee assistance programs as discussed earlier in this chapter under organizational context.

Support and Encouragement

In high performing teams, members and leaders support and encourage one another as professionals and technical experts as well as personally. This may include sharing relevant information to facilitate the accomplishment of work tasks, providing backup as necessary, and/or "covering" for those members attending professional conferences or training programs (Scholtes, 1988). Members also help one another cope with challenging, difficult, or stressful work situations such as preparing for a briefing with management or with site visitors evaluating a special hospital program. When a team member faces a personal crisis or challenge, other members rally around in support of him or her and ensure the team's continued functioning. For example, during an illness or death in the family, other members express feelings of consolation and adjust the workload of the team to compensate for the time the member in crisis is absent from work.

The team orients new members and new student trainees to a positive team culture in which support and encouragement among members are the expected norms.

Commitment to Team, Members, and Teamwork

Commitment to the team's purpose and goals is critical to its success. When members are bound both personally and professionally to an ideal or course of action, the likelihood of consistent positive team outcomes increases. Team members must be willing, at times, to subordinate their personal goals to the goals of the team (Mackie & Goethals, 1987). This does not mean that team members should be encouraged to lose sight of their individual goals or identities. Rather, they should realize that successful teamwork requires recognition of and sustained commitment to the team's vision, mission, and goals. The returns on investment in and commitment to the team include increased motivation, enthusiasm, and perception of the work as interesting and important as well as increased cohesion and sense of unity among members. When the team is functioning well, its goals and those of its individual member's often coincide.

Cohesion, Unity, and Team Identity

Cohesion refers to a sense of solidarity and unity among team members. It develops as they work together over time, develop mutual trust, and become adept at using one another's skills and abilities appropriately. As cohesion develops, a cooperative group identity also emerges (Tuckman, 1965). Members have a sense of belonging to the team, and cliques and individual competition become less apparent. In teams where members are cohesive, processes improve, and members work together more collaboratively and efficiently. They function as a collective unit and create a more supportive treatment environment for patients (Moos & Moos, 1998).

Team Spirit, Morale, Energy, and Enthusiasm

Once team members become cohesive and a sense of team identity develops, they experience high levels of morale, energy, and enthusiasm (Ancona, 1987; Porter-O'Grady & Wilson, 1998). The sense of group identity and feelings of being a valued part of the team increase members' excitement and motivation. They develop more confidence in the team and believe it can take on challenging and complex tasks and complete them successfully. Confidence leads to increased team spirit, and productivity increases as well as the quality of accomplishments.

Perceptions of Interesting, Challenging, and Important Work

When members have a voice in determining the team's mission, goals, and objectives and understand how their team's work activities contribute to the organization as a whole, they are more likely to perceive their work as interesting, challenging, and important. Members, who have positive perceptions of their work, are more likely than others to be task-oriented and concerned about the quality of their and the team's work. They also are more likely to be committed to the team, to its customers, and to the organization (Lichtenberg, Strzepek, & Zeiss, 1990). Perceptions of work as meaningful often result in improved relationships with customers such as patients, their family members, and their informal caregivers. Job satisfaction improves among team members, and satisfaction with care and services improves among the team's patients.

Pride and Satisfaction with Colleagues, Team, and Teamwork

A final element of team context is developing pride and satisfaction with colleagues, the team, and teamwork. When members are proud of their team, they tend to have high morale and feel a personal sense of enjoyment about being part of the team. They also are willing to help each other find personal satisfaction from the team's work. They are satisfied with their roles in the team and the kind of work they do as team members. They feel good about where the team is headed, the interactions among members, and the way the work gets done. They are productive and often express a sense of satisfaction with the team's leadership, its overall performance, and its accomplishments.

SUMMARY

The context within which teamwork takes place has been the focus of considerable writing and research. The quality of support for teams from the organization in which they function is crucial to their ability to develop into coordinated, effective working units. Organizations provide this support through managers modeling the team approach, providing resources to teams so they can pursue their mission effectively, and providing recognition and rewards for effective teamwork. Within teams, a positive context of trust, commitment, respect, warmth, and willingness to support one another is essential. Team members can promote such a climate by getting to know one another and developing a sense of mutual trust, cohesion, and team identity. When these contextual conditions are met, members become energized and motivated. The stage is set for effective, coordinated, interdependent efforts, high levels of productivity, and quality accomplishments.

REFERENCES

Ancona, D.G. (1987). Groups in organizations: Extending laboratory models. In C Hendrick (Ed.), *Group processes* (pp.207-230). Newbury Park, CA: Sage Publications, Inc.

Baehr, M.E. (1999). *Organizational Survey System (OSS) sample report for health care: Nursing staff.* Minneapolis, MN: National Computer Systems, Inc.

Barczak, N. (1996). How to lead effective teams. *Critical Care Nursing Quarterly, 19*, 73-82.

Chartier, M.R. (1991). Trust-Orientation Profile. In J.W. Pfeiffer (Ed.), *The 1991 annual: Developing human resources* (pp. 139-148). San Diego, CA: Pfeiffer & Company.

Dyer, W.G. (1977). *Team building: Issues and alternatives*. Reading, MA: Addison-Wesley Publishing Company.

Farrell, M.P., Heinemann, G.D., & Schmitt, M.H. (1986). Informal roles, rituals and styles of humor in interdisciplinary health care teams: Their relationship to stages of group development. *International Journal of Small Group Research, 2*, 143-162.

Furnham, A., & Goodstein, L.D. (1997). The Organizational Climate Questionnaire (OCQ). In *The 1997 annual: Volume 2, consulting* (pp. 163-181). San Francisco: Pfeiffer, an imprint of Jossey Bass, Inc.

Gibb, J.R. (1977). TORI Group Self-Diagnosis Scale. In J.E. Jones & J.W. Pfeiffer (Eds.), *The 1977 annual handbook for group facilitators* (pp. 73-81). San Diego, CA: Pfeiffer & Company.

Hall, J. (1969). *Conflict Management Survey: A survey of one's own characteristic reaction to and handling of conflicts between himself and others*. Conroe, TX: Teleometrics International.

Heinemann, G.D., Schmitt, M.H., Farrell, M.P., & Brallier, S.A. (1999). Development of an Attitudes Toward Health Care Teams Scale. *Evaluation & the Health Professions, 22*, 123-142.

Janis, I.L. (1972). *Victims of Groupthink: A psychological study of foreign policy decisions and fiascos*. Boston, MA: Houghton Mifflin.

Janis, I.L., & Mann, L. (1977). *Decision making*. New York: Free Press.

Lichtenberg, P.A., Strzepek, D.M., & Zeiss, A.M. (1990). Bringing psychiatric aides to the treatment team: An application of the VA's ITTG model. *Gerontology & Geriatrics Education, 10*, 63-73.

Mackie, D.M., & Goethals, G.R. (1987). Individual and group goals. In C. Hendrick (Ed.), *Group processes* (pp.144-166). Newbury Park, CA: Sage Publications.

Mechanic, D. (1962). Sources of power of lower participants in complex organizations. *Administrative Science Quarterly, 7*, 349-364.

Moos, R.H., & Billings, A.G. (1991). Understanding and improving work climates. In J.W. Jones, B.D. Steffy, & D.W. Bray (Eds.), *Applying psychology in business: The handbook for mangers and human resource professionals* (pp. 552-562). Lexington, MA: D.C. Heath.

Moos, R.H., & Moos, B.S. (1998). The staff workplace and quality and outcome of substance abuse treatment. *Journal of Studies on Alcohol, 59*, 43-51.

Moos, R.H., & Schaefer, J.A. (1987). Evaluating health care work settings: A holistic conceptual framework. *Psychology and Health, 1*, 97-122.

Parker, G.M. (1990). *Team players and teamwork: The new competitive business strategy*. San Francisco: Jossey-Bass Publishers.

Phillips, S.L., & Elledge, R.L. (1989). *The team building sourcebook*. San Diego, CA: University Associates, Inc.

Porter-O'Grady, T., & Wilson, C.K. (1998). *The health care team book*. St. Louis, MO: Mosby.

Pritchett, P., & Pound, R. (1993). *Team reconstruction: Building a high performance work group during change*. Plano, TX: Pritchett Rummler-Brache.

Scholtes, P.R. (Ed.). (1988). *The team handbook: How to use teams to improve quality*. Madison, WI: Joiner Associates, Inc.

Shockley-Zalabak, P. (1981). The effects of sex differences on the preference for utilization of conflict styles of managers in a work setting: An exploratory study. *Public Personnel Management Journal, 10*, 289-295.

Shortell, S.M., Zimmerman, J.E., Rousseau, D.M., Gillies, R.R., Wagner, D.P., Draper, E.A., Knaus, W.A., & Duffy, J. (1994). The performance of intensive care units: Does good management make a difference? *Medical Care, 32*, 508-525.

Tuckman, B.W. (1965). Developmental sequences in small groups. *Psychological Bulletin, 63*, 384-399.

Wheelan, S.A. (1993). *The Group Development Questionnaire: A manual for professionals.* Philadelphia, PA: GDQ Associates.

Zeiss, A.M., & Steffen, A. (1996). Interdisciplinary health care teams: The basic unit of geriatric care. In L.L. Carstensen, B.A. Edelstein, & L. Dornbrand (Eds.), *The handbook of clinical gerontology* (pp. 423-450). Thousand Oaks, CA: Sage Publications, Inc.

CHAPTER 6
TEAM PROCESS

Linda O. Nichols, Ph.D.
VA Medical Center, Memphis, TN. VISN 9

Alice M. DeFriese, Ph.D., R.N.C.
VA Northern California Health Care System, Sacramento, CA, VISN 21

Charlotte C. Malone, M.A.
Navy Recruiting Command, Memphis, TN

Process refers to how the team functions (i.e., how members work to carry out the mission and goals of the team) and whether the team and its members grow, develop, and improve over time. In our model of team performance, the domain of process is dynamic and action-oriented. Process influences and is influenced by both team structure and context, covered in Chapters 4 and 5, respectively. This reciprocal influence also applies to accomplishments and outcomes, covered in Chapter 7.

Despite the importance of effective process, many organizations and teams, especially in the U.S., do not provide adequate time for developing and maintaining it. With the present emphasis on productivity and outcomes, American society and its organizations often lack appreciation for the role of process in determining quality results. Management in some U.S. organizations believes that developing teams is a waste of time and unrelated to quality of services high productivity (Donnellon, 1996; Dumaine, 1990; Nahavandi & Aranda, 1994). Such beliefs devalue team process and result in unreasonable limits on the amount of time organizations permit teams to grow, develop, improve, and become collaborative working units. During periods of downsizing and cost containment, teams often fail to take the time to develop their process activities. This can result in inefficiency and reduced productivity of the team.

In this chapter, we address the two dimensions of process in our model of team performance, interdependence and growth and development. We also explore the elements within each dimension as they relate to performance.

INTERDEPENDENCE

Interdependence is the hallmark of teamwork (Kormanski & Mozenter, 1987; Reilly & Jones, 1974). When team members collaborate and are truly interdependent, the team develops a synergy that facilitates its functioning and its productivity. The interdependence dimension of team process includes a considerable number of elements such as utilizing the team's resources and team members' abilities to communicate, cooperate, work together, and share the workload effectively. Participation and sharing leadership in making decisions, solving problems, and managing conflict also are part of interdependence. Finally, being task-oriented, implementing tasks efficiently, balancing task and process activities, and using the appropriate process for a particular situation are elements of interdependence.

Utilizing Resources and Team Members

Ideally, teams should be composed of individuals who have the appropriate skill sets to accomplish its mission. Members bring a variety of knowledge bases, skills, and expertise to the team, and when the team functions well, these individual strengths complement one another (Given & Simmons, 1977). "The team as a whole, rather than each of its members, must possess the desired attributes" (Hammer & Stanton, 1995, p, 61). Thus, the resources each member brings to a team can be forged into team competence. This requires that members take the time to identify one another's skills and abilities and participate in and contribute to the team's efforts. A team is unproductive when it fails to utilize members' capabilities and contributions for the benefit of the team as a whole (Hackman, 1999).

Diversity, professional, cultural, and demographic (e.g., age and gender), among team members provides a variety of perspectives for decision-making, problem solving, and creativity. Diversity also expands the team's spectrum of skills, resources, and experiences (Bryan, 1999; Ilgen, 1999; Kirchmeyer & Cohen, 1992; McClelland, 1999; Ovretveit, 1996). The relationship between diversity and team functioning, however, may be curvilinear in that too little diversity can lead to "groupthink" and too much can inhibit the ability of team members to develop common goals and shared understandings (Ilgen, 1999; Lichtenstein, Alexander, Jinnett, & Ullman, 1997). According to Kirchmeyer and Cohen (1992), training in the management of disagreement and conflict that accompany diversity increases the decision-making effectiveness of culturally diverse groups. As a result of such training, minority members, in particular, become more active and contribute divergent points of view that provide broader perspectives, more options for consideration, and potentially better decisions. Thus, teams and work groups that learn to utilize the diverse resources of their members function more effectively.

Participation and Workload Sharing

Once team members become committed to the team and its mission and feel comfortable with one another, they are more likely to participate in the team's activities. That is, they more readily use their skills and abilities to further the team's goals; they accept responsibility for specific tasks and "pitch in" to share the work of the team with other members. The active participation of all members increases the quality of the team's process activities (e.g., communication, collaboration, and decision-making) and the quality of its accomplishments. Conversely, when team members do not "pull together" some become overworked and burn out while others never become committed to the team and its goals. Team process suffers, and the team is less efficient and less productive as a result.

Communication

Quality communication is a prerequisite for every aspect of team performance (Dickinson & McIntyre, 1997; Johnson & Johnson, 1991). Communication can be oral, written, and nonverbal. The ability of the clinical team to provide care and treatment to its patient population depends upon members exchanging information effectively with one another and with the team's customers. The better the communication within the team and with other teams and units in the organization, the better the team is likely to perform. Conversely, poor communication can impede team performance by adding to workload stress, mental effort, fatigue, and time and cost pressures (Bowers, Braun, & Morgan, 1997; Casali & Wierwille, 1983).

In teams that communicate well, members minimize the use of discipline-specific jargon and develop a common language, where terms have the same meaning for all members. The development of a common language helps unify team members and facilitates open, honest, and accurate communication among them. Reciprocity is an important part of communication; dialoging together is much more effective that one-sided presentations of information. When members are communicating well, they present information clearly and concisely, and no one holds back relevant pieces of information. They do not interrupt one another or begin side conversations when a particular member "has the floor." Members listen carefully to make sure they understand one another. Other ways to ensure understanding include paraphrasing the speaker's message, asking questions for clarification, and summarizing the speaker's main points. Finally, members are not made to feel defensive or embarrassed in public since such feelings create barriers to effective communication.

Team members' nonverbal communication should match verbal content. Voice tone or actions (e.g., eye contact, posture, standing or sitting, gesturing) should make sense in the context of the oral/verbal message. Consideration should be given for cultural differences in the meaning and appropriateness of nonverbal communication (e.g., the meaning of direct eye contact and the physical proximity of individuals during communication); these nonverbal cues often differ from culture to culture. In written communication, the nonverbal cues include the use of emphases such as underlining, highlighting, punctuation, and capitalizing.

Legibility and accessibility also are important with regard to written communication. Patients' data, whether hard copy charts or computerized data files, should be available to team members when needed. Lost charts and computer systems that are "down" much of the time interfere with effective communication among team members.

Giving and Receiving Feedback

Feedback is a critical component of teamwork (Dickinson & McIntyre, 1997). If members are to take corrective actions with regard to improving the team or improving themselves as team members, they must learn how to give and receive feedback. Good communication skills are a must, and the norms established regarding feedback are equally important. First, both strengths and areas for improvement should be addressed so negative criticism does not predominate. Second, feedback should never be presented to embarrass, "put down," or demoralize; rather, it should be given in the spirit of facilitating improvement in the team and one another as team members. Third, team members must learn to assess, accept, and act on feedback given to them rather than overly personalize it (McIntyre & Salas, 1995). Finally, the ability to accept feedback often depends on the way it is presented and whether suggestions are made for improvement. Thus, the giver of feedback should be supportive of the person receiving it and should acknowledge positive changes in behavior observed in response to the feedback (Kraiger & Wenzel, 1997).

Giving and receiving feedback can be problematic in health care teams and natural work groups where members do not function as equals. In these circumstances, the majority of feedback experiences on the job are set within a superior/subordinate relationship (e.g., supervisor/employee). Consequently, the communication models for feedback often do not incorporate the concept of equals sharing information about behavior, peer to peer, as occurs in a well functioning, interdisciplinary team.

Although it is more difficult to assess the dynamics and process activities of the team than it is to identify individual team member's strengths and weaknesses, some team members feel less threatened hearing feedback when it is directed at the team rather than at themselves. In such situations, it is best for team members to focus on the team or work group when critiquing strengths and weaknesses initially. As they become more comfortable with this process, they can begin to give one another feedback as well. It also is important that team members distinguish between the team's and individual team member's strengths and weaknesses. The team should not be blamed when a particular team member has not worked up to his or her potential. Nor should particular team members become "scapegoats" and always blamed for problems arising at the level of the team (e.g., unclear roles, lack of rules and procedures, or a tense or hostile atmosphere).

Collaboration

Collaboration occurs when team members need one another to complete assignments and associated tasks (Kormanski & Mozenter, 1987). It requires that they trust, complement, help, and support one another as they work together (Hayes, 1997). In effective teams, members share and participate in its process activities. They take collective responsibility for using the team's resources, and they work in concert to achieve its goals (Ovretveit, 1996; Williams & Laungani, 1999).

Given the American cultural context of valuing and rewarding individual effort (Nahavandi & Aranda, 1994; Reagan, 1996), fostering the notion of collaboration can conflict with team members' and managers' preferences for individual autonomy in U.S. organizations (Donnellon, 1996). In the health care setting, this barrier can be amplified by the technical or professional nature of team members' specialty areas and the limited training in collaborative practice that students in the medical and health care professions receive (Baldwin, 1996). Freeth (2001) also identified barriers to sustaining collaboration over time. These include structural differences between organizations, complex communication demands, team member turnover and the need to form strong links with the new members, regular evaluation, and shared planning among team members. Teams that manage to overcome these barriers are more likely to demonstrate effective, interdependent process behaviors and activities.

Cooperation, Coordination, and Efficiency

In well functioning teams, members cooperate with one another and coordinate their efforts. Duplication and fragmentation diminish and the results are a more efficient work group. When cooperation, coordination, and efficiency are key elements in a team's process, its members also tend to share leadership responsibility, and the team becomes a self-managed work group. Teams, whose members are unable to cooperate and coordinate their efforts, often become fixated in the second or conflict stage of development. Their efficiency and cost-effectiveness suffer. Under these circumstances, an educational program or consultation may be necessary to facilitate their maturation to a higher level of functioning.

Power and Leadership Sharing

Power Sharing

Well functioning teams de-emphasize power differentials among members and work to balance the different types of power across members. Power should be a function of the expertise among team members as they collaborate and contribute to attaining the team's goals (Johnson & Johnson, 1991). Members are more likely to share power and positively influence one another when they perceive working together as meaningful and rewarding.

Power differences within the team come from multiple sources, including formal organizational position (e.g., supervisor, team coordinator/leader), work or professional status (e.g., professional, specialist), individual factors related to the job (e.g., competence, information, skills, expertise, experience, work ethic), and an employee's personality (e.g., charisma, friendliness). Power differentials are always present, and all human interaction involves the use of power or influence. The activation and use of power differentials unrelated to expertise can affect teamwork negatively (Poulton & West, 1999). Such power differences within hospitals and within teams also can negatively affect the management of conflict (Skjørshammer, 2001). When power belongs to a single member or faction within the team or to a supervisor outside the team, commitment, participation among members, and productivity suffer. Donnellon (1996) describes linguistic strategies for minimizing the use of power (e.g., requests, politeness, and disclaimers) as opposed to strategies that maximize its use (e.g., dominating the discussion, demanding, and directing). When power flows from gender, status, or other characteristics apart from expertise, the ability of team members to work collaboratively and interdependently is diminished.

Leadership Sharing

In some teams, management assigns and fills formal leadership positions; in others, supervisors appoint team leaders, and in still others, leaders emerge and are legitimated by team members. Teams require the performance of certain leadership functions in order for them to achieve their goals, maintain themselves, and relate effectively to the surrounding work environment (Hamaoui & Nichols, 1993; Johnston, Smith-Jentsch, & Cannon-Bowers, 1997). Very rarely are all of the skills necessary to move the team forward embodied in one member of the team. Thus, the sharing of leadership permits the different leadership skills of members to complement one another and helps ensure that any given situation in the team will be met with the appropriate leadership style. Thus, leadership sharing is vital for quality team performance.

Utilizing Leadership Skills

Leadership skills include serving as a team representative and team advocate within the health care organization (i.e., serving as a conduit between management and members of the team). This involves requesting needed resources, providing progress reports of the team's activities and accomplishments, and informing team members about new organizational directions and policies that impact them and their work. A good leader facilitates the coordination and planning of the team's activities and serves as a mediator and calming force for its members. Other leadership skills include setting high standards and clear expectations for members; demonstrating trust and confidence in members' abilities; listening to and supporting their ideas, suggestions, and opinions; encouraging their learning, growth, and creativity; creating an environment for trust and collaboration; and recognizing and rewarding their performance. Finally, good leaders match their respective leadership styles with the requirements of the situation at hand and encourage the participation of other team members in leadership activities (Dimock, 1987; Ducanis & Golin, 1979; Dyer, 1977; Kormanski & Mozenter, 1987; Larson & LaFasto, 1989).

In teams with formal leaders, the ability of members to share leadership is highly dependent on the style of the formal leader. An overly assertive, authoritarian leadership style stifles other members' commitment and involvement, creates a climate of apathy or conflict related to authority in the team, and can negatively affect team functioning. Conversely, when formal leaders set expectations for shared leadership as well as nurture and model effective leadership behavior, team members develop these skills, take responsibility for leadership activities, and use their skills appropriately.

Decision-Making and Problem Solving

Quality decision-making and problem solving activities require input and participation from all members of the team. A team has reached consensus when it is able to articulate a proposal that all team members can accept and support. Consensus has little to do with voting or with all team members being completely satisfied (Scholtes, 1991). Consensus involves at least three phases. First, brainstorming is the sharing of ideas, the more the better, without any evaluation. Second, members prioritize these ideas along with a rationale for the rankings. Finally, they choose the best two options as Plan A and Plan B. Consensus decision-making and problem solving are most appropriate when issues are complex and when there is adequate time for a comprehensive discussion. In situations where team members have widely divergent initial opinions or are in conflict, they can use a five-phase approach to come to consensus (Fisher, Ury, & Patton, 1991). This approach is described under the conflict management section of this chapter.

Teams that never develop the skills associated with reaching consensus become vulnerable to conflict when critical, unpopular, or emotion-laden decisions must be made (Hamaoui & Nichols, 1993). If all team members are not involved in making the decision, the best decision may not be reached due to missing pieces of information. Additionally, a decision made without consensus may later be sabotaged or ignored by those members dissatisfied with the decision-making process or with the decision itself.

Another danger for team decision-making is groupthink or premature concurrence of group members prior to considering all relevant information and options critically (Janis, 1972; Janis & Mann, 1977). In groupthink, members do not identify alternatives to a suggested solution and minimize any doubts raised about the decision. They make poor decisions that undermine members' confidence, morale, and outcomes. Groupthink usually occurs in newly developing teams, in teams with an overly directive leader, and teams insulated from experts and other organizational teams and units (Heinemann, Farrell, & Schmitt, 1994).

Consensus is not always the most appropriate methodology for making a group decision or solving a problem. Some issues are not complex or important enough to require it, or the team may not have a broad enough time frame to utilize it. In the latter instance, the team's leader(s) should initiate a short, focused discussion to gain an understanding of members' views and opinions about the issue.

Conflict Management

Conflict is a normal part of group development (Farrell, Heinemann, & Schmitt, 1986; Tuckman, 1965; Tuckman & Jensen, 1977; Wheelan, 1993). Disagreement and conflict provide opportunities for members to define their roles more clearly and develop common norms and values. If managed appropriately, they provide energy and facilitate the development of trust, cohesion, and collaboration (Wheelan, 1993).

Without effective mechanisms for conflict management, conflict can lead to misunderstandings, anger, and hostility among team members and between members and leaders. Conflict management and resolution require a balancing of extreme views or positions and establishing a unified direction for the team and its members. They also require that communication and other interpersonal skills be practiced and used on a regular basis if conflict is to be constructive rather than destructive for the team. Team members are more likely to facilitate conflict resolution when they feel safe expressing diverse opinions and disagreeing with one another (Hochberger & Tedeschi, 1998). Suppressed or unresolved conflict can fester and increase hostility in the team as well as polarize its members (Hamaoui & Nichols, 1993). In polarized teams, members expend their energies fighting and arguing with one another rather than addressing the needs of their patients or other customers.

Five styles of conflict resolution can be identified on the basis of one's responses to assertiveness and cooperativeness (Johnson & Johnson, 1991; Thomas, 1992). Assertiveness refers to concern for one's own needs, and cooperativeness refers to concern for the needs of the other party or parties in the conflict situation. Persons use the avoidance style in conflict situations when they ignore both their own and the other party's needs (i.e., when they are most unassertive and most uncooperative). In the competing style, persons are highly assertive regarding their own needs, but ignore the needs of the other party. The reverse of the competing style is the accommodating style in which persons attempt to satisfy the needs of the other party to the exclusion of their own needs. All three of these styles tend increase anger and frustration as well as escalate rather than resolve the conflict.

Midway between the competing and accommodating styles is the compromising style. Persons using this style are moderately assertive and moderately cooperative (i.e., they give up some of their needs to get others met). The ideal style in dealing with conflict is the collaborating style; here persons are highly assertive regarding their own needs and highly cooperative regarding the needs of the other party. They come to view the conflict as a mutual problem.

Teams skilled at resolving conflict will utilize the style appropriate for a given situation and the individuals involved. For example, the compromising style is appropriate when a team is working under a tight deadline. The collaborating style is most effective given enough time to identify the concerns of all parties in the conflict. This style facilitates improved relationships between the parties in conflict and the development of a solution that creatively integrates the needs of all parties. It also can save time in that once resolved, these issues, with appropriate monitoring, do not result in major conflicts again. Unfortunately, Skjørshammer (2001) found, in a case study of one Norwegian hospital, that avoidance is the most common style used by health professionals in dealing with conflict. Some health professionals were embarrassed by conflict, and others did not view its management as urgent given their other hospital priorities.

The basic tool for conflict resolution is negotiation. In developing a process to manage conflict, teams must be aware of the characteristics of good negotiation (Fisher, Ury, & Patton, 1991). Effective negotiation is efficient and durable; improves or does not damage the relationship between negotiators; meets both parties' legitimate interests; takes the interests of the team, organization, and customers into account; and resolves conflicting interests fairly.

Fisher, Ury, and Patton (1991) describe a five-phase approach to resolving conflict. First, the parties involved delineate clearly the disagreement while being respectful to the concerns of each party. Second, each party clarifies his/her interests. What does each hope will happen or fear might happen? This phase is vital to the success of the process; it requires parties to the conflict to temporarily set aside their positions and focus on the outcomes they hope to achieve. Next, using brainstorming techniques, they collaboratively generate new action options that address all of the expressed interests. Fourth, using objective criteria, they select the option that best addresses the problem and satisfies their interests. Finally, they identify a "fall-back" position if no option satisfies the needs of all parties. This last phase is rarely needed if the approach has been followed in good faith.

Utilizing Appropriate Team Process Activities

In well performing teams, members use the most appropriate process activity for a given situation. When issues are unclear, they communicate; when numerous activities must be completed simultaneously, they prioritize, plan, and coordinate their efforts; when patients present complex needs, they collect relevant information, share it with one another, and problem solve. Leaders do not make hasty decisions regarding complex issues when time permits members to discuss a variety of options and make a better decision. Conversely, members do not waste time in consensus decision-making when one member of the team can make a simple, straightforward decision. Utilizing appropriate process activities improves both the efficiency and effectiveness of the team.

Task-Orientation and Effective Task Implementation

Effective teams are task-oriented, and members expect one another to have a strong work ethic. They plan and implement activities related to their mission, purpose, and goals. Usually the activities of teams in health care settings refer to the care, treatment, and services provided to patients and related customers. Members plan proactively, come to meetings prepared to participate, stay focused, and implement plans of action collaboratively and efficiently in order to accomplish their goals. They also report their outcomes and accomplishments to management systematically and implement suggestions for maximizing the quality of their treatment, care and services.

Balance Between Task and Process Activities

As stated in Chapters 1 and 4, well functioning teams attend to both task and process goals. On one hand, they stay focused on the work to be done and carry out activities to this end. On the other hand, they monitor the way in which members work together and take action to improve their process and the team's functioning as needed. In high performance teams, members must learn to balance these two sets of goals. They must be able to attend to the tasks related to their patients and/or customers, use appropriate process activities, and, at the same time, be responsive to actions that detract from effective interpersonal relationships and group dynamics.

GROWTH AND DEVELOPMENT

In order for the members of a team to work interdependently, growth and development must occur at two levels–at the level of the team and at the level of individual team members. Teams change over time. Members leave the team, and new ones replace them. The team takes on new patients with new problems and needs, and new standards of practice replace old ones as knowledge and technology expand clinical expertise and capabilities. These kinds of changes can alter the mission and goals of the team as well as the dynamics within the team. The ongoing process of growth and development is essential for teams to function optimally and to ensure their accountability to stakeholders and customers (Hackman, 1987; Montebello, 1994).

The ability to grow and develop is influenced by a number of factors. Teams in organizations that value learning have fewer barriers to growth and development in comparison to other organizations (Senge, 1990; Senge, Kleiner, Roberts, Ross, & Smith, 1994). Supportive leadership, from the organization and from within the team, is a driving force for growth and development. Shared ideals, values, and working relationships among team members also facilitate growth and development. Support and sharing give members a sense of ownership with regard to the team and the organization (Fullan, 1986). Additionally, team members must maintain and update their respective technical and/or discipline-specific knowledge bases and skills and keep abreast of the new, "cutting edge" techniques and procedures for clinical treatment and care. Each of them also should learn and implement the skills of teamwork.

The growth and development dimension of process includes: (a) skills mastery and its maintenance; (b) utilizing feedback and learning from mistakes; (c) role bending and cross-training; (d) flexibility; and (e) creativity, risk-taking, and innovation.

Skills Mastery, Maintenance, and Application

When the team and its leadership value continuous learning, it becomes an automatic expectation. Under these circumstances, individual members are able to capitalize on opportunities for growth and development with regard to both professional and team competencies. Each team member reflects on his/her strengths and weaknesses and attempts to improve in areas where weaknesses are evident. With regard to professional competencies, some professions mandate a certain number of continuing education hours per year for upgrading technical qualifications and keeping up-to-date about new and changing technologies. Such new learning enhances professional growth and development and, ultimately, team productivity.

While most team members become well versed in their respective professional/work areas, many have not had training in the skills of teamwork. It is necessary to learn how to work effectively with team members from other professions and work areas with regard to both the team's task and process activities (Barr, 1998). The members themselves often determine when team skills are lacking or need to be improved. Keeping lines of communication open with coworkers outside the team and attending educational programs offered in the local community or their respective professional organizations can not only facilitate growth and development among team members, but also help prevent insulation and faulty decision-making by the team.

Regardless of how team members become leaders or under what conditions they accept leadership responsibility, they must possess leadership skills and expertise relevant to the team's mission and goals if the team is to function well and be successful. For example, in team meetings a number of leadership roles are important (e.g., chairperson, recorder/scribe, timekeeper, process facilitator). Initially, team members take turns "trying on" and practicing any or all of these roles; later, as the team matures, they selectively volunteer for only those roles that coincide with their skills, comfort level, and effectiveness in carrying them out.

Informal Learning, Utilizing Feedback, and Learning from Mistakes

Opportunities for team members to grow and develop are available if they learn from one another as they work together, utilize feedback about the team and themselves as members, and have leaders who encourage learning from mistakes.

The team setting itself maximizes opportunities for informal learning since employees are exposed to new knowledge bases and skill sets as they work together on a regular basis. These opportunities are enhanced even more when all members of the team participate in the team's activities and share information and express ideas and opinions openly with one another. Leaders and supervisors can facilitate informal learning by taking advantage of "teachable moments" with team members during the work day and setting expectations related to members learning from one another, meeting new challenges, and striving for improvement. Teams, functioning as feedback systems, as described in Chapter 1, also enhance informal learning by reviewing previous work, and refining it.

It is not enough that team members are able to give and receive feedback appropriately. They must use the feedback from one another, the team's leadership, and sources outside the team to help them and the team become better functioning. Well performing teams often use continuous quality improvement techniques, discussed in Chapter 1, as well as self-monitoring strategies, discussed in Chapter 7, to ensure constructive feedback is considered and used to help members build upon their strengths, learn from their mistakes, and improve the team's ability to function effectively. Viewing mistakes as a way to learn and improve encourages team members' creativity, risk-taking, and innovation. Leaders, who view mistakes as rationale for punitive, reduce inquisitiveness and informal learning among team members.

Preventing Insulation

Insulation occurs when team members close off ideas and opinions from outside the team. Insulation can stifle new perspectives and creative ways of thinking and acting. It also can lead to groupthink or "decision fiascos" in teams (Heinemann, Farrell, & Schmitt, 1994; Janis, 1972; Janis & Mann, 1977). Teams and their members are more likely to grow and develop if they do not isolate themselves from other teams, units, and programs in the hospital or from resources and expertise outside the organization. Working in a vacuum can be avoided by inviting consultant team members and content experts to team meetings for their ideas and feedback. Using outside facilitators trained in the techniques of reflection, inquiry skills, and dialogue facilitation also can prevent insulation (Senge, Kleiner, Roberts, Ross, & Smith, 1994).

Role Bending and Cross-Training

As team members work together over time, they learn from one another. They bend their roles beyond the limits of their respective disciplines and professions, and as a result, they expand their knowledge bases and skill sets. Role bending is especially important in teams where members do not have equal access to the patients (e.g., primary care or home care). For example, in a home care team, the social worker may be the contact person seeing a particular patient during a given time period. He/she must serve as the eyes and ears for all of the other professionals on the team and alert them to any patients' needs or symptoms related to their respective areas of expertise. Having learned from one's team members makes this task much easier.

In natural work groups, members receive cross-training to increase their flexibility within the group and be able to "fill in" for one another or take on additional duties. Such cross-training permits the team to maintain consistent levels of efficiency and productivity during vacation periods, workload peaks, or periods of high turnover. Members of both natural work groups and clinical teams must constantly guard against taking on broader roles than their training or professional scope of practice allows them to handle safely and effectively.

Flexibility

Flexibility is the ability to adapt to new or changing situations readily, handle multiple inputs and tasks, be open to others' ideas, and maximize limited resources. Flexibility is important at the team level, especially with the development of regional health care organizations, hospital integrations, restructuring of hospitals from hierarchical to more horizontal structures, and the new technologies available. During periods of rapid change, teams must be able to redefine themselves, shift resources and attention quickly, and adapt their goals, priorities, and work methods to meet new conditions and demands.

Team members, too, need to be flexible if the team is to perform well. Leaders and members must learn to adapt to the changing needs of the team. For example, as a team develops over time, leaders should adapt their leadership styles to meet the changing needs of members (Kormanski & Mozenter, 1987). When the team's workload increases, members should take on new and additional task assignments willingly. As members work together, they should look at issues and situations from different perspectives and be flexible in their approaches to decision-making, problem solving, and task implementation.

The team's size can influence its flexibility. Teams lose flexibility when they become either too small or too large (Ilgen, 1999; McCullough, 1995). Approximately eight to 10 team members is optimal for maximal flexibility according to Elwyn and colleagues (1998). Obviously the size also depends on the range of tasks and expertise needed for the team to carry out its mission and achieve its goals. If a team's size is not optimal, it should be especially sensitive to procedures to maintain flexibility and good working relationships. Small teams can enhance their flexibility by cross-training members (Anderson, 1993); large teams can work in smaller subgroups, reduce the number of student members on the team at any given time, or educate management regarding the optimal number of employees to assign to a team.

Creativity, Uniqueness, Innovation, and Risk-Taking

For quality team performance, members should be able to think and act creatively, look beyond the current reality, challenge assumptions, be innovative and take risks, and encourage creativity and innovation in one another. The support of organizational managers coupled with strong professional identities of team members maximize collaborative creativity within the team (Molyneux, 2001). To exercise their creativity and develop innovative approaches to problem solving, teams often must take risks. Risk-taking becomes less threatening if mistakes are forgiven and not held against members and when conformity to traditional or rigid rules and procedures is minimized.

Team members also should encourage one another in their creative and innovative approaches to decision-making and problem solving. At the same time, management should foster and reward creative and innovative teams within the organization. Bryan (1999) contends that diversity among team members further encourages creativity. Finally, employees in health care settings, who are "open to innovation and change are more likely to work well as a team, structure their work more effectively, and be more effective in their health care delivery" (Poulton & West, 1999, p. 16).

SUMMARY

Team process is the domain in our model of team performance most often included in instruments assessing teams. In many ways, this is entirely appropriate since the dimension of interdependence probably captures the qualities that most define the parameters of an interdisciplinary health care team (i.e., a group that works collaboratively to plan, implement, and improve health care delivery). The ability of teams to communicate well; share work, power, and leadership; and make quality decisions that solve problems and resolve conflicts leads to the delivery of holistic health care. Further, the ability of teams to continuously grow and develop in order to carry out up-to-date, well-coordinated health care is essential in a dynamic, constantly changing health care environment. Growth, development, and improvement within the team and the organization facilitate productivity and quality outcomes, especially when members are flexible, creative, innovative, and willing to take risks.

REFERENCES

Anderson, L. (1993). Teams: Group processes, success, and barriers. *Journal of Nursing Administration, 23*, 15-19.

Baldwin, D.C., Jr. (1996). Some historical notes on interdisciplinary and interprofessional education and practice in health care in the USA. *Journal of Interprofessional Care, 10*, 173-188.

Barr, H. (1998). Competent to collaborate: Towards a competency-based model for interprofessional education. *Journal of Interprofessional Care, 12*, 181-188.

Bowers, C., Braun, C., & Morgan, B., Jr. (1997). Team workload: Its meaning and measurement. In M. Brannick, E. Salas, & C. Prince, (Eds.), *Team performance assessment and measurement* (pp. 85-110). Mahwah, NJ: Lawrence Erlbaum Associates.

Bryan, J.H. (1999). The diversity imperative. *Executive Excellence, 16*, 6.

Casali, J., & Wierwille, W. (1983). A comparison of rating scale, secondary-task, physiological, and primary-task workload estimation techniques in a simulated flight task emphasizing communications load. *Human Factors, 25*, 623-641.

Dickinson, T., & McIntyre, R. (1997). A conceptual framework for teamwork measurement. In M. Brannick, E. Salas, & C. Prince, (Eds.), *Team performance assessment and measurement* (pp. 19-44). Mahwah, NJ: Lawrence Erlbaum Associates.

Dimock, H.G. (1987). *Groups: Leadership and group development.* San Diego, CA: University Associates, Inc.
Donnellon, A. (1996). *Team talk: The power of language in team dynamics.* Boston, MA: Harvard Business School Press.
Ducanis, A.J., & Golin, A.K. (1979). *The interdisciplinary health care team: A handbook.* Germantown, MD: Aspen Systems Corp.
Dumaine, B. (1990). Who needs a boss? *Fortune* (May), 52-59.
Dyer, W.G. (1977). *Team building: Issues and alternatives.* Reading, MA: Addison-Wesley Publishing Company.
Elwyn, G.J., Rapport, F., & Kinnersley, P. (1998). Primary health care teams re-engineered. *Journal of Interprofessional Care, 12*, 189-198.
Farrell, M.P., Heinemann, G.D., & Schmitt, M.H. (1986). Informal roles, rituals and styles of humor in interdisciplinary health care teams: Their relationship to stages of group development. *International Journal of Small Group Research, 2*, 143-162.
Fisher, R., Ury, W., & Patton, B. (1991). *Getting to yes: Negotiating agreement without giving in.* New York: Penguin Books.
Freeth, D. (2001). Sustaining interprofessional collaboration. *Journal of Interprofessional Care, 15*, 37-46.
Fullan, M. (1986). *World yearbook of education: The management of change.* London: Evans Bros.
Given, B., & Simmons, S. (1977). The interdisciplinary health-care team: Fact or fiction? *Nursing Forum, 16*, 165-185.
Hackman, J.R. (1987). The design of work teams. In J.W. Lorsch, (Ed.), *Handbook of organizational behavior* (pp. 315-342). Englewood Cliffs, NJ: Prentice-Hall, Inc.
Hackman, J.R. (1999). Thinking differently about context. In R. Wageman (Ed.), *Research on managing groups and teams: Groups in context, Vol. 2.* (pp. 233-247). Stamford, CT: JAI Press, Inc.
Hamaoui, E., & Nichols, L. (1993). The nutrition support team: Organization and dynamics. In J.L. Rombeau & M.D. Caldwell, (Eds.), *Clinical nutrition: Parenteral nutrition* (pp. 284-309). Philadelphia, PA: WB Saunders.
Hammer, M., & Stanton, S. (1995). *The reengineering revolution: A handbook.* New York: Harper Collins.
Hayes, N. (1997). *Successful team management.* London: International Thompson Business Press.
Heinemann, G.D., Farrell, M.P., & Schmitt, M.H. (1994). Groupthink theory and research: Implications for decision making in geriatric health care teams. *Educational Gerontology, 20*, 71-85.
Hochberger, J., & Tedeschi, K. (1998). Reassigning staff: Effects on team members. *Nursing Management, 29*, 38-40.
Ilgen, D.R. (1999). Teams embedded in organizations: Some implications. *American Psychologist, 54*, 129-139.
Janis, I.L. (1972). *Victims of Groupthink: A psychological study of foreign policy decisions and fiascos.* Boston, MA: Houghton Mifflin.
Janis, I.L., & Mann, L. (1977). *Decision making.* New York: Free Press.
Johnson, D.W., & Johnson, F.P. (1991). *Joining together: Group theory and group skills.* Englewood Cliffs, NJ: Prentice Hall.
Johnston, J., Smith-Jentsch, K., & Cannon-Bowers, J. (1997). Performance measurement tools for enhancing team decision-making training. In M. Brannick, E. Salas, & C. Prince, (Eds.), *Team performance assessment and measurement* (pp. 311-330). Mahwah, NJ: Lawrence Erlbaum Associates.
Kirchmeyer, C., & Cohen, A. (1992). Multicultural groups: Their performance and reactions with constructive conflict. *Group and Organizational Management, 17*, 153-170.

Kormanski, C., & Mozenter, A. (1987). A new model of team building: A technology for today and tomorrow. In J.W. Pfeiffer (Ed.), *The 1997 annual: Developing human resource* (pp. 255-268). San Diego, CA: Pfeiffer & Company.

Kraiger, K., & Wenzel, L. (1997). Conceptual development and empirical evaluation of measures of shared mental models as indicators of team effectiveness. In M. Brannick, E. Salas, & C. Prince, (Eds.), *Team performance assessment and measurement* (pp. 63-84). Mahwah, NJ: Lawrence Erlbaum Associates.

Larson, C.E., & LaFasto, F.M. (1989). *TeamWork: What must go right/What can go wrong.* Newbury Park, CA: SAGE Publications, Inc.

Lichtenstein, R., Alexander, J.A., Jinnett, K., & Ullman, E. (1997). Embedded intergroup relations in interdisciplinary teams: Effects on perceptions of level of team integration. *Journal of Applied Behavioral Science, 33*, 413-434.

McClelland, B. (1999). Team players. *Executive Excellence, 16*, 18.

McCullough, D. (1995). Teams in the workplace: The way to power them to productivity. *Hospital Materiel Management Quarterly, 16*, 70-75.

McIntyre, R.M., & Salas, E. (1995). Measuring and managing for team performance: Emerging principles form complex environments. In R. Guzzo & E. Salas (Eds.), *Team effectiveness and decision-making in organizations* (pp.9-45). San Francisco: Jossey-Bass.

Molyneux, J. (2001). Interprofessional teamworking: What makes teams work well? *Journal of Interprofessional Care, 15*, 29-35.

Montebello, A. (1994). Teamwork in health care: Opportunities for gains in quality, productivity, and competitive advantage. *Clinical Laboratory Management Review, 8*, 91-105.

Nahavandi, A., & Aranda, E. (1994). Restructuring teams for the re-engineered organization. *Academy of Management Executive, 8*, 58-68.

Ovretveit, J. (1996). Five ways to describe a multidisciplinary team. *Journal of Interprofessional Care, 10*, 163-172.

Poulton, B., & West, M. (1999). The determinants of effectiveness in primary health care teams. *Journal of Interprofessional Care, 13*, 7-18.

Reagan, G. (1996). U.S. Style Teams (USST) Inventory. In J.W. Pfeiffer, (Ed), *The 1996 annual: Volume 2, consulting* (pp. 141-159). San Diego, CA: Pfeiffer & Company.

Reilly, A.J., & Jones, J.E. (1974). *Team-building.* In J.W. Pfeiffer & J.E. Jones (Eds.), The 1974 annual handbook for group facilitators. San Diego, CA: University Associates.

Senge, P. (1990). *The fifth discipline: The art and practice of the learning organization.* New York: Doubleday.

Senge, P., Kleiner, A., Roberts, C., Ross, R., & Smith, B. (1994). *The fifth discipline field book.* New York: Doubleday.

Scholtes, P.R. (1991). *The team handbook.* Madison, WI: Joiner Associates.

Skjørshammer, M. (2001). Co-operation and conflict in a hospital: Interprofessional differences in perception and management of conflicts. *Journal of Interprofessional Care, 15*, 7-18.

Thomas, K.W. (1992). Conflict and negotiation processes in organizations. In M.D. Dunnette & L.M. Hough (Eds.), *Handbook of industrial and organization psychology* (2nd ed., Vol. 3). Palo Alto, CA: Consulting Psychologists Press.

Tuckman, B.W. (1965). Developmental sequences in small groups. *Psychological Bulletin, 63*, 384-399.

Tuckman, B.W., & Jensen, M.A.C. (1977). Stages of small group development revisited. *Group and Organizational Studies, 2*, 419-427.

Wheelan, S.A. (1993). *The Group Development Questionnaire: A manual for professionals.* Philadelphia, PA: GDQ Associates.

Williams, G., & Laungani, P. (1999). Analysis of teamwork in an NHS community trust: An empirical study. *Journal of Interprofessional Care, 13*, 19-28.

CHAPTER 7
TEAM PRODUCTIVITY

Martha S. Waite, M.S.W.
VA Greater Los Angeles Healthcare System, Sepulveda, CA, VISN 22

Stephanie B. Hoffman, Ph.D.
James A. Haley VA Hospital, Tampa, FL, VISN 8

Productivity includes both the strategies teams use to achieve their goals and fulfill their mission and their accomplishments. In productive teams, members are collaborative, interdependent, and complete tasks efficiently. Teams or natural work groups that fail to maximize productivity often are characterized by questionable or poor processes (Steiner, 1972). The survival of today's and tomorrow's teams depends more and more upon their ability to be productive, and while improving process is important to this end, positive outcomes and high productivity levels are key (Brannick, Salas, & Prince, 1997). As a result, teams in health care settings are developing strategies to maximize productivity, document outcomes, and ensure quality accomplishments. Future team performance instruments will need to capture these kinds of performance activities as well as process activities.

STRATEGIES

In order to be productive, teams utilize many strategies. These strategies include formal planning involving various levels within the organization, the appropriate use of new technologies, and information management. Additionally, marketing team care and services to appropriate patient/client populations, time management, education and training, and self-monitoring and evaluation contribute to successful accomplishments. Finally, incentives, rewards, and celebrations within the team can set expectations for and reinforce high quality accomplishments among members of a team.

Action Planning

Action planning is important at all levels of the organization. It involves the development, implementation, monitoring, and fine-tuning of formal plans to achieve goals and resolve problems. Action planning in teams can focus on the team's needs and challenges, patients' needs and problems (i.e., patient care plans), and/or an individual team member's needs with regard to professional and work-related growth and development (i.e., individual development plans). Action planning permits teams to be proactive rather than continuously reacting to crises. Action planning, too, can be used to address larger organizational system issues.

Action Plans

A team's action plan is a formalized, written blueprint, developed by its members, to help them achieve both long-term and short-term goals related to the team's mission. Action plans can focus on either task-oriented or process goals as defined in Chapter 1. The first component of an action plan is a list of issues to be addressed. For each issue, a number of components must be developed, including realistic, measurable goals; approximate dates for goal achievement, required interventions; and identification of the team members responsible for implementing the interventions. Once the plan is developed, team members must agree and commit to it. The team, then, implements the plan and reviews progress toward goal achievement and/or problem resolution on a regular basis. A clinical team might create action plans around such issues as increasing the number of patients or clients it serves, developing orientation and procedure manuals for new members of the team, or becoming better role models and educators for students assigned to the team.

A natural work group of front-line employees might develop an action plan addressing the need for cross-training among its members, how to foster cooperation rather than competition, or how to empower members to function as a self-managed work team that requires less direct oversight from a supervisor. Action planning in natural work groups may require a consultant or educator to facilitate the process since employees may be unfamiliar with the rationale for the expected changes or with the action planning process itself. Supervisors, too, should work with employees of natural work groups during action planning.

A continuous quality improvement (CQI) team might develop and implement an action plan related to decreasing the number of wound infections among post-surgical patients or decreasing the number of accidents and injuries among employees on the job.

Patient Care Plans

The Joint Commission on Accreditation of Healthcare Organizations (JCAHO, 1998) mandates that patient care plans be interdisciplinary (i.e., show evidence of shared, collaborative, interdependent development and implementation among team members). This helps ensure consistency of care and treatment and decreases duplication of effort. The care plan should be the most frequently consulted part of the patient's record (Siegel & Fischer, 1981). Despite its importance, there can be resistance to developing and documenting it, in part, because health professionals do not learn the skills of accurate and succinct recording of information about patients in their respective formal educational programs (Grant, 1981).

The well functioning team uses a holistic, biopsychosocial approach to patient care planning. The four steps involved in devising a care plan are assessment, identification of needs and problems, planning (i.e., setting goals and determining interventions), and evaluation post implementation (Galasso, 1987). In geriatrics, the initial assessment typically addresses the physical, mental, and social functioning of the patient as well as his/her medical and health-related problems, disease prevention, health promotion, and quality of life issues. The assessment includes a medical history, physical examination, laboratory results, a social history (e.g., family supports, financial status, need for or use of community services), and other relevant assessment information from team members (e.g., nutritional status, speech and hearing deficits, rehabilitative potential, home safety, and emotional and cognitive functional levels). Team members often work together to assess other environmental, cultural, or spiritual issues that can be important parts of a patient's plan of care. From the assessment information, they identify the patient's strengths (e.g., adequate finances, access to supportive family members, highly motivated to function independently) and use them in the plan of care.

Problem identification involves breaking down a patient's particular diagnosis into the specific behavioral components and situational stressors that require intervention by the team. Diagnosis per se is not appropriate as a problem descriptor for two reasons. First, a diagnosis does not differentiate levels of severity and functional ability that vary from patient to patient. Second, a diagnosis is usually too broad to permit team members to identify their potential roles in developing and implementing the plan of care. For example, daytime drowsiness, noncompliance with medications, combative behavior, and potential for malnutrition are symptoms with behavioral components that can be more readily addressed by the team than can a diagnosis of Alzheimer's Disease.

Goals are statements that describe behaviorally what the patient will be able to do as a result of the team's intervention. Because goals serve as outcome criteria, they must be both realistic and measurable. Goals can be long-term and short-term. An example of a long-term goal for combative behavior might be,

"The patient will not use abusive language toward staff or family members by the time of discharge." Examples of short-term goals for daytime drowsiness might be, "The patient will remain awake during stimulating activities, will report feeling rested during the day, and will sleep five or more consecutive hours during the night."

Interventions are actions that accomplish goals, meet patients' needs, or resolve their health problems. While goals refer to what the patient will be doing, interventions refer to what team members will be doing. Team members from several professions work together to implement interventions if the care plan is truly interdisciplinary. Examples of interventions for combative behavior might include, "Staff will interact with the patient in a calm, matter-of-fact manner, identify antecedents or causes of such behavior, and reinforce appropriate behavior." For many of the interventions, the patient or family caregiver should be informed about and become committed to them prior to implementation.

Once implemented, the team revisits care plans periodically. This review and evaluation involves reassessing the patient and determining the effectiveness of the interventions in relation to the goals. The inability to achieve goals may indicate the goal is unrealistic, the interventions are ineffective, or the patient is not committed to the plan. Including patients and or family caregivers in the care planning process can result in more efficient and effective teamwork.

Individual Development Plans

The purpose of individual development plans (IDPs) is to facilitate employees' professional and career management and to help them advance to more challenging positions within their respective teams or the larger organization (VA Assistant Deputy Administrator for Personnel & Labor Relations, 1981). Individual team members, in conjunction with their team leader or supervisor, identify developmental needs, prepare and implement the IDP, and periodically review goals and performance to determine whether any adjustments need to be made. In a sense, IDPs are the building blocks individual team members use to enhance their own and the team's productivity.

Use of Technology

Technology has resulted in new infrastructures for communication and information sharing. Their use can improve collaboration, efficiency, and effectiveness within and across teams. In the age of down-sizing (i.e., reducing the number of employees in the hospital), restructuring, and merging of hospitals, application of technology in teams offers a solution to the difficulty of coordinating health care providers' varying schedules and multiple site practices

(Kovacich, 1996). Technology, too, is responsible for new advances in modes of treatment and care for patients.

New Technologies

Through the use of new technologies, members of a team have more options for communicating with one another. Phone or voice mail and electronic mail (e-mail) as well as face-to-face meetings provide more flexibility with regard to sharing information. In fact, using such mechanisms for agenda setting and planning can improve the quality and effectiveness of a face-to-face meeting. Using audio and audiovisual teleconferencing permits the inclusion of team members who are at other hospital sites, on travel, or on leave; they can maintain contact with the team and participate in its regular meetings and decision-making processes from a distance. A typical scenario for sharing information in a team might involve: using e-mail to generate meeting agenda items, sending the final agenda to team members as an attached document to e-mail, and conducting the meeting via video-conferencing augmented by computer generated aids (e.g., Power Point, graphics, video clips, Internet examples).

Mankin, Cohen, and Bikson (1996) note that technology-based information systems, ranging in complexity from voice mail and e-mail to more advanced hand held computers and "groupware" applications, can be important mechanisms for teams to accomplish their tasks. They work especially well for developing memos and newsletters and collecting data via interviews and surveys. Such use of technology can reduce time and costs for the team. These technologies facilitate communication and collaboration across teams and enable members to locate information to make decisions once reserved only for management (Mohrman, Cohen, & Mohrman, 1995). Internet access is one of the most important advances for clinical teams in the new millennium. It gives them access to new and cutting edge knowledge and additional sources of "expert opinion" about patients' conditions. It also provides information about resources available for team training and development.

These new technologies are changing teams and teamwork and will continue to do so in the future. The term "virtual team" is being touted as a practical way to provide more comprehensive and timely care to patients. Virtual team members can collaborate across remote locations even when members have diverse and conflicting schedules. Team members have rapid access to the same information, especially when patients' records are computerized. New technologies also enable virtual teams to function via teleconferencing, videoconferencing, and computer networking (Mankin, Cohen, & Bikson, 1996). This permits members to work efficiently and to accomplish their goals more effectively. Appropriate use of technology will become an important component in evaluating how well future teams are performing.

Appropriate Use of Technology

There is growing evidence that new communication mechanisms, such as voice and e-mail require skill and training to be used effectively in teams. When using voice mail, it is important to avoid long, involved and unfocused messages. Such messages are counterproductive because recipients tend to delete them without listening to the content (Kaiser Permanente & UCLA, 1999). Many voice mail systems have time and date stamps; some systems include the name of the sender. When these features are in place, they do not need repetition in the body of the message. Conference calls, too, can save time and cost as long as a system is in place for making decisions and coming to closure.

Use of e-mail for teams has become widespread and has its own challenges. While e-mail can assist with developing agenda and patient lists for clinics and inpatient units, it is not a good medium for disagreements, humor, and emergency or privileged communications. Some forms of e-mail can be used to set up and confirm attendance at meetings. As with voice mail, e-mail messages should be clear and concise. These messages can be forwarded beyond the intended audience and can be retrieved after they have been deleted.

With regard to communicating via the Internet, team members need to impose order for multiple, parallel threads of communication by creating folders for each topic since some persons communicate more effectively if they can attend to one topic at a time. Leadership, too, requires definition since fewer persons assume leadership "on-line" than in face-to-face meetings. Because persons come on-line at different times, norms for frequency of involvement must be developed. Likewise teams need to set norms for absences since members sometimes forget to inform the team about vacations or illnesses. For some teams, members participate more equally on-line since women tend to participate more than they do in face-to-face meetings (Vroman, 1999).

Information Management

With increasing emphasis on accountability, data driven outcomes, and new technologies for gathering, transmitting, and storing information, health care teams must learn to manage and retrieve large amounts of information quickly (Greenes, Sato, Schaffer, & Dixon, 1998). For clinical teams, computerized patient records and care plans improve the efficiency of information sharing among members and across teams. Additionally, teams increasingly operate in an "extended enterprise" milieu in which they interact not only with patients and numerous other clinicians and patient care providers, but also hospital managers, vendors, researchers, educators, and external review organizations (Greenes, 2000). Often the systematic presentation of data about the team's work and performance is required in these interactions. Information especially important to retrieve, share, and present includes patients' outcomes or responses to care and treatment, cost data, customer service data, and team performance data.

Computerized Patient Records and Care Plans

The Computerized Patient Record System (CPRS) in the VA system serves as one example of changes in managing information about patients. This system permits all patients' records, previously located in the "hard copy" chart, to be documented and stored in the computer. These computerized records make patients' information accessible to practitioners across a health care facility and permit continuity of care for patients receiving treatment and services at several hospital sites within a regional network. Initially clinical team members must invest time to learn how to use the CPRS and how to assess the patient and input data simultaneously. Once mastered, it offers improved communication and efficiency to local and virtual health care teams and, ultimately, better quality care and service to patients.

In an effort to create more accessible, legible, and interdisciplinary patient care plans, many teams, especially those in long-term care, have begun to computerize them. This process saves considerable time when templates for various health problems have been developed and standardized with measurable goals and specific disciplines responsible for interventions. The standardized templates can be individualized for each patient, and revisions in the plan can be highlighted to track patients' responses (Waite & Harker, 1997). Members unable to be present at the team meeting can enter important information for the team to consider and discuss during the meeting. This document is easily shared with consultant team members and other experts, as well as with the patient and family members, to encourage their input and commitment to the plan.

Patient Outcome and Cost Data

Once patients' records are computerized, teams can monitor a variety of outcome data for the patients they serve. Information of special importance includes number and length of hospitalizations, health promotion/disease prevention programs attended and any resulting changes (e.g., improved dietary habits or smoking cessation), functional status improvements, maintenance of independent living, and nursing home placements. Teams can monitor these data for given time periods to assess how their plans of care and treatment are impacting their respective patient populations.

Clinical teams also can track some of the costs of treatment and care to patients, such as how often laboratory and other diagnostic tests are ordered and how often prescription medications are utilized. Linking costs of treatment and care with patients' responses can provide the team with important information about the appropriateness and effectiveness of treatment and services that they provide. Natural work groups, too, benefit from monitoring cost data. For example, the hospital pharmacy might keep records of medication purchases over the quarters of a fiscal year. Acquisitions and materials management might monitor costs of purchasing equipment and materials for the hospital, compare the costs of different vendors for similar types of equipment, or compare the yearly cost totals to previous years' totals.

Customer Service and Team Performance Data

With the increased emphasis on providing quality customer service, many health care organizations are educating and sensitizing their employees about this issue. Additionally, they are collecting data to ascertain their customers' satisfaction and to identify areas in need of improvement. Clinical teams conduct patient and family satisfaction surveys about a wide array of topics such as patients' access to care, ability to get timely appointments, waiting time to see a care provider, quality of services provided, helpfulness and courtesy of employees, and employees' respect for patients' privacy. Additionally, some health care organizations survey team members and other employees to determine how satisfied they are with their working relationships, their working conditions within the hospital or health care facility, and the organization's management and leadership.

Effective teams often collect and discuss information related to their respective strengths and weaknesses. More formal assessment instruments generate information regarding facets of team performance, which can be monitored over time. Teams can computerize these data and present them in summary tables, charts, and graphs to upper level management during yearly program briefings and evaluations. Collecting and monitoring systematic data about the team over time permits members to plan, make adjustments as necessary, and better meet the expectations of management. In fact, presenting clearly depicted information to management about the team as a working unit can facilitate an understanding of the need to recognize and reward not only individual employees, but also teams themselves.

Marketing

Shycon (1991) noted that quality service results in a consistent pattern of increased market share and revenues. The greater the service quality, the greater the marketability of the team. A number of teams use the hospital's database to locate eligible patients and distribute information to them about the team program and its related services. Rubenstein and colleagues (1984), in their work with Geriatric Evaluation Unit (GEU) teams, found that patients' outcomes improve when team care is targeted to the patients who would benefit most from an interdisciplinary approach to care. Thus, teams are likely to have better outcomes if they market to appropriate target groups of patients. Other formal marketing strategies include the use of newsletters to patients, the hospital's newsletter, and the community newspapers, radio, and television. Some health care facilities employ a public relations specialist to take responsibility for these marketing campaigns. Such a position permits expanded marketing to the community via displays or health fairs in community settings such as shopping malls, grocery stores, or at county and state fairs.

Time Management

Time management requires the planning, organization, and coordination of intentions into efficient actions. Time management also involves breaking projects down into a series of tasks and prioritizing them (Eagle International Institute, 1998). The time invested in each task must be evaluated in terms of its relevance to the number and quality of the team's accomplishments. Effective teams organize their resources and activities in order to accomplish their tasks within established time frames (Fleishman & Zaccaro, 1992). These teams also set expectations regarding the pacing of activities. Finally, some teams encourage members to attend time management workshops. In such programs, they learn how to plan and prepare for the following day's and week's activities, keep important phone numbers and e-mail addresses with them during the work day, and make needed appointments early so as not to delay their work. Effective time management results in lower levels of stress and increased creativity among team members (Eagle International Institute, 1998).

Time management can be especially important during team meetings. Often a team member takes the role of timekeeper in order to prevent digression and ensure that the full agenda is covered. The team member chairing the meeting also has responsibilities regarding timing (e.g., making sure that one or two members do not monopolize all of the time to the exclusion of other members).

Self-Monitoring, Review, and Evaluation

Well performing teams almost always monitor, review, and evaluate both their task and process activities. Documenting and monitoring patients' outcomes and costs of care provide data regarding task effectiveness. With regard to process activities, self-monitoring can be accomplished through informal discussions among members to identify what the team does well and where it needs to improve or by collecting members' perceptions of the team using one of the multidimensional instruments presented in this book. Teams, especially newly developing ones, beginning the self-monitoring strategy should use a team consultant to assist in setting the appropriate tone (i.e., an open, honest, nonthreatening climate for discussion) and helping the team develop rules of trust. Each member of the team has responsibility for participating in assessing and evaluating the team (Bradford & Cohen, 1997). Once members have identified where the team needs to improve, developing an action plan can help ensure continuing attention to performance and productivity issues. When members are comfortable and skilled at assessing the team, they can begin to assess one another's performance as team members. Effective teams make use of this strategy at regular intervals–every quarter, six months, or year, depending on their level of development and functioning.

Education, Training, and Consultation

Education, training, and consultation are necessary strategies for teams to learn more about the disease entities of their patients, new and cutting edge treatment modalities, and team development and dynamics. Making use of these strategies to improve skills permits teams and natural work groups to be more productive and enables the clinical team to give better care to its patients.

Team members do not know intuitively how to lead or participate effectively in teams. Too often managers and team members make the erroneous assumption that such skills come naturally. The skills of teamwork must be learned either through formal educational programs, consultations, in-service education, and/or informal learning on the job. Although customized training is more costly, a quality intervention designed for a specific team can be more effective than a general "canned" program (Waite, Harker, & Messerman, 1994). Wheelan and colleagues (Wheelan, 1993) demonstrated in two studies that customized educational interventions are effective strategies in moving teams from a lower to a higher stage of development and, thus, improving their performance.

Teams in different stages of development often respond differently to educational interventions. Team training is especially effective for newly developing teams; it can decrease members' dependency on the leader, help them develop a mission statement, clarify their roles, and facilitate their getting to know one another professionally and personally. Conversely, a team trapped in the conflict stage is much more difficult to move to a more advanced developmental stage via educational programming in comparison to teams in other stages of development (Farrell, Schmitt, & Heinemann, 1988). In the conflict stage, members are quick to blame one another and view group problems as interpersonal problems because they have not yet become a collaborative group with shared responsibility. In such instances, their training should include an understanding and appreciation of the group as a system, how the larger organizational system functions, and how system problems can impact group performance (Wheelan, 1993). In addition, teams in the conflict stage or teams functioning poorly often perceive educational programs as formal acknowledgement by management that they are not meeting expectations and/or that they are being punished. Such perceptions diminish the positive impact of these programs.

Incentives, Rewards, and Celebrations

Apart from the organization's reward system, teams themselves can provide incentives and rewards to their members for outstanding efforts and successful accomplishments. Team members can express their appreciation for one another's efforts with cards, certificates, parties, or other social gatherings. Some teams celebrate special events in members' lives such as birthdays, births of children, or retirements; they also celebrate special events related to the team itself such as a team's anniversary or the departing of members and student trainees (Farrell, Heinemann, & Schmitt, 1986). Finally, teams benefit from celebrating their successes. For example, one home care team kept records of their successes with complex patients; when they had three or more successes in a given month, the members treated themselves to lunch at a nice restaurant. For CQI teams, celebrating acknowledges to others in the organization what the team has accomplished. It also serves as a positive rite of passage for terminating the team and gives members the opportunity to say "goodbye" and "job well done" to one another.

While these informal incentives, rewards, and celebrations should not take the place of formal, organizational recognition and rewards, they do much to boost the morale of team members, reinforce expectations, and improve and/or maintain enthusiasm for and commitment to the team approach.

ACCOMPLISHMENTS

Ultimately a team's accomplishments are the achievement of goals and successful completion of tasks related to its mission and goals. Other more short-term accomplishments set the stage for long-term ones. Examples of short-term accomplishments include meeting effectiveness, the effectiveness of the team's leadership, and improved quality of relationships with other teams. Having positive outcomes with regard to patients and trainees and a positive impact on the larger organization are important long-term accomplishments of the team.

These accomplishments are dependent upon the quality of all of the other dimensions and elements in our model of team performance described earlier in this book.

Achievement of Goals and Successful Completion of Tasks

Teams that are task-oriented and purposeful with regard to implementing their plans are more likely to achieve goals and complete tasks successfully. Success in this regard refers to completing tasks on schedule, within budget, and at the required level of quality. Teams that use formal action planning as a strategy have many of their goals and implementation strategies documented. Content analyzing these plans and the resulting outcomes can provide teams with indicators of how successful they have been. Analyzing responses to treatment and care from patients' records also can indicate whether the team's outcomes coincide with its and the organization's expectations.

Effective Meetings

Conducting effective meetings is an important team accomplishment. Meetings provide a forum for members to come together to communicate, make major decisions, and develop action and patient care plans. As discussed in earlier chapters, successful team meetings require organizational support (e.g., provision of a conference room in which to conduct meetings). Other requirements include an agreed upon procedure for conducting meetings, an open, comfortable climate, and effective team processes (e.g., communication, decision-making). Effective meetings also are a precursor to other successful team outcomes such as quality care to patients.

Components of effective meetings include adequate preparation prior to the meeting and information sharing among members during the meeting. Members' active participation in discussions related to decision-making and problem solving also is necessary. A results-driven structure ensures that members understand what the meeting accomplished and what their responsibilities are with regard to implementing plans and interventions.

Ineffective meetings can be a tremendous waste of time and money to the team and the larger organization in which it functions. Hoffman (1995), in a VA hospital study, identified two barriers to effective team meetings: (a) teams and work groups meeting when there is no need to do so and (b) team members lacking skills necessary to conduct successful meetings. While positive outcomes did arise from team meetings, many members lacked the ability to chair meetings, problem solve effectively, and specify follow-up responsibilities.

Members came to meetings inadequately prepared, which led to the presentation of unnecessary and/or erroneous information and poor use of meeting time. Additionally, there were poor locations and conditions of meeting rooms, late starts, late arrivals, interruptions, members' absences (particularly physicians), inattentiveness to discussion, and paper signing and shuffling during meetings. Her findings suggest the need to assess how well teams use their meeting time and to teach meeting effectiveness skills to team members when indicated.

Teams can assess their meeting effectiveness using some of the instruments presented in this volume. Results from the assessments can help identify the need for education and training in conducting and "getting the most" from meetings. Results monitored over time can help determine whether or not the team is improving its meeting effectiveness and whether meetings are contributing in a positive way to its accomplishments and productivity.

Effective Leadership and Self-Management

Effective leadership in teams and work groups relies on members sharing leadership roles, using the style of leadership most appropriate to a given situation and/or stage of a team's development, and modeling leadership skills. When formal leaders are not present, the team continues to function and accomplish its tasks as members share responsibilities. Effective leadership facilitates the team or work group's growth and improved performance over time. It helps members focus on tasks related to the mission of both the team and the organization and be productive. Effective leadership promotes feelings of enthusiasm, energy, and unity among members, which enable them to utilize their full potential in producing quality results and outcomes.

When members of teams and work groups learn to take responsibility and share leadership, they become self-directed or self-managed rather than being controlled from outside the team. They, rather than managers or supervisors, make decisions and define what needs to be done to achieve their goals and accomplish their mission and purpose. Supervisors, in turn, become role models, coaches, and mentors, and they have more time to facilitate informal learning among employees and within the team and/or work group at the work site.

The use of self-managed teams in industry has become widespread. Lawler, Mohrman, and Ledford (1992) surveyed Fortune 1000 companies and found that 47% of them use self-managed work teams with some of their employees. In a quasi-experiment within the telecommunications industry, Cohen and Ledford (1994) showed that self-managed teams are more effective than traditionally managed groups. They found modest improvements in product quality, cost savings, productivity, employee satisfaction, and quality of work life from case studies of several companies.

Effective Team Functioning

Effective team functioning is equivalent to a well performing team in the fourth or "performing" stage of development. In these teams, members are collaborative and interdependent. They work together smoothly and efficiently, and the team is synergistic. Effective teams continually assess their functioning since both external and internal factors can impinge upon them and create barriers to high performance. They function as interdisciplinary/interprofessional or self-managed teams as described in Chapter 1.

While all of the elements identified in our model of team performance have the potential to affect team functioning or performance, not all of them have been investigated systematically. Heinemann, Schmitt, and Farrell (1994) identified seven factors from the literature they believe influence team performance. These include characteristics of the team as well as its members. Team characteristics include its size, the stability of its membership, its workload or patient census, the number of stressful events it experiences in a given time period, and the resulting level of stress in the team. Characteristics of team members include their degree of heterogeneity, whether they are embedded in their team culture or their respective discipline-specific culture, and physicians' attitudes toward teams. Shortell et al. (1994) found that intensive care units (ICUs) with team-oriented cultures, supportive nursing leadership, timely communication, effective coordination, and collaborative approaches to problem solving were significantly more efficient than other ICUs in moving patients in and out of the unit. Johnson and Johnson's (1992) meta-analyses of studies showed that working in teams results in higher individual productivity than does working competitively or individually on verbal, mathematical, and procedural tasks. Other non-task effects that teams produced were better relationships, more social support, greater psychological health, and higher self-esteem.

While quality functioning within teams is essential, functioning across teams must also be effective. Teams must actively cultivate relationships with other teams and work groups in the organization and across organizations. These relationships must be positive and productive. That is, teams and work groups must work together successfully in carrying out the organization's mission and, in health care settings, providing quality care and treatment to patients. For example, a clinical inpatient team might set a goal for a bed-bound patient to prevent skin breakdown; part of the plan includes a high protein diet. This plan must be communicated to the nursing staff on the unit. The nursing staff orders the diet and makes sure the patient receives and eats it. Members of the nursing team also must be sure the patient is turned frequently and the patient's skin is kept clean and dry. The dietary and food service work group must purchase the food and prepare the meals, ensure their attractive presentation, and deliver them to the unit in a timely manner. Communication and coordination among these different groups is essential to best serve the patient and to achieve the goal of maintaining skin integrity.

Effective relationships between teams and management permit mutual trust and confidence to develop. A trusting, positive climate increases a team's ability to get the information and resources it needs to be productive and the recognition and rewards it deserves for quality performance.

Effective Customer Relations

A significant accomplishment of teams and work groups is satisfied customers. A clinical team's most important customers are its patients and their family members. Teams with good customer relations provide quality treatment, care, and services to their patients and appropriate patient/family education in a courteous, timely, and respectful manner. Team members respect patients' confidentiality and, at times, their need for privacy. They listen to, empathize with, and make appropriate referrals for them.

With all of the current reorganization and restructuring in health care, patients require updating on new locations of services and directions to their destinations. In order to meet these needs, some hospitals have instituted "greeter programs," where trained employees spend time in the hospital's main entrance or lobby to welcome, give directions to, and answer questions of patients, family members, and visitors. Some hospitals also provide complimentary shuttle service between their respective entrances and parking areas and shuttle service between segments of the facility that are geographically dispersed. In some hospitals, posters and bulletin boards announce the importance of these customers with such slogans as: "We put patients first," and "Customer service is our goal." In still other health care organizations, suggestion boxes are prominently displayed or a "patient advocate" is hired to address patients' complaints and difficulties negotiating the health care system. These programs attempt to improve quality of and satisfaction with care and services to patients and their family members.

All of the employees in the health care facility (i.e., the members of the team itself and all of the other employees with whom they come in contact, from professional colleagues to cafeteria and environmental management workers) are also customers of the team. Some of the other customers of a health care team include suppliers, vendors, colleges and universities, other health facilities and other consultants in the same geographic area. Courtesy, respect, patience, and mutual assistance are important components of these relationships.

As noted in the "strategies" section of this chapter, it is important to survey periodically both individuals using the health care organization about their satisfaction with care and services and employees in the organization about their working conditions and work relationships. Management can monitor these data over time in order to identify where the team and the organization are meeting needs and where they need to improve.

Positive Outcomes and Impact

Outcomes Related to Patients

Quality care that results in positive outcomes for both patients and the organization is a major accomplishment of the clinical team. An impressive and continuously increasing body of evidence supports such outcomes for a variety of different types of patients receiving both inpatient and outpatient care. Research findings support positive outcomes for geriatric and long-term care, intensive care, rehabilitation, and mental health and substance abuse care.

In a randomized experiment of patients' outcomes in four long-term care teams, Feiger and Schmitt (1979) and Schmitt, Watson, Feiger, and Williams (1982) found that the degree of equality of participation in team meetings was related to positive changes in patients after a one year period. Rubenstein and colleagues demonstrated that effective geriatric care, via a team approach, significantly reduced morbidity and mortality rates among older patients (Rubenstein et al., 1984; Rubenstein, Stuck, Siu, & Weiland, 1991). Reuben and colleagues confirmed that for outpatients, a comprehensive geriatric assessment followed by a "multiple discipline" adherence regimen favorably impacted physical functioning, energy, social functioning, and physical health of patients (Ruben, Frank, Hirsch, McGuigan, & Maly, 1999). The clinical team administering the assessments and making recommendations included a geriatric physician or nurse practitioner, a social worker, and a physical therapist.

Gavett, Drucker, McCrum, and Dickinson (1985) found that poor communication and coordination among health care providers resulted in unnecessarily high cost hospital stays. In ICUs, increased interaction and coordination between nurses and physicians positively influenced effectiveness of care to patients (Knaus, Drapper, Wagner, & Zimmerman, 1986). Additionally, greater collaboration between these health professionals regarding transferring patients from the ICU resulted in fewer readmissions and deaths among patients (Baggs, Ryan, Phelps, Richison, & Johnson, 1992). Shortell et al. (1994) also found that a team-oriented culture and quality team processes (e.g., communication, problem solving) in ICUs were related to lower length of stays among patients and higher perceived technical quality of care by ICU staff.

Zeiss and Okarma (1984) compared two interdisciplinary team approaches to multidisciplinary care for outpatients with rheumatologic-spectrum disease. Both types of interdisciplinary team care, when compared to multidisciplinary care, resulted in more improved outcomes among patients on measures of quality of life and health care utilization. Another study of rheumatology patients in

Sweden (Ahlmen, Sullivan, & Bjelle, 1988) compared interprofessional care versus standard care by a rheumatologist by examining outcomes in older women with rheumatoid arthritis. While there were no differences in joint function or disease activity at the end of the intervention period, overall health improved significantly over a one-year period for women followed by the interprofessional team. A one-year follow-up by the same authors (Ahlmen, Bjelle, & Sullivan, 1991) showed sustained positive impact of team care and also helped identify the predictors of this impact (e.g., clinical, social, and self-assessed health data).

Patients in various types of rehabilitation programs also have benefited from team care. Grahn, Ekdahl, and Borgquist (1998) compared patients receiving rehabilitation from an interprofessional team for prolonged musculoskeletal disorders with those receiving standard care, largely multidisciplinary in nature. The patients were comparable at baseline, but after six months of treatment, the patients in the interprofessional rehabilitation program showed greater improvement on a number of measures of health-related quality of life. At the two-year follow-up (Grahn, Ekdahl, & Borgquist, 2000), the interprofessional rehabilitation program showed even stronger effects, particularly in improved health-related quality of life, emotional response to chronic illness, pain-related movement, and need for pain medication. In another study, care delivered by an interdisciplinary team was compared to standard nursing care for Swedish patients who were being discharged after a medical inpatient hospital stay and who had at least one chronic medical condition and impairment on at lease one activity of daily living. Care provided by the interdisciplinary team resulted in substantially greater benefit with regard to independent functioning, mortality, and change in psychosocial functioning (Melin, Wieland, Harker, & Bygren, 1995). In the area of cardiac rehabilitation, Fridlund, Hogstedt, Lidell, and Larsson (1991) conducted a longitudinal study in which they randomly assigned post heart attack patients to an interprofessional rehabilitation program and to usual care rehabilitation. After six months, the patients in the interprofessional program showed significant improvements in their health condition, health habits, and cardiac health knowledge compared to the usual care patients, and these results were sustained and strengthened two years after the initial intervention (Lidell & Fridlund, 1996).

In the area of mental health and substance abuse, one group of researchers (Aberg-Wistedt, Cressell, Lidberg, Liljenberg, & Osby, 1995) followed schizophrenic patients assigned randomly to either a team-based intensive case management program or to standard psychiatric services. Over a two-year period, patients in the interprofessional team-based care program had significantly fewer emergency visits and developed increased social networks. Additionally, their relatives reported a significantly reduced burden of care. In another study of the use of psychotropic drugs in nursing homes, Swedish researchers compared 15 nursing homes that instituted interprofessional team discussions of medications and alternative treatment options to 18 nursing homes that continued standard, multidisciplinary care with no coordinated treatment meetings (Schmidt, Claesson, Westerholm, Nilsson, & Sverstad, 1998). After one year of intervention, the experimental nursing homes had decreased significantly the use of antipsychotic medications, benzodiazepine hypnotics, and antidepressants compared to the standard care homes. Finally, Drake, Yovetich, Bebout, Harris, and McHugo (1997) studied the impact of interprofessional care versus standard care to homeless adults with dual diagnoses of substance abuse and severe mental illness. The program provided integrated delivery of mental health, substance abuse, and housing interventions for patients and compared them to matched controls in standard care (i.e., receiving services from various programs). After 18 months of treatment, the patients receiving integrated, interprofessional care showed significantly fewer days of institutional care, more days in stable housing, and more progress toward recovery from substance abuse.

Outcomes Related to Trainees

The Pew Commission (1995) reported that the changing health care system mandates new teaching and learning approaches for future health care providers. Education must take place across professions with modeling of effective team integration and delivery of efficient high quality care to patients. Integrating students into clinical health care teams is critical to attracting and sustaining a future workforce with the knowledge and skills to maximize health care outcomes (Hansen & Hayes, 1998) and productivity (Gordon et al., 1996). Kirkpatrick (1994) identified four aspects of a systematic evaluation of learners that can be addressed in determining these outcomes. They are the learners' reactions to the program (e.g., positive responses, satisfaction), actual learning having taken place (e.g., modification of attitudes and perceptions, knowledge and skill acquisition), change in behavior, and results (e.g., increased production, improved quality, decreased costs, benefits to patients). For change in behavior to occur, the person attending the program must desire to change, know what to do and how to do it, work in a climate that is right for change, and be acknowledged or rewarded for change.

Given that many health care team settings serve as clinical sites for the education of medical and health professional trainees, some of the team's outcomes are related to how successful members are as teachers and mentors. Positive outcomes with trainees include the proportion of trainees recruited and hired as employees in the teams where they trained; the proportion desiring, seeking out, and accepting jobs in other team care settings; and improvement in trainees' abilities to collaborate with professionals from disciplines other than their own. Such collaboration includes being able to anticipate some of the needs of these other team members, involve them appropriately in the treatment and care of patients, and defer to their judgments in decision-making situations in which they are the experts.

The VA health care system has had considerable success in hiring a wide array of health professionals who, as trainees, interns, residents, and fellows, completed clinical affiliations and rotations on VA health care teams through the Geriatric Fellowship, Interdisciplinary Team Training and Development (ITT&D), and Primary Care Education Programs. Such hiring has infused the team approach to care throughout the VA culture and ensured that clinical employees have the appropriate skills to deliver care and services using this approach. Others have had considerable success using problem-based learning to teach interdisciplinary material. In one pilot project, students reported the learning experience helped them collaborate more effectively and gave them a better understanding of the roles of other disciplines and professions (Lary, Lavigne, Muma, Jones, & Hoefl, 1997). Harman, Carlson, and Darr (1996) reported that an interdisciplinary training program resulted in students developing commitment to a systems approach, shared leadership and commitment to the team, greater sensitivity to diversity, openness to learning and changing, trust, effective conflict resolution, and improved focus on client outcomes.

In the business arena, Depree (1990) noted that successful training programs taught respect for diversity, which helped participants develop trust, integrate personal and professional values, use consensus decision-making, and value people over structure. Finally, some of the most successful interdisciplinary training programs have emphasized a collaborative partnership between the academic institution and the clinical affiliation sites of the students. In such programs, the knowledge and skills of collaboration and teamwork are reinforced across sites.

Impact on the Organization

A final accomplishment of teams and work groups is to produce effective and valuable results that have an impact on the organization itself or contribute to its success. Positive results include high quality work, positive reports of performance, favorable productivity compared to other teams, and satisfaction of management and supervisors with performance. Indications of a team's impact on the organization, especially CQI teams, include acceptable, realistic recommendations that can be implemented easily and require minimal changes. Some of the best outcome data regarding impact come from Continuous Quality Improvement (CQI) teams as described in Chapter 1. For example, one CQI team was chartered to improve the complex perioperative system at an academic medical center (Davie, 1993). The team improved operating room start time by

25 minutes, increased room utilization by over 5%, decreased staff cost, and increased admissions and revenue.

SUMMARY

In this chapter, we presented the two dimensions of productivity–strategies for productivity and the accomplishments of teams and work groups. Productivity is strongly influenced by the other domains, dimensions, and elements in our team performance model. The domain of productivity is less well assessed in formal team performance instruments in comparison to other domains and dimensions of performance that focus specifically on what happens in the team itself (e.g., team structure and context, process). Some of the instruments designed for clinical teams have begun to measure perceived outcomes related to patients; however, both of the dimensions of productivity require more systematic assessment as teams and health care, itself, evolve and change.

REFERENCES

Aberg-Wistedt, A., Cressell, T., Lidberg, Y, Liljenberg, B., & Osby, U. (1995). Two-year outcome of team-based intensive case management for patients with schizophrenia, *Psychiatric Services, 46*, 1263-1266.

Ahlmen, M., Bjelle, A., & Sullivan, M. (1991). Prediction of team care effects in outpatients with rheumatoid arthritis. *Journal of Rheumatology, 18*, 1655-1661.

Ahlmen, M., Sullivan, M., & Bjelle, A. (1988). Team versus non-team outpatient care in rheumatoid arthritis. A comprehensive outcome evaluation including an overall health measure. *Arthritis & Rheumatology, 31*, 471-479.

Baggs, J.G., Ryan, S.A., Phelps, C.E., Richison, J.F., & Johnson, J.E. (1992). The association between interdisciplinary collaboration and patient outcomes in medical intensive care. *Heart and Lung, 21*, 18-24.

Bradford, D. L., & Cohen, A.R. (1997). *Managing for excellence: The guide to developing high performance in contemporary organizations*. New York: John Wiley & Sons, Inc.

Brannick, M., Salas, E., & Prince, C. (1997). *Team performance assessment and measurement: Theory, methods, and applications*. Mahwah, NJ: Lawrence Erlbaum Associates, Inc.

Cohen, S.G., & Ledford, G.E., Jr. (1994). The effectiveness of self-managing teams: A quasi-experiment. *Human Relations, 47*, 13-43.

Davie, R.N. (1993). Cross-functional clinical teams: Significant improvement in operating room quality and productivity. *Journal of the Society for Health Systems, 4*, 34-47.

Drake, R.E., Yovetich, N.A., Bebout, R.R., Harris, M., & McHugo, G.J. (1997). Integrated treatment of dually diagnosed homeless adults. *Journal of Nervous & Mental Disease, 185*, 298-305.

Depree, M. (1990). *Leadership is an art*. New York: Bantam/Doubleday/Dell.

Eagle International Institute, Inc. (1998). Time Management. Workshop presented at VA Western New York Healthcare System, Buffalo, NY.

Farrell, M.P., Heinemann, G.D., & Schmitt, M.H. (1986). Informal roles, rituals, and styles of humor in interdisciplinary health care teams: Their relationship to stages of group development. *International Journal of Small Group Research, 2*, 143-162.

Farrell, M.P., Schmitt, M.H., & Heinemann, G.D. (1988). Organizational environments of health care teams: Impact on team development and implications for consultation. *International Journal of Small Group Research, 4*, 31-53.

Feiger, S.M., & Schmitt, M.H. (1979). Collegiality in interdisciplinary health teams: Its measurement and its effects. *Social Science and Medicine, 13A*, 217-229.

Fleischman, E.A., & Zaccaro, S.J. (1992). Toward a taxonomy of team performance functions. In R.W. Swezey & E. Salas (Eds.), *Teams: Their training and performance* (pp. 31-56). Norwood, NJ: Ablex.

Fridlund, B., Hogstedt, B., Lidell, E., & Larsson, P.A. (1991). Recovery after myocardial infarction. Effects of a caring rehabilitation programme. *Scandinavian Journal of Caring Sciences, 5*, 23-32.

Galasso, D. (1987). Guidelines for developing multidisciplinary treatment plans. *Hospital and Community Psychiatry, 38*, 394-397.

Gavett, J.W., Drucker, W.R., McCrum, M.S., & Dickinson, J.C. (1985*). A study of high cost in-patients in Strong Memorial Hospital*. Rochester, NY: Rochester Area Hospital Corporation and the University of Rochester.

Gordon, P.R., Carlson, L., Chessman, A., Kundrat, M.L., Morahan, P.S., & Headrick, L.A. (1996). A multisite collaborative for the development of interdisciplinary education in continuous improvement. *Academic Medicine, 71*, 973-978.

Grahn, B., Ekdahl, C., & Borgquist, L. (1998). Effects of a multidisciplinary rehabilitation programme on health-related quality of life in patients with prolonged musculoskeletal disorders: A 6 month follow-up of a prospective controlled study. *Disability & Rehabilitation: An International Multidisciplinary Journal, 22*, 639-654.

Grahn, B., Ekdahl, C., & Borgquist, L. (2000). Motivation as a predictor of changes in quality of life and working ability in multidisciplinary rehabilitation. A two-year follow-up of a prospective controlled study in patients with prolonged musculoskeletal disorders. *Disability & Rehabilitation: An International Multidisciplinary Journal, 20*, 285-297.

Grant, R.L. (1981). The capacity of the psychiatric record to meet changing needs. In C. Siegel & S.K. Fischer (Eds.), *Psychiatric records in mental health care* (p. 319). New York: Brunner/Mazel.

Greenes, R.A. (2000). Decision systems group. [On-line web home page: http://dsg.harvard.edu]. Boston, MA: Harvard Medical School and Brigham and Women's Hospital (Producer and Distributor).

Greenes, R.A., Sato, L., Schaffer, J.L., & Dixon, C.M. (1998). The PartnerWeb project: Developing an infrastructure for facilitating enterprise-wide communication and access to information resources for patients and providers. *Asian Hospital Magazine* (March), 22-24.

Hansen, M.C., & Hayes, P.A. (1998). Integrating students into interdisciplinary teams: Extending the caring circle. *Seminars for Nurse Managers, 6*, 214-218.

Harman, L.B., Carlson, L., & Darr, K. (1996). Blessed are the flexible. *Joint Commission Journal of Quality Improvement, 22*, 188-197.

Heinemann, G.D., Schmitt, M.H., & Farrell, M.P. (1994). The quality of geriatric team functioning: Model and methodology. In J.R. Snyder (Ed.)*, Interdisciplinary health care teams: Proceedings of the sixteenth annual conference, Chicago* (pp. 77-91). Indianapolis, IN: School of Allied Health Sciences, Indiana University School of Medicine.

Hoffman, S.B. (1995). Zero-based meetings [Abstract]. Program book from the 17th Annual Interdisciplinary Health Care Team Conference (p. 25) in Pittsburgh, PA.

Johnson, D.W., & Johnson, R. (1992). *Positive interdependence: The heart of cooperative learning*. Edina, MN: Interaction Book Company.

Joint Commission on Accreditation of Healthcare Organizations. (1998). *Comprehensive accreditation manual for long-term care*. Oakbrook Terrace, IL: Author.

Kaiser Permanente & UCLA (1999). *Voice Mail Messages, Brief Team Lesson #16*. (Unpublished training manual from the Geriatric Interdisciplinary Team Managed Care Training of Trainers Project, California Geriatric Education Center, 10945 Le Conte, Suite 2339, Los Angeles, CA 90095-1687).

Kirkpatrick, D.L. (1994). *Evaluating training programs*. San Francisco, CA: Berret-Koehler Publishers.

Knaus, W.A., Drapper, E.A., Wagner, D.P., & Zimmerman, J.E. (1986). An evaluation of outcomes in intensive care in major medical centers. *Annals of Internal Medicine, 104*, 410-418.

Kovacich, J. (1996). Interdisciplinary team training on the information superhighway. *Journal of Interprofessional Care, 10*, 111-119.

Lary, M.J., Lavigne, S.E., Muma, R.D., Jones, S.E., & Hoefl, H.J. (1997). Breaking down the barriers: Multidisciplinary education model. *Journal of Allied Health, 26*, 63-69.

Lawler, E.E., Mohrman, S.A., & Ledford, G.E., Jr. (1992). *Employee involvement and total quality management: Practices and results in Fortune 1000 companies*. San Francisco: Jossey-Bass.

Lidell, E., & Fridlund, B. (1996). Long-term effects of a comprehensive rehabilitation programme after myocardial infarction. *Scandinavian Journal of Caring Sciences, 10*, 67-74.

Mankin, D., Cohen, S.G., & Bikson, T.K. (1996). *Teams and technology: Fulfilling the promise of the new organization*. Boston, MA: Harvard Business School Press.

Melin, A.L., Wieland, D., Harker, J.O., & Bygren, L.O. (1995). Health outcomes of post-hospital in-home care: Secondary analysis of a Swedish trial. *Journal of the American Geriatrics Society, 43*, 301-307.

Mohrman, S.A., Cohen, S.G., & Mohrman, A.M. (1995). *Designing team-based organizations: New forms for knowledge work*. San Francisco: Jossey-Bass Publisher.

Pew Health Professions Commission. (1995). Critical challenges: Revitalizing the health professions for the twenty-first century. San Francisco: Author.

Reuben, D.B., Frank, J.C., Hirsch, S.H., McGuigan, K.A., & Maly, R.C. (1999). A random clinical trial of outpatient comprehensive geriatric assessment coupled with an intervention to increase adherence to recommendations. *Journal of the American Geriatrics Society, 47*, 269-276.

Rubenstein, L.Z., Josephson, K.R., Wieland, G.D., English, P.A., Sayre, J.A., & Kane, R.L. (1984). Effectiveness of a geriatric evaluation unit: A randomized clinical trial. *New England Journal of Medicine, 311*, 1664-1670.

Rubenstein, L.Z., Stuck, A. E., Siu, A.L., & Wieland, D. (1991). Impacts of geriatric evaluation and management programs on defined outcomes: Overview of the evidence. *Journal of the American Geriatrics Society–Suppl., 39*, 8S-16S.

Schmidt, L., Claesson, C.B., Westerholm, B., Nilsson, L.G., & Sverstad, B.L. (1998). The impact of regular multidisciplinary team interventions on psychotropic prescribing in Swedish nursing homes. *Journal of the American Geriatrics Society, 46*, 77-82.

Schmitt, M.H., Watson, N.M., Feiger, S.M., & Williams, T.F. (1982). Conceptualization and measuring outcomes of interdisciplinary team care for a group of long-term, chronically ill, institutionalized patients. In J.E. Bachman (Ed.), *Interdisciplinary health care: Proceedings of the third annual interdisciplinary team care conference* (pp. 169-182). Kalamazoo, MI: Center for Human Services, Western Michigan University.

Shortell, S.M., Zimmerman, J.E., Rousseau, D.M., Gillies, R.R., Wagner, D.P., Draper, E.A., Knaus, W.A., & Duffy, J (1994). The performance of intensive care units: Does good management make a difference. *Medical Care, 32*, 508-525.

Shycon, H.N. (1991). Measuring the payoff from improved customer service. *Prism, 1*, 71-81.

Siegel, C., & Fischer, S.K. (1981). *Psychiatric records in mental health care*. New York: Brunner/Mazel.

Steiner, I. (1972). *Group process and productivity*. New York: Academic Press.

Veterans Administration Asst. Deputy Administrator for Personnel and Labor Relations. (1981). *Individual development planning in the VA*. VA Pamphlet 05-67. Washington, DC: Author.

Vroman, K. (1999). Interdisciplinary collaboration using the Internet: Theory vs. reality [Abstract]. Program book from the 21st Annual Interdisciplinary Health Care Team Conference (p. 24) in Louisville, KY.

Waite, M.S., & Harker, J.O. (1997). Team training in diversity for interdisciplinary nursing home teams: Wherein lies diversity? *Continuum: An Interdisciplinary Journal on Continuity of Care, 17*, 15-20.

Waite, M.S., Harker, J.O., & Messerman, L.I. (1994). Interdisciplinary team training and diversity: Problems, concepts and strategies. *Gerontology and Geriatrics Education, 15*, 65-82; also in D. Weiland, D. Benton, B.J. Kramer, & G.D. Dawson (Eds.), *Cultural diversity and geriatric care: Challenges to the health professions (pp. 65-82)*. New York: The Haworth Press, Inc.

Wheelan, S.A. (1993). *The Group Development Questionnaire: A manual for professionals*. (Available from GDQ Associates, 144 N. Bread Street, Philadelphia, PA, 19106).

Zeiss, A.M., & Okarma, T.B. (1984). Effects of interdisciplinary health care teams on elderly Arthritic patients: A randomized prospective trail of alternative team models. In P.W. Gillespie, R. Erickson, J. Lewis, C. Polifroni, M. Podurgiel, & H. Palmer (Eds.), *Interdisciplinary health team care: Proceedings of the sixth annual conference, Hartford, CT (pp. 21-35)*. Storrs, CT: The University of Connecticut.

PART II
REVIEWING AND EVALUATING TEAM PERFORMANCE INSTRUMENTS

CHAPTER 8
CRITIQUING AND SUMMARIZING INSTRUMENTS

Sara A. Brallier, Ph.D.
Coastal Carolina University, Conway, SC

Steven Lovett, Ph.D.
VA Palo Alto Health Care System, Palo Alto, CA, VISN 21

Thomas F. Miller, Ph.D.
William S. Middleton Memorial VA Hospital, Madison, WI, VISN 12

This chapter serves as an introduction to the second part of this book. In it, we provide an overview of the process and guidelines used to critique the 66 instruments measuring team performance and some trends found across the instruments with regard to the guideline categories. Next we discuss the statistical criteria used in evaluating the psychometric testing. Finally, we explain the tables used to summarize the instruments in the following chapters.

PROCESS AND GUIDELINES FOR CRITIQUING

The editors divided the instruments into four groups based upon their breadth of coverage of the eight dimensions of our model of team performance described in Chapter 3. Focused instruments (Chapter 9) measure one to three dimensions of team performance. Middle-range instruments (Chapter 10) measure four or five dimensions; broad-spectrum instruments (Chapter 11) measure five or six dimensions, and full-spectrum instruments (Chapter 12) measure seven or eight dimensions. These four chapters begin with an overview of the instruments followed by a summary table and their critiques. Five additional critiques appear in Chapter 13; these supplemental instruments have the potential for adaptation for teams in health care settings, but none of them measures team performance directly or uses the definition of team that we have employed in this volume.

At least two experts in the area of health care teams/teamwork critiqued each instrument. At times, one of the reviewers was a developer of the instrument or had experience using it with health care teams. In such instances, the other reviewer served as the unbiased evaluator. In other instances, one of the reviewers communicated directly with the developer by phone, letter, or e-mail. These close links with the developers helped us better understand the instruments and their respective purposes.

In order to ensure the critiques were consistent and standardized, the editors developed a set of guidelines and a standardized reporting format. Each critique includes an abstract or critique summary, a description of the conceptual or theoretical framework used as a basis for developing the instrument, a description of the instrument itself (i.e., purpose, item and response formatting, and how it is scored), and its reliability and validity data. Reviewers also provide an evaluation of the instrument, information about its status and availability, and any publications related to its development. Instruments marked with asterisks in the critiques are considered "best measures;" we discuss them further in Chapter 14.

Abstract

Each critique begins with an abstract or reviewers' summary. It includes a description of the instrument, highlights from the evaluation, and recommended uses. The abstracts permit the reader to identify quickly the instruments of interest to him or her.

Conceptual Framework

The framework includes a description of the conceptual or theoretical model that guided the instrument's development and the metaphor or descriptors used by developers to define a team.

The majority of instruments included in this volume were developed from specific models of team performance. Most common are the stages of small group development and the team as a work unit within a large, complex organization. In addition to a conceptual framework, many developers present an explicit or implicit metaphor or descriptor of the team. Common team metaphors or descriptors include the team as a small group that matures over time, a living organism, a system or subsystem, a link or bridge between employee and organization, and a self-managed work group. Less common metaphors are the team as a family, a bundle of energy, a rope, and a shamrock.

Description of Measure

In each critique, the reviewers provide a description of the instrument including its purpose, the components of team performance it measures both as conceptualized by the developers and with respect to our model of team performance, the formatting of items and response choices, and the procedures for scoring responses.

Many developers designed their instruments as education and consultation tools to help teams identify their strengths and weaknesses and develop action plans for improvement. Others designed instruments as part of research projects. Many of these instruments measure team members' perceptions of the quality of specific team processes; some can be used to evaluate the impact of educational interventions. A third set of instruments, expeditious learning tools, provides teams with a quick picture of what they do well and where they need to improve. A number of the instruments are appropriate for multiple purposes.

Where possible, the purpose also includes the original target group and the setting where developers piloted or first used the instrument. Many developers designed instruments for use in a variety of organizational settings. Others focused specifically on health care settings. Similarly, some instruments are generic and suitable for use with multiple types of groups or teams, while others focus on one particular type of team (e.g., geriatric clinical teams).

Components of team performance measured frequently are those related to within-team functioning–the elements within team structure, team context, and interdependence. Least likely components measured are those related to the organization in which the team functions and the domain of productivity.

Item and response formats and scoring procedures vary considerably across the instruments. For most items, the respondent is asked to indicate how representative a statement, phrase, or series of descriptors is of his or her attitudes, experiences, or behaviors. Answer choice options include a Likert format ranging from strongly agree to strongly disagree, dichotomous true/false choices, ratings along a continuum, ranking choices, or a distribution of a given number of points over several answer choices.

Developers usually provide written scoring instructions or a template that accompanies the instrument to facilitate scoring. Alternatively, some proprietary instruments require results be sent to the company for scoring and analysis. The majority of instruments are precoded (i.e., each answer choice is given a numeric code to circle or write in a blank). For other instruments, respondents make check marks beside their answer choices, and their answers are converted to numeric responses via a scoring template. Information from most instruments is summed and averaged to provide a team score or multiple team scores as the unit of analysis. The quantifying of information from answers to items of an instrument results in an overall scale score, several subscale scores, or a set of means and ranges from an item analysis. In instruments using both positively and negatively worded items and the same numeric answer choices for both, one set of items must be reverse coded before they can be summed. Some instruments explain this step while others use a template that automatically does the reverse coding.

A small number of developers provide directions for converting subscale scores to standardized scores or have established normative averages or norms. For instruments containing several subscales of varying lengths, standardizing the subscales so they have the same average and/or range facilitates their comparison. Using norms, one can interpret the meaning of a team's or team member's score(s) more effectively.

Psychometric Testing: Reliability and Validity

The next section of the guidelines summarizes the available data on the instrument's reliability and validity. These concepts are described in detail in Chapter 2. Data supporting an instrument's reliability and validity establish confidence that the instrument consistently measures what it is intended to measure. With regard to the instruments, three types of reliability are addressed–internal consistency, test-retest, and inter-rater. Internal consistency is the most frequently tested type of reliability, and inter-rater reliability is the least frequently tested since the majority of the instruments are self-administered.

The types of validity included in the critiques are content or face, concurrent, construct, predictive, and discriminant. Content validity is the most frequent type of validity addressed. A number of the research instruments also have concurrent and construct validity data. Only a small number have predictive or discriminant validity data available.

Evaluation

In the evaluation section, the reviewers discuss the instrument's strengths and weaknesses related to such issues as conceptual soundness, conceptual breadth and depth, and psychometric testing. Reviewers also address the length of time needed to complete the instrument, the clarity and readability of the items, the ease of responding to items, and the complexity of the scoring procedures. They address the suitability of the instrument for different types of teams (especially health care teams) and appropriate uses (e.g., research, educational evaluation, education and improvement). Reviewers also note when normative data are available for an instrument and how scores are compared to these norms (e.g., tables providing percentile ranks, calculation of standardized scores, etc.).

In order for an instrument to be valid, its items should be clearly worded and communicate the intended meaning to the respondents (Schutt, 1999). In the critiques, the reviewers report when an instrument's items contain complex or unclear wording, colloquialisms, or are written at a high reading level that may not be appropriate for all employees in a team or work group. Additionally, reviewers have identified several reoccurring methodological errors in item construction. First, some developers have included "double-barreled" items (i.e., an item that includes more than one question or issue, but allows for only one response). Second, some instruments contain items in which the setting is not clearly specified. That is, should the respondent answer in terms of his/her team or the larger organization in which the team works? Third, in a number of instruments, all of the items are worded either positively or negatively. This can create response bias if respondents get into a pattern of responding affirmatively or negatively and fail to read all of the items carefully. Another potential for response bias occurs in instruments that present items using a continuum with verbal anchors at each end. Usually, all positive anchors are on one side of the page and all negative anchors on the other side. If there are large numbers of items, respondents sometimes circle the answer codes without seriously considering the items themselves. Inserting an open-ended question that breaks up the long series of items can help minimize this type of response bias.

The evaluation also includes reviewers' suggestions for improving the instrument, remedying methodological errors in item construction, or adapting it for use with health care teams. Finally, if either of the reviewers has used the instrument for education, consultation, or research, they describe their experience and offer suggestions regarding its use.

Status/Availability

This section indicates whether the instrument is in the public domain, copyrighted, or proprietary. Most instruments in the public domain can be reproduced and used without charge. Some instruments must be obtained directly from the developers or can be used only with their permission. Many copyrighted instruments and the proprietary instruments must be purchased. Some of the proprietary instruments must be used in conjunction with a consulting firm. We have provided the name of the developer, publisher, copyright holder, and/or consulting firm and some means of contacting them (e.g., mailing addresses, phone numbers, e-mail addresses) to facilitate readers having access to instruments relevant to their needs.

Relevant Publications

This section includes references for the instrument itself, accompanying manuals, articles or book chapters about its development and/or its theoretical underpinnings, and research articles that lend support to its psychometric properties.

STATISTICAL CRITERIA FOR PSYCHOMETRIC TESTING

The determination of what constitutes adequate reliability and validity depends on the nature of the instrument and its intended use. Here we provide a brief review of the most frequently reported statistics in the critiques. The critiques also offer some guidance for interpreting psychometric data.

The correlation coefficient is most often used to assess the psychometric properties of the instruments. Correlation coefficients reflect the strength and direction of the relationship or association between two variables. For example, a correlation coefficient between individuals' original scores on a test and their scores on the same test taken a week later reflect the measure's test-retest reliability. The numeric value of a correlation coefficient ranges from −1 to +1. The closer it is to one in either direction, the stronger the relationship between the two variables; the closer the coefficient is to zero, the weaker the relationship. In general, a correlation coefficient of .70 or greater indicates a very strong relationship. A coefficient between .50 and .70 indicates a strong relationship; one between .20 and .50, indicates a moderate relationship, and one between .10 and .20, a weak relationship. A coefficient less then .10 indicates no or a negligible relationship (Fox, 1995). A positive coefficient indicates that high scores on one variable are associated with high scores on the second variable, and low scores on one are associated with low scores on the other variable. A negative coefficient indicates that high scores on the first variable are associated with low scores on the second variable and vice versa.

Cronbach's alpha is the most frequently used measure of internal consistency for scales and subscales. The coefficient for Cronbach's alpha ranges from zero to one; the closer it is to one, the stronger the relationship among items is and the higher the likelihood is that a scale or subscale measures a single construct rather than combining dissimilar ones (Norusis, 1992). Generally, alphas below .60 are considered unacceptable.

Another, more complex statistical procedure for identifying relationships among variables is referred to as a factor analysis. Factor analysis is commonly used to test the assumption that scale or subscale scores on a measure actually reflect different and independent components of team performance in the manner in which they were designed to do. There are many procedures for conducting a factor analysis and equally varied criteria for interpreting the results. Generally, items that do not have a factor loading above .40 should be dropped from a scale and instrument. Factors with an eigenvalue greater than one and that can be interpreted meaningfully should be retained as scales or subscale. Reviewers offer suggestions for interpreting factor analytic results based on the nature of the specific measure and its intended use.

Some types of validity are most easily established by demonstrating that average scores for different groups of respondents differ in an expected way. For example, demonstrating that highly productive team members perceive their team to be better functioning on a measure of team performance than nonproductive team members would provide evidence for the validity of the measure. Analysis of variance (ANOVA) is the statistical test used most often to establish the difference of means for two or more groups (Knoke & Bohrnstedt, 1994).

Typically, the results of statistical procedures include information about their statistical significance, usually reported as a probability value (p). The accepted levels of statistical significance are probability less than or equal to $(p \leq)$ .05, .01, and .001. This means that these results would occur by chance less than five out of a hundred times, less than one out a hundred times, and less than one out of a thousand times, respectively.

SUMMARIZING TEAM PERFORMANCE INSTRUMENTS

A number of tables summarizing the team performance instruments appear in the second part of this book. Because so many instruments have similar names, all tables list the instruments in alphabetical order by the developer's last name. These tables, when used in conjunction with our model of team performance (Table 3.1 in Chapter 3), give the reader a quick summary of the team performance concept and the instruments that measure various facets of it (also see Table 14.3 in Chapter 14). These tables should help the reader identify relevant instruments for his or her situation and where to find more detailed information about them quickly and efficiently. Chapters 9 through 12 each include a summary table of the instruments critiqued in them. These summary tables report the name of the instrument, its developer(s), the number of items it includes, its purpose or purposes, the target group for which it is intended, and the status of its psychometric testing.

Chapter 13 includes three tables of instruments used in health care settings. Table 13.1 depicts instruments designed for use with health care teams. Table 13.2 depicts instruments adapted for use with health care teams, and Table 13.3 lists generic instruments with a history of frequent use in health care settings. A fourth table (Table 13.4) summarizes information about instruments that can either be used in conjunction with team performance measures or be adapted, with permission, to measure team performance. All of the tables in Chapters 9 through 13 identify, in bold face print, the instruments we have selected as "best measures." The column labeled instrument "type" in the Chapter 13 tables permits the reader to backtrack and locate other chapters where these instruments are critiqued and discussed.

Chapter 14 includes three tables. Table 14.1 identifies the state-of-the-art instruments and Table 14.2 lists the honorable mention instruments. Each of these tables provides a rationale for each instrument's selection as a "best measure." Table 14.3 presents a list of all of the team performance instruments critiqued in this volume and which of the eight dimensions of our model of team performance each measures. The column labeled instrument "type" in the Chapter 14 tables guides the reader to other chapters where the instruments are critiqued and discussed.

REFERENCES

Fox, W. (1995). *Social statistics: An introduction using MicroCase*. Bellevue, WA: MicroCase Corporation.

Knoke, D., & Bohrnstedt, G.W. (1994). *Statistics for social data analysis* (3rd ed.). Itasca, IL: F.E. Peacock Publishers, Inc.

Norusis, M.J. (1992). *SPSS for windows: Professional statistics release 5*. Chicago, IL: SPSS Inc.

Schutt, R. (1999). *Investigating the social world: The process and practice of research* (2nd ed.). Thousand Oaks, CA: Pine Forge Press.

CHAPTER 9
FOCUSED INSTRUMENTS

Ruth Ann Tsukuda, M.P.H.
VA Medical Center, Portland, OR, VISN 20

This chapter provides an overview of the 11 focused instruments measuring one to three dimensions of our model of team performance (see Chapter 3). Following the overview, Table 9.1 summarizes these instruments with regard to the developer(s), number of items, purpose, target group, and psychometric testing. The instruments in this table are alphabetized by the name of the developer(s). We designated the instruments in bold face type as "best measures." The critiques of each instrument follow the summary table. An instrument designated as a "best measure" has an asterisk after its title at the beginning of the critique.

OVERVIEW

For the most part, the focused instruments measure what occurs within the team (i.e., the quality of the team's processes, the quality of relationships among its members, and the developmental level of the team itself). Two instruments assess collaboration among members; three assess participation in team meetings or effectiveness of meetings, and four assess level of team functioning more generally. Additionally, one instrument measures general attitudes toward teams, and another measures the acquisition of teamwork skills in geriatric teams. Items are heavily concentrated in the team context and interdependence dimensions of team performance although team structure and growth and development also are addressed. The team's role within the organization and relationships across teams are largely ignored.

With regard to purpose, the instruments fall into two groups, those designed for research and evaluation (seven) and those designed to assess and improve team functioning or performance (four). Some of the research instruments also have been used or have the potential for use for education and improvement (see Table 9.1). Six instruments are applicable to many different types of teams; five specifically target health care teams; this latter group is discussed in more detail in Chapter 13.

The instruments are relatively short and easy to complete. The number of items ranges from a low of eight to a high of 27. All instruments are self-administered or have a self-administered component (i.e., completed anonymously by members of a team). Two instruments have an observational component or option as well. The instruments have good readability–all eighth grade level or below with one exception. Baggs' Collaboration and Satisfaction about Care Decisions has a higher readability level and, as a result is targeted to health care professionals only.

Most instruments require respondents to select one answer per item from a Likert-formatted set of answer choices. Two instruments require respondents to rank answer choices, and one requires the distribution of points over two answer options. We provide examples of item formatting in the "formatting and scoring" sections of the critiques for a number of the nonproprietary instruments.

Two of the educational instruments, Pfeiffer and Jones' Postmeeting Evaluation Form and Weisbord's Team Development Rating Scale are labeled expedient. Expedient measures are short, less formally structured instruments that have undergone no psychometric testing and can be modified to meet the specific needs of a team. We designated five of the 11 focused instruments as best measures and discuss them in more detail in Chapter 14.

Unique Features of the Instruments

Several of the instruments have unique features. Baggs' Collaboration and Satisfaction about Care Decisions measures collaboration in specific decision-making situations. Rating Individual Participation in Teams, developed by Bailey and Helsel-DeWert, collects both self-report and observational data, and Dimock's Survey of Team Development can be completed by either independent observers or team members. The former instrument is appropriate for monitoring or tracking performance over time. Heinemann, Farrell, and Schmitt's Attitudes Toward Health Care Teams Scale measures general attitudes toward teams, including whether or not physicians should have a central role of authority in teams. Hepburn, Tsukuda, and Fasser's Team Skills Scale measures perceived skills of team members or trainees. This latter measure is the only instrument in this volume that measures one dimension of our model of team performance. It is included because it measures team members' skills, part of the growth and development dimension of team performance. Additionally, it is a useful evaluation tool for determining the impact of educational interventions. Pfeiffer and Jones' Postmeeting Evaluation Form assesses general characteristics of and individual behaviors in team meetings; it asks respondents to answer in terms of how they perceived the meeting and their respective behaviors in the meeting.

Proportion with Psychometric Testing

Eight of the eleven instruments have undergone some psychometric testing. As one would expect, the instruments designed for research and evaluation have undergone the most testing. Four instruments have strong to good reliability and/or validity. Five have undergone preliminary testing or such testing is incomplete to date due to the newness of the instrument (see Table 9.1).

Implications for Use

The brevity of these instruments makes them appropriate for use among teams of busy health professionals and work group members. The research instruments are especially appropriate for large-scale surveys where space and time must be conserved. All of the educational instruments can be used by the teams themselves and do not require the presents of an outside consultant for administration unless the team is a newly developing one and is not yet comfortable assessing its own level of functioning. Teams can use the results from the educational instruments to develop action plans for improvement.

Table 9.1. Summary of Focused Instruments

Instrument	Developer(s); Adapter(s)	# Items	Purpose	Target Group	Psychometrics
Team Collaboration Index	Aram, Morgan & Esbeck	16	Research; assess & help improve functioning	Generic work groups/teams	Good reliability, preliminary validity
Collaboration & Satisfaction about Care Decisions	Baggs; adapted by Schmitt, Heinemann & Farrell	9	Research	Physician/nurse in ICUs; core members of clinical teams	Good reliability & strong validity
Rating Individual Participation in Teams	Bailey & Helsel-DeWert	17	Assess, monitor, & help improve functioning (participation in team meetings); research	Clinical, direct care teams	Strong reliability & validity
Survey of Team Development	Dimock	13	Assess & help improve functioning; identify stage of development	Generic teams with formal leader	Preliminary reliability only
Team Development Scale	Dyer	10	Assess & help improve functioning; research	Generic work groups/teams	Good preliminary reliability & validity
Team Anomie Scale	Farrell, Schmitt & Heinemann	23	Research; assess & help improve functioning	Clinical/professional teams, esp. new teams	Strong reliability & validity
Team Meeting Assessment	Harper & Harper	27	Assess & help improve functioning (meeting effectiveness)	Generic work groups/teams	None
Attitudes Toward Health Care Teams	Heinemann, Schmitt & Farrell	20	Research; evaluate educational intervention	Clinical teams	Strong reliability & validity
Team Skills Scale	Hepburn, Tsukuda & Fasser	17	Evaluate educational intervention	Geriatric clinical teams & trainees	Preliminary reliability & validity
Postmeeting Evaluation Form	Pfeiffer & Jones	20	Assess & help improve functioning (expedient measure of meeting effectiveness)	Generic work groups/teams	None
Team Development Rating Form	Weisbord	8	Assess & help improve functioning (expedient measure)	Generic work groups/teams	None

TEAM COLLABORATION INDEX*

Developed by John D. Aram, Cyril P. Morgan, and Edward S. Esbeck, 1971
Reviewed by Glenda F. Brown and Gloria D. Heinemann

The Team Collaboration Index is a 16-item measure of collaboration among members of product line groups/teams. It includes three subscales: Problem Solving through Support and Integration; Open, Authentic Communication; and Knowledge-Based Risk-Taking. The Index is based on a model of organizational adaptation that emphasizes collaboration and consensus for promoting the goals of both individual employees and the organization in which they are located. It is short, easy to administer and score, and has good reliability data. Additional psychometric testing should be undertaken, however. It is appropriate for educational, consultative, and research use with health care teams, especially those in organizations undergoing structural change from hierarchical departments or services to more horizontal product or care lines.

Conceptual Framework

The Index is based on Shepard's (1965) theory of the social organization as an "adaptive organism" in linking interpersonal relationships and the survival of the organization as a collectivity. According to Shepard, human adaptation may be primary, where the individual is concerned for self-interest, or secondary, where the individual is concerned for the interest of the collectivity (i.e., organization, group, or team). In primary adaptation, the relationship of the organization to the individual is coercive-compromising as the individual exhibits cooperative behavior in order to attain personal advantage; such behaviors are only minimally adaptive for the organization. In secondary adaptation, collaboration and consensus characterize the relationship between the organization and the individual. Others are viewed as valuable, and interpersonal relationships involve openness and trust. Secondary adaptation provides satisfaction to individual employees and promotes the goals of the organization.

Developers perceive the team as an "adaptive organism" linking interpersonal relationships of employees with the organization in which they work. Relationships are played out in the work place among employees of the work group to promote self-interest and/or the interest of the organization.

Description of Measure

Developers constructed this instrument as part of a research project to test assumptions about Shepard's theory (i.e., that collaboration and consensus in interpersonal relations benefit both the individuals and the organization) among work group members in an industrial organization. The Index was part of a larger data collection instrument administered to 110 scientists, engineers, and laboratory technicians organized into 16 product-line groups in a research and development center of a major industrial organization. In addition to its use in research, it has potential as an educational and consultative tool for groups engaged in team development activities, especially those interested in assessing and attempting to improve collaboration. Group members complete the instrument anonymously.

Components of Team Performance Measured

The 16-item instrument includes three subscales, each measuring a component of the collaboration concept: (a) Problem Solving through Support and Integration (six items); (b) Open, Authentic Communication (six items); and (c) Knowledge-Based Risk-Taking (five items). One item appears in two of the subscales (see scoring section).

The Index measures three dimensions (team context, interdependence, and growth and development) in two of the domains (context and process) of our model of team performance.

Formatting and Scoring

Each of the 16 items appears as a stem with two alternative ending phrases; one indicates a collaboration-consensus orientation and the other, a coercion-compromise orientation. Each respondent distributes five points between the two alternatives in a way that best represents his/her perceptions of the group/team during the past year (see item example below).

1. When we are working for solutions to task-related problems, the team seems to be most concerned with ...
    a. finding the best solution.
    b. whose solution is accepted.

    A   B
    1. ___ ___

Reprinted by permission of developers.

Responses allocated to the collaboration-consensus orientation are summed for each subscale score. Note that item 12A is included in both the second and third subscales. We recommend that it be dropped from the third subscale.

The scores for the Problem Solving through Support and Integration and Open, Authentic Communication Subscales range from 0 to 30; for the Knowledge-Based Risk-Taking Subscale, scores range from 0 to 25. The total Collaboration Scale scores range from 0 to 80. The higher the score on any subscale or scale, the more collaborative the team is perceived to be. To compare collaboration levels among teams of varying sizes, divide each team's three subscale scores and its total collaboration score by the number of members of the team.

Psychometric Testing

Internal Consistency Reliability

Developers began with 18 items from the organizational literature on interpersonal relationships in project teams. Factor analysis techniques resulted in three factors or subscales for team collaboration. Two items did not load on any of the three factors and were dropped from the scale. Item 12A loaded on both factors two (.59) and three (.48) and was retained in both of these subscales.

For factor one, the Problem Solving through Support and Integration Subscale, six items loaded from .78 to .64; for factor two, the Open, Authentic Communication Subscale, six items loaded from .78 to .46; and for factor three, the Knowledge-Based Risk-Taking Subscale, five items loaded from .79 to .43. For factors one, two, and three, the correlations between each factor and the total team collaboration score were .86, .88, and .89, respectively.

The reliability coefficients for internal consistency are .87, .80, and .80 for the factors/subscales, respectively, and .91 for the total score. If the duplicate item 12A is dropped from the third subscale as recommended, its reliability coefficient and the one for the total score could decrease slightly.

Test-Retest/Inter-Rater Reliability

No data are available regarding test-retest reliability, and testing for inter-rater reliability is inappropriate since the measure is self-administered.

Content or Face Validity

The Problem Solving through Support and Integration Subscale and the Open, Authentic Communication Subscale have good face validity. The Knowledge-Based Risk Taking Subscale is less focused than the other two; three of its factor loadings are below .50.

Concurrent Validity

None of the three subscales was related significantly to an observational/ranking measure of team effectiveness made by three judges for 16 product line groups. This may be a result of either a small sample size or collaboration being only one facet of an overall measure of team effectiveness. Thus, concurrent validity was not supported.

Construct/Predictive/Discriminant Validity

No data are available regarding these three types of validity.

Evaluation

The instrument has good theoretical underpinnings and is easy to administer and score. Factor loadings on the subscales are strong. As stated earlier, we recommend dropping item 12A from the Knowledge-Based Risk-Taking subscale since it loads stronger on the Open, Authentic Communication one. This item includes the term, "level" to mean "openly express." This is a colloquial meaning that may not have wide applicability among respondents. We suggest this item be reworded for clarity. The instrument is a reliable measure of collaboration; however, it needs additional testing for validity. Although its conceptual framework and team metaphor/descriptors address the team within the organization, the actual items in the instrument measure only "within team" elements of performance.

It is appropriate for use as a research, education, and consultation measure with health care teams, especially those in organizations restructuring along product or care lines and for teams wanting to become more collaborative.

Status/Availability

This Index is in the public domain. Information about its development appears in the 1971 publication by Aram, Morgan, & Esbeck. For additional information, contact Cyril Morgan, Washington State University, Department of Management and Systems, College of Business and Economics, Pullman, WA 99164; (509) 335-7527.

Relevant Publications

Aram, J.D., Morgan, C.P., & Esbeck, E.S. (1971). Relation of collaborative interpersonal relationships to individual satisfaction and organizational performance. *Administrative Science Quarterly, 16*, 289-296.

Shepard, H.A. (1965). Changing interpersonal and intergroup relations in organizations. In J.G. March (Ed.), *Handbook of organizations* (pp. 1115-1143). Chicago, IL: Rand McNally.

COLLABORATION AND SATISFACTION ABOUT CARE DECISIONS*

Developed by Judith G. Baggs, 1992; adapted for health care teams
by Madeline H. Schmitt, Gloria D. Heinemann, and Michael P. Farrell, 1994.
Reviewed by Elizabeth Fox and Gloria D. Heinemann

The Collaboration and Satisfaction about Care Decisions includes a six-item Collaboration Subscale, a one-item, global measure of collaboration, and a two-item Satisfaction Subscale. The original instrument measures collaboration between nurses and physicians working in intensive care units (ICUs) around decisions to transfer patients out of the ICU. The instrument was adapted to include the core team of health professionals (nurse, physician, and social worker) in geriatric team settings. The adapted instrument measures collaboration around the decision to discharge patients from inpatient and/or outpatient geriatric team programs. The original instrument has strong theoretical underpinnings and good reliability and validity. Psychometric testing for the adapted instrument is underway at the present time. The instrument is unique in that it links collaboration to specific decision-making situations. An additional strength is its brevity, which makes it especially appropriate for busy health professionals. Its high readability level indicates that it is best used with professionals rather than front line staff. Both the original and adapted versions are research instruments.

Conceptual Framework

In designing this instrument, Baggs used the model of collaboration developed by Thomas (1976), who identified two major facets of collaboration, cooperativeness and assertiveness. That is, when collaborating, a person has concern for the others and his/her own interests simultaneously. Collaboration is essential where the parties have common interests and the stakes are high. In such situations, collaborative solutions maximize the satisfaction of the parties involved. Other critical attributes for collaboration between nurses and physicians in intensive care units (ICUs) include cooperative working together and sharing responsibility for problem solving and decision-making to formulate and implement plans of care for patients (Baggs & Schmitt, 1988). According to the developer, the more ICU physicians and nurses collaborate, the more satisfied they will be with decision-making and the better their patients' outcomes will be.

Description of Measure

Baggs developed the instrument to measure nurse-physician collaboration and satisfaction about care decisions in ICUs and to study the relationship of

ICU transfer decisions and patients' outcomes. She notes that the instrument could be used in other patient care settings, specifically around decisions related to the discharge of patients.

The adapted version, also a research instrument, expands the number of health professionals from two to three by focusing on the core team of nurse, physician, and social worker in geriatric team settings. It measures collaboration around discharging rather than transferring patients. The adapted instrument was used as part of a VA Cooperative Studies Project evaluating geriatric care versus usual care. Core team members of both inpatient and outpatient Geriatric Evaluation and Management (GEM) Teams in ten VA hospitals completed it.

Components of Team Performance Measured

The first six items of both the original and adapted instruments make up the Collaboration Subscale. They elicit information regarding the six critical attributes of collaboration (i.e., joint planning, open communication, shared decision-making responsibilities, cooperation, consideration for the different professionals' concerns, and coordination). The seventh item is a global measure of the amount of collaboration that occurred in making the decision to transfer the patient out of the ICU (original instrument)/collaboration that occurred in making the decision to discharge the patient (adapted instrument). Items eight and nine make up the Satisfaction Subscale (i.e., satisfaction with the decision-making process as well as satisfaction with the actual decisions made).

The original and the adapted instruments measure two domains (context and process) and two dimensions (team context and interdependence) of our team performance model. It is unique in its measurement of collaboration around specific decision-making situations.

Formatting and Scoring

For both the original and adapted instruments, the developers use a seven-point set of answer choices with verbal anchors for each of the extreme scores. The Likert formatted responses range from 1 = low collaboration/satisfaction to 7 = high collaboration/satisfaction (see item example below). The number of items was kept to a minimum so busy providers could complete the instrument as they worked and relatively soon after a decision was made and implemented.

1. Core team members <u>cooperated</u> in making these decisions.
   Strongly   Strongly
   Disagree . . . 1   2   3   4   5   6   7 . . . Agree

Reprinted by permission of developer, J.G. Baggs ©1992.

Actual changes made to the original version of the instrument were minimal. Adapters substituted "among core team members" for "between nurses and physicians" in three of the six subscale items and in the one-item, global measure of collaboration. They substituted "core team" for "nurses and physicians" in two of the six subscale items and "medicine, nursing, and social work concerns" for "nursing and medical concerns" in one subscale item. No changes were made to the two satisfaction items. For each item, the content of the question was preserved. Baggs' original instrument asked two additional questions specific to ICU care decisions; these were dropped in the adapted version.

For both the original and adapted instruments, subscale items are summed and mean scores calculated for each subscale in order to determine the relationship between collaboration with decision-making and satisfaction with it. The Collaboration Subscale has a potential range from 6 to 42; the potential range of the Satisfaction Subscale is from 2 to 14. The higher the score, the higher is the perceived collaboration and satisfaction with it. For the original and adapted measures, different health professionals' scores can be compared and contrasted, or they can be averaged for a team score.

Psychometric Testing

Internal Consistency Reliability

For the original instrument, an unrotated factor analysis confirmed that all six items making up the Collaboration Subscale had strong factor loadings on one factor; they loaded between .82 and .93. This held when the factor analysis was run on nurses, residents, and the total sample. This factor explained 75% of the variance in collaboration. Cronbach's alpha was 0.95. Intercorrelations among the six items ranged from .52 to .83. The two items making up the Satisfaction Subscale correlated .64; they had different correlations with the global measure of collaboration, r = .78 and .50, respectively.

Test-Retest/Inter-Rater Reliability

No data are available regarding test-retest reliability, and testing for inter-rater reliability is inappropriate since the measure is self-administered.

Content or Face Validity

For the original instrument, 12 nursing and medical experts on collaboration and interdisciplinary teams reviewed the items. They judged the majority of them as very relevant to the concept of collaboration; none of the items was found to be non-relevant. Additionally, eleven nursing and medical ICU providers agreed that the items measured collaboration, that they had the information to respond to the items, that the items were understandable, and that responses would vary in different patient decision-making situations. Finally, the use of a conceptual model and a thorough review of the literature contributed to content validity.

Concurrent Validity

Concurrent validity is supported in that Baggs' global measure of collaboration correlated .87 with the total of the six critical attribute items making up the Collaboration Subscale. Additionally, the global measure of collaboration correlated significantly and positively with the Weiss and Davis' Collaborative Practice Scale in one of Baggs' (1994) previous studies.

Construct Validity

Construct validity was supported in that the original Collaboration Subscale correlated with the Satisfaction Subscale (r = .66.). The Collaboration Subscale correlated differently with each item in the Satisfaction Subscale, as expected. The correlation between the Collaboration Subscale and the satisfaction with the decision-making process item was higher than the correlation between this subscale and satisfaction with the decision itself, r = .69 and .50, respectively.

Predictive/Discriminant Validity

No data are available for these two types of validity.

Evaluation

Baggs based the instrument on a strong theoretical framework. It is unique in that it measures collaboration targeted to a specific decision-making situation rather than global collaboration. The Satisfaction Subscale measures both satisfaction with the process of decision-making and with the decision itself. Although it includes only two items, we believe it is sufficient given that it measures both of these facets of decision-making satisfaction. The instrument also is unique in that its brevity does not compromise its soundness. Its short, clearly written items make it amenable to completion by busy health professionals. It has strong reliability and validity data, which we believe "hold up" for the adapted version since only minor changes were made in the items. Psychometric testing on the adapted version is proceeding, however.

The instrument is a strong measure of collaboration, and we highly recommend its use in research. Given that it measures collaboration related to decisions made for specific patients, it is especially useful in studies where the number of teams is limited, but the number of patients is large. The instrument is not recommended for use with large teams. Health professionals should complete the instrument relatively soon after their decisions are made (i.e., within 48 hours), and in large teams this may not always be possible. Because of the complexity of wording of some of the items, it is not recommended for use with nonprofessional, front line employees.

Status/Availability

Judith G. Baggs holds the copyright for the instrument; she can be reached at the University of Rochester, School of Nursing (716) 275-8879. There is no fee for using the instrument; however, the developer and/or adapters would appreciate receiving reliability and validity data or a copy of the raw data. To obtain a copy of the adapted instrument, contact Madeline H. Schmitt, University of Rochester, School of Nursing, Box SON, 601 Elmwood Avenue, Rochester, NY 14624; (716) 275-8889; e-mail, madeline_schmitt@urmc.rochester.edu.

Relevant Publications

Baggs, J.G. (1994). Development of an instrument to measure collaboration and satisfaction about care decisions. *Journal of Advanced Nursing, 20*, 176-182.

Baggs, J.G., & Schmitt, M.H. (1988). Collaboration between nurses and physicians. *Image, 20*, 145-149.

Thomas, K. (1976). Conflict and conflict management. In M.D. Dunnette (Ed.), *Handbook of industrial and organizational psychology* (pp. 889-935). Chicago, IL: Rand McNally College Publishing Company.

RATING INDIVIDUAL PARTICIPATION IN TEAMS*

Developed by Donald Bailey and Marjorie Helsel-DeWert, 1981
Reviewed by Sara A. Brallier, Gloria D. Heinemann, and Linda O. Nichols

Developers designed this instrument to measure the participation and collaboration of direct care team members in the team meeting. The instrument includes 17 items and five subscales–Preconference Preparation, Providing Information, Participating in Group Process, Distractions, and Nonverbal Behavior. A unique feature of this measure is its combining team members' perceptions with observational data. It measures behaviors and provides meaningful feedback for training and improving collaborative behavior among team members. Tests of reliability and validity indicate the instrument is a sound measure of group participation. Given its strong psychometric data, it is appropriate for both educational and research purposes.

Conceptual Framework

The developers view team effectiveness as a developmental process that takes place over time with the help of education and consultation. Teams move through stages from newly developing to well functioning. Along the way, various dysfunctions can occur that are specific to particular stages of development. Not only is there a developmental sequence to team functioning per se, but also to team meetings. Individual team members must learn to participate and collaborate effectively in team meetings in order to meet the team's goals and better serve its clients.

The team is a developing and changing entity, a set of subsystems, and a functioning unit. The team's success and effectiveness are determined, in part, by the behavior of its individual members, especially during team meetings.

Description of Measure

Developers designed the instrument to measure team members' participation in the team meeting. Their instrument combines self-reported data with observational data. It provides meaningful feedback by identifying aspects of the interdisciplinary process that require additional training and evaluation to improve collaboration among team members. Developers designed the instrument for use in a residential institution for severely developmentally disabled persons. Team members included nursing personnel, social workers, educational staff, paraprofessionals, unit managers, support personnel such as psychologists and physical therapists, and parents/guardians. Used mostly as an educational instrument, it also has potential for research purposes.

Components of Team Performance Measured

Using 17 items organized into five subscales, developers measure five components of an individual's behavior in team meetings–preconference preparation (three items), the quality and quantity of information provided by the individual (three items), participation in the group process (seven items), distracting behavior (two items), and nonverbal behavior (two items).

The instrument measures two domains (context and process) and three dimensions (team context, interdependence, and growth and development) of our team performance model. Unique features measured are preparation for the meeting, the use of jargon, and non-verbal communication.

Formatting and Scoring

The first three items of the instrument (the Preconference Preparation Subscale) are based on self-reports from team members. The remaining 14 items are scored on the basis of direct observation. Each item is rated from one to five, with behavioral descriptors for ratings of one, three, and five.

I. **PRE-CONFERENCE PREPARATION**

A. Preparing reports prior to conference

1	2	3	4	5
Fails to complete any required reports or assessments.		Partially completes required reports or assessments.		Completes all required reports or assessments.

Reprinted by permission of developers.

Developers provide a template to assist with recording observational data about team members' behaviors. The items within each subscale are summed to produce subscale scores. The Preconference Preparation Subscale ranges from 3 to 15; Providing Information Subscale, from 3 to15; Participation in the Group Process Subscale, from 7 to 35; Distractions Subscale, from 2 to 10, and Nonverbal Behavior Subscale, from 2 to 10. High scores indicate behaviors facilitating meeting effectiveness. Each item also can be examined independently to identify specific areas of meeting participation that require improvement.

Psychometric Testing

Internal Consistency Reliability

Using principal components factor analysis with varimax rotation, developers identified five factors with eigenvalues greater than one. The factor analysis confirmed the five groupings of items, identified by the developers during the instrument's construction.

Test-Retest Reliability

Developers assessed the generalizability of the scale using 16 team members, observed at two different meetings. Results indicated that there is considerable variability in individual participation across team meetings. They concluded that multiple observations are required to determine typical behavior over time.

Inter-Rater Reliability

Two observers attended 23-team meetings. Team members were divided into two groups, and each observer rated his or her respective half of the team. As a reliability check, both observers at each team meeting rated one individual. The process yielded the comparison of 322 items (14 items x 23 subjects). Results showed 64% of the comparisons in exact agreement, 24% off by one rating; 8% off by two ratings, 3% off by three ratings, and in only one instance, were the comparisons off by four ratings.

Content or Face Validity

Eleven professionals with extensive expertise in team process assessed the content validity of a preliminary version of the instrument. They rated the relevance of each item to quality participation in interdisciplinary team meetings on a scale of 1 = strongly disagree to 5 = strongly agree. The mean rating for all items was 4.56; the experts agreed that the content of the scale was relevant. However, their suggestions regarding the issues of overall clarity and feasibility of scoring led to several modifications–expanding the scale from 10 to 17 items; grouping the subscale items together to ease recording of observational data; and reducing the number of answer choices from seven to five.

Concurrent Validity

The developers compared the observational scores with Yoshida and colleagues' (1978) self-reported measure of participation. The moderate correlation of the scales ($r = .34$) suggests they measure a common construct.

Construct Validity

As predicted, the findings from an ANOVA indicated that participation in team meetings corresponds with status in the job hierarchy. Professionals contributed the most, followed by paraprofessionals, and nonprofessional staff had the lowest levels of participation.

Predictive/Discriminant Validity

No data are available for these two types of validity.

Evaluation

This is a well-designed instrument assessing the effectiveness of team meetings. It is conceptually sound and includes many facets of collaboration in meetings. However, it was developed as part of a larger study in which leadership in team meetings was measured using another instrument; thus, any measure of leadership in meetings is omitted from this instrument. Reliability and validity testing indicate that it is a robust measure of participation in team meetings. An additional study, (Bailey, Thiele, Ware, Helsel-DeWert, 1985) added further support to its reliability and validity.

The items are well constructed and methodologically sound. One exception is the item about submitting reports prior to the meeting. In order to receive a rating of five, team members must submit all required reports at least one week prior to the meeting. This time frame was chosen because of the specific requirements at the institution where the scale was first developed. The actual time frame assigned to this item may vary according to local agency regulations; in hospitals this time frame may need to be shortened. Apart from this, the instrument is directly applicable to other clinical and direct care teams.

This measure combines observational and self-report data and takes the measurement of participation beyond merely counting the number of verbal comments or questions. It can help identify aspects of team meeting behavior that require improvement. Researchers also can use it to monitor participation over time and compare levels of participation of different groups (e.g., men and women, professionals and front line employees) within the team. Data suggests that members' behaviors are not always consistent across team meetings; thus, developers caution that one observation is not sufficient to obtain an accurate picture of typical participation; at least two observations are necessary.

Status/Availability

This instrument is unpublished and may be obtained by writing Donald Bailey, Division of Special Education, Peabody Hall 037-A, University of North Carolina, Chapel Hill, NC 27514.

Relevant Publications

Bailey, D.B., & Helsel-DeWert, M. (1983). Rating individual participation on the interdisciplinary team. *American Journal of Mental Deficiency, 88*, 247-254.

Bailey, D.B., Thiele, J.E., Ware, W.B., & Helsel-DeWert, M. (1985). Participation of professionals, paraprofessionals, and direct-care staff members in the interdisciplinary team meeting. *American Journal of Mental Deficiency, 89*, 437-440.

SURVEY OF TEAM DEVELOPMENT

Developed by Hedley G. Dimock, 1987, revised 1991
Reviewed by Ruth Ann Tsukuda and Gloria D. Heinemann

The Survey of Team Development is a 13-item instrument that assesses the stage of a team's development. Designed for use by either an independent observer or team members, it is based on a strong theoretical framework and is relatively easy to complete. It would benefit from some rewording of items, clearer distinction between the four answer choices for the items, clearer description of how to score the instrument, and further psychometric testing. It is a team building instrument for consultative and/or educational activities. The developer suggests using it along with several of his other measures (e.g., leadership inventory and peer rating scale).

Conceptual Framework

Dimock weaves a number of concepts from several developmental frameworks as the basis for this instrument's development. He argues that five interrelated aspects of group development, taken together, account for most of the dynamics occurring within groups. A group can improve its performance by attending to these five developmental areas–physical and emotional climate, involvement, interaction, cohesion, and productivity. Roles also are important for development of the team. These are divided into (a) task roles such as defining problems, seeking information, giving information, seeking opinions, giving opinions, and testing feasibility and (b) group-building and maintenance roles such as coordinating, mediating-harmonizing, orienting-facilitating, supporting-encouraging, and following. Additionally, some individual roles (e.g., blocking, and digressing) may be present in the early stages of development. These roles are nonfunctional to the group and are not present in well performing ones. Group members who learn to use roles flexibly and appropriately help the group grow and develop.

Like individuals, the group must deal with inclusion, control, and intimacy or openness in a sequential manner as it grows and develops. Groups that have resolved concerns in these three areas become cohesive, share leadership among members, and become well functioning. To become mature and well functioning, groups also must work through roles and relationships with the authority figure or group leader. The more emotional the content involved in working out authority issues, the lower is the level of work accomplished by the group. Groups tend to exhibit high emotional content in the early stages of development; that is, they tend to respond to authority in the following sequential ways–concern about authority, tension and hostility, cohesion and solidarity, and openness and authenticity. Trust is the final component of this framework. As the group grows and develops, trust should develop as members learn to trust themselves and other members.

The developer views the team is a social system with structure, norms, values, and procedures. Education and training facilitate team development, growth, and productivity.

Description of Measure

The instrument has been used extensively to help groups and teams assess and analyze their level of functioning. It provides a set of categories or questions for formalized observations of team development from meeting to meeting or across activities. It can be used to assess a team's current stage of development and changes in development over time. Dimock recommends that an observer or team members complete the instrument about the team immediately after one of its meetings or activities. Average scores for each item give a profile of the team's level of development.

Components of Team Performance Measured

This 13-item instrument includes the components–unity, self-direction, team climate, distribution of leadership, distribution of responsibility, problem solving, resolving disagreements, basic needs, variety of activities, depth of activities, leader-member rapport, role of the formal leader, and stability.

The instrument addresses two (context and process) of the four domains and three (team context, interdependence, and growth and development) of the eight dimensions in our model of team performance.

Formatting and Scoring

For each of the 13 items, there are four descriptive answer choices. The respondent or observer places a check mark on the blank to the left of the item that most closely describes his or her perception of the team. An example of the item formatting appears below.

No scoring instructions accompany the instrument. The developer indicates that numeric scores can be given to the answer choices on the basis of desirability for team development; scores range from 1 (least desirable stage) to 4 (most desirable stage); however, there is no indication given as to which answer choices coincide with which stages of development.

11. **Leader-Member Rapport:** the extent to which relations between the team and its formal leader are productive.

   _____ a. The team members are generally antagonistic or resentful toward the formal leader.
   _____ b. The team members are generally indifferent or noncommunicative toward the formal leader; friendship is neither sought nor rejected.
   _____ c. The team members are generally friendly toward and interested in the formal leader; they are attentive to the leader's suggestions.
   _____ d. The team members have close relationships with the formal leader; there is strong rapport, openness, and sharing.

In J.W. Pfeiffer & C. Nolde (Eds.), *The encyclopedia of team development activities* ©1991. Reprinted by permission of the developer and Jossey-Bass, Inc., a subsidiary of John Wiley & Sons, Inc.

Psychometric Testing

Internal Consistency/Test-Retest Reliability

No data are available for these types of reliability.

Inter-Rater Reliability

The developer reports that independent observers had high inter-rater reliability (significant at .05 level) and that ratings by members, leaders, and supervisors correlated at the same high level of significance.

Validity

No data are available regarding the instrument's validity.

Evaluation

Strengths of the instrument include good theoretical underpinnings, relative ease of completion, and its assessment of multiple facets of leadership. The instrument lends itself to two methods of collecting data–from observers or team members. Activities outside of team meetings can be difficult to assess by an observer, however. These reviewers believe team members make the better respondents with regard to some team activities. Another option would be to have both observers and team members complete the instrument.

Several weaknesses related to design are evident. First, the instrument includes only one item to measure each facet of group development and omits assessing goals/objectives and roles, two of the most common elements of team performance measured in similar instruments. Second, some wording problems exist in some of the answer choices. For example, "clique" in item 2c, "detriment" in item 3c, "rapport" in item 11d, and "stimulus" in item 12c are difficult or sophisticated words, and "external factors" in item 1b, "self-propulsion" in item 2b, "pet idea" in item 6b, and "scratch the surface" in item 10a are unclear. Such wording can result in differing interpretations by respondents, inconsistent responses, and poor quality data.

Additionally, instructions for scoring the instrument are unclear. Even more importantly, from item to item, it is not clear how to rank the answer choices. For nine of the 13 items, "a" appears to be the least desirable (i.e., the least developed team), "b" the second least desirable, "c" the second most desirable, and "d" the most desirable (i.e., the most developed team) answer choice. However, for the other four items (i.e., items 2, 3, 5, 6), these reviewers could not come to consensus on the ranking of answer choices "b" and "c."

Finally, the reviewers question the instrument administration after a specific activity of the team since it is measuring team development generally. Finally, the instrument would benefit from further psychometric testing, especially test-retest reliability if it is to be used to monitor development over time. It also would be interesting to know if the 13 items are scalable.

Status/Availability

The instrument is copyrighted. It is published as the Survey of Group Development, 1987 by University Associates and as the revised Survey of Team Development, 1991 by Pfeiffer & Company (see references below). It can be duplicated and used (100 copies or less) for educational/training purposes. Written permission must be obtained to use over 100 copies. Contact University Associates at (619) 578-5900 and/or Pfeiffer & Company at (800) 274-4434.

Relevant Publications

Dimock, H.G. (1987). *Groups: Leadership and group development*. San Diego, CA: University Associates, Inc.

Dimock, H.G. (1991). Survey of Team Development. In J.W. Pfeiffer & C. Nolde (Eds.), *The encyclopedia of team development activities* (pp. 243-246). San Diego, CA: Pfeiffer & Company.

TEAM DEVELOPMENT SCALE

Developed by William G. Dyer, 1977
Reviewed by Stephen K. Harmon and Ruth Ann Tsukuda

The Team Development Scale is a 10-item instrument that addresses two major aspects of team development, positive affect/cohesion and sharing/interdependence. It is relatively short and easy to read, complete, and score. It can be used for item analysis or as two subscales. It also has good preliminary reliability and validity data. We recommend its use in educational consultations and evaluations of educational impact. While not developed specifically for health care teams, the instrument has been used widely with health care teams in the VA system.

Conceptual Framework

Dyer's framework is based on the work of numerous organizational and management theorists from the 1960s (see Dyer, 1977). The major focus of this framework is that the human group is a mechanism for integrating individuals into organizations. Many important activities in organizations are better accomplished by groups or teams rather than by supervised individuals, and managers would be more effective managing groups rather than individuals. Differentiated groups within an organization need to be tied together through integrating or coordinating teams (e.g., management teams). Using participatory management, groups can bring about change within an organization at both the individual and organizational levels. Team development is needed at all levels of an organization to build effective working relationships and develop effective, highly functioning work groups or teams.

The work group or team integrates people into organizations. The collaboration and interdependence among work group members provide the most appropriate means for accomplishing the work of the organization.

Description of Measure

Dyer designed the instrument primarily for consultation to facilitate team members' self-examination and the identification of conditions that keep the work group from functioning effectively. It has been used in National Training Laboratories settings, professional group management training, and corporate settings with organizations such as Exxon, Arco, and General Foods. Overall, use of the instrument is associated most frequently with business and corporate settings. The instrument has been administered to groups of mangers and teams in corporate settings in conjunction with management training curriculum. The instrument also has been widely used in management graduate education and in the VA health care system. Individual members of the work group or team complete the instrument.

Components of Team Performance Measured

The instrument measures inclusion/membership (one item), climate (two items), decision-making (one item), goal clarity (one item), task accomplishment (one item), planning and organization (one item), assuming responsibility (one item), conflict (one item), and team reactions to leadership (one item).

It measures three of the four domains (structure, context, and process) and three of the eight dimensions (team structure and context and interdependence) of our team performance model. Although the theoretical model emphasizes the team within the organization, the instrument addresses "within team" issues.

Formatting and Scoring

The instrument consists of 10 items, each with answer choices from 1 to 5 along a continuum. Each answer choice has a verbal anchor below the continuum. Six items are designed so 1 = worst functioning and 5 = best functioning. For the other four items, 1 = best functioning and 5 = worst functioning.

7. Our planning and the way we operate as a team is largely influenced by:

1	2	3	4	5
One or two team members.	A clique.	Shifts from one persons or clique to another.	Shared by most of the members, some left out.	Shared by all members of the team.

In Dyer, W.G. *Team Building* ©1987 and S.L. Phillips & R.L. Elledge (Eds.), *The team building sourcebook* ©1989. Reprinted by permission of Pearson Education, Inc. Upper Saddle River, NJ.

The developer recommends an item analysis. Scores for each item are summed across team members, and mean scores and ranges are compared across items to identify areas for improvement. Findings from research using this instrument (Stahelski & Tsukuda, 1990) showed that the items are scaleable. After reverse coding items so answer choice 5 is always most positive, items 4 and 6-9 can be summed to create an Interdependence Subscale. Items 1-3, 5, and 10 can be summed to create a Positive Affect or Cohesion Subscale. Both subscales range from 5 to 25; the higher the score the more developed is the team. Subscale scores can be averaged for team scores.

Psychometric Testing

Internal Consistency Reliability

The second reviewer and her research colleague used this instrument to investigate factors influencing cooperation in geriatric health care teams. Their factor analysis revealed that the ten items in Dyer's instrument load together on two factors. The stronger factor includes five items (see previous section for specific items); the factor loadings ranged from .49 to .75. They named this factor work structure; these items measure elements of interdependence in our model. The remaining five items loaded on the second factor named team cohesion; the loadings ranged from .47 to .90.

Test-Retest/Inter-Rater Reliability

No data are available regarding test-retest reliability, and testing for inter-rater reliability is inappropriate since the measure is self-administered.

Content or Face Validity

A panel of experts from the fields of business, management, and organizational behavior and reviewers and experts from National Training Laboratories established the instrument's face validity. In all cases, the experts were asked to indicate the appropriateness of each item and the relevance of each item to team functioning. The 10 items are the result of their efforts.

Concurrent Validity

No data are available.

Construct Validity

The second reviewer's research showed that the larger the size of the team, the lower the cooperation in work structure or interdependence, and as the number of team members who are staff, as opposed to trainees, increases, team cohesion or positive affect within the team increases.

Predictive/Discriminant Validity

No data are available for these two types of validity.

Evaluation

The strengths of the instrument are its practical applications in business and health care settings and the ease of administration and scoring. Unlike many of the instruments designed for education and consultation, there are good preliminary psychometric data supporting its reliability and validity. Weaknesses include some colloquial, confusing, and difficult wording of items (e.g., "under wraps" in item 3, "coasts" in item 6, and "clique" in item 7). The use of a verbal anchor for each answer choice increases the amount of reading for the respondent, but adds to the clarity of potential responses. Aptly named, the instrument addresses two major aspects of team development, positive affect/cohesion and sharing/interdependence. We recommend its use in educational consultations and evaluations of educational impact. It has potential as a research instrument as well.

Status/Availability

Pearson Education, Inc. holds the instrument's copyright. It appears in the 1987 and 1989 publications below. To purchase the 1989 publication, contact University Associates, Inc., at (619) 578-5900. Alternatively, contact Pearson Education, Inc., One Lake Street, Upper Saddle River, NJ 07458.

Relevant Publications

Dyer, W.G. (1977). *Team building: Issues and alternatives.* Reading, MA & Menlo Park, CA: Addison-Wesley Publisher.

Dyer, W.G. (1987) *Team building: Issues and alternatives* (2nd ed.). Reading, MA & Menlo Park, CA: Addison-Wesley Publisher.

Dyer, W.G. (1989). Team Development Scale. In S.L. Phillips & R.L. Elledge (Eds.), *Team-building source book* (pp. 16-17). San Diego, CA: University Associates, Inc.

Dyer, W.G. (1995). *Team building: Current issues and new alternatives* (3rd ed.). Reading, MA & Menlo Park, CA: Addison-Wesley Publisher.

Stahelski, A., & Tsukuda, R.A. (1990). Predictors of cooperation in health care teams. *Small Group Research, 21,* 220-232.

TEAM ANOMIE SCALE*

Developed by Michael P. Farrell, Madeline H. Schmitt, and Gloria D. Heinemann, 1992
Reviewed by Gloria D. Heinemann and Antonette M. Zeiss

The Team Anomie Scale is a 23-item instrument measuring lack of clarity in the team's structure and culture (i.e., mission, goals, roles, norms, rules, and procedures). It has strong theoretical underpinnings and is easy to read and complete. This unidimensional scale has strong reliability and validity data. Two items in the instrument were revised slightly between the two large-scale surveys in which it has been used. Additional psychometric testing is in progress with regard to the revised version. Developers designed the instrument for purposes of research with geriatric health care teams; it also has potential as an educational tool, especially for newly developing teams and those that recently have experienced stressful events or disruptions.

Conceptual Framework

This measure is based on a small group development framework. Task-oriented small groups move through four stages of development: (a) testing and dependency or forming; (b) conflict or storming; (c) cohesion and consensus or norming; and (d) functional role relatedness or performing (Tuckman & Jensen 1977; Farrell, Heinemann, & Schmitt, 1986). Anomie is a sociological concept that refers to lack of purpose and identity or normlessness in a person or society. When applied to health care teams, it refers to uncertainty or lack of clarity regarding the team's structure and culture (i.e., its mission, purpose, goals, roles, norms, and rules/procedures for operating). Teams in early developmental stages, before mission and roles are clear, or teams having experienced stressful events or disrupted physical environments should score high on this scale.

The team is a task-oriented, small group that develops over time. Development is not a linear progression; the team can experience stress and disruption that require it to revisit the fundamentals of mission, role clarity, and development of a culture.

Description of Measure

Developers used the measure in two large scale surveys–an NIA-funded, Quality of Geriatric Team Functioning Study of over 100 geriatric health care teams in 34 VA hospitals and a VA-funded Cooperative Studies Project in 10 VA hospitals evaluating geriatric care versus usual care. Designed for use in research, it measures lack of clarity in the team's structure and culture. Individual members of the team complete it. The instrument has potential as an educational or consultative tool to improving team performance in newly developing teams or those having recently experienced major disruptions such as stressful events or major changes in the team's physical environment. Team members' scores can be compared to the team's average score. Additionally, average team scores permit different teams to be compared and contrasted.

Components of Team Performance Measured

Developers designed the instrument to measure ambiguity related to lack of mission and role clarity and role tensions among team members.

The instrument measures three of the four domains (structure, context, and process) and three of the eight dimensions (team structure, team context, and interdependence) of our model of team performance.

Formatting and Scoring

The unidimensional scale includes 23 positively and negatively worded Likert-formatted items. For each item, there are six answer choices ranging from strongly agree = 5 to strongly disagree = 0.

Strongly Disagree	= SD
Moderately Disagree	= MD
Somewhat Disagree	= SWD
Somewhat Agree	= SWA
Moderately Agree	= MA
Strongly Agree	= SA

	SD	MD	SWD	SWA	MA	SA
1. My team's basic mission is clear to me	0	1	2	3	4	5

Reprinted by permission of developers.

Positively worded items (1, 2, 3, 7, 9, 10, and 11) are reverse-coded; all items are summed to create one scale that ranges from 0 (no anomie) to 115 (high anomie). The higher the score, the more anomic the members perceive the team. Team members' scores can be summed and averaged to obtain a team score.

Psychometric Testing

Internal Consistency Reliability

Early exploratory and confirmatory factor analysis ($N = 189$) resulted in a unidimensional scale of 23 items. Cronbach's alpha was .90, and the item-to-

150 TEAM PERFORMANCE IN HEALTH CARE

scale correlations ranged from .35 to .72. Cronbach's alpha for the version used in the Quality of Geriatric Team Functioning Study ($\underline{N}$ = 973) was .88. A confirmatory factor analysis indicated that the items form a single factor (Goodness of Fit Index = .92; Comparative Fit Index = .93). Factor loadings ranged from .40 to .75; the two items with the lowest loadings were reworded slightly for clarity.

Test-Retest/Inter-Rater Reliability

No data are available regarding test-retest reliability, and testing for inter-rater reliability is inappropriate since the measure is self-administered.

Content or Face Validity

Developers generated items measuring the dimensions of the anomie construct based upon a review of the literature, observations of teams, interviews with team members, and psychometric testing with four team experts.

Concurrent Validity

No data are available.

Construct Validity

Initial steps in assessing construct validity showed that the more anomie reported, the less respondents felt that teams contribute to the quality of care patients receive and the more they saw teams as unrealistic, ineffective, powerless, dull, and disorganized. Perceived anomie was negatively correlated with Clutter and Sachs' (1990) Semantic Differential, a measure of attitudes toward teams ($\underline{r}$ = -.40).

In the Quality of Geriatric Team Functioning Study, the scale correlated as anticipated with theoretically related scales with known validity and reliability. It correlated negatively and significantly with the modified Moos' Cohesion Subscale ($\underline{r}$ = -.64), modified versions of the Shortell and colleagues' (1989) Quality of Communication Subscale ($\underline{r}$ = -.75) and Task Effectiveness Subscale ($\underline{r}$ = -.61), and the Heinemann and colleagues' Quality of Care/Process Subscale of the Attitudes Toward Health Care Teams Scale (1992) ($\underline{r}$ = -.35).

The instrument was positively and significantly correlated with number of stressful events in the team's recent history ($\underline{r}$ = .20), and level of stress these events generated ($\underline{r}$ = .21). It correlated positively and significantly with

Maslach's (1986) Emotional Exhaustion Scale ($r = .38$) and Depersonalization Scale–the degree to which professionals depersonalize clients ($r = .32$).

Predictive Validity

No data are available.

Discriminant Validity

Responses to the instrument were investigated for a number of demographic variables to determine if team members were responding differently on the basis of these characteristics. Developers found no significant differences.

Evaluation

The instrument has a strong theoretical basis; psychometric testing indicates that it is conceptually sound. It is clear and straightforward; brevity facilitates its use with busy health professionals and in large-scale research projects. The first reviewer's experiences using it in research, indicate that completed responses should be edited carefully to avoid accidentally skipped items.

Further testing of the instrument should address the following three issues. First, with regard to concurrent validity, does high anomie relate to observations of the team by skilled raters confirming that the team is in forming or storming stages of development, and conversely, does low anomie relate to ratings of the team as being in more advanced stages of development? Second, regarding the development of norms, what exactly are "high" and "low" scores for this measure? Norms would allow teams or trainers working with teams to obtain more specific feedback to guide planning for team training. The third issue is related to additional scoring options. To date, only the mean score for the team has been utilized. A measure of internal variability in the team also could be calculated by examining how much the team is in agreement regarding items measured. This would provide information about consensus on perception of the team and might yield sensitive information about the level of storming within it.

Status/Availability

This instrument is in the public domain. Developers request a copy of the raw data and/or reports of its reliability and validity. For additional information about the instrument, contact Michael P. Farrell at (716) 645-2417, extension 456; e-mail, ofarrell@acsu.buffalo.edu.

Relevant Publications

Farrell, M.P., Schmitt, M.H., Heinemann, G.D., & Roghmann, K.J. (2001). The Team Anomie Scale: An indicator of poor functioning in health care teams. Unpublished manuscript.

Farrell, M.P., Heinemann, G.D., & Schmitt, M.H. (1992). A measure of anomie in health care teams. In J.R. Snyder (Ed.), *Interdisciplinary Health Care Teams: Proceedings of the Fourteenth Annual Conference in Chicago* (pp. 186-197). Indianapolis, IN: School of Allied Health Sciences, Indiana University School of Medicine, Indiana University Medical Center.

Farrell, M.P., Heinemann, G.D., & Schmitt, M.H. (1986). Informal roles, rituals, and styles of humor in interdisciplinary health care teams: Their relationship to stages of group development. *International Journal of Small Group Research, 2*, 143-162.

Tuckman, B.W., & Jensen, M.A.C. (1977). Stages of small group development revisited. *Group and Organization Studies, 2*, 419-427.

TEAM MEETING ASSESSMENT

Developed by Ann Harper and Bob Harper, 1992
Reviewed by Sara A. Brallier and Gloria D. Heinemann

The Team Meeting Assessment, a 27-item measure of a team or work group's meeting effectiveness, addresses communication and decision-making in considerable depth. Omitted from the instrument is measurement of outcomes or results of meetings. The measure facilitates the identification of the team's strengths and weaknesses regarding meetings and helps members plan to improve the weaknesses. Its simple, clear language makes it appropriate for work groups at any level of the organization. No psychometric testing has been done to date.

Conceptual Framework

Team meetings are major arenas where members work together. Regularly scheduled meetings provide opportunities to problem solve, schedule work, share ideas and information, plan for the future, and discus relevant issues. In meetings, members get to know one another, make decisions together, and. identify the team's strengths and weaknesses in order to improve productivity. Members also can practice team skills (i.e., listening, giving and receiving feedback, disclosure).

The team is a self-directed work group within a complex organization.

Description of Measure

Developers designed the instrument to identify strengths and weaknesses of the organizational work group's regular meetings and to stimulate discussion about improving meeting effectiveness. Team members complete the instrument anonymously.

Components of Team Performance Measured

The instrument focuses on communication; decision-making; participation of team members; rules, procedures, and roles related to the meeting; climate in the meeting; and efficiency.

It measures three of the four domains (structure, context, and process) and three of the eight dimensions (team structure, team context, interdependence) of our model of team performance.

Formatting and Scoring

The instrument includes 27 positively worded items whose Likert-formatted answer choices range from 0 = never to 4 = always (see item example below).

	Never	Seldom	Usually	Frequently	Always
1. Everyone understands the purpose of the meeting	0	1	2	3	4

In Harper, A., & Harper B. *Skill-building for self-directed team members* ©1992. Reprinted by permission of MW Corporation.

Developers suggest using an item analysis and a total score analysis. The total score is calculated by summing the responses for all 27 items. The higher the score, the more effective the meetings. Total scores can range from 0 to 108.

Psychometric Testing

Reliability

No reliability data are available.

Content or Face Validity

No formal testing for content validity has been conducted; however, the items included are relevant to measuring effective team meetings. Most of the items focus on communication and decision-making in meetings; the instrument does not address whether positive outcomes or results emerged as a consequence of the meetings.

Concurrent/Construct/Predictive/Discriminant Validity

No data are available for these types of validity.

Evaluation

The instrument's coverage of the elements of meeting effectiveness is very good. Its clear wording and easy readability make it appropriate for work groups in many levels of an organization. Results can be used to facilitate discussion and action planning for improving meetings. It lacks a strong theoretical framework, and superlative verbal anchors are used for the extreme answer choices ("never" and "always"), which respondents sometimes are reluctant to select. More appropriate answer choices might be "almost never" and "almost always." Given that all items are positively worded, there is potential for response bias. The developers also suggest summing the items for a total score without evidence of internal consistency. Psychometric testing and minor modifications would improve the instrument. Meeting effectiveness is only one of the many topics covered for quality team performance in the publication listed below. The publication is extremely useful as a workbook for developing and improving teams and work groups in complex organizations.

Status/Availability

The full-service consulting firm, MW Corporation, holds the instrument's copyright. The instrument appears in the publication below. To order it or other books and videos on teams, contact MW Corporation at (914) 962-2933.

Relevant Publications

Harper, A., & Harper B. (1992). *Skill-building for self-directed team members: A complete course* (pp. 88-90). New York: MW Corporation.

ATTITUDES TOWARD HEALTH CARE TEAMS*

Developed by G.D. Heinemann, M.H. Schmitt, and M.P. Farrell, 1991
Reviewed by Gloria D. Heinemann and Glenda F. Brown

The Attitudes Toward Health Care Teams Scale is a 20-item research measure of general attitudes about teams. The measure contains two subscales, Quality of Care/Process, and Physician Centrality in teams. Tests of reliability and validity demonstrate that each subscale is a strong measure of its respective underlying concept. The instrument's purposes include: (a) comparing attitudes of team members from different disciplines; (b) comparing attitudes among different types of teams; and (c) testing hypotheses about the interrelationships between attitudes and such variables as education, participation of team members, tenure on the team, and team functioning. The measure has strong psychometric data and has been used successfully as a pre/post test instrument for evaluating educational interventions with teams.

Conceptual Framework

Developers use the stages of small group development as the basis for this instrument. Members' attitudes toward teams, especially toward physician authority in teams, are often related to stage of their respective team's development. Teams in the early stages of development often include members who favor strong physician authority due to lack of commitment, unclear roles, and hesitancy to participate in the team's activities.

Developers view the team as a small group or differentiated feedback system. Noise, such as negative attitudes toward teams, can get in this feedback system and inhibit effective team functioning.

Description of Measure

Designed for research with geriatric health care teams, the instrument permits the comparison of attitudes of team members from different disciplines and the comparison of attitudes among different types of teams. Developers also used it to test hypotheses about the interrelationships between attitudes and such variables as education, participation of team members, tenure on the team, and team functioning. Team members complete the instrument. Heinemann, with research colleagues, Schmitt and Farrell, used the instrument in an NIA-funded research project attempting to identify factors influencing quality of functioning among over 100 geriatric health care teams in the VA system. The sample consisted of 973 health professionals working on teams.

Brown (1996) used the earlier version of the instrument that included three subscales in her study of attitudes among VA employees in one medical center.

Her sample included 200 health professionals (i.e., physicians, nurses, social workers, and pharmacists), the majority of whom worked on health care teams. The Geriatric Interdisciplinary Team Training (GITT) researchers used this same version as a pre/post test to determine the impact of an educational intervention with health/medical professional trainees (Fulmer & Hyer, 1998; Hyer, Fairchild, Abraham, Mezey, & Fulmer, 2000).

Components of Team Performance Measured

The instrument addresses general attitudes toward health care teams with regard to quality of team care and processes and physician centrality in teams.

It addresses two domains and two dimensions (team structure and team context) of our model of team performance. It is unique in that it measures general attitudes toward the quality of care and processes of the health care team and attitudes toward how central the role of physician should be within the team.

Formatting and Scoring

An earlier version of this scale included three subscales–Quality of Care, Costs of Team Care, and Physician Centrality. In the final version, the first two subscales were combined resulting in two subscales, Quality of Care/Process (14 items) and Physician Centrality (six items–4, 6, 8, 12, 15, and 17). This final version is made up of 20 items, both positively and negatively worded. The items are Likert-formatted. For each item, there are six answer choices ranging from strongly agree = 5 to strongly disagree = 0 (see item example below).

Strongly Disagree	=	SD
Moderately Disagree	=	MD
Somewhat Disagree	=	SWD
Somewhat Agree	=	SWA
Moderately Agree	=	MA
Strongly Agree	=	SA

	SD	MD	SWD	SWA	MA	SA
18. The team approach makes the delivery of care more efficient	0	1	2	3	4	5

Reprinted by permission of developers.

After reverse coding negative items, the items are summed for each subscale. The Quality of Care/Process Subscale ranges from 0 to 70; a high score indicates the perception of high quality of care/process from teams. The Physician Centrality Subscale ranges from 0 to 30; a high score indicates a positive view of physician authority in the team, which is indicative of an early stage of team development (i.e., forming or storming). Team averages also can be calculated.

Psychometric Testing

Internal Consistency Reliability

Using factor analysis with varimax rotation, developers identified two factors/subscales with eigenvalues above one that could be interpreted meaningfully–the Quality of Care/Process Subscale and the Physician Centrality Subscale. Cronbach's alphas were .83 and .75, respectively. The item-to-total scale correlations for the Quality of Care/Process Subscale ranged from .48 to .62; and for Physician Centrality, from .38 to .59.

Test-Retest Reliability

A subset of nurses ($N = 27$) completed the earlier version of scale (three subscales) on two separate occasions six weeks apart. The test-retest correlation for the Quality of Care Subscale was .71 ($p < .001$), for Cost of Team Care, .42 ($p < .05$), and for Physician Centrality, .36 ($p < .05$). Additional testing with professionals other than nurses might yield higher reliability for the latter two subscales.

Inter-Rater Reliability

This type of reliability testing is not applicable since the instrument is self-administered.

Content or Face Validity

As part of the development of this scale, four experts rated items on appropriateness and assignment to subscale domains. The level of agreement for the entire scale resulted in a Content Validity Index of .95 for appropriateness of items and .91 for assignment of items to domains.

Concurrent Validity

The three earlier subscales were correlated with a Semantic Differential Scale, developed by Clutter and Sachs, also measuring attitudes toward health care teams. For Quality of Care the correlation was .60 ($p < .001$); for Costs of Team Care, $r = -.57$ ($p < .001$). The Semantic Differential Scale was not correlated with the Physician Centrality Subscale (Heinemann, Schmitt, Farrell, & Brallier, 1999).

Construct Validity

According to social exchange theory, physicians would be expected to have more negative perceptions of team care and see greater costs to this approach in comparison to other health professionals since physicians have the potential of losing prominence and autonomy, while others have the potential to gain in these areas. As predicted, Brown (1996) found physicians have significantly lower perceptions of the quality of care provided by teams and significantly higher perceptions of the costs of team care. Heinemann and colleagues' (1999) analysis replicated the trends found by Brown, although the differences were not statistically significant. In an ANOVA comparison of health professionals, physicians scored significantly higher than other health professionals on the Physician Centrality Subscale, as expected (Schmitt, Heinemann, & Farrell, 2001). Brown (1996) replicated these findings in an independent study.

As a further measure of construct validity, nurses' scores on the earlier three subscales were correlated with the "nurse section" of the Weiss and Davis (Heinemann et al., 1999) Collaborative Practice Scale. The more collaborative nurses perceived their current relations with doctors, the more they believed that teams contribute to the quality of care ($r = .21$, $p < .05$), the less they perceived teams as costly and inefficient ($r = -.21$, $p < .05$), and the more they valued physician centrality in the team ($r = .24$, $p < .01$).

One might hypothesize that in better functioning teams, members have more positive attitudes toward teams. As expected, the Quality of Care/Process Subscale correlates $-.35$ ($p < .001$) with a Team Anomie Scale that measures lack of mission and role clarity in teams and $.39$ ($p < .001$) with a measure of team effectiveness adapted for health care teams from Shortell & Rousseau's Intensive Care Unit Study (Heinemann et al., 1999).

Predictive/Discriminant Validity

No data are available for these types of validity.

Evaluation

For a relatively new instrument, the reliability and validity testing is extensive. The psychometric data indicate that the instrument is a robust measure of attitudes toward health care teams. Moreover, the scales are well constructed and the instrument is easy to administer. The final version of the instrument is appropriate for use in research. GITT researchers believe the three-subscale version gives more specific information for evaluating educational interventions (Hyer et al., 2000). In the latter instance, we expect scores on the Quality of Care Subscale to increase from baseline and scores on the Costs of Care and Physician Centrality Subscales to decrease from baseline post intervention.

Status/Availability

This instrument is in the public domain. There is no fee for using it; however, the developers would appreciate receiving reliability and validity data or a copy of the raw data. For additional information about the instrument, contact Gloria D. Heinemann at (716) 862-6091 or gloria.heinemann@med.va.gov.

Relevant Publications

Brown, G.F., & Chamberlin, G.D. (1996). Attitudes toward quality, costs, and physician centrality in health care teams. *Journal of Interprofessional Care, 10*, 63-72.

Heinemann, G.D., Schmitt, M.H., Farrell, M.P., & Brallier, S.A. (1999). Development of an Attitudes Toward Health Care Teams Scale. *Evaluation & the Health Professions, 22*, 123-142.

Fulmer, T., & Hyer, K. (1998). Evaluating the effects of geriatric interdisciplinary team training. In E.L. Siegler, K. Hyer, T. Fulmer, & M. Mezey (Eds.), *Geriatric interdisciplinary team training* (pp. 115-146). New York: Springer Publishing Company.

Hyer, K., Fairchild, S., Abraham, I., Mezey, M., & Fulmer. T. (2000). Measuring attitudes related to interdisciplinary training: Revisiting the Heinemann, Schmitt and Farrell 'attitudes toward health care teams' scale. *Journal of Interprofessional Care, 14*, 249-258.

Schmitt, M.H., Heinemann, G.D., & Farrell, M.P. (2001). Professional differences in attitudes and perceptions of teamwork and job stress in geriatric health care teams. Unpublished manuscript.

TEAM SKILLS SCALE

Developed by Kenneth Hepburn, Ruth Ann Tsukuda, and Carl Fasser, 1996
Reviewed by Kathryn Hyer, Gloria D. Heinemann, and Terry Fulmer

The Team Skills Scale, one of the core measures of the Hartford Foundation-funded Geriatric Interdisciplinary Team Training (GITT) Program, is a 17-item measure of the team skills essential for geriatric health care professionals. The measure is a self-report of interpersonal skills (e.g., ability to handle conflict, draw out inactive members, and communicate succinctly), discipline-specific skills, and geriatric care skills. Developers designed the instrument to capture change in the self-reported skills of health care providers after exposure to a geriatric team-training program. It can be used to measure baseline skills for clinicians and to help educators tailor training based upon the self-perceived needs of team members. Psychometric testing is in the early stages and indicates the instrument has good reliability. An additional strength is its brevity and ease of administration. It includes unique items related to care planning.

Conceptual Framework

For a health care team to function effectively, its members must learn and use both the interpersonal skills of teamwork and the skills of their respective disciplines. Both sets of skills are necessary for developing and implementing interdisciplinary care plans. The process of care planning involves identifying a patient's needs and health problems and negotiating the priorities for intervention. In addition, the patient's and his/her family members' perceptions and preferences must be considered and included in a plan of care. This requires quality communication among clinicians themselves and among clinicians and the patient and family. The final, individualized care plan should be agreeable to all members of the team, the patient, and his/her family.

The team is a group of health care professionals who create and implement interdisciplinary care plans for geriatric patients. They can improve their skills and the team's performance through education and training interventions.

Description of Measure

Hepburn and associates developed this instrument to measure changes in the skills of geriatric health care team members before and after a team training intervention. Developers adapted the instrument from Tsukuda and Stahelski's (1990) longer Team Skills Questionnaire (reviewed in Chapter 11). Developers used the instrument to assess the impact of a major educational intervention for medical and health professional trainees in eight sites throughout the country that participated in the Hartford Foundation-funded GITT initiative. Student trainees and/or health care clinicians working in teams complete the instrument.

Components of Team Performance Measured

The instrument measures the skills of teamwork, especially with regard to care planning. It includes the ability to represent one's own discipline in care planning meetings, draw out inactive team members, and treat team members as colleagues. It also addresses the ability to apply geriatric principles to care of older persons, communicate and participate effectively, manage differences and conflict among team members, recognize when the team is not functioning well, and intervene effectively to improve team functioning.

The instrument addresses one domain (process) and one dimension (growth and development) in our team performance model. The instrument is unique in that it measures perceived skills of individual team members and trainees.

Formatting and Scoring

The instrument includes 17 Likert formatted-items. Each item represents a task; respondents rate their perceived skill level for each task from poor to excellent by circling the appropriate answer choice (see example below).

	Poor	Fair	Good	Very Good	Excellent
11. Develop an interdisciplinary care plan	1	2	3	4	5

In E.L. Siegler, K. Hyer, T. Fulmer, & M. Mezey (Eds.), *Geriatric interdisciplinary team training* ©1998. Reprinted by permission of the GITT Resource Center and Springer Publishing Company.

For the GITT project, answer choices were formatted such that circles were filled in with a number two pencil and answers were summarized using a scanning device.

Items are summed, and the scale ranges from 17 to 85; the higher the score, the higher is the self-reported skill level. At baseline, the instructor can review average item scores to identify areas of low skill levels and design training to address them. After the training intervention, evaluators compare baseline scores to post training scores to determine the effectiveness of the training intervention. Individual scores can be averaged for a team score.

Psychometric Testing

Internal Consistency Reliability

Using factor analysis with varimax rotation, Hyer, Fairchild, Abraham, Mezey, & Fulmer (2000) identified one factor; the factor loadings for the 17 items ranged from 0.62 to 0.81. The variance explained by the factor was 53%. Cronbach's alpha was .94. Item-to-total scale correlations ranged from .58 to .78.

Test-Retest/Inter-Rater Reliability

No data are available regarding test-retest reliability, and testing for inter-rater reliability is inappropriate since the measure is self-administered.

Content or Face Validity

Nationally renowned clinical experts and educators, who were the Principal Investigators and Project Evaluators for Hartford-funded GITT Program and Resource Center, met to finalize the common core measures. The initial list of skills was drawn from the learning objectives of the proposed GITT sites and from the Teams Skills Questionnaire developed by Tsukuda and Stahelski (1990). Using discussion and voting, experts rank ordered the most important skills for geriatric health care professionals. The result is the 17 items entitled Team Skills Scale. Since the items are self-reported skills that should change after an educational intervention, the test is expected to capture these changes.

Concurrent/Construct/Predictive/Discriminant Validity

No data are available for these types of validity.

Evaluation

The instrument is clearly worded, easy to administer, and easy to score. It is geared specifically for health care professionals and trainees. It is unique it that it focuses on a number of skills omitted from other instruments. These include interdisciplinary care planning, including the preferences of the patient and family members in the care plan; understanding the varied disciplines' roles on the team; applying knowledge in the clinical setting; and linking the team's goals to patient care.

Status/Availability

This instrument is copyrighted. There is no fee for using it; however, the GITT Research Center would appreciate receiving reliability and validity data. Permission to use the scale can be secured by contacting Terry Fulmer, R.N., Ph.D., FAAN, Professor, New York University, Department of Nursing, 246 Greene Street, 5th Floor, New York, NY 10003; http://www.GITT.org.

Relevant Publications

Hepburn, K., Tsukuda, R.A., & Fasser, C. (1998). Team Skills Scale, 1996. In E.L. Siegler, K. Hyer, T. Fulmer, & M. Mezey (Eds.), *Geriatric interdisciplinary team training* (pp. 264-265). New York: Springer Publishing Company.

Hyer, K., Fairchild, S., Abraham, I., Mezey, M., & Fulmer, T. (2000). Unpublished factor analysis.

Tsukuda, R.A., & Stahelski, A.J. (1990). *Team Skills Questionnaire*. Unpublished instrument and guidelines.

POSTMEETING EVALUATION FORM

Developed by J. William Pfeiffer and John E. Jones, 1974; revised by developers, 1991
Reviewed by Sara A. Brallier and Gloria D. Heinemann

The PostMeeting Reaction Form is a 20-item measure of members' perceptions of a recent team meeting and their own behavior in the meeting. Developers designed this expeditious instrument to provide teams with immediate feedback after a meeting and to stimulate discussion about improving meetings. Despite its brevity, it conceptualizes and operationalizes meeting effectiveness well. Because it is short and easy to administer, teams can use it without the presence of an outside consultant. It has no reliability or validity data; however, developers do not scale the items. It was not designed for research purposes.

Conceptual Framework

The ability of a team to meet effectively is a reflection of the mastery of a series of teamwork skills including maintaining a positive team climate, communicating effectively, sharing power, and participating appropriately. The ability to meet effectively also is an important component of team performance because the team meeting is the time when professionals gather to exchange information and collectively develop goals, objectives, and action plans.

The developers view the team as a small group that works to accomplish specific tasks.

Description of Measure

The measure is used to evaluate meetings and to help the team identify facets of the meeting that need improvement. Team members complete the instrument, which is generic and, therefore, appropriate for a wide variety of teams.

Components of Team Performance Measured

Developers designed this instrument as a two-part measure. The first part measures characteristics of the meeting such as climate, participation, leadership, communication, task orientation, and attention to process issues. The second part measures individual behaviors such as friendliness, participation, focus on the meeting, leadership, politeness, irritation, and aggression.

The instrument includes two domains (context and process) and two dimensions (team context, and interdependence) of our model of team performance.

Formatting and Scoring

The instrument consists of 10 positively and negatively worded items measuring meeting effectiveness and 10 positively and negatively worded items measuring individual behavior in the meeting. Respondents rank-order the 10 statements in each part of the instrument from 1 (most like the meeting/behavior) to 10 (least like the meeting/behavior). Respondents write the appropriate number on the blank to the left of each statement.

Using an item analysis, individual's responses for each item can be compared to identify team members' strengths and weaknesses and to see if there is consensus regarding perceptions of the team.

Psychometric Testing

No reliability or validity data are available.

Evaluation

Teams themselves can use this instrument to evaluate and improve their meeting effectiveness. The instrument is easy to administer, and respondents can complete it quickly. For a short, expeditious instrument, it conceptualizes and operationalizes meeting effectiveness well. Item 20 could be improved by substituting the word assertive for aggressive since aggression may be viewed negatively by team members. No psychometric testing has been conducted. Such testing would improve the instrument; however, developers do not scale the items.

Status/Availability

University Associates, Inc. holds the instrument's copyright. The most recent version of it appears in the Pfeiffer and Jones 1991 publication below. To purchase it, contact University Associates, Inc. at (619) 578-5900.

Relevant Publications

Pfeiffer, J.W., & Jones, J.E. (1974). Postmeeting Reactions Form. In J.E. Jones & J.W. Pfeiffer (Eds.), *A handbook of structured experiences for human relations training, Volume III* (p. 30). San Diego, CA: Pfeiffer & Company.

Pfeiffer, J.W., & Jones, J.E. (1991). Postmeeting Evaluation Form. In J.W. Pfeiffer (Ed.), *The encyclopedia of team-development activities* (p. 233) San Diego, CA: University Associates, Inc.

TEAM-DEVELOPMENT RATING FORM

Developed by Marvin R. Weisbord, 1987, 1991
Reviewed by Linda Nichols and Sara A. Brallier

The Team Development Rating Form is a self-administered, eight-item instrument. The facets of team development measured are purpose, membership, elbow room, discussion, use of skills, support, conflict, and influence. The instrument has a sound conceptual framework and is easy to administer and score. It is appropriate for use in developing newly formed teams and to stimulate discussion of strengths and weaknesses in more advanced teams. Reviewers recommend minor revisions of several items. No psychometric testing has been conducted to date; therefore, it is inappropriate for research purposes.

Conceptual Framework

The theoretical underpinnings of the instrument originate from Weisbord's work with organizations and Michael Blansfield's Team Effectiveness Theory (Weisbord, 1987). The key to building an effective team is to focus on its task and process issues. This theory outlines three interrelated levels of team effectiveness–team issues, structure, and results. Team issues include whether team members feel as if they belong, are valued, and have tasks that are important to the team. Also included are the extent to which members' skill are used, the extent to which members feel they have power and control over team decisions, and the quality of communication among team members. Structure encompasses the extent to which team goals, procedures, and members' roles are clear; the use of feedback to identify members' strengths and weaknesses related to team functioning; and how conflict is handled. Dealing effectively with team issues and optimizing team structure lead to results including higher productivity, better quality, more profits, and lower costs. When results are not forthcoming, many mangers and organizations tend to blame and/or try to manipulate structures. Weisbord suggests that most interventions should focus on team issues to improve effectiveness and results. The developer views the team as an organizational work group.

Description of Measure

Weisbord designed the instrument to assess a team's level of development, identify its strengths and weaknesses, and facilitate discussion among members about steps they might take to improve its performance. Individual members of organizational work groups or teams complete the instrument.

Components of Team Performance Measured

Weisbord addresses eight facets of team development. These include purpose (clear about the team's purpose versus uncertain), team membership ("in or out"), elbow room (crowded or comfortable), and discussion (cautious and guarded or open and free). Also included are the use of skills (poor or full), support (team members support themselves versus team members support all members), conflict (avoided or worked on), and the extent to which influence is shared among team members (few have versus all have).

The instrument includes three domains (structure, context, and process) and three dimensions (team structure, team context, and interdependence) of team performance in our model.

Formatting and Scoring

The eight-item instrument is self-administered. Each item has an answer choice continuum from 1 (low or negative score) to 5 (high or positive score). For each item, a descriptive heading appears above the continuum, and two verbal statements anchor the extreme answer choices below the continuum (see item example below).

The developer provides no instructions for scoring. We recommend an item analysis given that no psychometric testing has been conducted. Individual responses, then, can be compared to one another or the team average.

1. The Team's Purpose

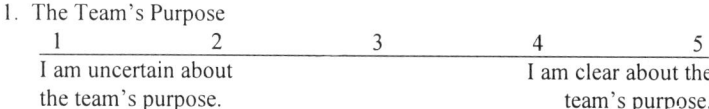

1	2	3	4	5
I am uncertain about the team's purpose.			I am clear about the team's purpose.	

In J.W. Pfeiffer & C. Nolde (Eds.), *The encyclopedia of team-development activities* ©1991. Reprinted by permission of Jossey-Bass, Inc., a subsidiary of John Wiley & Sons, Inc.

Psychometric Testing

No reliability or validity data are available.

Evaluation

The instrument is easy to administer and score. It is an improvement over some of the other expedient measures of team effectiveness because it is based on a conceptually sound framework. There is an inconsistency between the instructions and the wording of several of the items. The instructions indicate that respondents should rate the team's position on the continuum for each item, but three of the items (purpose, membership, and elbow room) ask for a rating on the individual team member. Additionally, items contain some colloquial (items 2 and 3) and unclear language (item 5). Minor revision of these items would improve the measure.

This instrument is appropriate for educational and consultative purposes, especially to help teams identify their strengths and weaknesses. It also could be used by teams, without a consultant, as a springboard for discussion regarding structure and team issues requiring improvement. No psychometric testing has been conducted on this measure.

Status/Availability

The copyrighted instrument may be reproduced for small scale education and training purposes (up to 100 copies per year). For large-scale administration, written permission from Jossey-Bass and Marvin R. Weisbord is required and a fee is charged. To obtain the 1991 publication below, contact Jossey-Bass Publisher, (800) 274-4434.

Relevant Publications

Weisbord, M.R. (1987). *Productive workplaces: Organizing and managing for dignity, meaning, and community*. San Francisco: Jossey-Bass Publisher.

Weisbord, M.R. (1991). Team-Development Rating Form. In J.W. Pfeiffer & C. Nolde (Eds.), *The encyclopedia of team-development activities* (pp. 249-250). San Diego, CA: Pfeiffer & Company, an imprint of Jossey-Bass.

CHAPTER 10
MIDDLE-RANGE INSTRUMENTS

Stephanie B. Hoffman, Ph.D.
James A. Haley VA Hospital, Tampa, FL, VISN 8

This chapter addresses the 11 middle-range instruments. Each instrument measures four of the eight dimensions of our model of team performance (see Chapter 3). Table 10.1 summarizes relevant information about these instruments. In this table, instruments are alphabetized by the name of the developer(s). We designated the instruments in bold face type as "best measures." They are discussed in more detail in Chapter 14. The critiques of each of these instruments follow the summary table. An instrument with a "best measures" designation has an asterisk after its title at the beginning of the critique.

OVERVIEW

Like the focused instruments, the majority of middle-range instruments measure "within team" performance, especially related to team structure, context, and processes. Five of the eleven instruments are expedient in that they permit a quick identification of a team's strengths and weaknesses and can be individualized to meet the needs of a specific team; two of these measures assess meeting effectiveness. Four other instruments assess performance for purposes of improvement; one focuses specifically on trust climate; another addresses task and maintenance orientations, and two are more general measures of performance. One instrument assesses the stage of the team's development; and another focuses on within team integration (see Table 10.1).

Most of these instruments are educational or consultation tools designed to identify problem areas needing improvement. Only two instruments, Kormanski and Mozenter's Team Development Rating Scale and Lichtenstein and colleague's Team Integration Measure, are research measures. The former instrument also can be used to assess and improve team performance. Ten of the instruments are generic; one was developed specifically for psychiatric treatment teams.

Generally speaking, these instruments are easy to read and complete. Two instruments (Hall's Teamness Index and Pfeiffer and Jones' Group-Growth Evaluation Form) are especially appropriate for new teams. Two other measures (Goodstein, Cooke, and Goodstein's TOBI and Varney's Team Profile Questionnaire) require a relatively high reading level and should be used with professional teams only.

The number of items included in the middle range instruments varies from five to 56; most instruments include between 10 to 20 items. Five of the instruments are weak with regard to a theoretical framework. All are self-administered. The majority requires respondents to select one answer per item from a Likert-formatted set of answer choices or across a continuum. One instrument requires respondents to rank answer choices, and one requires the distribution of points over two answer options.

Two of the 11 instruments, Kormanski and Mozenter's Team Development Rating Scale and Lichtenstein and colleagues' Team Integration Measure were designated as "best measures" and are discussed in Chapter 14.

Unique Features of the Instruments

Six of the middle-range instruments have unique features. Three of them measure either more than one facet of performance or measure it from different perspectives. Burns and Gragg's Work-Group-Effectiveness Inventory measures perceptions of three different kinds of effectiveness–team members' perceptions of their own behavior, their fellow team members' behaviors, and the team's performance. Goodstein, Cooke, and Goodstein's TOBI assesses values and skills with regard to both task and maintenance orientations. Kormanski and Mozenter's Team Development Rating Scale measures both task-oriented and relationship-oriented outcomes in determining the team's stage of development

Three other instruments measure elements of team performance not often measured. Chartier's Trust Orientation Profile includes items about trust among team members. Hall's Teamness Index includes rewarding team performance. Lichtenstein and colleague's Team Integration Measure includes participation among team members and accomplishments of the team.

Proportion with Psychometric Testing

Middle range instruments have had very limited, if any, psychometric testing. Only three of the eleven measures have preliminary psychometric data. Even though most instruments require an item analysis to summarize responses, psychometric testing would facilitate the identification of items requiring revision in some of the instruments. For example, some items measure more than one concept, and some are redundant from one subscale to the next. The wording of others is complex and still others don't counterbalance positive and negative items. Answer choices are, at times, unclear, and labels and items don't always match. Of the three with preliminary psychometric data, two are strong research instruments (see Table 10.1)

Implications for Use

Because most of the educational instruments are fairly brief, they can be administered quickly and easily to obtain a "snapshot" of the team at one point in time. Either the team itself or a consultant, working in conjunction with the team, can use the information provided by the instruments to design interventions to improve team functioning. Kormanski and Mozenter's Team Development Rating Scale has been used successfully to monitor stage of development at several points in time. The brevity of both research instruments permits their use in large-scale research and with busy health professionals. Lichtenstein and colleagues' instrument is used with psychiatric treatment teams that often include both professional and nonprofessional members. Two of the instruments are especially appropriate for new teams, and two are best used with professional teams. The other instruments in this category can be used with most types of teams and work groups (see Table 10.1)

Table 10.1 Summary of Middle-Range Instruments

Instrument	Developers	# Items	Purpose	Target Group	Psychometrics
Meeting Evaluation Scale	Burns & Gragg	11	Assess & help improve functioning (expedient measure of meeting effectiveness)	Generic work groups/teams	None
Work-Group-Effectiveness Inventory	Burns & Gragg	20	Assess & help improve functioning (perceptions of self, fellow team members & team)	Generic work groups/teams	None
Trust Orientation Profile	Chartier	24	Assess & help improve functioning (trust climate)	Generic work groups/teams	None
PostMeeting Reaction Form	Dimock	5	Assess & help improve functioning (expedient measure of meeting effectiveness)	Generic work groups/teams	None
The Team Orientation and Behavior Inventory (TOBI)	Goodstein, Cooke & Goodstein	56	Assess & help improve functioning (values & skills within task & maintenance orientations)	Generic professional teams	Preliminary reliability & validity
Teamness Index	Hall	24	Assess & help improve functioning	Generic work groups/teams (esp. new teams)	None

Table 10.1 Summary of Middle-Range Instruments (continued)

Instrument	Developers	# Items	Purpose	Target Group	Psychometrics
Team Development Rating Scale	Kormanski & Mozenter	10	Assess, monitor & help improve functioning; identify stage of development using task & relationship outcomes; research	Generic work groups/teams	Preliminary reliability & validity
Team Integration Measure	Lichtenstein, Alexander, Jinnett & Ullman	19	Research (within team integration)	Psychiatric treatment teams	Good preliminary reliability & validity
Group-Growth Evaluation Form	Pfeiffer & Jones	20	Assess & help improve functioning (expedient measure)	Generic work groups/teams (esp. new teams)	None
Criteria of Group Maturity	Schein	10	Assess & help improve functioning (expedient measure)	Generic work groups/teams	None
Team Profile Questionnaire	Varney	19	Assess & help improve functioning (expedient measure)	Generic professional teams	None

MEETING EVALUATION SCALE

Developed by Frank Burns and Robert Gragg, 1981
Reviewed by Sara A. Brallier and Glenda F. Brown

The Meeting Evaluation Scale, an 11-item measure of respondents' perceptions of meeting effectiveness, addresses three facets of meeting effectiveness–effective communication, clearly defined roles and expectations, and the ability to operate in a timely, organized manner. It provides a quick and easy method of describing and quantifying a group or team's experience in meetings and allows the group to focus on processes that can be improved for greater meeting effectiveness. It would benefit from psychometric testing and the revisions of several items.

Conceptual Framework

Burns and Gragg did not specify a conceptual framework for this instrument; however, it is apparent that the ability to meet effectively is crucial if teams are to accomplish their assigned tasks. Participants need to have adequate time and information to prepare for the meeting; team members' roles need to be clearly defined; and they need to communicate effectively.

Developers view the team is a small group whose members meet on a regular basis and work together to accomplish specific tasks.

Description of Measure

Developers designed the instrument for educational and consultative purposes related to team meetings–to evaluate meetings, critique the meeting process, assess meeting quality, and facilitate planning. Team members complete the instrument. It is generic in nature and appropriate for a variety of types of teams.

Components of Team Performance Measured

The instrument measures quality of communication, clarity of roles, shared understanding of procedures and expectations, conflict management, and participation in relation to meeting effectiveness.

It includes items in all four domains and four of the eight dimensions (team structure and context, interdependence, and accomplishments) of our model of team performance.

Formatting and Scoring

The instrument includes 11 items measuring meeting effectiveness. The items, all worded positively, are Likert formatted. For each item, there are five answer choices ranging from strongly agree = 5 to strongly disagree = 1 (see example below).

	Strongly Disagree	Disagree	Undecided	Agree	Strongly Agree
1. I was notified of this meeting in sufficient time to prepare for it	1	2	3	4	5

In J.E. Jones & J.W. Pfeiffer (Eds.), *The annual handbook for group facilitators* ©1981. Reprinted by permission of Jossey-Bass, Inc., a subsidiary of John Wiley & Sons, Inc.

An item analysis can identify particular strengths and weaknesses of the meeting. That is, an average score for the team is calculated for each item. High average scores indicate strengths, and low average scores indicate weaknesses. Individual team member's scores also can be compared to the team's average scores. Whether items can be scaled is unknown given the lack of psychometric testing.

Psychometric Testing

No reliability or validity data are available.

Evaluation

This instrument's strengths include its focus on meeting effectiveness, an important component of team performance, and the ease with which it can be administered and scored. It would benefit from minor revisions and reliability and validity testing. All items are positively worded, which could lead to response bias. Additionally, many of its items inappropriately measure two concepts (e.g., I understood what was expected of me as a participant and what was expected of other participants) simultaneously. The reviewers suggest the instrument be revised so that each item measures only one underlying concept. Overall, the developers conceptualized the components of meeting effectiveness well and, with minor revisions, the instrument has the potential to be a useful tool for assessing meeting effectiveness for teams.

Status/Availability

The instrument is copyrighted. It appears in the publication below and may be reproduced up to 100 copies without prior written permission. To purchase the publication, contact Pfeiffer & Company at (800) 274-4434.

Relevant Publications

Burns, F., & Gragg, R. (1981). Brief diagnostic instruments. In J.E. Jones & J.W. Pfeiffer (Eds.), *The annual handbook for group facilitators* (pp. 87-93). San Diego, CA: Pfeiffer & Company.

WORK-GROUP-EFFECTIVENESS INVENTORY

Developed by Frank Burns and Robert Gragg, 1981
Reviewed by Sara A. Brallier and Glenda F. Brown

The Work-Group-Effectiveness Inventory is a 20-item instrument measuring team members' perceptions of their own behavior, the behavior of other members, and the behavior of the team as a whole with regard to effectiveness. Work group effectiveness is a multifaceted concept requiring members' attention to team development, proficient communication skills, and the ability to be flexible in a changing work environment. Although not based on a strong conceptual framework, the instrument is easy to administer and score. It would benefit from some revision since some of the items measure more than one concept, and items measuring perceptions of the team are redundant with those measuring perceptions of self and other team members. Developers have not conducted psychometric testing. It serves as a guide for education and consultation.

Conceptual Framework

The developers identify several components of work group effectiveness (i.e., the ability of members to communicate openly and directly, listen effectively and provide constructive feedback, clearly define team goals and roles of members, establish flexible operating procedures, and monitor team effectiveness). They emphasize that for the team to maximize its effectiveness, these skills and goals must be attended to by all team members and be valued by the team as a whole.

The team or work group is composed of members, whose commitment to performance and mastery of teamwork skills is critical for its effectiveness.

Description of Measure

The instrument's purpose is educational and consultative (i.e., facilitating a team's self-assessment and team building). The comparisons of members' assessments of themselves, other team members, and the team as whole can be used to identify discrepancies in perceived contributions to team performance. Team members complete the instrument anonymously.

Components of Team Performance Measured

The facets of team effectiveness measured include communication skills (i.e., direct and open communication, careful listening, provision of feedback), the clarity of team members' roles and the team goals, team flexibility regarding operating procedures and organization, and the monitoring of team effectiveness. The items are written to ascertain team members' perceptions of their own behavior as it contributes to team effectiveness (five items), members' perceptions of the behavior of fellow team members (three items), and members' perceptions of team performance (12 items).

The instrument includes items in three of the four domains (structure, process, and productivity) and four of the eight dimensions (i.e., team structure, interdependence, growth and development, and strategies for productivity) of our model of team performance.

Formatting and Scoring

For each of the 20 positively worded items, there are five answer choices ranging from strongly disagree = 1 to strongly agree = 5 (see item example below).

	Strongly Disagree	Disagree	Undecided	Agree	Strongly Agree
7. I have been asking for and receiving constructive feedback regarding my influence on the team	1	2	3	4	5

In J.E. Jones & J.W. Pfeiffer (Eds.), *The annual handbook for group facilitators* ©1981. Reprinted by permission of Jossey-Bass, Inc., a subsidiary of John Wiley & Sons, Inc.

The developers do not provide any guidelines for scoring, although Likert formatted items are usually summed. Given that no psychometric testing has been conducted, we recommend an item analysis within each of the three grouping–own behavior, other members' behaviors, and the team's performance. For an item analysis, members' responses are summed and divided by the team size to obtain average team scores for each item. The higher the average score the more positive are the team members' perceptions.

Psychometric Testing

No reliability or validity data are available.

Evaluation

This instrument would benefit from reliability and validity testing to determine whether the three groupings of items can be scaled. Additionally, some of the items require minor revisions. We recommend some negatively worded items to avoid response bias. Additionally, many of the items measure two concepts (e.g., Members of this team have been listening carefully, and we have been paying special attention to strongly expressed values). The reviewers suggest that the instrument be revised so that each item measures only one underlying concept. Finally, the items related to perceptions of the team as a whole are redundant given that other items elicit information about members' perceptions of themselves as team members and of other team members. This makes the instrument confusing to respondents and could negatively impact the response rate and/or quality of the responses. Reviewers recommend using either the eight items related to self and other team members or the 12 items related to perceptions of the team as a whole.

Status/Availability

The instrument is copyrighted. It appears in the publication below and may be reproduced and used up to 100 copies without prior written permission. To purchase the publication, contact Pfeiffer & Company at (800) 274-4434.

Relevant Publications

Burns, F., & Gragg, R. (1981). Brief diagnostic instruments. In J.E. Jones & J.W. Pfeiffer (Eds.), *The annual handbook for group facilitators* (pp. 87-93). San Diego, CA: Pfeiffer & Company.

TRUST ORIENTATION PROFILE

Developed by Myron R. Chartier, 1991
Reviewed by Amy L. Noe and Gloria D. Heinemann

The Trust Orientation Profile is a 24-item instrument developed to measure the "trust climate" in interpersonal relationships within a team or organization. It is a tool for team-building and team development. After they have identified their trust deficits, teams may choose to pursue skills training that might ameliorate them (e.g., assertiveness training, communication skills training, etc.). The instrument's construction is based on the theory that trust is an integral facet of team effectiveness. It is easy to use and score, but would benefit from psychometric testing and some rewording of items to improve clarity.

Conceptual Framework

This measure is grounded in the premise that trust is necessary for effective communication, and once trust has been established, many facets of teamwork naturally fall into place. For example, Chartier contends that as trust is established, people begin to accept others' attitudes and feelings. They begin to communicate clearly and efficiently and to take risks. Information flows openly and in an uninhibited manner, and team members gather data quickly and make decisions effectively.

Chartier views teams as collections of individual personalities whose personal characteristics, attitudes, and behaviors create a climate of either trust or mistrust. The climate within the team affects its level of functioning.

Description of Measure

The primary purpose of this instrument is to measure the trust climate present in a team and to help educate members regarding the degree to which they display or espouse trust-building characteristics. Feedback from the measure can serve as a springboard for team-building sessions or be used for action planning for improvement. Team members complete the instrument anonymously.

Components of Team Performance Measured

This instrument measures members' feelings toward their roles in the team and their roles in relation to other members' roles. Chartier describes these tendencies as being open (i.e., sharing ones thoughts and feelings versus keeping thoughts/feelings to oneself) and supportive (i.e., being encouraging, reassuring, and understanding of others versus being concerned with ones own desires and wishes). Other tendencies include being willing to take risks, respectful, genuine, and cooperative. Still others are a desire for two-way communication and power sharing, being problem centered (i.e., working together to define problems, explore alternatives, and arrive at solutions), being accepting and warm, and being dependable. Finally, having knowledge and experience in an area or specific areas as well as being personally responsible and following through on assignments also are important.

The instrument measures three of the four domains (structure, context, and process) and four of its eight dimensions (organizational and team structure, team context, and interdependence). Several of the items are unique in that they focus on trust among team members.

180 TEAM PERFORMANCE IN HEALTH CARE

Formatting and Scoring

The instrument contains 24 items, each consisting of two opposing statements. Respondents distribute five points between the two statements based upon their perceptions of themselves as team members or of the team itself. Respondents write the points allocated to each item on the blank to the left of the statement (see item example below).

13. _____ (A) My co-workers and I cooperate with one another.

_____ (B) My co-workers and I compete with one another.

In J.W. Pfeiffer (Ed.), *The 1991 Annual: Developing human resource*
©1991. Reprinted by permission of Jossey-Bass, Inc., a subsidiary of
John Wiley & Sons, Inc.

A scoring matrix permits the assignment of items to one of 12 facets of trust; each facet includes two items. Each team member can compute his/her own trust/mistrust ratio for each of the 12 facets. For each member, total trust and mistrust scores are calculated; the mistrust score is subtracted from the trust score for a "trust orientation" score. An average team score also can be computed. A trust orientation score of -60 or greater indicates mistrust whereas a score of +60 or greater indicates trust.

Psychometric Testing

No reliability or validity data are available. The developer believes the measure has face validity. Items appear relevant to establishing a trusting environment; however, empirical support is lacking.

Evaluation

The instrument lacks a strong theoretical framework and conceptual depth in that each of the twelve facets of trust is measured by only two items, and some items are redundant (e.g., items 1 and 19). With regard to conceptual soundness, some of the items measure facets of team performance (e.g., cooperation, problem solving) that are related to, but not necessarily components of trust. It is easy to use and score and can be helpful in sensitizing teams to develop a more trusting climate; however, its lack of conceptual soundness, and psychometric testing prevent its use in evaluating educational interventions or other research.

The instrument would benefit from some revision of items. The use of colloquialisms (e.g., items 5B and 8), complex wording, and attempting to measure more than one concept per item (e.g., items, 1, 3, and 19) should be minimized.

Status/Availability

The instrument is copyrighted. There is no fee for using it. A copy of the instrument appears in the reference below and may be reproduced and used up to 100 copies without prior written permission. Contact Pfeiffer & Company at (800) 274-4434.

Relevant Publications

Chartier, M. R. (1991). Trust-Orientation Profile. In J.W. Pfeiffer (Ed.), *The 1991 Annual: Developing human resources* (pp. 135-148). San Diego, CA: Pfeiffer & Company.

POSTMEETING REACTION FORM

Developed by Hedley G. Dimock, 1987
Reviewed by Ruth Ann Tsukuda and Gloria D. Heinemann

The PostMeeting Reaction Form is an expedient, five-item instrument measuring perceptions of team members regarding their meeting effectiveness. Its strength lies in its brevity and usefulness to stimulate discussion about the meeting at its end. It would benefit from some clarification of wording in some of the answer choices. No psychometric testing has been conducted. It is useful for sensitizing the team to the importance of effective meetings.

Conceptual Framework

As a basis for the instrument, the developer integrates a number of concepts from several developmental frameworks. He believes that teams can grow and develop effectively if they assess the effectiveness of their programs and activities, including their regularly scheduled meetings.

The team is a social system with structure, norms, values, and procedures. Education and training can facilitate team growth and productivity.

Description of Measure

The instrument assesses the members' perceptions of the effectiveness of the team meeting. Results can stimulate discussion of strengths and weaknesses in conducting and participating in the meeting and for planning to improve meeting performance. Individual team members complete the instrument.

182 TEAM PERFORMANCE IN HEALTH CARE

Components of Team Performance Measured

This instrument measures five dimensions of meeting effectiveness–task accomplishment, team cohesiveness, clarity of goals, team cooperation, and team productivity. It also seeks suggestions for improvement in each of these areas.

It covers all four domains and four of the eight dimensions (team structure and context, interdependence, and accomplishments) of our model of team performance.

Formatting and Scoring

All five items are stated in the form of questions. Respondents rate them from 1 (most negative) to 5 (most positive) along a continuum. Each item has a descriptive label above the continuum and a verbal anchor for each answer choice below the continuum (see item example below).

1. How well did we do today in accomplishing our task?
   Task Accomplishment

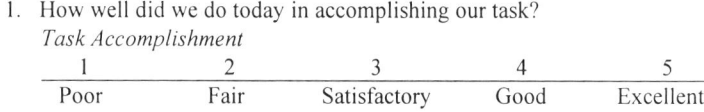

Suggestions for improving task accomplishment:

In J.W. Pfeiffer (Ed.), *The encyclopedia of team-development activities* ©1991. Reprinted by permission of the developer and Jossey-Bass, Inc., a subsidiary of John Wiley & Sons, Inc.

We recommend an item analysis for this instrument. For each item, responses are averaged for a team score; individual responses can be compared to the team averages. No overall score is calculated for the instrument.

Psychometric Testing

No reliability or validity data are available.

Evaluation

The instrument provides a quick assessment of how well a team accomplishes work during meetings; it can be used to stimulate discussion about how to improve future meetings. Weaknesses include unclear language in some of the answer choice descriptors. For example, in the third item, Clarity of Goals, the distinction between answer choices, "confused" and "unclear" is problematic.

Status/Availability

The instrument is copyrighted and appears in the 1991 publication below. It may be reproduced for education and training purposes (100 copies or less). To order the publication, contact Pfeiffer & Company at (800) 274-4434.

Relevant Publications

Dimock, H.G. (1987) *Groups: Leadership and group development.* San Diego, CA: University Associates.

Dimock, H.G. (1991). PostMeeting Reaction Form. In J.W. Pfeiffer (Ed.), *The encyclopedia of team-development activities* (pp. 231-232). San Diego, CA: Pfeiffer & Company.

TEAM ORIENTATION AND BEHAVIOR INVENTORY (TOBI)

Developed by Leonard D. Goodstein, Phyliss Cooke, and Jeanette Goodstein, 1983
Reviewed by Linda O. Nichols and Martha S. Waite

The TOBI is a self-administered, 56-item instrument designed to measure team members' skills in and valuing of task and maintenance orientations (i.e., the work of the team and the processes and interpersonal relationships of the team). The instrument includes four subscales: Task Values; Task Skills; Maintenance Values; and Maintenance Skills. Although it is somewhat lengthy, it is relatively easy to administer, and scoring instructions are clear. It has preliminary reliability and validity data; reviewers suggest additional psychometric testing. The "values" subscales can help newly developing teams set goals, and the "skills" subscales can facilitate the identification of problems and areas for improvement. The instrument is appropriate for use with college educated groups for education/consultation.

Conceptual Framework

The work group is a subsystem of the organization, and the team leader links its members with other facets of the organization. The developers conceptualize a well functioning work group or team as one that maintains a balance between both task and maintenance orientations. Task orientation ensures the completion of the group's work; maintenance orientation ensures that the group continues to function by focusing on interpersonal relationships and team processes (e.g., how the work is accomplished and whether team members are working well together). Each of these orientations includes two components–values and skills. Well functioning groups have members who highly value task and maintenance roles and have high skills in both.

Success in team development includes understanding where the problems exist and working with deficiencies in values and skills in both orientations. For example, team members might have high values, but need skills training in either or both orientations. Members with high maintenance values and skills may not value task sufficiently to facilitate the work of the group. Members with high task values and skills may not understand the importance of good interpersonal relationships among members and a climate that permits open communication. Members who are not invested and have no interest in the group tend to score low on values and skills for both task and maintenance orientations. In this latter instance, team development activities should begin with the development of positive values and commitment to both task and maintenance orientations.

The team is a work group, the most important element of any organization. The team, through its leadership, links individual employees with other facets of the organization and the organization as a whole. The work group provides an affective climate for employees and carries out the work of the organization.

Description of Measure

The instrument's purpose is to help the team or the educational consultant distinguish issues of values from issues of skills. It assesses how much the team needs to work on each of the task and maintenance orientations to be well functioning. The developers suggest that it can be used for team development or research to assess the task and maintenance values and skills of the team and its members, to assess and compare differences across teams, and to assess the impact of team development activities by collecting pre- and post data. Additionally it can identify, prior to team development, the attitudes and behaviors the team would like to achieve and examine team profiles in different work settings. Individual team members complete the instrument; scores can be used to compare individuals or to profile the team as a whole.

Components of Team Performance Measured

The TOBI focuses on two important aspects of performance: task orientation (i.e., concerns related to work and its completion) and maintenance orientation (i.e., consideration for people and processes–how work gets done). It measures team members' values or commitment and skills in each of these orientations.

The instrument addresses three of the four domains (structure, context, and process) and four of the eight dimensions (team structure, team context, interdependence, and growth and development) of our model of team performance. Unique features of the instrument are items measuring the balance between task and process or maintenance and its assessment of skills and values.

Formatting and Scoring

The four subscales measured are–task values, task skills, maintenance values, and maintenance skills. The 56 items are divided equally among the four subscales so each includes 14 items of which four are negatively worded. The items are general statements, worded both positively and negatively; they measure skills of individual team members, attitudes/values about groups generally, and attitudes/values about "my group." Answer choices for the items range from "strongly disagree or very unlike me" = 1 to "strongly agree or very like me" = 7, a Likert-type response format. They appear at the top of each page of the instrument.

Scores on each of the four subscales are summed and can range from 14 to 98; the higher the scores, the higher is the perceived value or skill in that area. Developers provide a scoring template that simplifies reverse coding of negatively worded items and summing subscale items. A profile sheet permits each respondent to plot his/her subscale scores to facilitate interpretation.

Psychometric Testing

Internal Consistency Reliability

The alpha coefficients for the four subscales indicate that the scales are reliable. The alpha coefficients are: task values, .74; task skills, .79; maintenance values, .81; and maintenance skills, .83.

Test-Retest/Inter-Rater Reliability

No data are available regarding test-retest reliability, and testing for inter-rater reliability is inappropriate since the measure is self-administered.

Content or Face Validity

No data are available.

Concurrent Validity

Teams rated as well functioning and effective by observers tend to have scores in the high 70s and low 80s on all four subscales. These teams show little difference in their four scores of task values and skills and maintenance values and skills. Teams rated as moderately effective tend to have scores on all four subscales in the high 60s. These results suggest that task and maintenance values and skills are related to functioning.

Construct/Predictive/Discriminant Validity

No data are available for these types of validity.

Evaluation

The TOBI is somewhat lengthy and includes sophisticated language. Its scoring instructions are clear, and preliminary reliability data indicate that the instrument is reliable. The preliminary validity data suggest that the subscales have validity as measures of team effectiveness.

There are some problems with the instrument's design. First, the similarity of the four subscale scores obtained when measuring effectiveness (see concurrent validity above) suggests that the subscales may be highly intercorrelated and, therefore, may not be measuring unique concepts. That is, team members may place higher value on the task and maintenance skills, which they personally possess. Or the similarity of items across the skills and values subscales suggests they may be measuring the same thing. Secondly, some of the items within both the values and skills subscales are confusing. The two "values" subscales address the group generally, while others address "my group." This could be confusing to respondents, especially when the instrument is used to develop a specific group. Additionally, within the skills subscales, some items measure behaviors while others measure skills. Third, some of the negatively worded statements in all four subscales tend to duplicate other positively worded ones and, therefore, are redundant. Fourth, the use of seven, rather than six, answer choices allows respondents to be noncommittal (i.e., frequently choosing code four, neither agree nor disagree). A forced choice, six-point answer format might provide more variability among responses.

The reviewers suggest further testing of the instrument's reliability and validity, including a factor analysis of the items to ensure that the subscales are measuring four distinct facets of team performance and that the items are assigned appropriately to their respective subscales. We do not recommend its use to monitor team performance over time or to determine the impact of an educational intervention until adequate test-retest reliability has been conducted.

Despite the concerns regarding psychometric testing and scale design expressed above, the instrument has some unique features. The breakdown into task and maintenance and values and skills can help pinpoint problems and areas in need of improvement. It has potential as both an educational and research instrument. The instrument should be used with college educated groups due to the complexity of item wording and sentence structure.

Status/Availability

The TOBI is copyrighted and available in the publication below. The instrument can be reproduced and used for small administrations up to 100 copies per year free of charge for education and training purposes. To purchase this publication, contact Jossey-Bass Publisher at (800) 274-4434.

Relevant Publications

Goodstein, L.D., Cooke, P., & Goodstein, J. (1983). The Team Orientation and Behavior Inventory (TOBI). In L. Goodstein & J.W. Pfeiffer (Eds.), *The 1983 annual for facilitators, trainers and consultants* (pp. 103-114). San Diego, CA: Pfeiffer & Company, an imprint of Jossey-Bass Publishers.

TEAMNESS INDEX

Developed by Jay Hall, 1988
Reviewed by Linda O. Nichols and Sara A. Brallier

The Teamness Index assesses four minimal conditions of team functioning (i.e., shared commitment to goals and objectives; team structure; standards, values and norms of performance; and positive identification with the team, its members, and work). There are 24 Likert-formatted items, six for each condition of teamwork. The Index identifies conditions of teamwork that require improvement. It is especially relevant for newly formed teams interested in team development. It has a strong theoretical basis, and the developer provides guidelines for team development activities. There are no reliability and validity data. The Index would benefit from psychometric testing and some revision prior to its use.

Conceptual Framework

The instrument is based on the theory that there are four basic or minimal conditions, identified by Sherif and Sherif (1969), necessary for individuals to function as a team and for the team to function effectively. For individuals to function as a team, they must share and be committed to: (a) team goals and objectives; (b) team structure; (c) team standards, values, and norms of performance; and (d) positive identification with the team, its members, and its work.

The first condition, "shared goals and objectives," focuses on the team's purpose and the objectives related to that purpose. Members must agree about the purpose and commit to it. The second condition, "team structure," refers to the team's ability to coordinate efforts and individual resources. Members must agree about how to integrate their contributions, how their roles relate to one another, and how leadership is handled. After the structure is in place, members develop "standards, norms, and values of performance," the third condition. Performance ground rules (i.e., evaluation criteria, guidelines for procedures, and shared values) allow members to know what are the appropriate actions to take and how to evaluate them. Agreed upon goals and objectives, structure, and performance guidelines should lead to the fourth condition, "identification and attraction." This emotion-based condition takes into account how much team members look to each other as sources of interpersonal rewards and satisfactions, identify with the team, and are concerned for one another. This shared sense of community leads to a commitment to one another and to the team as an entity.

The team is conceptualized as a work group whose purpose is the completion of specified goals and objectives. Members develop teamwork skills over time.

Description of Measure

The developer designed the instrument to assess the four conditions of teamness within work groups. It can be used for education and consultation with teams to identify their strengths and weaknesses. Individual team members complete it; their scores can be compared to team scores for each item.

Components of Team Performance Measured

The Index measures four conditions of teamness—goals and objectives; structure; standards, norms, and performance; and identification and attraction.

The instrument addresses three of the four domains (structure, context, and process) and four of the eight dimensions (organizational and team structure, team context, and interdependence) of our model of team performance.

Formatting and Scoring

Hall provides 24 positive statements, each of which is followed by an opposing statement (e.g., I feel that my contribution plays an essential role in team performance, as opposed to feeling the team could get along just as well without me). Respondents use Likert-type answer choices ranging from 1 = never true to 9 = true all the time to indicate how accurately the statement reflects their situation. Respondents write their numbered response in a box to the right of each item.

Each team member's responses are recorded on a scoring summary sheet, and an average or team score is computed for each item. The team scores are plotted on the Teamness Profile sheet as a value from one to nine. Values of 1-3 indicate separateness (i.e., the work group is a collection of people who function independently). Values of 4-6 indicate transition or some movement toward teamness, and values of 7-9 indicate teamness (i.e., the work group meets the four conditions of teamwork).

On the Teamness Profile sheet the 24 items are grouped so that six-items measure each of the four conditions of teamness. When the team scores within a condition are low, indicating separateness, the developer recommends the team take corrective actions to help it meet the condition. Team members also plot their own responses on the Profile to compare themselves with the team.

Psychometric Testing

No reliability or validity data are available.

Evaluation

The Teamness Index is based on a solid theoretical framework. Its unique features include attention to the basic principles of teamwork and an understanding that some facets of team performance are not necessarily training issues. In other words, team members do not become committed to the team or gain a shared understanding of its purpose and goals solely through skills training.

The developer gives the respondent both the positive and the negative sides of each item. In comparison to instruments using one-statement items in which the positive or negative statement is implied, this is a more objective way of presenting the material and may result in more accurate responses. Scoring of the instrument is straightforward, and directions for completing it are clear.

A useful feature of the Index is the provision of supporting material that emphasizes moving beyond the assessment to identification of problems and corrective actions. It includes sample profiles of common team problems to help teams unfamiliar with team diagnostic procedures to identify problems they may be facing. It also includes guidelines for team development activities for each of the four conditions, symptoms/characteristics of malfunction, and suggested corrective action steps.

There are several design problems that make administration moderately difficult. The items are wordy and awkward; many also are overstated and superlative (e.g., item 20, which asks if the team is the respondents' primary source of satisfaction and fellowship). The range of answer choices is too wide and some choices are not distinct from others (e.g., "true frequently" and "true quite often"). Last, the answer choices are presented on the cover page of the instrument, but not on the pages that contain the items. This may make completion of the instrument awkward for respondents, as they must refer to the cover page continuously.

There also are some conceptual and methodological problems with the instrument. Several items are assigned inappropriately to one of the four conditions of teamness. For example, the developer placed item five, a measure of rewards for performance, within the "shared goals" condition, while the reviewers believe it is conceptually consistent with the "standards, norms and values of performance" condition. Item 15, within the "standards, norms, and values" condition, is measuring role clarity, which according to the theoretical framework is part of the "team structure" condition. Two items measure the same concept (e.g., items two and three both measure the fit between personal and team goals). Last, item 19 is measuring two concepts, agreement with team goals and commitment to the team.

There are no reliability or validity data for the instrument. Tests of the instrument's internal consistency, the appropriate assignment of the items to conditions of teamness, and the ability of the instrument to measure adequately the four identified conditions of teamness should be empirically tested.

This measure is useful for teams attempting to identify components of teamwork requiring improvement. Because of its focus on the minimum conditions required for team functioning, it is especially relevant for newly formed teams. The reviewers recommend revising it to address the conceptual and methodological problems outlined above.

Status/Availability

The Index is copyrighted. The reproduction of any part of it in any way is a violation of domestic and international copyright laws. It can be purchased from Teleometrics International, 1755 Woodstead Court, The Woodlands, Texas, 77380, (713) 367-0060.

Relevant Publications

Hall, J. (1988). *Teamness Index: An assessment of your team's readiness for effective team work* [Assessment tool]. The Woodlands, TX: Teleometrics International.

Sherif, M., & Sherif, C.W. (Eds.). (1969). *Interdisciplinary relationships in the social sciences.* Chicago, IL: Aldine.

TEAM DEVELOPMENT RATING SCALE*

Developed by Chuck Kormanski and Andrew Mozenter, 1987
Reviewed by Glenda F. Brown and Gloria D. Heinemann

Kormanski and Mozenter designed the 10-item Team Development Rating Scale to track team development patterns and to identify performance outcomes (task and relationship) at each stage of development. Using it, teams can monitor their progress through the various stages of development. The instrument is well grounded in a theoretical framework that takes the appropriate leadership style into account for each stage of development. Its items are well conceptualized, and it is easy to use and score. Preliminary psychometric testing has been conducted; however, the instrument would benefit from further testing and some minor revisions. It is appropriate for a wide variety of work groups and teams and can be used for research purposes.

Conceptual Framework

The developers integrate group development theory into a team-building model. Each of the five stages of development has both task and relationship outcomes. The five developmental stages and their respective outcomes (in parentheses) are: stage one, awareness (commitment and acceptance); stage two, conflict (clarification and belonging); stage three, cooperation (involvement and support); stage four, productivity (achievement and pride); and stage five, separation (recognition and satisfaction). Each stage of development also has an appropriate leadership style related to the readiness level of team members. Leaders, who use the appropriate leadership style for the team's stage of development, facilitate its achievement of outcomes for that stage. For example, in the newly developing team, a leader should use a high task, low relationship style (i.e., telling) since members are inexperienced, hesitant, and have a low readiness level. In contrast, a well functioning team in the fourth stage of development is best supported by a delegating leadership style (low task and low relationship) since members are experienced, willing, and have a high readiness level. Team building, then, is a process for developing work groups into effective teams whose members have a common purpose and are empowered to create positive organizational change.

In innovative organizations, teams, rather than individuals, are the units for accomplishing tasks and achieving desired outcomes due to the increasing complexity of the work. Teams are made up of members or "mutual followers" who require leadership and management. In fact, an important management skill is the ability to build, nurture, lead, and disband teams. Leaders facilitate the development of team members, while managers facilitate the team's "getting the job done."

Description of Measure

The instrument identifies team outcomes, both task-oriented and relationship-oriented, and permits team members to assess their team's effectiveness. A generic measure, it provides an internal measure of the effectiveness of the team (i.e., team members' perceptions) that can be used to complement external assessments of goal accomplishment. Individual team members complete the instrument. Responses are averaged for team scores. The instrument has been used in business, industrial, educational, volunteer, and sports settings. It can be used for research as well as to assess team development and functioning.

Components of Team Performance Measured

Each of the 10 items measures a task or relationship outcome of the team to ascertain its stage of development. The five odd-numbered items address task outcomes (i.e., commitment, clarification, involvement, achievement, and recognition), and the five even-numbered items address relationship outcomes (i.e., acceptance, belonging, support, pride, and satisfaction).

The instrument includes all four domains and four dimensions (team structure and context, interdependence, and strategies for productivity) of our model of team performance. It is one of the few instruments that addresses team members, themselves, rewarding team performance.

Formatting and Scoring

All ten items are positively worded. Answer choices from 1 (low) to 10 (high) are formatted along a continuum for each item (see item example below). No verbal anchors accompany the answer choices; respondents are instructed that 10 is the high score, and 1 is the low score.

   3. Clarification
      Team members acknowledge and confront conflict openly.

    10   9   8   7   6   5   4   3   2   1

In J.W. Pfeiffer (Ed.), *The 1987 annual: Developing human resources* ©1987. Reprinted by permission of Jossey-Bass, Inc., a subsidiary of John Wiley & Sons, Inc.

An average team score is calculated for each item. Item scores also are summed for a total score ranging from 10 to 100 points. Total scores are plotted on a graph to reveals patterns of development over time.

Psychometric Testing

Internal Consistency Reliability

Developers correlated each item with the total score for each of five rating periods; the correlations ranged from .65 to .90. Cronbach's alpha ranged from .92 to .96 over the five rating periods.

Test-Retest/Inter-Rater Reliability

No data are available regarding test-retest reliability, and testing for inter-rater reliability is inappropriate since the measure is self-administered.

Content or Face Validity

The items were selected from a thorough review of group development theories and team building models. Therefore, face validity appears good although no formal validity studies have been reported.

Concurrent Validity

No data are available.

Construct Validity

Over a five-week period, the developers found that new teams rated themselves relatively high on outcomes due to high expectations of success. As expected, over time teams' ratings decreased (stage two), and later effective teams (stages four and five) showed increasingly higher ratings (N = 23).

Kormanski used this instrument to investigate the development of learning teams in an academic setting. A total of 29 teams of five to seven members each were assessed over a period of five weeks. He identified three patterns of development from his findings. The majority of his teams (21) showed a typical "roller coaster" pattern of team development in that they scored high initially, lower in the conflict stage, and alternating highs and lows in subsequent stages, but always with a slight upward trend. Two of the teams scored high initially, lower in the conflict stage, and never seemed to recover from this stage in that they continued to score lower and lower over time. Finally, six teams functioned as ideal teams in that their scores progressed higher and higher over the stages of development, almost in a linear fashion. As expected, the teams' means for the three different patterns of development were not significantly different in the early rating periods, but toward the end of the five weeks, the means were significantly different. These findings mirror the expectations of group development theory. The majority of teams has ups and downs with regard to development over time. A minority has little difficulty with the conflict stage and continues to improve over time, and a very small minority becomes fixated in the conflict stage and continues to function poorly.

Predictive/Discriminant Validity

No data are available for these types of validity.

Evaluation

The instrument has solid theoretical underpinnings, compatible with the major theories of group development. It is unique in that it measures both task-oriented and relationship-oriented team outcomes. It is easy to complete and score and has been subjected to preliminary psychometric testing; however, additional testing would strengthen it, especially with regard to tracking performance over time. In a phone interview with the first reviewer, Kormanski reported additional, unpublished, validity data utilizing graduate student groups, nursing home supervisory staffs, and restaurant management teams. The developers used a five-week period to examine team development in their study. This is a relatively short time frame for completing all five stages of the team development for health care teams. Kormanski stated, and these reviewers agree, that additional data from groups in a variety of settings and time frames are still needed to further substantiate the team development patterns.

With regard to construction, the extreme verbal anchors for answer choices one and 10 might be better labeled "strongly agree" and strongly disagree" rather than "high" and "low." Additionally, some discrepancy exists between several item titles the actual content of the items (e.g., 3. Clarification: Team members acknowledge and confront conflict openly). Finally, because all items are worded positively, the potential for response bias exists.

The instrument's brevity makes it appropriate for large-scale research and to assess the functioning of busy professionals on clinical teams. It can be used with many types of work groups and teams.

Status/Availability

The instrument is copyrighted. Systematic or large-scale reproduction or distribution (more than 100 copies) or inclusion of items in publications for sale require prior written permission. The instrument appears in the 1987 publication below. To purchase it, contact University Associates at (619) 578-5900.

Relevant Publications

Kormanski, C. (1990). Team building patterns of academic groups. *The Journal for Specialists in Group Work, 15*, 206-214.

Kormanski, C. (1998). *The team: An exploration in group process.* Denver, CO: Love Publishing Company.

Kormanski, C., & Mozenter, A. (1987). A new model of team building: A technology for today and tomorrow. In J.W. Pfeiffer (Ed.), *The 1987 annual: Developing human resources* (pp. 255-268). San Diego, CA: University Associates, Inc.

TEAM INTEGRATION MEASURE*

Developed by R. Lichtenstein, J.A. Alexander, K. Jinnett, and E. Ullman, 1997
Reviewed by Gloria D. Heinemann and Patricia L. Evans

Designed for use in psychiatric settings, this 19-item research measure of within team integration includes three subscales–Participation, Role Clarity, and Team Functioning. The instrument is based on a strong theoretical framework and is unique in its measurement of accomplishments related to team functioning and patients. It has good preliminary reliability and validity, easy readability, and it is easy to complete. The instrument's brevity makes it especially appropriate in large-scale research projects.

Conceptual Framework

Two theories serve as the basis for this instrument's development, social identification theory (Tajfel, 1982) and embedded intergroup relations theory (Alderfer, 1987). Team integration, a multidimensional concept, refers to how team members function within the team and how they work with and relate to one another. In the "well integrated" team, members understand and are comfortable with their roles, are comfortable sharing their perspectives, participate freely in team activities, and feel positively about the team and its goals. Diversity in a team has both rewards and costs. When members are professionally and personally diverse, they bring different knowledge bases, skills, abilities, and perspectives to the team. Such diversity facilitates problem solving and decision-making; however, it also can be a barrier to team identity and quality processes such as the development of cohesion, communication, coordination, and consensus building. Diverse teams often reach better outcomes, but have difficulty doing so. Often their members tend to be competitive, hostile toward one another, and frequently in conflict; these teams or groups are "poorly integrated."

Members of teams have a number of social identities (e.g., occupation, age cohort, gender, race, and ethnicity). Additionally they have things in common with a number of employees within the organization (e.g., length of service, department) apart from fellow team members. When a team's boundaries are overly permeable with the environment outside the team, members tend to be influenced more by their social identities and other organizational identities. As a result, they have difficulty establishing a strong team identity. Instead, they often are in conflict, and the team functions poorly.

Psychiatric treatment teams are predominately "underbounded" (i.e., boundaries are too permeable). Their members identify with organizational and social identities outside their respective teams. In addition, these teams are underbounded because they lack formal responsibility within the hospital's authority structure. That is, supervising, evaluating, and setting work schedules for team members comes from outside the team.

Description of Measure

Designed for use in research in psychiatric settings, the instrument's purpose is to measure the level of integration within the team as perceived by members. The instrument was used in a large-scale study of 1004 individuals working on 105 treatment teams in a national sample of 29 VA psychiatric hospitals. It also has potential to help teams improve team identity and within team integration of members. Individual team members complete the instrument.

Components of Team Performance Measured

The instrument measures three facets of team integration–member participation (seven items), role clarity (four items), and team functioning (eight items). Participation involves the frequency and comfort of contributing to the team's activities. Role clarity refers to knowing what is expected of the employee as a team member and knowing what can be expected from other team members. Team functioning involves team members' perceptions of cooperation, coordination, and quality of decision-making in the team as well as the quality of the team's outcomes.

The instrument includes items in all four domains and four dimensions (team structure, team context, interdependence, and accomplishments) of our model of team performance. It is unique in its measurement of participation of team members and accomplishments of the team.

Formatting and Scoring

Respondents rated each of the 19 items on a seven-point scale. For the Participation Subscale, the answer choices range from strongly agree to strongly disagree. For the Role Clarity Subscale, they range from never to always, and for the Team Functioning Subscale, they range from very accurate to very inaccurate. The first and third subscales include a neutral category as an answer choice. A unique feature of the instrument formatting is the shading of every other item to help ensure that respondents do not accidentally skip one. Below is an item example from the Participation Subscale.

	Strongly Agree	Agree	Slightly Agree	Neither Agree nor Disagree	Slightly Disagree	Disagree	Strongly Disagree
d. I feel free to participate actively	1	2	3	4	5	6	7

Reprinted by permission of R. Lichtenstein. Some items in this instrument were adapted from an earlier instrument developed by Davis-Sacks.

Prior to summing item responses for each subscale, some of the items are reverse coded so that, for all items, 1 = most negative and 7 = most positive. Subscale scores range as follows: Participation Subscale, from 7 to 49; Role Clarity, from 4 to 28; and Team Functioning, from 8 to 56. The higher the scores, the more positive is the measure of the respective underlying concept.

Psychometric Testing

Internal Consistency Reliability

Developers adapted a number of items for this instrument from an instrument used to study multidisciplinary psychiatric teams in a VA hospital by Davis-Sacks (1991). The Davis-Sacks' instrument included items from other well-established instruments; it was pretested to improve item wording and clarity. Cronbach's alphas for its nine scales (Role Clarity, Goal Clarity, Control, Participation, Interdependence, Performance, Ward Involvement, Skill Utilization, and Satisfaction) ranged from .64 to .87.

Using principal components factor analysis with varimax rotation, the developers identified three factors/subscales–Participation, Role Clarity, and Team Functioning. Cronbach's alphas were .90, .90, and .91, respectively. A minimum factor loading of $\geq$ .60 was used as criteria for including items on a factor. Correlations between the three factors ranged between .38 and .55.

Test-Retest/Inter-Rater Reliability

No data are available regarding test-retest reliability, and testing for inter-rater reliability is inappropriate since the measure is self-administered.

Content or Face Validity

We are unaware of any formal testing of face validity; however, the reviewers believe the items in each subscale are relevant to the respective concepts being measured.

Concurrent Validity

No data are available.

Construct Validity

As expected, the larger the team and the more diversity in it with regard to age, the lower is the perceived participation on the team. The larger the team and the more diversity in it with regard to hospital tenure, and age, the lower is the perceived level of role clarity in the team. The larger the team and the more diversity in it related to occupation, position tenure, and age, the lower is the level of perceived team functioning. These relationships were significant at the .05 and .01 levels of significance. Two individual level variables, tenure in the hospital and being a member of a lower status, non core occupation on the team (i.e., members other than the physician, nurse, or social worker), related to perceived level of participation in the team as one would expect. Employees with considerable tenure perceived high levels of participation in the team, while employees in lower status or less visible occupations perceived lower levels of participation in the team.

Physicians and social workers perceived role clarity and team functioning to be significantly better than did nurses. Physicians also were significantly more positive than nurses regarding their perception of participation on the team. These findings are as expected given the negativity on the part of nurses might be due to their frequently experiencing the negative consequences that teams' decisions have on patients and/or their uncertain sense of professional identity in comparison to physicians in the health care system.

Predictive Validity

No data are available.

Discriminant Validity

Consistent with other research, age was positively related to team functioning. That is, older team members rate team integration significantly more positively than younger members do. No gender differences were found in the perceptions of team integration.

Evaluation

The instrument has strong theoretical underpinnings and good preliminary reliability and validity testing. It has good readability and is easy to complete. It is unique in its assessment of members' perceptions of interdependence within the team and how well the team functions, especially with regard to its patients. Its use of shading every other item also is a unique way to prevent unanswered items. The range of answer choices is broad (1 to 7), and for two of the three subscales, it does not require a forced choice answer from respondents; this could, in some instances, have a negative impact on data quality. Its brevity makes it an especially appropriate instrument for large-scale research projects. Its use as an educational instrument is untested.

Status/Availability

The instrument is part of a larger Job Satisfaction Survey used to study inpatient and outpatient teams in VA psychiatric hospitals. Items included in it appear in the article below by Lichtenstein and colleagues. For additional information, contact Richard Lichtenstein at email, lichto@umich.edu.

Relevant Publications

Alderfer, C.P. (1987). An intergroup perspective on group dynamics. In J.W. Lorsch (Ed.), *Handbook of organizational behavior* (pp. 190-222). Englewood Cliffs, NJ: Prentice Hall.

Davis-Sacks, M.L. (1991). *Final report: Evaluation of collaborative program in psychiatry.* Ann Arbor, MI: VA Great Lakes Region Health Services Research and Developmental Program.

Lichtenstein, R., Alexander, J.A., Jinnett, K., & Ullman, E. (1997). Embedded intergroup relations in interdisciplinary teams: Effects on perceptions of level of team integration. *Journal of Applied Behavioral Science, 33*, 413-434.

Tajfel, H. (1982). Social identity and intergroup relations. Cambridge, MA: Cambridge University Press.

GROUP-GROWTH EVALUATION FORM

Developed by J. William Pfeiffer and John E. Jones, 1974
Reviewed by Gloria D. Heinemann and Sara A. Brallier

The Group-Growth Evaluation Form is a 20-item expedient measure, developed to help teams assess and their performance. It addresses four domains of performance–climate, data flow (communication), goal formation, and control (e.g., getting the job done responsibly versus using manipulation) in the team. It is most appropriate for newly developing teams attempting to set goals and improve their group processes/dynamics. It is not recommended for research purposes since several domains include only two to three items, and it has undergone no psychometric testing.

Conceptual Framework

The instrument seems to be based on McGregor's Theory Y although this is not stated explicitly. Work within an organization is best accomplished in interactive groups or teams rather than hierarchical interaction between the worker and his/her supervisor. When employee goals coincide with organizational goals, the work group is committed to the organization and carries out tasks enthusiastically. Experiential exercises and instruments documenting team members' perceptions of the level of team performance can facilitate work group development. The team should monitor its performance on a regular basis and attempt to improve it.

Developers view the team as a human relations group that has the potential to grow and develop over time.

Description of Measure

The instrument assesses a team's current performance level; discussion of results can facilitate improvement. Team members complete it, and averaging ratings for each item provide team scores.

Components of Team Performance Measured

Four broad dimensions of teamwork are measured by this instrument–climate (nine items), data or communication flow (two items), goal formation (five items), and control within the team (three items). An additional item (item 10) is included under climate to ascertain if the respondent is answering honestly.

This instrument measures three domains (structure, context, and process) and four dimensions (team structure and context, interdependence, and growth and development) of our team performance model.

Formatting and Scoring

A seven-point rating scale is used to record team members' responses on each of the 20 items such that 1 = lowest score and 7 = highest score. Respondents record answers to each item twice (i.e., how they perceive the group initially and at the present time) by writing the appropriate number on the blanks to the left of the statement (see example below). No visual aids or verbal anchors are provided for answer choices.

Data Flow
  Initially   Now

_____   _____ 11. I am willing to share information with other members of this group.

In J.W. Pfeiffer & J.E. Jones (Eds.), *A handbook of structured experiences for human relations training: Volume III* ©1974. Reprinted by permission of Jossey-Bass, Inc., a subsidiary of John Wiley & Sons, Inc.

There are no specific instructions for scoring. Developers state that once the form is completed by each team member, the data should be posted for discussion. We recommend scoring the responses via an item analysis (i.e., averaging team members' ratings for each item and also presenting the highest and lowest rating).

Psychometric Testing

No psychometric data are available for this instrument.

Evaluation

This instrument is appropriate for use in education/consultation sessions in which newly developing teams assess their level of performance and discuss how to improve it. Teams can use it for their own internal assessment of performance as long as one team member is a skilled facilitator for the discussion; however, new teams may not have developed enough trust among members to successfully critique the team without a neutral consultant.

The instrument measures only four areas of performance, and the conceptual soundness of three of them is questionable. The definitions of climate and goal formation are overly broad. "Climate" includes several items that measure group processes and growth and development among team members, and "goal formation" includes several items that address problem solving and dealing with problems. The definition of "data flow" is narrow in that it addresses only communication flow within the team; it could be improved by including items about documenting information, managing large amounts of data, and the use of technology in handling data. Both "data flow" and "control" include a small number of items. Additional weaknesses include unclear answer choices and lack of scoring instructions.

Respondents are asked to report earlier perceptions of the team's performance; we do not recommend such retrospective recall since retrospective responses are not always accurate. The reviewers believe it is better to administer an instrument to collect baseline data and use repeated administrations over time for comparison; however, this instrument is not appropriate for this since it has no test-retest reliability data. The developers suggest revising the instrument according to the needs of the team. It is inappropriate as a research instrument.

Status/Availability

University Associates, Inc. holds the instrument's copyright. The instrument may be reproduced for educational/training purposes. Large-scale reproduction requires prior written permission. The instrument appears in the Pfeiffer & Jones handbook referenced below. Contact Pfeiffer & Company at (800) 274-4434 to purchase the publication.

Relevant Publications

Pfeiffer, J.W., & Jones, J.E. (Eds.). (1974). *A handbook of structured experiences for human relations training: Volume III* (pp. 26-27). San Diego, CA: University Associates, Inc.

CRITERIA OF GROUP MATURITY

Developed by E.H. Schein, 1988
Reviewed by Antonette M. Zeiss and Gloria D. Heinemann

This expedient 10-item instrument assesses a group or team's strengths and weaknesses with regard to the maturation of its group processes. It is theoretically based, short, relatively easy to complete, and easy to score. It is best used with a consultant or by a team that is relatively sophisticated about group processes since a number of its group process terms are not defined in the items. It can be useful as a quick way to assess the team's growth and development at a given point in time.

Conceptual Framework

As team members work together, they develop norms, procedures, and, ultimately, the team's culture. Through learning and coping, teams grow, develop, and become more effective. An effective team learns to deal with the environment; establishes basic agreement about mission, goals, and values; has the capacity for self-knowledge; and optimizes resources. It accomplishes its goals by using integrated internal processes, and members' work experiences provide learning opportunities. That is, new information is assimilated into the team, and responses to such information are flexible. If the team is to learn from its experiences, certain steps must be negotiated. They include sensing change in the internal or external environment, bringing relevant information into the group and analyzing it, changing internal processes based upon that information, creating new behaviors or products to responds to changes, and obtaining feedback about the fit between the new responses and the environmental change.

The team is an organizational work group that grows and develops over time. It moves from the early stages of "getting acquainted" to the mature stages of effective, smooth functioning. Ultimately it becomes stable and stagnates. Formal and informal learning facilitate its functioning. Schein views team maturity as analogous to individual maturity; thus, his criteria for a mature team are taken from the criteria that define the personality of a mature individual.

Description of Measure

Schein designed this instrument to assess the group's maturation level and how effective its processes are. This expedient instrument is best use in education and consultation sessions or for self-assessment by team members themselves. It helps them identify their strengths and weaknesses at a given point in time. It is a generic instrument appropriate for a wide variety of groups. Individual group or team members complete the instrument.

Components of Team Performance Measured

The instrument measures 10 components of effective functioning. Some of these criteria were originally developed for judging individual personality. They include clear, agreed upon goals; shared participation in leadership functions; feelings of interdependence with persons in authority; maximum use of resources; acceptance of minority views and persons; cohesion; flexibility with regard to organization and procedures; and adequate mechanisms for communication, decision-making, and getting feedback.

The instrument measures three domains (structure, context, and process) and four dimensions (team structure, team context, interdependence, and growth and development) of our model of team performance.

Formatting and Scoring

For each of the 10 items, answer choices range from 1 = immature, ineffective process to 5 = mature, effective process. Answer choices are formatted along a continuum with verbal anchors provided below the continuum for the extreme ends (1 and 5) and the middle choice (3 = average) on the continuum (see item example below).

The developer does not provide scoring instructions. The reviewers recommend an item analysis. The range of individual scores indicates whether or not there is consensus among members regarding their perceptions of the team. Individual scores can be compared to the average team score for each item.

A mature group possesses:

1. Adequate mechanisms for getting feedback:

| Poor feedback mechanisms | 1 | 2 | 3 Average | 4 | 5 | Excellent feedback mechanisms |

In Schein, E.H. *Process consultation: Role in organization development* ©1988. Reprinted by permission of Pearson Education, Inc. Upper Saddle River, NJ.

Psychometric Testing

No reliability or validity data are available.

Evaluation

This expedient instrument is theoretically based, and its items relate well to team effectiveness. It is short, relatively easy to complete, and easy to score. It provides a quick assessment of a team's strengths and weaknesses with regard to group processes and effectiveness. Several of its items require respondents have an understanding of team processes in that there is little definition provided (e.g., phrases such as feedback mechanisms, decision-making procedures, optimal cohesion, and high interdependence). As a result, the instrument is best used with a consultant or by a relatively sophisticated team. Given that answer choice five is always positive and one is always negative, there is some potential for response bias. Additionally, the verbal anchors for the most positive responses are not consistent (e.g., excellent and optimal versus very adequate).

Status/Availability

The instrument is copyrighted; it appears in the 1988 publication below.

Relevant Publications

Schein, E.H. (1988). *Process consultation: Role in organization development* (2nd ed., pp. 76-83). Reading, MA & Menlo Park, CA: Addison-Wesley Publisher.

TEAM PROFILE QUESTIONNAIRE

Developed by Glenn H. Varney, 1989, 1991
Reviewed by Sara A. Brallier and Thomas F. Miller

This 19-item instrument identifies aspects of teamwork that require improvement. It measures components of team structure, context, processes, growth and development; the majority of items focus on team processes. No psychometric testing has been conducted to date. The instrument can be completed in ten minutes or less, and responses can be summarized easily. Results facilitate the action planning to improve the team's effectiveness.

Conceptual Framework

Varney uses Rubin, Fry, and Plovich's (1978) model as a conceptual framework for all his instruments included in this volume (see also the reviews of the Teamwork Survey and Analyzing Team Effectiveness). Team productivity is the result of indicators (i.e., effective team processes) and causes (i.e., a well-defined team structure). Indicators include open communication, minimal mistakes, low levels of conflict, cooperation, responsibility, and minimal complaints. Causes include clear and accepted team roles, clear and agreed upon goals, positive relationships, well-defined processes and procedures as well as effective leadership. Results of indicators and causes include capitalizing on opportunities, correct decisions, deadlines met, decreased costs, effective use of time, and innovative and effective problem solving. Rubin and associates view teamwork as a dynamic process in which team members and leaders continually assess, analyze, and improve indicators and causes in order to maximize results.

Teams are work groups within organizations. They are living entities in that they come to life, grow, develop, mature, and eventually die.

Description of Measure

Varney developed the instrument to assist teams with the identification of problem areas of teamwork that need to be addressed and improved. Results facilitate problem solving and action planning. Individual team members and the team as a whole are targets of assessment.

Components of Team Performance Measured

The instrument measures components of team structure (clarity of goals and roles), team context (a supportive environment/level of trust), interdependence (effective use of resources, planning, collaboration, communication, effective leadership, problem solving, decision-making, conflict management) and growth and development processes (creativity, risk-taking). The majority of the items focus on team processes.

The instrument measures three of the four domains (structure, context, and process) and four of the eight dimensions (team structure and context, interdependence, and growth and development) of our team performance model.

Formatting and Scoring

Team members indicate their level of agreement with each of the 19 items by writing a number (1 = strongly disagree through 5 = strongly agree) on the blank to the right of each item (see example).

> 7. Mistakes are not punished but rather viewed as opportunities to learn; risk is accepted as a condition of growth and change. _____
>
> In J.W. Pfeiffer (Ed.), *The encyclopedia of team-development activities* ©1991. Reprinted by permission of Jossey-Bass, Inc., a subsidiary of John Wiley & Sons, Inc.

Each item is analyzed separately. Varney recommends using visual graphics such as bar charts or percentage distributions to summarize the data and present it to the team. Mean scores for each item also can be generated. The reviewers recommend those items on which respondents score lower than three or items with a mean score lower than three should be examined closely as potential problem areas.

Psychometric Testing

No reliability or validity data are available.

Evaluation

The instrument is easy to administer and can be used to identify areas of teamwork that require improvement. It is useful as a starting point for action planning. Varney presents the instrument as an example of a standardized measure useful for identifying team strengths and weaknesses. He acknowledges that standardized measures do not always examine all of the relevant factors and may include terminology that is not relevant for the organization or team being surveyed. Thus, he suggests adapting and revising the instrument to address issues and use terms relevant for the team being examined. For example, item 16 uses the term "boss," while for many teams the term "team leader" or "supervisor" may be more appropriate. For use with nonprofessional teams, item wording should be simplified given the number of complex words used in the original version. Additionally, all of the items are positively worded, which can create a response bias. Although the instrument measures the structure, context, and processes of the team fairly well, it omits any elements of organizational impact (e.g., organizational structure or context) and has no items addressing team productivity. The instrument is appropriate for teams of professionals interested in discussing and improving their teamwork. It is not recommended for use as part of an organizational assessment or for research.

Status/Availability

The instrument is copyrighted and appears in the 1991a and 1991b (adapted version) publications below. To order the 1991a publication, contact Jossey-Bass Publisher at (800) 274-4434. To order the 1991b publication that includes the adapted version, contact University Associates at (619) 578-5900.

Relevant Publications

Rubin, I., Fry, R., & Plovich, M. (1978). *Managing human resources in health organizations*. Reston, VA: Reston Books.

Varney, G.H. (1991). *Building productive teams: An action guide and resource book* (pp. 29-30). San Francisco: Jossey-Bass Publisher.

Varney, G.H. (1991b). Team-Profile Questionnaire (adapted). In J.W. Pfeiffer (Ed.), *The encyclopedia of team-development activities* (pp. 247-248). San Diego, CA: University Associates.

CHAPTER 11
BROAD-SPECTRUM INSTRUMENTS

Martha S. Waite, M.S.W.
VA Greater Los Angeles Healthcare System, Sepulveda, CA, VISN 22

Linda O. Nichols, Ph.D.
VA Medical Center, Memphis, TN. VISN 9

This chapter introduces 23 broad-spectrum instruments, each of which covers five or six dimensions of our model of team performance presented in Chapter 3). Table 11.1, summarizing the main features of these instruments, and the critiques of each instrument follow the overview. We selected instruments presented in bold face type in the table and marked with asterisks in the critiques as "best measures."

OVERVIEW

In comparison to the instruments presented in Chapters 9 and 10, the broad-spectrum instruments are, on average, longer and have both a broader and more in-depth coverage of the dimensions and elements of team performance. They more often measure both the facets of performance within the team and the team's relationship to the organization within which it functions. Some instruments also address team outcomes and productivity.

Broad-spectrum instruments have three different purposes. Nineteen focus on assessing and improving team performance. One of the nineteen (Alexander's) is an expedient measure in that it is short, easy to use, and can be altered to meet the needs of a specific team. Another one (Moos and Humphrey's GES) has a duel purpose in that it also is a research instrument. Two additional instruments are research measures (Anderson and West's TCI and Schmitt and colleagues' adaptation of the ICU Nurse/Physician Instrument. The former instrument addresses support for innovation; the latter assesses geriatric team functioning.

One common theme of the broad-spectrum instruments is their collection of data and comparison of results from more than one perspective. For example, Gibb assesses trust at the individual and team levels. Parker assesses perceptions of performance and the importance that members place on the various facets of performance. Lazar and Brown measure members' perceptions of ideal and actual performance. Hoevemeyer and Moos/Humphrey both compare team members' and leaders' perceptions. Alexander's instrument is the only one designed for data collection from a team, an outside observer, or both; the latter choice facilitates comparison of internal and external perceptions.

Four of the 23 instruments discussed in this chapter were designated as "best measures. They are Anderson and West's TCI, Jones and Bearley's GDA, McGregor's Analyzing Team Effectiveness, and Schmitt and colleagues' adapted version of the ICU Nurse/Physician Instrument, originally developed by Shortell and Rousseau. These instruments are presented again in Chapter 14.

Unique Features of the Instruments

Several instruments have unique features. The instruments designed by Jones and Bearley and Carew and associates both assess a team's current stage of development, and Anderson and West's instrument is unique in its measurement of support for innovation. Lawler, Cammann, Nadler, and Jenkins' Work Group Module can be administered independently or as one of several modules that assess organizational performance. Reagan's inventory has the unique perspective of assessing teamwork in relation to U.S. culture to help teams determine hidden values, behaviors, and norms that could hamper members' working together. Tsukuda and Stahelski measure, in considerable detail, the skills acquired for quality geriatric team care by team members and trainees.

Proportion with Psychometric Testing

Two of the broad-spectrum instruments and their adaptations have strong reliability and validity data. Two other instruments have preliminary reliability and good validity data. Four instruments have only preliminary data on reliability and/or validity, and 15 instruments have not been subjected to any psychometric testing (see Table 11.1).

Implications for Use

The broad-spectrum instruments are applicable to a wide audience in that most target generic groups or teams. Of the generic instruments, those with high readability levels should be used with professional teams only. Parker recommends that his Survey of Cross-Functional Teams be used only with experienced teams (see Table 11.1). Two other generic instruments (Gibb and Moos/Humphrey) assesses family, therapy, and/or support groups; often such instruments include items and subscales that do not translate easily to clinical health care teams and natural work groups in hospital settings. Three other instruments target health care teams specifically. Some of these instruments are applicable to clinical teams only, while others are appropriate for all types of teams in health care settings.

These instruments also are broadly applicable because they are easy to complete and score, are readily availability, and do not have to be purchased although permission is needed from the developer or holder of the copyright to use some of them. The longer ones should be used with caution among some teams and work groups. They can fatigue respondents, and uncommitted members of teams can quickly lose interest in completing them. Both of these situations can compromise the quality of data collected.

Disappointing is the lack of test-retest reliability data for these instruments. As a result, we do not know their capability to monitor or track team performance over time. Most of them can be used by the teams themselves or with a consultant.

Table 11.1 Summary of Broad-Spectrum Instruments

Instrument	Developer(s); Adapter(s)	# Items	Purpose	Target Group	Psychometrics
Team Effectiveness Critique	Alexander	10	Assess & help improve functioning (expedient measure)	Generic work groups/teams	None
Team Climate Inventory (TCI)	Anderson & West	38	Research (support for innovation)	Generic professional teams	Good preliminary reliability & good validity
Team Success Survey	Bader, Bloom & Chang	12	Assess & help improve functioning	Generic work groups/teams	None
Team Development Stage Assessment (TDSA)	Carew, Parisi-Carew, Stoner & Blanchard	7	Assess & help improve functioning; identify stage of development	Generic work groups/teams	None
Team Maturity Scale	Dyer	22	Assess & help improve functioning (level of maturity)	Generic work groups/teams	None
Modified Family Assessment Device for Teams (MFADT)	Waite & Harker's adaptation from Epstein, Baldwin & Bishop's FAD	54	Assess & help improve functioning	Generic clinical or direct care teams	Preliminary reliability & validity
TORI Group Self-Diagnosis Scale	Gibb	96	Assess & help improve functioning (trust at individual & group levels)	Close primary groups such as families or therapy & support groups	None
Team Effectiveness Inventory	Hoevemeyer	20	Assess & help improve functioning (members' & leader's perceptions of effectiveness)	Generic work groups/teams	None

Table 11.1 Summary of Broad-Spectrum Instruments (continued)

Instrument	Developer(s); Adapter(s)	# Items	Purpose	Target Group	Psychometrics
Group Development Assessment (GDA)	Jones & Bearley	40	Assess & help improve team functioning; identify stage of development along task & process dimensions	Generic professional teams	Preliminary reliability; no validity
Work Group Functioning Module (4)	Lawler, Cammann, Nadler & Jenkins	14	Assess & help improve functioning	Generic work groups/teams	Preliminary reliability & good validity
Team Excellence Questionnaire	Lazar	10	Assess & help improve functioning	Generic work groups/teams	None
Factors Influencing Productivity & Excellence in Team Work	Brown adaptation of two of Lazar's instruments	30	Assess & help improve functioning	Generic work groups/teams	Preliminary reliability & validity
Analyzing Team Effectiveness	McGregor	10	Assess & help improve functioning	Generic work groups/teams c	None
Group Environment Scale (GES)	Moos & Humphrey; adapted by Schmitt, Heinemann & Farrell	27	Assess & help improve functioning (original–members' & leader's perceptions); research (original & adapted)	Generic work groups/teams; therapy & support groups	Strong reliability & validity
Survey of Cross-Functional Teams	Parker	20	Assess & help improve functioning	Generic work groups/teams (esp. experienced teams)	None

213

Table 11.1 Summary of Broad-Spectrum Instruments (continued)

Instrument	Developer(s); Adapter(s)	# Items	Purpose	Target Group	Psychometrics
Team-Development Survey	Parker	12	Assess & help improve functioning	Generic professional teams	None
High-Performance Work Team Questionnaire (HPWTQ)	Preziosi	48	Assess & help improve functioning	Generic work groups/teams	None
U.S. Style Teams (USST) Inventory	Reagan	33	Assess & help improve readiness to implement the team approach	Generic work groups/teams	None
ICU Nurse/Physician Instrument	Shortell & Rousseau; adapted by Schmitt, Heinemann & Farrell	23	Research	Clinical teams	Strong reliability & validity
Team Skills Questionnaire	Tsukuda & Stahelski	49	Assess skills level of team members & trainees	Geriatric clinical teams & trainees	None
Analyzing Team Effectiveness	Varney	12	Assess & help improve functioning	Generic work groups/teams	None
Teamwork Survey (TWS)	Varney	33	Assess & help improve functioning	Generic work groups/teams	Preliminary reliability, no validity
Team Communication, Cooperation & Contribution Surveys	Zoglio	35	Assess & help improve functioning	Generic work groups/teams	None

TEAM EFFECTIVENESS CRITIQUE

Developed by Mark Alexander, 1985, 1989
Reviewed by Sara A. Brallier and Ruth Ann Tsukuda

The 1989 version of the Team Effectiveness Critique is a 10-item instrument measuring team development and effectiveness. The developer designed this instrument to identify strengths and weakness in team functioning. Its strengths include ease of administration and scoring and the option of either an observer or team members completing it. Weaknesses include the measurement of more than one concept in several items and the lack of psychometric testing. With minor revisions, it has potential as an expedient assessment device in team education and consultation. It is not appropriate for statistical or research purposes.

Conceptual Framework

This instrument is based on the stages of team development framework. The developer asserts that in order for teams to function effectively, they must have accomplished a series of developmental tasks. In early development, they must establish clearly stated goals, objectives, procedures, and roles. They also must agreed upon approaches to problem solving and decision-making. As teams continue to develop, they need to cultivate an atmosphere that encourages trust, open and honest communication, creativity, and direct resolution of conflict. In well-developed teams, members share leadership and responsibility for team maintenance. Periodic monitoring and evaluation allows the team to examine its group processes and identify areas that need improvement; this facilitates team development.

The team is a work group with the potential to develop over time. Monitoring team performance and developing action plans for improvement facilitate effectiveness of the team.

Description of Measure

The instrument assesses group development and effectiveness. It is useful for targeting weaknesses and facilitating action planning for improvement. Individual team members complete the instrument anonymously. Team averages provide a picture of the team as a whole. Alternatively, an independent observer can complete the instrument to assess team effectiveness and identify problem areas in need of improvement.

Components of Team Performance Measured

The 1985 version of the instrument measures nine facets of team effectiveness–goals and objectives, utilization of resources, trust and conflict, leadership, control and procedures, interpersonal communications, problem solving/decision-making, experimentation/creativity, and evaluation. The revised instrument (1989) measures ten facets; for this version, developers added an additional item measuring roles and responsibilities.

The 1989 version addresses all four domains and five dimensions (team structure and context, interdependence, growth and development, and strategies for productivity) of our model of team performance.

Formatting and Scoring

Developers present a word or phrase identifying the element of performance being measured in each item. Items are rated on a seven-point continuum from 1, most negative to 7, most positive. Extreme answer choices (1, 7) have verbal descriptors (sentences) above the continuum (see item example below).

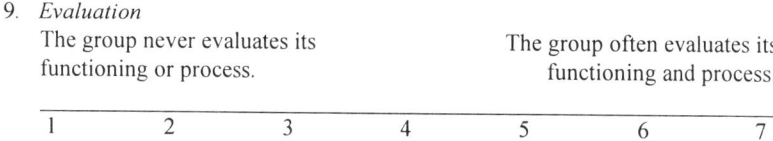

9. *Evaluation*
   The group never evaluates its functioning or process.   The group often evaluates its functioning and process.
   1   2   3   4   5   6   7

In S.L. Phillips & R.L. Elledge (Eds.), *The team building sourcebook* ©1989. Reprinted by permission of Jossey-Bass, Inc., a subsidiary of John Wiley & Sons, Inc.

Team averages are calculated for each item. Team members' responses are compared with one another and with the team averages. Discussion of results facilitates reaching consensus about areas of effectiveness needing improvement.

Psychometric Testing

No reliability or validity data are available.

Evaluation

This instrument's strengths include ease of administration and scoring and the option of an outside observer completing it. It also is useful for obtaining a quick, global impression of a team. A weakness is the measurement of more than one concept per item in the trust/conflict and control/procedures items. Data showing whether or not observers and team members rate the team in similar fashion would be useful.

Alexander (1985) provides descriptions of the concepts underlying each item; these descriptions should be presented to team members prior to administering the original instrument. With minor revisions, both versions of the instrument are appropriate for educational programs and consultations with teams.

Status/Availability

The instrument is copyrighted. The original version appears in the 1985 publication, and the revised version appears in the 1989 publication (see relevant publications below). To purchase the 1985 publication, contact Pfeiffer & Company at (800) 274-4434. To purchase the 1989 publication, contact University Associates at (619) 578-5900.

Relevant Publications

Alexander, M. (1985). The Team Effectiveness Critique. In L.D. Goodstein & J.W. Pfeiffer (Eds.), *The 1985 annual: Developing human resources* (pp. 101-106). San Diego, CA: Pfeiffer & Company.

Alexander, M. (1989). The Team Effectiveness Critique. In S.L. Phillips & R.L. Elledge (Eds.), *The team building sourcebook* (pp. 19-20). San Diego, CA: University Associates, Inc.

TEAM CLIMATE INVENTORY (TCI)*

Developed by Neil R. Anderson and Michael A. West, 1994
Reviewed by Steven Lovett and Antonette M. Zeiss

The Team Climate Inventory (TCI) is a theoretically based, well validated instrument that yields an overall scale score and subscale scores on five components of team performance–vision, frequency of interaction among team members, participative safety, task orientation, and support for innovation. There are two versions of the instrument–a 61-item version and a 38-item revision. Psychometric data and administration to health care teams indicate that the TCI is reliable, valid, and sensitive to differences across teams. Psychometric data do not address its utility as a longitudinal measure of change. Developers designed the instrument primarily to serve as a research tool. Its focus on climate for innovation is unique for a team performance measure. Wording complexity makes the instrument most suitable for well-educated professionals.

Conceptual Framework

The developers define a team's climate as a set of shared perceptions of organizational policies, practices, and procedures. They identify four facets of climate that predict innovation–vision, participative safety, task orientation, and support for innovation. "Vision" is a valued outcome or higher order goal that gives teams focus and direction; it must be clear, shared, and attainable. "Participative safety" is the degree to which involvement in decision-making is encouraged, reinforced, and occurs in an environment that is interpersonally non-threatening. "Task orientation" is commitment to high quality work with emphasis on accountability and assessing and modifying policies, procedures, and methods as needed. "Support for innovation" is the expectation, approval, and practical support for introducing new and improved ways of doing things in the work environment.

Teams are permanent or semi-permanent proximal work groups. Individuals are assigned to and come to identify with them.

Description of Measure

Developers designed the instrument for research to measure facets of team or work group climate that they believe to be related to innovation. Although individual team members complete the instrument, the real target of assessment is the team itself.

Components of Team Performance Measured

The TCI measures five facets of team climate (i.e., vision, participative safety, task orientation, support for innovation, and interaction frequency). The first four facets or subscales were derived from the theoretical framework. The fifth was derived from factor analytic procedures; it reflects the amount of interaction among team members. Participative safety has two components–team participation (i.e., members' frequency of interaction, degree of information sharing, and influence over decision-making) and safety (i.e., the level of perceived safety to communicate freely within the team). Task orientation also has two components–climate for excellence and constructive controversy. Climate for excellence refers to the extent to which team members interact in order to promote excellence in the team's work. Constructive controversy is the degree to which opposing ideas are discussed openly and collaboratively and attempts are made to integrate them into a high-quality, accepted solution.

In the shortened version, the 38 items are distributed across five subscales as follows: vision includes 11 items; participative safety includes eight items; support for innovation, eight items; task orientation, seven items; and interaction frequency, four items.

The instrument includes items in all four of the domains and five of the eight dimensions (team structure, team context, interdependence, growth and development, and strategies for productivity) of our model of team performance.

Formatting and Scoring

The original version includes 61 items; the revised version includes 38 items. Both have been used in published research studies. All items have Likert-formatted response choices. The Vision and Task Orientation Subscales have answer choices ranging from 1 to 7. The Team Participative Safety and Support for Innovation, and Interaction Frequency Subscales have answer choices ranging from 1 to 5 (see item example below).

	Strongly disagree	Disagree	Neither agree nor disagree	Agree	Strongly agree
21. People in this team are always searching for fresh, new ways of looking at problems	1	2	3	4	5

Reproduced with permission of the publishers, the NFER-NELSON Publishing Company Limited, Darville House, 2 Oxford Road East, Windsor, Berkshire SL4 1DF, England. Team Climate Inventory © Neil Anderson & Michael West, ASE 1996, 1999.

Subscale scores and a total score are obtained by summing the responses to the respective items. Some of the items must be reverse scored prior to summing. A high score on each subscale indicates a high perception of that concept. Team scores are calculated by averaging the scores of team members.

Psychometric Testing

Internal Consistency Reliability

In an exploratory factor analysis, 38 of the 61 items loaded above .50 on five factors. Confirmatory factor analyses using the 38-item version of the TCI validated the five-factor structure obtained on the 61-item, original version; the alphas for the subscales are Vision, .94; Participative Safety, .89; Support for Innovation, .92; Task Orientation, .92; and Interaction Frequency, .84.

Test-Retest/Inter-Rater Reliability

No data are available regarding test-retest reliability, and testing for inter-rater reliability is inappropriate since the measure is self-administered.

Content or Face Validity

The TCI has good face validity. A thorough review of the literature guided the instrument's development. Additionally, the developers culled some items from previously developed scales tapping similar concepts.

Concurrent Validity

No data are available.

Construct Validity

Comparisons of TCI scores across five separate samples of teams (i.e., hospital management teams, oil company teams, community psychiatric teams, primary health care teams, and social services teams) revealed significant differences in mean scores. This suggests that the inventory is sufficiently sensitive to detect differences in climate across teams in different settings.

Predictive Validity

Developers demonstrated the predictive validity of the instrument in a longitudinal study of team innovation. Expert and naive raters assessed the innovation demonstrated by work teams during the six months following their completion of the TCI. The results showed that team-level scores on the instrument were significant predictors of number of innovations, innovation novelty, and overall ratings of innovation.

Discriminant Validity

No data are available.

Evaluation

Designed for research, the TCI has a sound theoretical framework and has served as an effective measure in a number of studies including studies of health care teams. It is relatively easy to complete and score. Wording of items is generally straightforward and easy to understand although some items include complex wording. Occupation-specific jargon is virtually absent, which makes the TCI suitable for use with any type of professional team.

The considerable psychometric data available on the TCI indicate it is a very sound measure. Its internal consistency and the validity of its factor structure are well established. It is sufficiently sensitive to detect differences in team climate among various types of teams. Its ability to detect intra-team changes in climate over time has not been well established at this time, and data on test-retest reliability would be useful. No normative data have been established; therefore, it is difficult to define cut-off points for high and low scores.

The short version of the TCI is a well designed and validated self-report measure of several domains of team performance that can be used in virtually any organizational setting. Its focus on climate for innovation is unique for a team performance measure. It is an excellent choice for research, especially if there is interest in assessing innovation within teams.

Status/Availability

The TCI can be obtained from Assessment Services for Employment, NFER-Nelson-Nelson, Darville House, 2 Oxford Road East, Windsor, Berkshire, SL4 1DF, U.K. The items also have been published in the Anderson & West (1998) publication cited below. The instrument is copyrighted; however, use for research purposes is permitted.

Relevant Publications

Agrell, A., & Gustafson, R. (1983). The Team Climate Inventory and group innovation: A psychometric test on a Swedish sample of work groups. *Journal of Occupational and Organizational Psychology, 67*, 143-151.

Anderson, N.R., & West, M.A. (1994). *The Team Climate Inventory*. Windsor, U.K.: Assessment Services for Employment, NFER-Nelson.

Anderson, N.R., & West, M.A. (1996). The Team Climate Inventory: The development of the TCI and its applications in team-building for innovativeness. *European Journal of Work and Organizational Psychology, 5*, 53-66.

Anderson, N.R., & West, M.A. (1998). Measuring climate for work group innovation: Development and validation of the team climate inventory. *Journal of Organizational Behavior, 19*, 235-258.

West, M.A., & Anderson, N.R. (1996). Innovation in top management teams. *Journal of Applied Psychology, 81*, 680-693.

TEAM SUCCESS SURVEY

Developed by Gloria E. Bader, Audrey E. Bloom, and Richard Y. Chang, 1974
Reviewed by Linda O. Nichols and Martha S. Waite

The Team Success Survey is a 12-item instrument designed to help teams assess and improve their performance, motivate team members, and provide data for individual and team rewards within the organization. Developers suggest using it in conjunction with their other measurement instruments. The instrument is easy to complete and score. Several of the items would benefit from revision, and no reliability or validity data are available. The instrument is generic and appropriate for a variety of types of teams.

Conceptual Framework

There is no strong theoretical framework underlying this instrument. The developers acknowledge that in newly restructured organizations, work groups should function as teams, and teams should be evaluated on the basis of their operating processes and work outcomes. The team's work must coincide with the organization's business objectives, and the internal dynamics of the team must facilitate its productivity and outcomes. The developers believe assessment of team performance is an important facet of team development and helps motivate team members. Results of an assessment should be incorporated into the organization's rewards systems for both individuals and teams. Developers view the team as a work group of individuals attempting to achieve a common goal.

Description of Measure

The purpose of the measure is to assess a team's progress with regard to achieving goals, improving effectiveness, building motivation among members, and rewarding performance. It has been used for education, training, and consultation. The team and its members are the units of analysis.

Components of Team Performance Measured

The developers address 12 dimensions of performance–mission and goals; creative operation; results focus; roles and responsibilities; organization; building on individual strengths; support of leadership and each other; team climate; disagreement resolution; communication; decision-making; and evaluation of effectiveness. Each dimension is measured by one item.

The Survey measures all four domains and six of the eight dimensions (team structure and context, interdependence, growth and development, strategies for productivity, and accomplishments) of our team performance model.

Formatting and Scoring

The Survey has a seven-point rating continuum for each of the 12 items with 1 as the lowest or most negative score and 7 the highest or most positive score. The two extreme answer choices (1 and 7) are labeled verbally with descriptive sentences below the continuum (see item example below).

According to the developers, the 12 items do not constitute a scale. Team members' scores are averaged for each item. Members' scores are compared to one another and to the team averages (an item analysis).

6. *Builds upon individual strengths*

1	2	3	4	5	6	7
The knowledge, skills, and talents of team members are underutilized.					Members' knowledge, skills, and talents are put to good use.	

In Bader, G.E., Bloom, A.E., & Chang, R.Y. *Measuring Team Performance* ©1994. Reprinted by permission of Richard Chang Associates, Inc.

Psychometric Testing

No reliability or validity data are available.

Evaluation

Overall, this instrument is short, easy to complete, and covers a relatively wide range of performance elements. It is not theoretically based, and no psychometric testing has been conducted to determine its reliability and validity. Data regarding test-retest reliability would ascertain its usefulness for tracking performance over time. There are difficulties with several of the verbal descriptors. Item 3, "Focuses on results," attempts to measure three concepts (i.e., accomplishing objectives within budget, on schedule, and to the required level of quality) in one statement. The verbal descriptors in item 5, "Is well organized," do not refer to the same concept. The negative statement refers to whether team structure, policies, and procedures are disorganized, while the positive statement refers to whether team members support them. Item 7 does not address team members' support of one another as the label suggests. Item 11 has little to do with objectivity in decision-making; rather, it measures the presence or absence of consensus decision-making.

The instrument is appropriate for team education and consultation. It is straightforward enough that the team itself can use it without a consultant. The developers recommend using it in conjunction with several other methods of team assessment, some of which they present in the appendix of their book (see relevant publications below).

Status/Availability

The instrument is copyrighted. It is presented in the appendix of the developers' book (see publications below). To purchase this publication, contact the publisher at (800) 756-8096.

Relevant Publications

Bader, G.E., Bloom, A.E., & Chang, R.Y. (1994). *Measuring team performance: A practical guide to tracking team success.* Irvine, CA: Richard Chang Associates, Inc. Publications.

TEAM DEVELOPMENT STAGE ASSESSMENT (TDSA)

Developed by Don Carew, Eunice Parisi-Carew, Jesse Stoner, and Ken Blanchard, 1998
Reviewed by Alice M. DeFriese and Thomas F. Miller

The TDSA is a seven-item measure of team productivity and morale. It measures purpose, empowerment, relationships and communication, flexibility, optimal performance, recognition and appreciation, and morale. Individual team members complete the instrument. A team score is used to assess the team's stage of development. The instrument has strong theoretical underpinnings; however, there are no published data on its reliability or validity. It is appropriate for identifying the strengths and weaknesses of developing teams. Developers provide supporting literature to help the team create an action plan for continued development.

Conceptual Framework

The developers used Lacoursiere's (1980) five stages of group development as a basis for the TDSA. These stages include orientation, dissatisfaction, integration, production, and termination. Low productivity and moderately high morale characterize the orientation stage. During this stage, the team needs to develop a common understanding of its purpose, goals, norms, and procedures. In the second stage, dissatisfaction, morale decreases while productivity increases slowly. Members feel frustrated when they realize their initial expectations were unrealistic, and they discover their own and others' weaknesses as team members. During the third stage, resolution, productivity is moderately high and morale is variable or improving. Team members' task accomplishment and technical skills are improving, and there is an increased understanding of and commitment to the team's purpose and goals. As the team continues to work on its development during this stage, it should focus on shared leadership, conflict management, and evaluation of team performance. In stage four, production, morale and confidence are high. During this stage, team members' confidence in one another, both in terms of ability and compatibility, and commitment to the team's success increase. Leadership roles are shared and delegated based on expertise. Time limited groups are the only ones that experience the final or fifth stage.

The developers define teams as two or more individuals, who are working together to accomplish a common purpose and are accountable for the results. As teams grow from a group of individuals to a successful and productive team, they pass through a series of developmental stages. Metaphorically, the developers state that teams are complex living systems in which the whole is different from the sum of its parts.

Description of Measure

The TDSA assesses a team's stage of development, identifies areas in which the team needs to improve, and facilitates the development of an action plan for improvement. Each team member completes the instrument; their scores are averaged and used to determine the team's stage of development.

Components of Team Performance Measured

In order to determine a team's stage of development, the TDSA measures seven facets of morale and productivity. These are: (a) purpose and values; (b) empowerment; (c) relationships and communication; (d) flexibility; (e) optimal performance; (f) recognition and appreciation; and (g) morale.

This instrument includes items in all four domains and six of the eight dimensions (team structure and context, interdependence, growth and development, strategies for productivity, and accomplishments) of our team performance model.

Formatting and Scoring

The TDSA is a seven-item instrument. There are four statements (labeled a through d) describing each of the seven components of productivity and morale that it measures. The respondent circles the letter of the statement that best describes his or her perceptions of the team's level of performance.

The developers provide a scoring template to transform the letter responses into a numerical team development stage score. The scores range from 7 to 28; the higher the score the higher is the team's developmental stage.

Psychometric Testing

No reliability or validity data are available.

Evaluation

The instrument has strong theoretical underpinnings. For each stage of development, the developers describe the major issues faced by the team, the possible duration of the stage, and an outline of the team's needs during the stage. Although there are no reliability and validity data, the instrument appears to have considerable face validity. It is appropriate for use with teams who want to assess their stage of development or level of functioning and identify their strengths and weaknesses. The developers provide supporting literature to help the team create an action plan for improvement. They suggest teams use the TDSA in conjunction with their Situational Leadership II instrument to help them match the appropriate leadership behaviors with the needs of the team.

Status/Availability

The TDSA can be purchased from Blanchard Training and Development, Inc., 125 State Place, Escondido, CA 92029; (760) 489-5005 or (800) 489-8407 or http://www.blanchardtraining.com. This company holds the copyright.

Relevant Publications

Carew, D., Parisi-Carew, E., Stoner, J., & Blanchard, K. (1998). *Team Development Stage Assessment: Team Member Questionnaire*. Escondido, CA: Blanchard and Training Development, Inc.

Carew, D., Parisi-Carew, E., Stoner, J., Finch, F., & Blanchard, K. (1998). *Team Development Stage Assessment: Team Profile*. Escondido, CA: Blanchard and Training Development, Inc.

Carew, D., Parisi-Carew, E., Stoner, J., Finch, F., & Blanchard, K. (1998). *Team Development Stage Assessment: Leader's Guide*. Escondido, CA: Blanchard and Training Development, Inc.

Carew, D., Parisi-Carew, E., & Blanchard, K. (1998). Team Development and Situational Leadership II (article). Escondido, CA: Blanchard and Training Development, Inc.

Lacoursiere, R.B. (1980). *The life cycle of groups: Group development stage theory*. New York: Human Service Press.

TEAM MATURITY SCALE

Developed by William G. Dyer, 1995
Reviewed by Stephen K. Harmon and Glenda F. Brown

The Team-Maturity Scale consists of 22 items related to team maturity or level of functioning. The instrument identifies teams' strengths and weaknesses in the areas of team processes, interpersonal relations, and staff satisfaction. It also assesses team leadership and leadership styles. Focused discussions related to understanding and interpreting results can be valuable in helping team members recognize important aspects of team maturity. This instrument is appropriate for educational and consultative purposes; however, it would benefit from some minor revisions and psychometric testing to determine its appropriateness for monitoring team performance over time.

Conceptual Framework

The instrument is based on a group development framework in which the team has the potential to mature over time. A mature team is synonymous with a fully developed team that performs efficiently and effectively. According to Dyer, the leader and team members develop and mature, and the leader plays a key role in facilitating the team's development.

Dyer views the team as an interactive, interdependent work group that has the potential to grow and improve over time.

Description of Measure

The instrument's purpose is to assess how team members perceive the functioning of the team based on a range of maturity factors and criteria. The instrument is used in team training and consultation to help identify strengths and areas for improvement. Team members complete it individually; their perceptions contribute to an overall "picture" or profile of the team's maturity. The primary target of the instrument is the team as a whole. According to Dyer, the instrument is sensitive to changes that take place over time and allows for repeated assessments to monitor progress and outcomes related to maturity.

Components of Team Performance Measured

Developers measure 15 components of team maturity or effectiveness: goals; decision-making; collaboration; trust; leadership; communication; conflict; inclusion/involvement; commitment/support; evaluation; satisfaction with team functioning; team-building skills; risk-taking; productivity/effectiveness of interpersonal relations; and sensitivity to needs of team members.

Measurement of goals (four items) includes how they are established on the work unit, what the commitment is to achieving them, whether team members understand what they need from each other to achieve them, and whether members know how their work contributes to goals. Decision-making (one item) addresses how decisions are made; collaboration (one item) measures how well team members collaborate, and trust (one item) addresses members' trust in one another to carry out assignments, do their share, and help each other.

Facets of leadership addressed (three items) are the leader's management style, the extent to which the work unit is dependent on the leader, and whether the leader has team-building capabilities and skills. Communication (one item) measures whether communication is open and free in meetings; conflict (one item) measures how disagreement and conflict are handled in the team; inclusion/involvement (one item) assesses the degree to which members feel they are part of a team.

Measurement of commitment/support (three items) addresses team members' understanding of and commitment to implementing decisions and whether leaders and members are supportive of each other, willingly make personal sacrifices for the good of the team, and are sensitive to one another's needs. Evaluation (one item) assesses whether members critique how well they work together. One item measures how satisfied members are with team functioning, and one item measures whether members have team-building knowledge and skills. Whether members are willing to take risks and try new actions to improve the team are included in the measurement of risk-taking (one item). Balancing task and maintenance activities (one item) assesses whether members know how to get work done and maintain good relations at the same time.

The instrument addresses all four domains and six of the eight dimensions (organizational and team structure, team context, interdependence, growth and development, and strategies for productivity) of our model of team performance.

Formatting and Scoring

The 22 items are statements or questions to which the responses range from 1 = low team maturity to 5 = high team maturity. For each item, answer choices 1, 3, and 5 have verbal sentence descriptors to assist respondents (see item example below).

> 8. When people have differences or conflicts, how are they handled?
>
> | 1 | 2 | 3 | 4 | 5 |
> |---|---|---|---|---|
> | Conflicts are ignored, or people are told not to worry about them. | | Conflicts are sometimes looked at, but are usually left hanging. | | Conflicts are discussed openly and resolved. |
>
> In Dyer, W.G. *Team building: Current issues and new alternatives* (3rd ed.) ©1995. Reprinted by permission of Pearson Education, Inc. Upper Saddle River, NJ.

Each respondent sums his or her responses for the 22 items and divides the total by 22, the total number of items for his/her average maturity score. Individual scores are averaged to get the team's maturity score. Ratings of 3.75 or higher are evidence of an appropriate level of maturity. Scores between 2.5 and 3.75 indicate maturity that is mid-level with work still needed by the team to enhance team maturity. Scores between 1.0 and 2.5 indicate that the team is at an immature level and requires a great deal of team development.

An item analysis is useful to identify areas needing work to move the team to a higher maturity level.

Psychometric Testing

No data are available. Content validity experts in the field of team building and organizational management developed the items; thus, the instrument appears to have content or face validity.

Evaluation

The facets of team effectiveness measured are well conceptualized. The instrument is easy to complete and score. However, there is an inconsistency in use of terms across items. For example, unit and team are used interchangeably as are boss and leader. Some of the items attempt to measure more than one concept, which is problematic. Given that answer choices are formatted identically for each of the 22 items, there is some potential for response bias. The instrument is appropriate for team education and consultation; it would benefit from minor revisions and psychometric testing, especially to determine its reliability over time and whether items can legitimately be summed. Focused discussions related to interpreting results can helping members recognize important aspects of team maturity.

Status/Availability

Pearson Education, Inc. holds the instrument's copyright. It appears in the 1995 publication below. To purchase, contact University Associates, Inc., at (619) 578-5900. Alternatively, contact Pearson Education, Inc., One Lake Street, Upper Saddle River, NJ 07458.

Relevant Publications

Dyer, W.G. (1995). *Team building: Current issues and new alternatives* (3rd ed.). Reading, MA & Menlo Park, CA: Addison-Wesley Publisher.

McMASTER FAMILY ASSESSMENT DEVICE (FAD)/ MODIFIED FAMILY ASSESSMENT DEVICE FOR TEAMS (MFADT)

Developed by N. Epstein, L. Baldwin, and D.S. Bishop, 1983; adapted as the Modified Family Assessment Device for Teams (MFADT) by M.S. Waite and J.O. Harker, 1993
Reviewed by Martha S. Waite and Linda O. Nichols

The 60-item McMaster Family Assessment Device (FAD) assesses family functioning. Based on family systems theory, it measures problem solving, communication, roles, affective responsiveness, affective involvement, behavior control, and general functioning. It has long-term use in clinical, educational, and research settings, and psychometric testing shows it is reliable and valid. Waite and Harker adapted this instrument for teams, with permission, and renamed it the Modified Family Assessment Device for Teams (MFADT). Preliminary psychometric testing shows that the MFADT items are internally consistent, and it is a valid measure of team functioning. The 54-item MFADT is appropriate for identifying areas of team dysfunction that require intervention. It has potential as a pre- and posttest measure to evaluate the impact of interventions pending further psychometric testing.

Conceptual Framework

The FAD measures aspects of family functioning and distinguishes between healthy and unhealthy families. It is based on the McMaster Model of Family

Functioning, a clinically oriented conceptualization of families that includes structural and organizational properties and patterns of transactions among family members. Waite and Harker adapted the FAD for use with teams because of the conceptual similarity between teams and families (i.e., both are small primary groups) and because the FAD has strong psychometric data and longstanding use in clinical, educational, and research settings.

Both instruments use a general systems approach to identify problem areas. A general systems model holds that everyday action at the group level produces reactions in one or more of its members. The assumption underlying both measures is that family functioning and interdisciplinary team functioning are the result of complex interactions among variables. For health care teams, these interactions involve team members, patients, and the context in which the team works (e.g., the hospital, nursing home, or specific areas within them). These formal and informal interactions and the resulting feedback impact the team's goals, activities, and outcomes.

Developers conceptualized the team as a small, face-to-face primary group that functions as a system much like the family.

Description of Measure

The FAD and MFADT assess areas of healthy and unhealthy group functioning in families and teams, respectively. Their results provide feedback to help plan interventions and educational programs that are group specific. The FAD can be used for research and consultation; it can pinpoint areas of functioning to be evaluated before and after interventions to determine training effectiveness and changes in the system. Group members complete these instruments individually.

Components of Team Performance Measured

The 60-item FAD measures seven aspects of family functioning–problem solving, communication, roles, affective responsiveness, affective involvement, behavior control, and general family functioning. The 54-item MFADT assesses the same aspects in team settings; each aspect is a subscale. Problem Solving (six items) refers to the team's abilities to resolve problems within and outside the team at a level that maintains effective functioning. Communication (nine items) refers to whether communication in the team is clear and direct or indirect and vague. The Roles Subscale (nine items) addresses the extent to which teams have established patterns of behavior for handling their tasks. Affective Responsiveness (six items) refers to ability of members to respond to a range of situations with the appropriate quality and quantity of emotion. Affective Involvement (seven items) addresses the degree to which members are involved/interested in the activities of other members. Behavior Control (five items) refers to ways a team expresses and maintains standards of behavior for members. Finally, General Functioning (12 items) measures overall health of the team.

The adapted instrument addresses all four domains and five of the eight dimensions (team structure and context, interdependence, growth and development, and accomplishments) of our team performance model.

Formatting and Scoring

Items in the FAD and MFADT are single statements describing group functioning. For both instruments, the respondent rates the level of agreement with each item–strongly agree, agree, disagree, or strongly disagree–by checking the appropriate box to the right of the statement.

Waite and Harker modified the original FAD items as follows: (a) unmodified (30 items or 50%); (b) minor modifications (14 items or 23%); (c) adapted with greater modification (8 items or 13%); and (d) omitted or substituted (8 items or 13%). Unmodified statements from the FAD apply directly to teams in the MFADT, (e.g., "In times of crisis, we can turn to each other for support."). Statements needing only minor modifications ("family" replaced by "team") were easily adapted. Additional items from the FAD were adapted with greater modification (e.g., "You can easily get away with breaking the rules." became "You can easily get away with not coming to meetings."). Other items were substituted (e.g., We are reluctant to show our affection for each other." in the FAD became, "We are reluctant to express innovative ideas." in the MFADT). An example of an omitted item is: "We have rules about hitting people."

On a separate scoring sheet, items describing unhealthy functioning are reversed coded by subtracting their score from five. The responses for each subscale are summed and then divided by the number of items in the subscale to provide seven subscale scores, each having a positive range from 1 (healthy) to 4 (unhealthy). Team scores are obtained by averaging the sum of individual team member's subscale scores. The lower the score, the better functioning the team.

Psychometric Testing

Internal Consistency Reliability

Through successive iterations of intercorrelating items, subscales of the FAD were developed so that each subscale had a minimum Cronbach's alpha of .70.

The MFADT was administered to members of three interdisciplinary nursing homes teams (N = 27) in two VA hospitals. Cronbach's alphas were: Problem Solving, .67; Communication, .60; Roles, .74; Affective Responsiveness, .71; Affective Involvement, .68; Behavior Control, .47; and General Functioning, .84.

Test-Retest Reliability

Developers administered the FAD to 45 non-clinical individuals and readministered it to the same individuals one week later. The test-retest correlations for the FAD were problem solving .66, communication .72, roles .75, affective responsiveness .76, affective involvement .67, behavior control .73, and general functioning .71 (Miller, Epstein, Bishop, & Keitner, 1985). This type of reliability has not been determined for the MFADT.

Inter-Rater Reliability

This type of reliability testing is not applicable.

Content or Face Validity

No data are available.

Concurrent Validity

The FAD was compared to the Locke Wallace Marital Satisfaction Scale (Kabacoff, Miller, Bishop, Epstein, & Keitner, 1990). It predicted 27% (R^2 = .53) of the variance in the Marital Satisfaction Scale; this indicated the two instrument are measuring related phenomena.

Miller and colleagues (1985) correlated the FAD's subscales with the Family Unit Inventory, another measure of family functioning. Correlations above .50 for five of the seven subscales–Problem Solving, Communication, Affective Responsiveness, Affective Involvement, and General Functioning–support the FAD's concurrent validity. They also compared the FAD scores of 42 families with an experienced family therapist's clinical ratings. Families rated by the therapist as unhealthy had significantly higher FAD scores (poorer functioning) for every dimension except behavior control. These analyses support a relationship between clinical ratings of healthy and unhealthy families and six of the seven FAD subscales.

The MFADT subscales were correlated with a measure of team effectiveness developed by Norman–an adaptation of McGregor's Analyzing Team

Effectiveness, reviewed later in this chapter. Five of the seven MFADT subscales correlated significantly with this measure.

Construct Validity

Using the FAD, Epstein and colleagues predicted 22% ($R^2 = .47$) of the variance in morale, measured by Lawton's Philadelphia Geriatric Morale Scale, for one set of respondents and 17% ($R^2 = .41$) of the variance of another set of respondents (Kabacoff et al., 1990).

Predictive/Discriminant Validity

No data are available for these types of validity.

Evaluation

The MFADT is easy to complete, score, and interpret. It measures a broad range of team functioning elements and can help identify areas for intervention and improvement. While research shows the FAD is a reliable and valid measure, the MFADT is a new instrument and has not been thoroughly tested. It has been used only once as a pre- and posttest measure in a team study examining the impact of diversity training in interdisciplinary teams. Team members completed the questionnaire in approximately 15-20 minutes and did not raise questions about the instructions or the wording of items.

Minor revision of items and subscales would enhance the conceptual soundness of these measures as there is potential for response biases in two of the FAD and MFADT subscales. The Problem Solving Subscale consists of all positively worded items, and all items in the Affective Involvement Subscale are negatively worded. This may encourage "yea-saying" and "nay-saying" biases.

For the MFADT specifically, the Behavior Control Subscale might be more appropriately named "rules and procedures;" the General Functioning Subscale does not have a clear conceptual definition and contains items that seem relevant to the other subscales. In the Problem Solving Subscale, one of the six items refers to problem solving on the unit; it could be reworded to apply more generally to teams working in inpatient and outpatient settings as well as nonclinical teams. Several of its subscales could be streamlined since some of the items are redundant within and across subscales. Additionally, a number of the items seem more appropriate for groups where members have closer personal relationships than found in some clinical teams (e.g. support groups). Additional psychometric testing would facilitate establishing it as an evaluation tool.

Status/Availability

The copyrighted FAD must be purchased. For information regarding fees, contact Christine E. Ryan, Ph.D., Director, Brown University Family Research Program, Butler Hospital, 345 Blackstone Blvd., Providence, RI 02906. For information about the MFADT, contact Martha S. Waite at (818) 895-9311 or e-mail, marti.waite@med.va.gov. She would appreciate receiving reliability and validity data or a copy of the raw data from individuals using the MFADT.

Relevant Publications

Epstein, N.B., Baldwin, L.M., & Bishop, D.S. (1983). The McMaster Family Assessment Device. *Journal of Marital and Family Therapy, 9*, 171-180.

Kabacoff, R.I., Miller, J.W., Bishop, D.S., Epstein, N.B., & Keitner, G.I. (1990). A psychometric study of the McMaster Family Assessment Device in psychiatric, medical, and non-clinical samples. *Journal of Family Psychology, 3*, 203-208.

Miller, I.W., Epstein, N.B., Bishop, D.S., & Keitner, G.I. (1985). The McMaster Family Assessment Device: Reliability and validity. *Journal of Marital and Family Therapy, 11*, 345-356.

TRUST, OPENNESS, REALIZATION AND INTERDEPENDENCE (TORI) GROUP SELF-DIAGNOSIS SCALE

Developed by Jack R. Gibb, 1977
Reviewed by Sara A. Brallier and D. Erik Everhart

The TORI Group Self-Diagnosis Scale includes 96-items measuring the four facets of trust in its name. Using eight 12-item subscales, each of the four facets is measured at both the individual and group level. Gibb conceptualizes trust as part of the group development process, with the more developed groups having higher levels of trust. The instrument can be used to assess group development, and individual behaviors and feelings can be compared to perceptions of group norms. Gibb states that it also can be used as a pre/post test following an educational intervention; however, no test-retest reliability data are available for it. Based on a strong conceptual framework, the instrument is long, and some items include complex and unclear wording. It requires some revision to improve conceptual soundness, reduce redundancy of items, and for use with health care teams. It would benefit from psychometric testing as well.

Conceptual Framework

TORI's theory focuses on trust level as a key determinant of group effectiveness and productivity. Groups that have high levels of trust and whose members are accepting of one another are healthy and productive. TORI is an acronym for the four facets of trust that influence group development. The trust component focuses on trust and acceptance of other members. Members of teams with low levels of trust or acceptance are concerned with their adequacy as members and lack clear definition of their respective roles on the team. They may strive either to conform or to seek status within the team. As it develops and trust is established, the team becomes more supportive of its members, and they, in turn, become more willing to take risks and become more tolerant of diversity and nonconformity.

Openness refers to the flow of information within the team and the team's decision-making abilities. Teams in the early stages of development are often cautious, and communication is ambiguous or guarded. As the team develops, communication is clearer, more direct, and open. Members listen, share, and provide feedback to one another. Realization refers to consensual goal setting and goal-directed movement. Members of teams in the early stages of development often compete with one another or are apathetic and withdrawn. They lack self-motivation and are overly conforming to the team's expectations. In later stages of development, goals are shared, and team members are more involved, creative, cooperative, and enthusiastic. Finally, interdependence focuses on leadership, power, and structures that can be developed into more flexible forms. Teams in earlier stages of development are inflexible and rigid, counter-dependent, and adhere to formal rules. Teams in later stages are more informal and flexible. Members feel a sense of belonging, enjoy working and being with one another, and share leadership and power.

Each team is a unique organism. The team has its own "being and essence" since the whole is more than the sum of the parts. Additionally, the team is a small group that becomes more trusting over time, and trust is a key component to improved development.

Description of Measure

Teams can use the measure to assess group development or members' perceptions of group climate, to compare behaviors and feelings with group norms, or as a pre/post test. Team members complete the instrument individually. A group average is calculated and used to describe perceived trust and team climate within the team as a whole. Individual scores can be compared to group averages to identify discrepancies in perceived trust or team climate among members.

Components of Team Performance Measured

Eight 12-item subscales measure the four facets of trust at both the individual and group/team level. The Trust Subscales measure trust or self-acceptance at the individual level and the existence of a trusting environment at the group level. The Openness Subscales measure how free individuals are about expressing their attitudes and feelings. At the group level, openness is a measure of how open the group is to the expression of opinions and feelings, especially negative ones. The Realization Subscales measure how willing the individual is to take risks or be assertive. At the group level, the subscale measures how much freedom the group tolerates and how effectively it focuses on emergent and intrinsic goals. The Self-Interdependence Subscale measures the individual level of commitment to the group and its goals. At the group level, the subscale measures how effectively the group encourages conformity to its goals.

The instrument measures all four domains and five of the eight dimensions (team structure and context, interdependence, growth and development, and accomplishments) of our team performance model.

Formatting and Scoring

The scale contains 96 positively and negatively worded statements measuring levels of trust among individual group members and within the group as a whole. The items are Likert formatted. For each item, there are four answer choices ranging from strongly agree to strongly disagree (see item example below). Respondents write the appropriate letter or letters on the blank to the left of each item or statement.

      SD = strongly disagree   D = disagree   A = agree   SA = strongly agree

      _____   35. It is easy for me to take risks in this group.

In J.E. Jones & J.W. Pfeiffer (Eds.), *The 1977 annual handbook for group facilitators* ©1977. Reprinted by permission of Jossey-Bass, Inc., a subsidiary of John Wiley & Sons, Inc.

Gibb provides a template to assist with converting responses to numeric scores and reverse coding the negatively worded items and assigning items to their respective subscales. For each item, strongly agree = 3, agree = 2, disagree = 1, and strongly disagree = 0. Each subscale has a potential range from 0 to 36;

a high score indicates a positive perception of the construct being measured. Group averages also can be calculated for each subscale.

Psychometric Testing

No reliability or validity data are available.

Evaluation

This instrument measures two important components of team development–level of trust among group members and the extent to which the group climate is a trusting one. A unique feature is its measurement of both the perceptions of members' own feelings and behaviors and of the group's norms and behaviors related to trust. It has a strong theoretical underpinning; however, the reviewers believe that Gibb overemphasizes the importance of trust, to the exclusion of other important components of group development (e.g., managerial support, development of a team mission, goals, and objectives, etc.). Moreover, many of the items in the instrument measure components of development beyond trust. For example, some items measure goal setting and growth and development of team members. The instrument is especially appropriate for teams having difficulty developing trust and for new teams where trust has not developed yet.

Gibb did not design the instrument for health care teams or other types of work groups. It seems more appropriate for use with families or therapy and support groups. For example, many of the items (e.g., item 74) address levels of intimacy and expressions of personal feelings than are inappropriate for a work setting and/or teams in health care settings. Additionally, Gibb defines "role-playing" as a negative aspect of trust, (i.e., adhering to one's role out of fear instead of trusting one's self). This limited definition of the concept could be confusing to respondents since it also is defined as carrying our one's role effectively; for example, He played his role well.

The instrument has some conceptual and methodological problems. Items measuring Gibb's four facets of trust are not always conceptually distinct from one another. Redundancy also is a problem within subscales. For example, items 27 and 67 measure the same thing regarding goals; one item is merely the reverse of the other. Finally, some items contain colloquialisms that could be misinterpreted. Item 16, This groups really "has it together at a deep level," and item 61, It is easy to tell who the "in" people are in this group, provide prime examples. Test-retest reliability should be determined before using the instrument as a pre- posttest measure.

Status/Availability

This instrument is copyrighted. There is no fee for using it. It appears in the Gibb (1977) publication below. To purchase the publication, contact Pfeiffer & Company at (800) 274-4434.

Relevant Publications

Gibb, J.R. (1977). TORI Group Self-Diagnosis Scale. In J.E. Jones & J.W. Pfeiffer (Eds.), *The 1977 annual handbook for group facilitators* (pp. 73-81). San Diego, CA: Pfeiffer & Company.

Gibb, J.R. (1991). *Trust.* North Hollywood, CA: New Castle Publishing, Co., Inc.

TEAM-EFFECTIVENESS INVENTORY

Developed by Victoria A. Hoevemeyer, 1992
Reviewed by Stephanie B. Hoffman and Sara A. Brallier

The Team-Effectiveness Inventory, a 20-item measure of team effectiveness, includes five areas–team mission; goal achievement; empowerment; open, honest communication; and positive roles and norms–each with four items. The developer designed the instrument to compare members' and leaders' perceptions and to facilitate their coming to consensus about the team and what requires improvement. She recommends an item analysis within each of the five areas of team effectiveness and a total score comparison. The instrument seems conceptually sound and is easy to administer. The items are easy to read, and a template is provided for scoring. No reliability or validity data are available.

Conceptual Framework

Hoevemeyer used an atheoretical approach in developing this instrument. Through her experience as an organizational development consultant, she determined those factors most influential to a team's success. She stresses that team development is a continuous process and that measuring and monitoring performance is an important component of team development. She also emphasizes the importance of consensus between the team leader and members' perceptions regarding fulfilling customers' expectations, team processes, and empowerment of members. Employees on effective teams are more likely to be self-directed, have higher levels of morale and productivity, provide more timely and appropriate customer service, and value interdependence as a way of accomplishing tasks.

The developer views the team is an organizational work group with potential for improvement over time.

Description of Measure

Hoevemeyer designed the instrument to assess perceived team effectiveness by members and the leader. If differences exist regarding their perceptions, the instrument can be used as a springboard for discussion to improve consensus. Individual team members and leader(s) complete the instrument. Individual scores are averaged for each item and compared to the leader's scores.

Components of Team Performance Measured

The inventory measures five areas of team effectiveness: mission; goal achievement; empowerment; open, honest communication; and positive roles and norms.

The instrument includes items in three of the four the domains and six of the eight dimensions (i.e., organizational and team structure, organizational and team context, interdependence, and growth and development) of our model of team performance.

Formatting and Scoring

All 20 items are written in a positive direction. Respondents circle the one answer choice that matches their perceptions of the team on a five-point, Likert-formatted continuum from strongly agree = 5 to strongly disagree = 1 (see item example below).

5 = strongly agree, **4** = agree, **3** = neutral, **2** = disagree, and **1** = strongly disagree.

11. The team understands how it fits into the organization.   5   4   3   2   1

In Hoevemeyer, V.A. How effective is your team? *Training and Development, 47* ©1993. Reprinted by permission of the developer.

Each of the five areas includes four items. Within each area, members' scores for each item are averaged and compared to the leader's score (an item analysis). Total scores for members and leaders are summed and compared as well. Consensus ratings also are recorded between members' average scores and the leader's scores.

Psychometric Testing

No reliability or validity data are available.

Evaluation

The instrument is brief, straightforward, and easy to score. The accompanying scoring sheet facilitates the scoring process. Most of the items are clearly stated, and several of them address the team within a complex organization. The information generated from it could aid in conflict resolution between members and the leader as well as ensure that they are in agreement regarding their perceptions of the team's effectiveness. The instrument lacks strong theoretical underpinnings. There is no stated rationale for inclusion of certain areas of team performance rather than others; however, all five appear relevant to team effectiveness within a complex organization. Given that all items are positively worded, there is the potential for response bias. It would benefit from psychometric testing. Without psychometric data, we do not know if items are additive for a total score. Without test-retest reliability, we do not know if the instrument is appropriate for tracking effectiveness over time. It also would be interesting to know if the items within each content area can be scaled.

The definition of goals is too general for clinical health care teams, whose goals are defined more specifically than meeting customers' expectations; however, the instrument itself is quite appropriate for other work groups in health care settings. It does not require a consultant to assist with administration.

Status/Availability

The instrument and scoring template appear in the article referenced below. Hoevemeyer holds the instrument's copyright. A single reprint of the article may be obtained from the American Society of Training and Development (ASTD) for a fee. Contact ASTD Customer Support, 1640 King Street, Box 1443, Alexandria VA 22313-2043, (703) 683-9203.

Relevant Publications

Hoevemeyer, V.A. (1993). How effective is your team? *Training and Development, 47*, (September), 67-71.

GROUP DEVELOPMENT ASSESSMENT (GDA)*

Developed by John E. Jones and William L. Bearley, 1973, 1993
Reviewed by Glenda F. Brown and Martha S. Waite

The 40-item GDA identifies a group's current level of development along two dimensions–task behaviors and process behaviors. It serves as a diagnostic tool to help managers, leaders, consultants, and group facilitators determine how to improve group functioning. Action planning guides, accompanying the instrument, facilitate the development of the group into a productive team. The instrument is unique in its approach to identifying the stages of team development. It is most appropriate for professionals given its sophisticated language. It is long, and there are numerous steps to scoring, but the guidelines are clear and well written. The GDA has potential as a research tool pending adequate psychometric testing.

Conceptual Framework

The GDA is based on group development theory as outlined by Jones (1973, 1974) and Tuckman (1965). The group goes through predictable stages of growth as a result of interaction along two behavioral dimensions–task (i.e., how the work gets done) and process (i.e., personal/interpersonal behavior) behaviors. Each of the two types of behavior includes four developmental phases. For task behavior, the phases are orientation, organization, open data flow, and problem solving. For process behavior, they are dependency, conflict, cohesion, and interdependence. In order for a group to achieve optimal functioning, its members must engage simultaneously in consistently high levels of both types of behaviors (i.e., functioning at the problem solving and interdependence phases). If the group develops at the same rate in both behavioral dimensions, it moves through the four stages in a linear fashion from an immature group to a fractionated group, then a sharing group, and finally an effective team (stage four). Often, however, the group develops at different rates with regard to task and process behaviors. This results in what Jones refers to as "off diagonal" groups–six in which process behaviors are emphasized at the expense of task behaviors (above the diagonal) and six in which task behaviors are emphasized at the expense of process behaviors (below the diagonal). Once optimal functioning is achieved (stage four), the team must continue to work to maintain this level of development.

Developers view the team as a group of individuals who come together to perform specific tasks. The team goes through predictable, developmental phases with regard to its task and process behaviors as it moves from immature to well functioning.

Description of Measure

Developers designed the measure to help determine how to improve group functioning. More specific purposes include: (a) assessing how group members perceive the functioning of the group; (b) improving team performance and productivity through action planning; (c) acting as a learning exercise for group leaders; (d) guiding appropriate group leadership behavior; and (e) providing a mechanism for diagnosing level of functioning for use in team building. Individual group members complete the instrument. Their scores are used to identify their perceptions of the team's phases and stage of development and to create an overall team profile.

Components of Team Performance Measured

The instrument assesses both task and process behaviors. Each type includes four developmental phases. For task behavior, the phases measured are orientation, organization, open data flow, and problem solving. For process behavior, the phases are dependency, conflict, cohesion, and interdependence. Each of the eight phases is measured by five items.

The instrument includes items in four domains and six dimensions (organizational and team structure, team context, interdependence, growth and development, and strategies for productivity) of our model of team performance. It is unique in its measurement of both task and process behaviors. It also considers the intersection of these behavioral phases in identifying a team's stages of development.

Formatting and Scoring

The 40-item instrument includes eight developmental phases, each made up of five items. For each item, respondents circle the answer choice that best represents their perception of their group. Answer choices include DT or 1 = definitely true; T or 2 = true; TTT or 3 = tends to be true; TNT or 4 = tends not to be true; NT or 5 = not true; and DNT or 6 = definitely not true. Respondents record their answers on a response/scoring form provided with the instrument.

Respondents sum the five items for each of the eight developmental phases; scores can range from 5 to 30 for each. The scoring system permits them to organize their results into eight phases–four for the phases of task behavior and four for the phases of process behavior. Respondents, then, identify the phases in which they perceive their team at the present time (i.e., the highest score for task and the highest score for process). Finally, each respondent helps develop a group profile by initialing the cell in a four-by-four matrix box that corresponds to the intersection of his/her two highest scores. They discuss results, look for clusters of agreement, and try to come to consensus regarding the level of their group's development. Provided charts facilitate this process.

Psychometric Testing

Internal Consistency Reliability

Alpha coefficients for the GDA average 0.65. It is not clear on which items the alphas were calculated or how they were averaged (i.e., across alphas within one sample of respondents or across several samples). No intercorrelation of items or factor analysis are available to determine if the five items for each phase of development are related to one another or load on the same factor.

Test-Retest/Inter-Rater Reliability

No data are available regarding test-retest reliability, and testing for inter-rater reliability is inappropriate since the measure is self-administered.

Validity

No validity data are available. The GDA is based on a long-standing theory of group development and has undergone numerous iterations between 1973, when it was first published, and 1993. The item wording, scoring scheme, and interpretive materials were refined based on feedback obtained from work groups in a variety of organizational settings and training sessions. The face validity appears high although, no formal validity studies have been conducted.

Evaluation

The GDA has strong theoretical underpinnings. Its items include a considerable number of complex words, which limits its usefulness for work groups made up of nonprofessionals. For professionals, it is relatively easy to complete although a bit long. Scoring involves a number of steps; however, the instrument is accompanied by a well-designed facilitator's guide, scoring sheets, and charts. It's strength lies in inclusion of both task and process behaviors as a part of developing and improving team functioning. Additionally, it expands the traditional concept of group development by depicting 12 "off diagonal" stages in addition to the traditional four stages. This adds to the predictive value of the instrument in diagnosing stages of development and assists in determining appropriate interventions that facilitate improving team functioning. Its results also facilitate discussion about the team's level of development and action planning for improving it. The instrument lacks sufficient psychometric testing for use as a research tool, although it may have potential in this area.

Status/Availability

The instrument is copyrighted and published by Organization Design and Development, Inc. under an exclusive license from the copyright owners. Purchased through the HRDQ Company, King of Prussia, Pennsylvania, the GDA is packaged as a complete tool for facilitating the development of groups into teams. The Inventory, the Response/Scoring Form, Interpretive Guide, Group Profile, and Action Planning Guide are contained in a single booklet. Developers recommend that this booklet be purchased and available to all group members. A "facilitator's guide" also is available for purchase. To purchase materials, contact HRDQ at (610) 270-2002 or hrdq@hrdq.com.

Relevant Publications

Jones, J.E. (1973). A model of group development. In J.E. Jones & J.W. Pfeiffer (Eds.), *The 1973 annual handbook for group facilitators.* San Diego, CA: University Associates.

Jones, J.E. (1974). Group development: A graphic analysis. In J.W. Pfeiffer & J.E. Jones (Eds.), *A handbook of structured experiences for human relations training, Vol. II.* San Diego, CA: University Associates.

Jones, J.E., & Bearley, W.L. (1993). *Group Development Assessment.* King of Prussia, PA: Organizational Design and Development, Inc.

Jones, J.E., & Bearley, W.L. (1994). *Group Development Assessment: Facilitator guide.* King of Prussia, PA: Organizational Design and Development, Inc.

Tuckman, B.W. (1965). Development sequence in small groups. *Psychological Bulletin, 63,* 384-399.

WORK GROUP FUNCTIONING MODULE

Developed by E. Lawler III, C. Cammann, D. Nadler, and D. Jenkins, 1975
Reviewed by Stephanie B. Hoffman and Sara A. Brallier

The Work Group Functioning Module (4) is part of a larger organizational assessment instrument, the Michigan Organizational Assessment Questionnaire (MOAQ). The Module contains 14 items which are divided into five subscales–Group Homogeneity, Clarity of the Work Group's Goals, Group Cohesiveness, Open Group Process, and Internal Fragmentation. It is unique in that it can be used both independently and in conjunction with the other five modules of the MOAQ to assess team and organizational functioning. Psychometric testing suggests that the instrument has moderate construct validity; however, the assignment of items to their respective subscales was not supported by a factor analysis.

Conceptual Framework

The instrument is based on a model, developed by Hackman and Oldham (1976), which purports that employees' reactions to their work environment are influenced primarily by four factors. The first factor includes descriptors of critical aspects of the work environment, such as job characteristics, role characteristics, supervision, work group characteristics, pay system, decision-making, and influence. The second factor encompasses psychological states that affect the work environment, such as job challenge, job involvement, organizational involvement, and beliefs that rewards are contingent upon performance. The third factor includes individual-level outcomes or responses that are commonly valued by organizational members such as employee turnover, job effort, motivation, and satisfaction with job and rewards. The last factor addresses individual differences (e.g., demographic characteristics, preferences, personality, and importance of aspects of the job). In this theoretical framework, the work group or team is an important component of the work environment. The characteristics of the work group to which an employee belongs affect his or her perceptions of and feelings about the organization and work-related behavior.

Work groups are composed of employees who share the same work area, report to the same supervisor, and perform tasks that are similar or related.

Description of Measure

The developers designed the MOAQ as an organizational assessment instrument appropriate for use in a variety of organizational contexts with employees who have diverse characteristics and work in a wide range of situations. The six modules making up the instrument can be used together or independently. Apart from work group functioning, they assess: (a) employees' general attitudes toward the organization and their jobs; (b) job facets which measures employees' perception of a variety of potential job rewards; (c) task, job, and role characteristics; (d) supervision; and (e) pay, administration, and determination. The Work Group Functioning Module assesses the perceived level of functioning of work groups within complex organizations. Individual members of a work group complete the instrument. Team averages can be calculated and compared.

Components of Team Performance Measured

Developers grouped the 14 items of the instrument into five subscales measuring facets of work group performance. Items are assigned to subscales as follows: Group Homogeneity (items 4 and 8); Group Goal Clarity (items 2 and 6); Group Cohesiveness (items 1 and 11); Open Group Process (items 5, 7, 9, and 13); and Internal Fragmentation (items 3, 10, 12, and 14).

This instrument includes items in three of the four domains and five of the eight dimensions (organizational and team structure, team context, interdependence, and growth and development) of our team performance model.

Formatting and Scoring

The developers utilize a seven-point Likert rating format for each of the 14 items in this module such that 1 = strongly disagree, 2 = disagree, 3 = slightly disagree, 4 = neutral, 5 = slightly agree, 6 = agree, and 7 = strongly agree. These verbal anchors appear at the top of each page above the numeric answer choices in the instrument. Respondents circle the appropriate answer code for each item.

Item responses are averaged for each subscale. The Group Homogeneity, Goal Clarity, and Group Cohesiveness Subscale scores range from 2 to 14; Open Group Process and Internal Fragmentation Subscale scores range from 4 to 28. Prior to summing the items in the Open Group Process Subscale, item 5 must be reverse coded. The higher the score, the stronger is the perception of the construct being measured for each of the five subscales. Subscales can be averaged for work group comparisons.

Psychometric Testing

Internal Consistency Reliability

Based on a sample of 400 respondents, Cronbach's alpha coefficients for each of the five subscales are as follows: Group Homogeneity (.62), Group Goal clarity (.61), Group Cohesiveness (.64), Open Group Process (.72), and Internal Fragmentation (.79).

A factor analysis offered only partial support for the placement of the items into the five subscales. The two group homogeneity items loaded as a distinct factor. The group goal clarity items and group cohesiveness items and several of the open group process items loaded on a second factor. Finally, all of the internal fragmentation items loaded on a third factor along with two of the open group process items. (See evaluation for further discussion).

Test-Retest/Inter-Rater Reliability

No data are available regarding test-retest reliability, and testing for inter-rater reliability is inappropriate since the measure is self-administered.

Content or Face Validity

Based on an extensive review of relevant empirical and theoretical literature, the designers of the MOAQ generated an extensive list of potential items. Experts reviewed the potential items and discarded irrelevant, redundant, overly complex, or ambiguous ones. The final MOAQ results from at least two revisions based on the comments of experts and psychometric testing.

Concurrent Validity

No data are available.

Construct Validity

The subscales correlated as theoretically anticipated with a number of subscales from other modules of the MOAQ. Group Homogeneity is positively correlated with measures of job satisfaction ($r = .13$, $p<.01$) and job involvement ($r = .12$, $p<.05$). Group Goal Clarity is positively correlated with measures of job satisfaction ($r = .37$, $p<.001$), job involvement ($r = 22$, $p<.001$), social reward satisfaction ($r = .31$, $p<.001$), job challenge ($r = .15$, $p<.001$) and negatively correlated with measures of intention to turnover ($r = -.23$, $p<.001$) and role conflict ($r = -.28$, $p<.001$). Group Cohesiveness is correlated positively with measures of job satisfaction ($r = .48$, $p<.001$), job involvement ($r = .31$, $p<.001$), social reward satisfaction ($r = .58$, $p<.001$), and job challenge ($r = .48$, $p<.001$) and correlated negatively with measures of turnover ($r = -.31$, $p<.001$) and role conflict ($r = -.11$, $p<.05$). The Open Group Process Subscale is positively correlated with measures of job satisfaction ($r = .43$, $p<.001$), job involvement ($r = .24$, $p<.001$), social reward satisfaction ($r = .47$, $p<.001$), and job challenge ($r = .33$, $p<.001$); it is negatively correlated with measures of turnover ($r = -.31$, $p<.001$) and role conflict ($r = -.14$, $p<.01$). Internal Fragmentation is positively correlated with turnover ($r = .29$, $p<.001$) and role conflict ($r = .31$, $p<.001$) and negatively correlated with job satisfaction ($r = -.37$, $p<.001$), job involvement ($r = -.11$, $p<.05$), social reward satisfaction ($r = -.56$, $p<.001$), and job challenge ($r = -.18$, $p<.001$).

Predictive/Discriminant Validity

No data are available for these types of validity.

Evaluation

The Work Group Functioning Module is easy to complete and score and has strong theoretical underpinnings. It is unique in that it is part of a larger instrument measuring organizational performance. It can be used independently or in conjunction with the other five modules of the MOAQ.

The results of the factor analysis supported only one of the subscales, Group Homogeneity, set forth by the developers. They viewed homogeneity among group members as a positive facet of group functioning; however, most of the literature on teams acknowledges the importance of diversity among members for quality team performance. Additionally, the items in this subscale are worded and scored such that it is actually measuring group diversity rather than homogeneity. Thus, the subscale is misnamed and should be expanded to include more than two items.

The majority of the items making up the Group Goal Clarity, Group Cohesiveness and Open Group Process loaded together on a second factor that seems to measure members' preparedness and participation. The "internal fragmentation" items loaded on yet another factor, along with two of the "open group process" items, which do not have face validity here. We do not recommend using the original subscales in research. We suggest further revision of items and additional testing for internal consistency.

The alpha coefficients are acceptable, but not strong. The developers did go to considerable lengths to establish content and construct validity.

Status/Availability

The instrument appears on page 132 of the 1983 edited volume below. Contact John Wiley & Sons, Customer Service Center, 1 Wiley Drive, Somerset, NJ 08875-1272; (800) 225-5945 or e-mail, custserv@wiley.com.

Relevant Publications

Cammann, C., Fichman, M., Jenkins, G.D., & Klesh, J. (1983). Assessing the attitudes and perceptions of organizational members. In S.E. Seashore, E.E. Lawler III, P.H. Mirvis, & C. Cammann (Eds.), *Assessing organizational change*. New York: John Wiley & Sons.

Cook, J.D., Hepworth, S.J., Wall, T.D., & Warr, P.B (1981). *The experience of work: A compendium, and review of 249 measures and their use*. New York: Academic Press.

Hackman, J.R., & Oldham, G. (1976). Motivation through the design of work: Test of a theory. *Organizational Behavior and Human Performance, 16,* 250-279.

TEAM EXCELLENCE QUESTIONNAIRE

Developed by Richard G. Lazar, 1971
Reviewed by Glenda F. Brown and Gloria D. Heinemann

Lazar developed the Team Excellence Questionnaire for use by experienced consultants to help teams identify their strengths and weaknesses with regard to performance. The 10-item instrument is an appropriate consultation devise; consultants are encouraged to help team members and their managers develop action plans based upon scoring results. A unique strength of the instrument is the collection of team members' perceptions regarding how things are now in the team and how they ought to be. It has no theoretical underpinnings, has not been subjected to reliability and validity testing, and is not appropriate for use in research.

Conceptual Framework

Lazar designed the instrument for consultation; no theoretical framework is identified. Team consultation is sought when team performance is threatened; team-building efforts focus on interventions believed to enhance performance.

The team is a work group with a leader and a manager. It is not clear whether the manager is the team leader or a supervisor outside the team.

Description of Measure

Lazar designed the instrument to help team members and leaders/managers understand their current level of performance in comparison to where they think it ought to be. According to Lazar, data collected via this instrument provide a "snapshot-in-time" of the team. Consultants use the instrument to help teams identify strengths and weaknesses, identify need/desire to improve, and plan to improve performance. Individual team members complete the instrument.

Components of Team Performance Measured

The instrument measures 10 facets of team excellence or performance: (a) victory, the team's commitment to a common goal; (b) open information, information sharing; (c) belonging, feelings that team members can count on one another; (d) payoff, greater payoff to you when the team wins as opposed to competing with the team or its members; (e) healthy competition, members compete with themselves to improve; (f) shared success, how you feel when another team member is successful; (g) trust and confidence in the leader; (h) risk-taking; (i) team morale and spirit; and (j) teamwork, teamwork endures even when the leader is not around. One item measures each of these 10 facets. Each team member responds twice (i.e., feelings about how things are now and how they should be) to each item. Thus, the instrument collects information about actual and ideal perceptions of the team.

It includes three of the four domains (structure, context, and process) and five of the eight dimensions (team structure and context, interdependence, growth and development, and accomplishments) of our team performance model.

Formatting and Scoring

The instrument includes 10 positively worded items; answer choices for each range from 1 to 7 along a continuum such that 1 indicates perceptions of weak performance and 7 indicates perceptions of strong performance. Respondents indicate the response that best fits their feelings about each statement under two different situations: How strong is this feeling now? How strong do you think this feeling should be? (See the formatting example in the following critique of Brown's adaptation of two of Lazar's instruments.)

Team members' responses are averaged for both actual and ideal perceptions for each item. An individual member's responses can be compared to the team's average for a particular item, and team averages for actual and ideal perceptions can be compared within and across items (an item analysis).

A delta score (i.e., the difference between perception of group productivity currently and what the group believes their productivity should be) is calculated for each item. It indicates whether or not the group is comfortable with the status quo (low score) or aspiring to a greater standard (high score). Items with either a mean score lower than 4 or a delta score greater than 2 require close scrutiny because they indicate need or desire for improvement.

Psychometric Testing

No reliability or validity data are available.

Evaluation

The instrument provides a consultant with a relatively quick appraisal of a team, as members perceive it and as they believe it ought to be. Using the instrument, a consultant can help teams identify their strengths and weaknesses and develop plans to improve their productivity. A unique strength of the instrument is its ability to distinguish between team members' perceptions of actual and ideal team performance. Weaknesses include: (a) the increased chance of response bias given that all items are worded positively; (b) the use of the term "feeling" in the items when the term "perception" might be clearer to respondents; and (c) the lack of verbal cues at the extreme ends of the continuum of answer choices. The instrument is not theory based; it would benefit from reliability and validity testing. It should not be used for research purposes.

Status/Availability

Permission to use this copyrighted instrument must be obtained from The Lazar Group, Inc., 3043 Moore Avenue, Lawrenceville, GA 30244, (770) 979-9618.

Relevant Publications

Lazar, R.G. (1971). Team Excellence Questionnaire. Lawrenceville, GA: Management Skills International.

FACTORS INFLUENCING PRODUCTIVITY AND EXCELLENCE OF TEAM WORK

Developed Richard G. Lazar; adapted for health care teams by Glenda F. Brown, 1993
Reviewed by Glenda F. Brown and Gloria D. Heinemann

Lazar's Team Excellence Questionnaire and Personal Productivity and Excellence Potential Survey are instruments designed for consultants to assist teams and organizational employees, respectively, in identifying their strengths and weaknesses with regard to productivity. Brown used items from both instruments to design a 30-item measure of performance for teams located within an organization, where both internal and external factors impinge upon performance/productivity. The adapted instrument permits a consultant to quickly pinpoint strengths and weaknesses of a team and work with team members to develop a plan for improvement. Lazar's instruments have not been subjected to reliability and validity testing; Brown's adaptation has undergone some initial testing; it would benefit from additional testing. None of these three instruments was designed for research purposes.

Conceptual Framework

Lazar designed his instruments for consultation and educational initiatives with teams; no theoretical framework is identified for them. Brown's adaptation is based on the premise that teams are instruments of organizations that utilize them to complete work and objectives. The perceived productivity of any team and its contribution to the mission of the organization determine its viability within the organization. Consultation usually is sought when team productivity is threatened. Team-building efforts are focused on interventions believed to enhance productivity. The productivity of the team is related to both external and internal factors. The appropriateness of team-building interventions, then, depends upon careful assessment of what is occurring within groups and between the groups and their respective environments.

For Lazar, the team is a work group within an organizational setting; each team is made up of employees of the organization. For Brown, the team is a work group designed to meet the organization's goals.

Description of Measure

Lazar designed the Team Excellence Questionnaire (see previous critique) to assess the perceptions of team members and the leader/manager as to the team's actual and ideal levels of performance. He developed the Personal Productivity and Excellence Potential Survey to measure the extent to which individual employees feel that the organization and its management support their efforts for productivity and pursuit of excellence. Lazar uses both instruments to help teams and employees in organizations improve their productivity and leadership.

With Lazar's permission, Brown combined items from both instruments to create one measure of a team's level of functioning and the level of organizational support given to it. Her measure can be used to assist a consultant in identifying a team's strengths and weaknesses. She notes that it can be used to monitor team functioning over time. Brown used the adapted version with clinical teams in the VA health care system. Team members complete the instrument; their scores are averaged for team scores on each item.

Components of Team Performance Measured

Lazar's Team Excellence Questionnaire measures 10 facets of team performance–the team's commitment to a common goal, information sharing, feelings of belonging, rewards for teamwork, healthy competition within the team, shared success, trust and confidence, risk-taking, team morale and spirit, and teamwork; one item measures each of the 10 facets. Lazar's Personal Productivity and Excellence Potential Survey measures five facets of personal productivity–the environment for change and innovation, rewards and innovation, teamwork and support, forces that foster and/or inhibit productivity and excellence, and the individual's personal potential for productivity and improvement. Brown's adapted instrument measures the relationship between the team and management, the environmental milieu, rewards for teamwork, effective leadership within the team, interpersonal relationships among team members, and structural functional issues (e.g., working toward a common goal, information sharing). In all three instruments, team members indicate their perceptions of performance in the team now and how they believe it should be (i.e., the actual and the ideal).

The adapted instrument includes items in three of the four domains (structure, context, and process) and six of the eight dimensions (organizational and team structure, organizational and team context, interdependence, and growth and development) of our team performance model. Unique items include those measuring communication between management and teams, cost and time pressures, and objective rewards for teamwork.

Formatting and Scoring

Lazar's Team Excellence Questionnaire includes 10 positively worded items; his Personal Productivity and Excellence Potential Survey includes 28 positively and negatively worded items. Brown's adapted instrument is made up of 30 items. She included six items from the Team Excellence Questionnaire and 24 items from the Personal Productivity and Excellence Potential Survey. She modified the language of the items to be more understandable to health professionals and employees working in health care settings. Answer choices for all three instruments use a seven point rating format. Respondents indicate the response that best fits their feelings about each statement under two different situations (see example below). A response of 1 indicates perceptions of weak performance; a response of 7 indicates strong performance. There are no verbal anchors for the answer choices (see item example below).

    4. The feeling you have of trust and confidence in the team leadership
        a. How strong is this feeling now?
           (CIRCLE ONE)   1 2 3 4 5 6 7
        b. How strong do you think this feeling should be?
           (CIRCLE ONE)   1 2 3 4 5 6 7

        Reprinted by permission of adapter.

An item analysis is used to score all three instruments. For each of the 30 items in the adapted instrument, the consultant calculates the team's mean score for the two types of responses (i.e., actual and ideal). A delta score (i.e., the difference between perception of group productivity currently and what the group believes their productivity should be) also is calculated for each item. The delta score indicates whether or not the group is comfortable with the status quo (low score) or aspiring to a greater standard (high score). Items with either a mean score lower than four or a delta score greater than two require close scrutiny because they indicate need or desire for improvement.

In order to determine the strengths and weaknesses of the team, the consultant examines the items with the highest mean scores for how things are now (indicating their perceived strengths) as well as those items with the lowest mean scores (indicating their perceived weaknesses). A comparison of individual scores with the group mean for each item can determine whether a facet of performance is perceived as problematic by only one or two individuals or by majority of team members.

Brown believes that the six themes, identified under "dimensions of teamwork measured," facilitate the consultant's ability to interpret data. Group means can be rank-ordered to determine if there is any clustering of items around particular themes. Delta scores can be rank-ordered to determine if a particular team's desire for improvement coincides with any of these themes.

Psychometric Testing

Lazar's original instruments have undergone no psychometric testing.

Internal Consistency/Inter-Rater Reliability

No data are available for the adapted measure with regard to internal consistency. Testing for inter-rater reliability is not appropriate since the instrument is self-administered.

Test-Retest Reliability

In establishing the test-retest reliability for the adapted instrument, 30 members of interdisciplinary health care teams completed the instrument on two separate occasions at least three weeks apart. The results of a Wilcoxon Rank Sum Test ($p > .58$) indicate that there are no significant differences between the two sets of scores (i.e., responses were consistent across the two administrations of the instrument).

Content or Face Validity

Brown adapted the Lazar instruments to reflect productivity factors as they relate to health care teams functioning within a hospital setting. A panel of experts, actively involved in interdisciplinary team training and consultation with health care teams, responded to the applicability of each item to the measurement of team productivity and excellence. They also reviewed the initial adapted instrument for clarity of instructions and readability. Utilizing comments and suggestions from the experts, Brown reformatted the questionnaire into 54 statements. The experts reviewed each of these items to determine if it had an impact on the productivity and excellence of an interdisciplinary team, whether the impact was positive or negative, and the degree of the impact from one (minimal impact) to seven (maximum impact). The a priori criteria for inclusion of items in the final instrument were: (a) 100% agreement among the experts that the item had an impact on team productivity and excellence; (b) a mean impact score greater than five for single items; and (c) an overall mean impact greater or equal to 5.5. Thirty items met these criteria.

Concurrent/Construct/Predictive/Discriminant Validity

No data are available for these types of validity.

Evaluation

All three instruments are effective consultation tools. Strengths include providing the consultant with a "quick picture" of the team or group with which he/she is working and addressing both actual and ideal perceptions of productivity.

A major strength of the adapted instrument is its emphasis on the team within an organization. By combining the two Lazar instruments, Brown has expanded the dimensions of team performance measured, especially those elements related to organizational structure and context. She has piloted this instrument with teams in numerous VA medical centers. It has proved to be a quick and effective instrument to determine if factors impacting the productivity of a team stem from internal or external forces. It also is an effective stimulus for developing action plans that are within the control of the team to implement. Team members have remarked consistently about the speed and accuracy with which the consultant, using this instrument, has been able to pinpoint issues that are amenable to intervention. Results from its use have provided a springboard for team discussions and have helped identify areas of team performance which require improvement and/or in which the team desires to improve.

The adapted instrument would benefit from further reliability and validity testing and some rewording of items for clarity. The themes identified for this instrument have no empirical basis as no factor analysis or scaling of items has been attempted to date. The instrument is not appropriate as a research tool.

Status/Availability

The Lazar instruments are copyrighted; permission to use them must be obtained from the developer at The Lazar Group, Inc., 3043 Moore Avenue, Lawrenceville, Georgia 30244, (770) 979-9618. Permission to use the adapted instrument must be obtained from Brown. Contact her at (501) 988-1660 or glenda.brown2@med.va.gov.

Relevant Publications

Lazar, R.G. (1971). *Team Excellence Questionnaire*. Lawrenceville, GA: Management Skills International.

Lazar, R.G. (1985). *Personal Productivity and Excellence Potential*. Lawrenceville, GA: Management Skills International.

ANALYZING TEAM EFFECTIVENESS*

Developed by Douglas McGregor, 1967
Reviewed by Gloria D. Heinemann, Evelyn P. Mahairas, and Elizabeth P. Fox

Analyzing Team Effectiveness was developed by McGregor in the early 1960s to assist a managerial group at Union Carbide Corporation with its own team development. It has been influential in the development of other instruments, and it is directly applicable to the education and consultation of health care teams. It also could be used to compare perceived functioning levels of different teams. For a short, 10-item instrument, it includes a broad range of elements of team effectiveness, including the team's relationship to the organization in which it functions and the team's accomplishments. It is well-constructed and easy to use. The developer recommends an item analysis to ascertain the team's strengths and weaknesses. One of the oldest educational/consultation instruments, it remains one of the best. There are no reliability or validity data for it, and as a result, we do not recommend its use in research.

Conceptual Framework

McGregor espoused a management style of egalitarianism in which managers and employees demonstrate a high commitment to jointly developed objectives and a high degree of collaboration in achieving them (Theory Y) as opposed to hierarchical authority and control over unmotivated employees (Theory X). Within an organization, there are types of activities appropriate to the individual; others, appropriate to the dyad or pair; and still others, appropriate to larger groups or teams. According to McGregor, under the right conditions, there are positive advantages achievable from group effort; however, most managers and employees do not know how to accomplish objectives through group effort. Through education and consultation, members of teams can learn the skills of teamwork and how to assess and improve their team's level of performance.

McGregor viewed the organization as a social system and the team as a "sociotechnological" sub-system working within the organization. The team as a work group has the capacity to develop over time by applying teamwork skills and continually monitoring and attempting to improve its effectiveness.

Description of Measure

McGregor developed the instrument to assist a managerial group at Union Carbide Corporation with its own team development. It assesses the current performance level of a group/team and facilitates members' agreement on which characteristics should be improved. It is completed anonymously by team members; an item analysis is used for scoring and interpretation of responses.

Components of Team Performance Measured

The instrument measures eight elements of team effectiveness: (a) degree of mutual trust in the team (one item); (b) degree of mutual support in the team (one item); (c) communication (two items); (d) understanding of and commitment to team objectives (two items); (e) handling conflicts within the team (one item); (f) utilization of members' resources (one item); (g) control methods; and (h) organizational environment (one item). Both open, authentic communication and listening are addressed within communication. Control methods includes the degree to which control is imposed on the team versus the team controlling itself. Organizational environment refers to the degree to which the environment is restrictive with pressure toward conformity versus free and supportive with respect for individual differences.

The measure covers all four domains (structure, context, process, and productivity) and five of the eight dimensions (team structure, organizational and team context, interdependence, and accomplishments) of our model of team performance. It is unique in that it includes both organizational environment and accomplishments as part of team performance.

Formatting and Scoring

The instrument has a seven-point rating scale for each of the 10 items. For each item, 1 is the lowest or most negative score and 7, the highest or most positive score (see item example below).

1. Degree of mutual trust:
   High suspicion 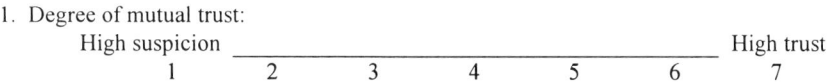 High trust
        1   2   3   4   5   6   7

In McGregor, D., Bennis, W.G., & McGregor, C. *The professional manager* ©1967. Reprinted by permission of McGraw-Hill, Inc.

For each item, team members' ratings are summed, and an average score is calculated. The average score as well as the high and low scores for each item are presented to the team for discussion. According to McGregor, the team should pay particular attention to items with means of 5 or below (indicating perceived poor functioning) or for which the range of individual ratings is particularly wide, indicating lack of consensus regarding functioning.

Psychometric Testing

Internal Consistency/Test-Retest Reliability

No data are available. With regard to test-retest reliability, McGregor noted that there is a tendency for members to rate the team unrealistically high the first time they complete the instrument, which suggests low test-retest reliability. To counteract this, he recommends that after discussion of initial ratings, the instrument be readministered a week or two later.

Inter-Rater Reliability

This type of reliability testing is not appropriate.

Validity

No data are available. While the instrument has no formal content validity established, it measures the concept of team effectiveness adequately for purposes of education and consultation. McGregor stated, "the purpose in using such devices is not precise measurement, but the provision of information that provokes analytic discussion" (McGregor, Bennis, & McGregor, 1967, p. 174).

Evaluation

The Analyzing Team Effectiveness instrument is one of the oldest of the educational/consultation measures, and many of the later instruments' developers have been influenced strongly by McGregor. The instrument is based on considerable social science and small groups research literature. It is well constructed and includes a broad range of elements of team effectiveness, including the team's relationship to the organization in which it functions. Scoring and interpretation of answers are easily accomplished and straightforward. The items are well constructed, and each measures a single dimension of the concept, team effectiveness. Item two uses "sexist" language, which is easily modifiable.

The first reviewer has used the instrument as part of a consultation with six geriatric teams; like McGregor, she found a tendency for team members to rate their team high on a one-time administration. This could be due to lack of trust regarding the use of their responses (i.e., giving answers that supervisors want to hear and that won't "get the team in trouble" and a lack of a shared understanding of the team's strengths and weaknesses. Because it is short, easy to administer, and answers are easily interpreted, it is appropriate in one-day workshops. In workshops, we have used it following task-oriented experiential exercises to emphasize that well functioning teams attend to both task-oriented and process goals (i.e., how and how well tasks are accomplished and how team members feel about the strategies and processes utilized in accomplishing the task). The measure was not constructed for and is not appropriate for research since it does not purport to be a precise measurement tool, and there are no reliability and validity data on it.

Relevant Publications

McGregor, D. (1960). *The human side of enterprise*. New York: McGraw-Hill, Inc.

McGregor, D., Bennis, W.G., & McGregor, C. (1967). *The professional manager* (Ch. 10, pp. 159-182). New York: McGraw-Hill, Inc.

GROUP ENVIRONMENT SCALE (GES)

Developed by Rudolph H. Moos and Barrie Humphrey, 1974; subscales adapted for health care teams by M.H. Schmitt, G.D. Heinemann, and M.P. Farrell, 1992
Reviewed by Stephanie B. Hoffman and Gloria D. Heinemann

The GES, developed by Moos and Humphrey (1974), is a 90-item measure of relationships, personal growth, and system maintenance/change within a group. It assesses the impact of a group's social environment on behavior. It includes ten subscales, each containing nine items. Schmitt and colleagues adapted four of these subscales (Cohesion, Leader Support, Expressiveness, and Anger and Aggression) for potential use with health care teams. The instrument is appropriate for education and consultation programs, research projects, and therapeutic settings. Because of its extensive use and the developers' careful attention to development, the measure has good validity and reliability. The disadvantages of the measure are its length and dichotomous, forced choice format for responses. Additionally, all of the subscales are not amenable to health care teams. The relationships and system maintenance/change subscales are especially applicable to them, while the subscales within the personal growth dimension are more appropriate for psychotherapy and support groups.

Conceptual Framework

According to the framework used in developing the GES, individual group members bring their life stressors, personal resources, personalities, coping abilities, and functioning abilities into the group. These variables, along with group dynamics themselves, influence the social environment of the group and how well it functions. Using a grounded theory approach to develop the measure, developers interviewed and observed a large number of groups to ascertain the facets of group performance–relationship, personal growth or goal orientation, and system maintenance/change.

The group creates a social environment that impacts individual members of the group, group leaders, and the group itself.

Description of Measure

There are three versions of this measure–the Real, Ideal, and the Expectations Forms. The forms differ only on the tense of the verbs. The real version measures members' perceptions about what is going on in the group. It facilitates the identification of a group's strengths and weaknesses, the understanding of individuals' (both leader and members) perceptions of their groups, and an understanding of the impact of the climate on performance or functioning. The ideal version measures what members want in a group, while the expectations version measures what they expect will happen before participating in the group. The subscales of the GES can be used to provide feedback to and educate individuals about important issues regarding their group's structure, process, and performance. Moos suggests that discrepancies between real and ideal or real and expected facets of group performance lead to dissatisfaction and poor functioning. Comparison of findings from these different forms identifies areas in need of change. Likewise, discrepancies between a group leader and members also reflect dissatisfaction or conflict within the group.

Researchers have used the GES to describe and compare groups, identify the components of group climates, and to examine the relationship between group climates and performance outcomes on both the group and individual levels. The real version was the one adapted for health care teams by Schmitt, Heinemann, and Farrell; they adapted four of the subscales (Cohesion, Leader Support, Expressiveness, and Anger and Aggression). Individual team members complete the instrument; their scores can be compared to one another, to the group leader's scores, or to their own scores over time. Team members' scores also can be averaged for a team score and monitored over time or compared to other teams' scores.

Components of Team Performance Measured

The GES measures ten facets of performance: (a) cohesion; (b) leader support; (c) expressiveness; (d) independence; (e) task orientation; (f) self-discovery; (g) anger and aggression; (h) order and organization; (i) leader control; and (j) innovation. Each facet is a nine-item subscale.

Subscales 1 through 3 refer to relationships. The Cohesion Subscale reflects members' commitment to the group and to each other. The Leader Support Subscale examines the helpfulness and friendship of the leader toward the group members. The Expressiveness Subscale reflects encouragement of the expression of feelings in the group.

Subscales 4 through 7 refer to personal growth. The Independence Subscale measures encouragement of autonomous actions by group members. The Task Orientation Subscale measures accomplishment of tasks through decision-making, planning, and new skills. The Self-Discovery Subscale examines self-disclosure about members' personal lives. The Anger and Aggression Subscale assesses the extent to which anger and disagreement are expressed openly in the group.

Subscales 8 through 10 address system maintenance/change. The Order and Organization Subscale examines the clarity of goals and procedures within the group. The Leader Control Subscale measures the leader's strength in terms of directing activities and making decisions. The Innovation Subscale measures routine versus creativity in the group.

The instrument includes items in all four domains and five of the eight dimensions (team structure and context, interdependence, growth and development, and accomplishments) of our model of team performance.

Formatting and Scoring

The 90 items are written as positively and negatively worded statements. Responses are forced choice "true" or "false." Instructions direct respondents to answer "true" if they believe a statement is true most of the time or true of most of the people in a work group on most days. They also are instructed to guess if unsure.

Each original subscale is given a real and standardized score. A respondent receives one point for agreeing with a positive statement or disagreeing with a negative statement. For each subscale, the scores are summed; they range from zero to nine (real scores) and from 20 to 80 (standard scores–standardizing the mean at 50 in order to compare the subscales with one another). A high score on a subscale indicates a strong positive perception of the concept being measured. All three forms of the GES are scored in the same way. An easy-to-use scoring template overlay accompanies the instrument. A standard scores conversion table is provided in the appendix of the *GES Manual* (see publications below).

The subscale scores are not totaled for an overall score. If the entire team completes the measure, a group or team average can be plotted on a social climate scale profile using standard scores. The group leader's score is often plotted separately on the same profile for comparison purposes.

For the four subscales adapted for health care teams, respondents circle the appropriate answer choice, 1 = true and 2 = false. In response to complaints about the dichotomous true/false choices, the Cohesion Subscale's answer choices were Likert formatted such that 4 = often, 3 = sometimes, 2 = seldom, and 1 = never in one research project.

For the four adapted subscales with dichotomous true/false answer choices, the negatively worded items were reverse coded so agreement with positively worded items and disagreement with negatively coded items all had a score of one; these scores were summed for each subscale. The Cohesion Subscale with Likert response formatting ranged from 9 to 36 with a high score indicating high or strong cohesion.

Psychometric Testing

Internal Consistency Reliability

The internal consistency of the subscales are all in the acceptable range– Cohesion, .86; Leader Support, .74; Expressiveness, .70; Independence, .62; Task Orientation, .72; Self-Discovery, .83; Anger and Aggression, .83; Order and Organization, .85; Leader Control, .73; and Innovation, .78. Item-to-subscale average correlations range from .30 for Independence to .53 for Cohesion.

The alpha reliabilities for the adapted subscales were .86 for Cohesion, .84 for Leader Support, .66 for Expressiveness, and .79 for Anger and Aggression. The item-to-subscale correlations ranged from .60 to .76 for Cohesion; from .45 to .75 for Leader Support; from .40 to .64 for Expressiveness; and from .43 to .69 for Anger and Aggression.

Test-Retest Reliability

Test-retest reliabilities for each original subscale are in the acceptable range, from .65 to .87. Re-tests were given one month following administration in seven groups. Stability of the overall GES profile was assessed for 10 staff teams at four months, eight months, one year, and two years (Brill, 1979; Duncan & Brill, 1977; Menard, 1974, 1976 as cited by Moos, 1994). Mean profile stability was .92 at four months, .91 at eight months, .84 at one year, and .78 at two years.

Inter-Rater Reliability

There is no inter-rater reliability needed since this is a self-report measure.

Content or Face Validity

Items were developed through interviews and observations of members/leaders in a variety of groups. Items were selected that measure one of the three underlying areas (i.e., relationships, personal growth, and system maintenance/change within a group), and provide some breadth as well.

Concurrent Validity

The Cohesion Subscale is highly correlated with a measure of group attraction (Evans & Jarvis, 1986 as cited by Moos, 1994) and is significantly related to the Perceived Depth of Interaction Scale that measures quality of group interaction (Rose & Bednar, 1980 as cited by Moos, 1994). With regard to the adapted subscales, the Expressiveness Subscale is correlated .32 with a Quality of Communication Subscale also adapted for health care teams (Schmitt, Heinemann, & Farrell, 1992).

Construct Validity

The measure discriminates among various kinds of groups on many of its subscales. Littlepage and associates (1989 as cited by Moos, 1994) found task groups scored higher on task orientation, order and organization, and leader control, while social groups scored higher on expressiveness, self-discovery, and innovation. In studies which included both observational and self-report data (Shadish, 1978, 1984 as cited by Moos, 1994), amount of interpersonal interaction in a support group correlated with more cohesion, expressiveness, independence, self-discovery, organization, and innovation.

With regard to the adapted subscales, the Cohesion Subscale correlated -.52 with a measure of anomie (lack of mission and role clarity) in teams, .62 with the Leader Support Subscale, .62 with a Quality of Communication Subscale, and .61 with a Team Effectiveness Subscale. Both of these latter two subscales were adapted for health care teams from Shortell and Rousseau's ICU Nurse/Physician Instrument (see critique later in this chapter). The Leader Support Subscale also correlated -.45 with the Team Anomie Scale, .48 with the Quality of Communication Subscale, and .49 with the Team Effectiveness Subscale (Schmitt, Heinemann, & Farrell, 1992).

Predictive Validity

In several studies (Giamartino, 1981; Giamartino & Wandersman, 1983; Prestby & Wandersman, 1985 as cited by Moos, 1994) information about social climate predicted the adequacy of organizational functioning one year later. Various studies also have been conducted to confirm predictions about group climate based on theoretical constructs concerning how a particular group should perform (Blair, 1989; Lavoie, 1981; Menard, 1976; Montgomery, Miller & Tonigan, 1993; Schramski et al., 1984; Toro, Rappaport, & Seidman, 1987 as cited by Moos, 1994).

Discriminate Validity

No data are available.

Evaluation

Both reviewers have used the GES in educational consultations or research with health care teams. Teams seem particularly eager to see how their average scores compare to group norms and how their scores differ from their leader's scores. These comparisons can be the beginning point for interventions to improve the functioning of the team. However, revealing scores to the group must be handled tactfully and carefully. Group leaders and members can become defensive about scores that differ from group norms and from each other. An experienced consultant/educator needs to explain GES outcomes and proceed with team training.

The second reviewer, with her research colleagues, has adapted four of the subscales (i.e., Cohesion, Leader Support, Expression, and Anger and Aggression) and used them in two survey research studies of health care teams. They found the Cohesion Subscale to be the strongest with regard to reliability and validity. Team members misinterpreted one item of the Expressiveness Subscale, "Team members think things out before saying anything;" they perceived a "true" answer to this item as positive rather than as inhibited expression. This accounts for the low correlation between this subscale and the other measure of communication in one of their studies. The Anger and Aggression Subscale was misinterpreted by team members in that they viewed the expression of anger, yelling, and hostility in the health care team as a negative reflection of team functioning, while Moos perceives such expression as positive in many psychotherapy and support groups. This is evident by the positive correlation between this subscale and the Team Anomie Scale (.47) and the negative correlations between this subscale and the Cohesion Subscale (-.31) and the Quality of Communication Subscale (-.39). The Anger and Aggression Subscale is not appropriate for health care teams.

The GES subscales in the relationship and system maintenance/change dimensions are reliable, valid, and useful in assessing and researching health care teams. The Cohesion Subscale is an exceptionally strong measure for this type of group. The instrument is especially useful in identifying and facilitating the resolution of conflict in teams, especially between leader(s) and team members. Also, it can be used in longitudinal research on teams and in outcome research about the effectiveness of group interventions.

Because there is such a rich and long history of research utilizing the GES, its reliability and validity have been particularly well documented (see Moos, 1994). Some factor analytic studies do not support the dimensions as conceptualized, but instead have found three to eight factors depending on the types of groups studied (Davis, 1980; Goetzel, 1982; Hartsough & Davies, 1986;

Meredith & Schmitz, 1986 as cited by Moos, 1994). In addition, developers assigned these subscales to the three facets of group environment–relationship (cohesion, leader support, expressiveness), personal growth (independence, task orientation, self-discovery, anger and aggression), and system maintenance/change (order and organization, leader control, innovation)–in an a priori fashion rather than through factor analysis. As a result, we question the conceptual soundness of the instrument and several of its subscales for some groups.

Completing the instrument is time consuming as each of its three forms has 90 items. Some of the original items are gender biased, and respondents often become frustrated by its dichotomous, forced choice format. The subscales within "personal growth" (e.g., Independence, Task Orientation, Self-Discovery, and Anger and Aggression) and the Expressiveness Subscale within "relationship" are more appropriate for psychotherapy and support groups than for groups or teams in a work environment with considerable clinical or task responsibilities. That is, functioning independently, discussing personal or family problems in the group, yelling, saying whatever you want, or letting off steam in the group may be positive indicators in the former types of groups, but are barriers to group effectiveness in the latter. Considerable caution should be taken adapting and using these subscales for health care teams. In fact, a subscale measuring interdependence among health care team members would be a better indicator of health care team functioning/effectiveness than Moos' Independence Subscale. Finally, the reviewers believe that the Self-Discovery Subscale is inappropriate for health care teams. Despite these weaknesses and in light of the current emphasis on quality improvement and increasing use of self-directed work teams, several subscales of the GES lend themselves to studies of employee empowerment and team performance.

Status/Availability

This is a copyrighted instrument; item booklets, answer sheets, and the scoring template are available for purchase from Consulting Psychologist Press, Inc., 577 College Avenue, Palo Alto, CA 94306; (650) 493-5000, x65925. For the adapted subscales, contact Madeline H. Schmitt, School of Nursing, University of Rochester, Elmwood Avenue, Box SON, Rochester, NY 14623; (716) 275-8889; e-mail, madeline_schmitt@urmc.rochester.edu.

Relevant Publications

Moos, R.H. (1994). *Group Environment Scale: Development, Applications, Research* (3rd ed.). Palo Alto, CA: Consulting Psychologists Press, Inc. (includes 1974 subscale items developed by Moos & Humphrey).

Schmitt, M.H., Heinemann, G.D., & Farrell, M.P. (1992). Unpublished questionnaire and data from the NIA-funded Quality of Geriatric Team Functioning Study.

SURVEY OF CROSS-FUNCTIONAL TEAMS

Developed by Glenn M. Parker, 1992, 1997
Reviewed by Stephen K. Harmon and Glenda F. Brown

The original Survey of Cross-Functional Teams (1992) is a 20-item instrument that measures factors contributing to the success or effectiveness of teams. A revised 20-item version and a shortened, 12-item version of the instrument also are available. A unique feature of the instrument is its measurement of the importance of the factors to team members and their assessment of how well their team does on each factor. The instrument has strong theoretical underpinnings, is conceptually sound, and easy to administer and score. It also includes unique items (e.g., communication technology, leadership effectiveness, customer satisfaction, and use of cultural/style diversity) not often measured in other instruments. No psychometric testing has been conducted to date. The instrument is appropriate for consultation with and development of teams. The developer recommends it for use with experienced teams.

Conceptual Framework

According to Parker, a cross-functional team includes people from different departments or disciplines. Its effectiveness is the result of a variety of interrelated factors, some external and some internal to the team. External factors are related to the team's requiring the support of organizational management to function effectively. A supportive management promotes team effectiveness by appointing appropriate leaders, assigning an appropriate number of members, giving teams the authority to make and implement decisions, addressing team participation as a component of employees' performance appraisals, and rewarding both effective team players and effective teams. Other factors internal to the team result from actions taken or not taken by members themselves. Teams ensure their own effectiveness by clarifying their goals among members, maintaining positive relationships within the organization (i.e., with management and other teams), and developing members' interpersonal skills such as communication or management and/or resolution of conflict.

According to the developer, members' combined efforts are necessary to accomplish the team's goals. The team is an important organizational vehicle; its whole is greater than the sum of its parts.

Description of Measure

Parker developed the original 20-item version of the instrument in 1992. Adapted 20 and 12-item versions were published in a *Cross Functional Teams Tool Kit* published by Jossey-Bass in 1997. Some of the elements were renamed and minor wording changes were made in the items themselves. The rationale for the adaptation of the 20-item instrument is not clear; however, the newer version does use more updated language. For example, authority becomes empowerment; leadership becomes leadership effectiveness, and clients become customers/clients. In some instances, item wording is improved somewhat (e.g., in item 10, "team meetings are well conducted" replaces "are well executed") in the adapted version. In other items, however, the adapted version tends to measure more than one concept per item; this was not a problem in the original instrument. The adapted 12-item version shares the same strengths and weaknesses of the longer one.

The instrument's purpose is to help teams and their managers or leaders assess current levels of success and identify areas needing improvement. Teams can use the instrument as a self-assessment tool to identify their strengths and weaknesses. Consultants can use it prior to a team-building or educational intervention to identify issues to be addressed and skills to be taught. The developer suggests using it with teams that have been in place for some time so there is experience on which to base the assessment. Individual team members complete the instrument. Team averages are used to describe the perceived importance of the facets of team success and the team's perception of its performance on each facet.

Components of Team Performance Measured

The original instrument includes 20 items measuring facets of success of cross-functional teams. These are leadership, authority, goals, decision-making, recognition, roles, boundary management, performance appraisal, team training, team meetings, communications technologies, team size, management support, co-location, customers and suppliers, cross-training, openness, conflict resolution, cultural/style differences, and client focus. The shorter, 12-item version includes leadership effectiveness, empowerment, shared goals, recognition, role clarity, boundary management, performance appraisal, team training, team size, management support, interpersonal excellence, and customer/client focus.

This instrument addresses all four of the domains and six of the eight dimensions (organizational and team structure, organizational context, interdependence, growth and development, and strategies for productivity) in our model of team performance. Many of its elements of performance are unique in that other instruments do not attempt to measure them.

Formatting and Scoring

The original instrument includes 20 positively worded items measuring elements of success in cross-functional teams. Team members rate each item twice: (a) their perception of how important each element is from 1 = unimportant to 5 = critically important and (b) their assessment of how well each item describes their own team, 1 = strongly disagree to 5 = strongly agree (see item example).

	IMPORTANCE	ASSESSMENT
	1. Somewhat unimportant	1. Strongly Disagree
	2. Unimportant	2. Disagree
	3. Important	3. Neutral
	4. Very important	4. Agree
	5. Critical	5. Strongly Agree
FACTOR		
1. Leadership Effectiveness The leader has high-level technical and team-management skills.	1 2 3 4 5	1 2 3 4 5

In Parker, G.M. *Cross-functional teams tool kit* ©1997. Reprinted by permission of Jossey-Bass, Inc., a subsidiary of John Wiley & Sons, Inc.

For each item, a team average is calculated for both "importance" and "assessment." Resulting scores identify team strengths and opportunities for improvement. Items that receive high scores (an average score of 4 or higher) for both importance and assessment identify the team's strengths. Opportunities for improvement are identified when an item is rated as important for the team's success (an average score of 4 or higher), but the team's assessment scores indicate poor performance (an average score of 3 or lower).

Psychometric Testing

No reliability or validity data are available.

Evaluation

The original instrument has many positive features. First, it is well constructed and easy to administer. Second, it measures both the importance of and performance on each facet of team success. This allows team consultants to identify both the areas team members' perceive as strengths and areas in which improvement is required. A third strength is Parker's broad conceptualization of team success. The instrument includes elements of team performance generally absent in many other instruments such as boundary management, use of communication technologies, leadership effectiveness, team size, cross-training and team training, use of cultural and style diversity, customer satisfaction, and the inclusion of teamwork in each member's performance appraisal.

The major weaknesses of the instrument are its lack of psychometric testing, its use of only one item to measure each success factor, and its receptivity to response bias since all items are positively worded. This instrument is appropriate for identifying areas for skill building and for facilitating action plans to improve the performance of experienced teams. The reviewers believe the original version is superior to and recommend its use over the adapted versions.

Status/Availability

The instrument is copyrighted. The original 1992 version of the instrument appears in Parker's 1994 book (see publications below). To purchase, contact Jossey-Bass at 350 Sansome Street, San Francisco, CA 94104; (415) 433-1740. Written permission must be obtained from Parker to use the instrument. The adapted versions of the instrument appear in the 1997 publication below. To purchase it, contact Pfeiffer & Company at (800) 274-4434.

Relevant Publications

Parker, G.M. (1994). *Cross-functional teams: Working with allies, enemies and other strangers*. San Francisco: Jossey-Bass.

Parker, G.M. (1997). *Cross-functional teams tool kit*. San Francisco: Pfeiffer & Company, an imprint of Jossey-Bass, Inc.

TEAM-DEVELOPMENT SURVEY

Developed by Glenn M. Parker, 1990
Reviewed by Carla Corral and Antonette M. Zeiss

The Team-Development Survey is a 12-item instrument measuring characteristics of effective teams. The instrument has strong theoretical underpinnings, and its items are conceptually sound. Completion of the instrument requires a relatively high reading level, and answer choices are somewhat confusing. Reliability and validity data are not available. It can be used to assist teams in identifying their strengths and weaknesses and in developing action plans for improvement.

Conceptual Framework

Based on an extensive literature review and his own research, Parker identified 12 characteristics of effective teams–a clear sense of purpose, an informal or comfortable climate, participation, listening, civilized disagreement, consensus, open communication, clear roles and work assignments, shared leadership, external relations, style diversity, and self-assessment.

Parker suggests that the 12 characteristics are indicators of a team's developmental level. Utilizing Tuckman's (1965) model of team development, he suggests teams in the performing stage function well on all effectiveness characteristics. As teams develop, they become effective on some of the characteristics and, at the same time, need work on others. Parker stresses the role that team members play in team effectiveness. Each of the characteristics of an effective team is supported by the actions of effective team players.

Teams are groups that change and develop over time. They consist of interdependent members working toward goal achievement and task completion.

Description of Measure

Parker developed the instrument to assess team development and effectiveness. It can be used to identify a team's strengths and weaknesses and develop action plans for continued improvement. Team members complete the instrument. Team averages are used to describe the team's effectiveness.

Components of Team Performance Measure

Each of the characteristics is represented by one item on the Team-Development Survey. The 12 characteristics/items include a clear sense of purpose, an informal climate, participation, listening, civilized disagreement, consensus, open communication, clear roles and work assignments, shared leadership, external relations, style diversity, and self-assessment.

This instrument addresses all four domains and six of the eight dimensions (team structure, organizational and team context, interdependence, growth and development, and strategies for productivity) of our model of team performance. Unique elements measured are informal climate, self-assessment, consensus decision-making, and style diversity of members.

Formatting and Scoring

Each of the 12 items consists of a statement describing a characteristic of an effective team. The respondent is asked to circle a number on the eight-point answer choice format: 1 or 2 = "seldom;" 3 or 4 = "sometimes;" 5 or 6 = "often;" and 7 or 8 = "very frequently." An example of item formatting follows:

Statements	Seldom	Sometimes	Often	Very Frequently
11. *Style Diversity:* The team has a broad spectrum of team player types including members who emphasize attention to tasks, goal setting, a focus on process, and questions about how the team is functioning. Comments: _____	1 2	3 4	5 6	7 8

Modified and reproduced by permission of the publisher, Consulting Psychologists Press, Inc., Palo Alto, CA 94303, from the *Team Development Survey* by G.M. Parker ©1992 by Xicom, Inc, a subsidiary of Consulting Psychologists Press, Inc. All rights reserved. Further reproduction is prohibited without written consent of the publisher.

Each of the 12 items is examined separately. Team averages are calculated for each item. A high score indicates a positive perception of team effectiveness.

Psychometric Testing

No reliability or validity data are available.

Evaluation

The instrument has strong theoretical underpinnings; items appropriately reflect the 12 characteristics of team effectiveness outlined by Parker. It includes some unique elements of performance not often included in other instruments. Weaknesses include its complex language that requires a high level of reading skills and comprehension such that respondents may need to read each statement more than once. Additionally, some of the items measure more than one concept. For example, in one item, the "clear purpose" statement queries whether the vision, mission, goal, and tasks of the team has been defined <u>and</u> are accepted by everyone <u>and</u> there is an action plan. Finally, the answer choice format is confusing since there is not a unique verbal descriptor for each numeric value. We believe a five point answer choice format (1 = almost never; 2 = seldom; 3 = sometimes; 4 = often, and 5 = almost always) would be more appropriate.

Status/Availability

Consulting Psychologists Press holds the instrument's copyright. To purchase the instrument, contact them at (800) 624-1765 or at <u>http://www.cpp-db.com/</u>. The instrument appears in Parker's book below. To purchase the publication, contact Jossey-Bass Publisher, 350 Sansome Street, San Francisco, CA 94104; (415) 433-1740.

Relevant Publications

Parker, G.M. (1990). *Team players and team work: The new competitive business strategy.* San Francisco: Jossey-Bass Publisher.

Tuckman, B.W. (1965). Developmental sequences in small groups. *Psychological Bulletin, 63,* 384-399.

HIGH-PERFORMANCE WORK TEAM QUESTIONNAIRE (HPWTQ)

Developed by Robert Preziosi, 1998
Reviewed by Glenda F. Brown and Stephen K. Harmon

The HPWTQ, a 48-item self-administered instrument, measures 12 characteristics of high performance work teams. It is useful as a consultation tool for identifying a team's strengths and weaknesses and stimulating discussion about improving team performance. Its strengths are its breadth of measurement and ease of administration and scoring. It lacks psychometric testing and has some methodological problems related to naming and measuring concepts, wording item, and response bias.

Conceptual Framework

Work teams are groups of individuals utilized by organizations to accomplish tasks and affect desired change. As organizations move away from traditional hierarchical control and toward participatory leadership and team empowerment, management expects teams to produce more valuable results than they did in the past. Preziosi believes that the greater the synergy among team members, the greater the productivity and quality of work produced by the team. He contends that highly productive teams exhibit certain characteristics that can be measured in terms of individual behaviors.

Preziosi perceives teams as work groups of individuals who are jointly commissioned by the organization to accomplish tasks and affect desired change.

Description of Measure

The HPWTQ provides a team leader or manager with an overall picture of the team's functioning on the 12 characteristics of high performance teams. It also gives a detailed picture of the perceptions of the team members and of the team. It can identify strengths of the team as well as areas requiring improvement. Team members complete it; results facilitate discussion and action planning.

Components of Team Performance Measured

The 12 characteristics of high performance teams measured by this instrument are interactive goals, resource optimizing, conflict management, interactive leadership, activity control, feedback mechanisms, decision style flexibility, mutual assistance, experimentation, self-evaluation, long-term commitment, and performance influence.

The HPWTQ includes all four domains and five of the eight dimensions (team structure and context, interdependence, growth and development, and strategies for productivity) of our team performance model. It includes some well-constructed items measuring decision-making and leadership sharing.

Formatting and Scoring

The instrument includes 48 statements addressing perceptions of the team, respondent as team member, and other team members. There are four statements or items for each of the 12 characteristics. Answer choices range from 1 to 6 and are Likert formatted such that 1 = agree completely, 2 = agree, 3 = agree somewhat, 4 = disagree somewhat, 5 = disagree, and 6 = disagree completely).

Answer choices and numeric codes appear at the top of the instrument's first page. Respondents write their answers on the blank to the left of each statement.

_____ 4. My team members have a common set of values.

In M. Silberman (Ed.), *Team and organization development sourcebook* ©1998. Reprinted by permission of McGraw-Hill, Inc.

The developer provides a scoring template that facilitates the calculation of an average score for each of the 12 characteristics. An average score of 5 or higher indicates a problem; a score of 2 or lower indicates an area of strength. Scores also can be analyzed on an item by item basis if more specific detail and discussion are desired. The same benchmarks apply.

Psychometric Testing

No reliability or validity data are available.

Evaluation

The instrument's strengths are its breadth of coverage and ease of administration and scoring. Results facilitate the identification of strengths and weaknesses in the team and stimulate discussion about improving team performance. Its major weakness is the lack of psychometric testing. Additionally, it is not apparent that the items grouped together actually measure their respective concepts (e.g., only two of the four items measuring interactive leadership are related to leadership; the other two address norms and values) or that they can be summed. In some instances, the concepts are not appropriately named (e.g., activity control might be more appropriately named roles and responsibilities). Finally, wording of some of the items could be improved; for example, in item 15, the phrases to "surface conflicts" and in item 35, to "feel positively obliged" could be confusing. Several items end in prepositions. Given that all 48 items are positively worded, there is potential for response bias.

Status/Availability

The copyrighted instrument is reproduced in the publication below. To obtain the publication, contact McGraw-Hill at (800) 2-MCGRAW.

Relevant Publications

Preziosi, B. (1998). How well is your work team functioning? In M. Silberman (Ed.), *Team and organization development sourcebook* (pp. 213-221). New York: McGraw-Hill, Inc.

U.S. STYLE TEAMS (USST) INVENTORY

Developed by Gaylord Reagan, 1996
Reviewed by Charles P. Broderick and Linda O. Nichols

Reagan developed the USST Inventory to assess organizations' readiness to implement the team approach. According to the developer, teams' structure and function must coincide with the particular culture of the society in which they operate. Designed to be easily utilized by organizations, this 33-item instrument has strong theoretical underpinnings and is easy to administer and score. Its major weaknesses include lack of psychometric testing, sophisticated wording of some items, and difficulty determining if some items refer to the organization or the team. We recommend its use in organizational consultations, but not in research until reliability and validity are established.

Conceptual Framework

Borrowing a theoretical framework from Nahavandi and Aranda (1994), Reagan emphasizes that teams have not been as effective in the U.S. as they have in Japan. This is due to seven characteristics of U.S. culture: (a) a belief that individual ingenuity and creativity result in performance improvement; (b) an emphasis on individual rights and nonconformity; (c) a high tolerance for conflict and competition; (d) a distrust of power, hierarchical structure, and management; (e) pride in attaining quick results; (f) preference for dynamic action; and (g) high levels of demographic diversity and heterogeneity. According to Nahavandi and Aranda, the type of team that functions most effectively in U.S. culture is the "shamrock" team. It has a stable core membership, specialized resource persons who join and leave the team as needed, and temporary or part-time members, utilized for short periods of time when the team needs additional expertise or manpower. In order to adopt this type of team and have it perform well, organizational managers and employees must adopt three behavioral norms: (a) value and endorse dissent among team members; (b) encourage fluidity of membership within teams; and (c) empower teams to address key organizational issues and implement their decisions.

278 TEAM PERFORMANCE IN HEALTH CARE

The team is a shamrock or Irish clover with three leaves per stem. Each leaf represents one of the components of the team. These components are: its core membership; its specialized, fluid membership; and its temporary or part-time membership.

Description of Measure

The developer designed the instrument to familiarize organizations with the need to utilize culturally sensitive team strategies, to assess perceptions of an organization's readiness to adopt a U.S. style team, and to assess an organization's readiness to implement teams. Employees of an organization, including management, complete the instrument individually. Employees working in teams are the targets of assessment.

Components of Team Performance Measured

The instrument measures the extent to which a person endorses the norms of U.S. teams: (a) values and endorsement of dissent among team members (11 items); (b) fluidity of membership within teams (11 items); and (c) ability to address key areas and implement team decisions (11 items).

The instrument includes three of the four domains (structure, context, and process) and five of the eight dimensions (organizational and team structure, organizational context, interdependence and growth/development) of our model of team performance. Unique elements in this measure include the team's boundaries and permeability and coalition formation.

Formatting and Scoring

The Inventory includes 33 items. The respondent checks the box to the left of each item if he/she perceives the organization as accurately described by the statement; otherwise, the box if left blank (see item example below).

☐ Disagreement is viewed as being the basis for creativity.

In J.W. Pfeiffer, (Ed.), *The 1996 annual: Volume 2* ©1996. Reprinted by permission of Jossey-Bass, Inc., a subsidiary of John Wiley & Sons, Inc.

Reagan provides a scoring key with instructions for reverse coding several items. Check marks ("yes" responses) are summed and multiplied by three for each norm; the three norm subscale scores also are summed to obtain a total score ranging from 0 to 99. Total scores ranging from 85 to 99 indicate strong organizational support for all three norms underlying U.S. style teams; scores of 75 to-84, indicate moderate support; scores of 65 to-74 indicate some support, and scores of 0 to-64, erratic, inconsistent support.

Psychometric Testing

Reliability

No reliability data are available.

Content of Face Validity

The developer notes that when used in research, the inventory has demonstrated high face validity with a range of respondents from executive managers to nonmanagement personnel.

Concurrent/Construct/Predictive/Discriminant Validity

No data are available for these types of validity.

Evaluation

The instrument has a strong theoretical framework and is relatively easy to administer and score. It is unique in that it measures organizational readiness to implement teams and bases that readiness on components of U.S. culture. Weaknesses include the lack of psychometric testing, overly sophisticated wording of some items, and difficulty determining if some items refer to the organization or the team. We recommend the use of this instrument in organizational consultation, but not in research until further psychometric testing is undertaken since there is no evidence that items making up the three subscale norms relate to one another in a way that would permit them to be summed.

The "shamrock" team is consistent with clinical teams in hospitals in that they usually include a core of regular members, rotating trainees from medicine and the health professions, and consultant team members used as patients' needs and problems indicate. Today's primary care teams in the VA system provide good examples of these "shamrock" teams.

Status/Availability

The instrument is copyrighted; it appears in the 1996 publication below. To purchase the publication, contact Pfeiffer & Company at (800) 274-4434.

Relevant Publications

Nahavandi, A., & Aranda, E. (1994). Restructuring teams for the re-engineered organization. *Academy of Management Executive, 8*, 58-68.

Reagan, G. (1996). U.S. Style Teams (USST) Inventory. In J.W. Pfeiffer, (Ed.), *The 1996 annual: Volume 2, consulting* (pp. 141-151). San Diego, CA: Pfeiffer & Company.

ICU NURSE/PHYSICIAN INSTRUMENT*

Developed by S.R. Shortell and D.M. Rousseau, 1989; subscales adapted for health care teams by Madeline H. Schmitt, Gloria D. Heinemann, and Michael P. Farrell, 1992
Reviewed by Gloria D. Heinemann, Sara A. Brallier, and Antonette M. Zeiss

Schmitt, Heinemann, and Farrell (1992) adapted subscales from the ICU Nurse/Physician Instrument for use with health care teams. The adapted subscales measure three facets of team performance: communication within teams; external relations or coordination of the team with other teams and services within the hospital; and overall team effectiveness. Tests of reliability and validity demonstrate that each subscale is a strong measure of its respective underlying concept. These subscales provide good outcome measures of team process and productivity; they are appropriate for use in large-scale survey research based on both their reliability and validity and the ease with which the scales can be administered to busy health professionals.

Conceptual Framework

According to Shortell and colleagues, managerial practices and organizational processes affect performance. Organizational culture and leadership facilitate effective communication, coordination, and problem solving approaches, which in turn, result in high cohesiveness and high performance of complex, interdependent tasks within teams. Improved team performance, then, results in a higher quality of care to patients. Critical care, provided in medical and surgical intensive care units, is influenced by both external and internal factors in the environment. External factors include efficiency and care outcomes. Quality internal factors or care provider interactions (e.g., culture, leadership, communication, coordination, problem solving, and conflict management) should be associated with both efficiency and high perceived quality of care.

Developers view the team as a vehicle for delivering quality care to patients. The original scales were adapted for geriatric health care teams where the team is viewed as a small group that develops over time and attempts to monitor and improve its quality of functioning.

Description of Measure

Shortell and associates developed this self-administered instrument to measure the managerial practices and organizational processes that promote the effective implementation of complex treatment plans in health care organizations, specifically the ICU. For the original subscales, nurses, physicians, and ward clerks working in the ICU were the targets of assessment.

The adapted scales were developed as outcome measures of team functioning in the areas of communication among members, quality of relationships between the team and groups in the organization, and overall perceived team effectiveness. All members of the health care team complete the adapted subscales; subscale scores are summed and averaged for team scores.

Components of Team Performance Measured

The original instrument contains a set of measures related to leadership, organizational culture, communication, coordination, problem solving/conflict management, unit cohesiveness, and unit effectiveness. The communication, coordination and unit effectiveness measures were adapted, with permission, by Schmitt, Heinemann, and Farrell. Both the original and adapted Communication Scales measure facets of communication including openness, accuracy, timeliness, understanding, and satisfaction.

The original Coordination between Units Scale measures the degree to which functions and activities between the ICU and other units in the hospital (i.e., the emergency room, operating room, and ancillary support services on the patient floors) are carried out to encourage cost-effective, continuous care. The adapted External Relations Scale measures the quality of a team's working relationships with other groups, teams, and services within the hospital.

The original Unit Effectiveness Scale measures perceptions of the technical quality of care provided in the unit, judgements of the unit's ability to meet family needs, and turnover of staff on the unit. The adapted Team Effectiveness Scale measures perceptions of the team's functioning in the above areas.

The adapted scales measure three of the four domain (context, process, and productivity) and five of the eight dimensions (organizational context, interdependence, growth and development, strategies for productivity, and accomplishments) of our model of team performance. The scales are unique in that they cover both communication and accomplishments in more depth than many other measures. Unique elements include timeliness of communication, communication with patients' families and other inpatient health professionals working on other shifts, relationships with other facets of the organization, marketing for recruitment of team members, accomplishment of goals, patients' outcomes, and retention of team members.

Formatting and Scoring

The original instrument contains 110 Likert-formatted items with answer choices ranging from 1 = strongly disagree to 5 = strongly agree. The Leadership Scale includes 16 items; the Coordination Scale, 13 items; the Communication Scale, 43 items; the Conflict Management Scale, 26 items; the Team Cohesion Scale, five items; and the Perceived Unit Effectiveness Scale, seven items.

The three adapted scales were modified from the original items. Adaptations were minor in that terms such as "nurses" and "physicians" in the original items were changed to "team members" and "unit" in the original items was changed to "team." The Quality of Communications Scale includes 10 items; the External Relations Scale, five items; and the Team Effectiveness Scale, eight items. The answer choices range from 0 = strongly disagree to 5 = strongly agree.

In both the original instrument and adapted scales, negative items are reverse-coded and each scale is summed. High scores indicate positive perception of the measured concept. The adapted Communication Scale ranges from 0 to 50; a high score indicates quality communication within the team. The adapted External Relations Scale ranges from 0 to 25; a high score indicates that the team has quality external relations. The adapted Team Effectiveness Scale ranges from 0 to 40; a high score indicates quality team effectiveness.

Psychometric Testing

Internal Consistency Reliability

Developers used three approaches to improve reliability. Multiple indicators were used (i.e., three or more questions addressing each concept). Additionally, the questions were alternated between positively and negatively worded items to avoid respondent bias. Last, for some scales, items from existing measures with known reliability were adapted. Cronbach's alpha for each scale is: Culture, .94; Leadership, .87 for nurses and .88 for physicians; Coordination, .75; Communication, .64; Problem Solving/Conflict Management, .82; Team Cohesion, .76 and Perceived Unit Effectiveness, .75 (Shortell et al., 1994).

The adapted scales also have considerable reliability, Cronbach's alphas are as follows: Quality of Communication, .87; External Relations, .71; and Team Effectiveness, .88 (unpublished data from Schmitt, Heinemann, & Farrell's NIA-funded study of geriatric health care teams in the VA system).

Test-Retest/Inter-Rater Reliability

No data are available regarding test-retest reliability, and testing for inter-rater reliability is inappropriate since the measure is self-administered.

Content or Face Validity

The original instrument was pilot tested in a five-medical surgical ICU's in four Chicago area hospitals. The items were revised to improve reliability. The instrument exhibits considerable face validity in that the items within each scale are clearly worded and appear to be measuring the respective underlying construct. Schmitt, Heinemann, and Farrell altered the scales only slightly; therefore, the adapted scales retain the face and content validity of the original measure.

Concurrent Validity

Two of the four primary investigators made on-site visits and conducted interviews with a representative sample of ICU staff. The developers substantiated instrument results that open and timely communication and effective coordination were associated with higher levels of performance. Shortell and associates report numerous other correlations and measures of validity for the original subscales (Shortell et al., 1991). There are no data available regarding concurrent validity for the adapted scales.

Construct Validity

As predicted by theory, all of the measures of communication and coordination were positively correlated with a measure of the strength of leadership/influence of nurses and physicians (i.e., the capacity of individuals to influence others toward the accomplishment of organizationally relevant goals); correlations ranged from .22 to .65.

Shortell and associates' (1991) findings indicate the relationships between the communication and coordination measures and ICU unit culture were in the theoretically predicted directions. They found effective communication and coordination to be positively correlated with a team satisfaction-oriented culture (i.e., a unit with norms emphasizing achievement, cooperation, and staff development); correlations ranged from .20 to .45. Conversely, effective communication and coordination were negatively correlated with people security-oriented (i.e., a unit with norms emphasizing approval, adherence to procedures/ conventions, dependence, and avoidance of conflict) and task security-oriented (i.e., a unit with norms emphasizing perfectionism, competition, opposition, and authoritarian control) cultures; correlations ranged from -.02 to -.20. All reported correlations were significant at the $p < .05$ level.

As expected, measures of performance (i.e., meeting family needs and technical quality of care) were positively correlated with nurse/physician leadership. This leadership included the extent to which unit leaders emphasized standards of excellence, communicated clear goals and expectations, were responsive to changing needs, and were aware of unit members' concerns. The correlations ranged from .27 to .48. Also, turnover among nurses was negatively related to the measure of nurse/physician leadership ($r = -.29$ and $-.31$).

A subsequent study by Shortell and associates (1994) found that units with timely communication and effective coordination are significantly more efficient in terms of moving patients in and out. Additionally, nurses and physicians believe that technical quality is higher when a team-oriented culture exists along with effective communication, coordination, and problem solving approaches. Shortell and associates found a positive association between the ability to meet needs of the family and a measure of ICU process (a composite measure of unit culture, leadership, communication, coordination, and problem solving/conflict management). Thus, high quality ICU care has an important service dimension involving the ability to listen to the needs of the family and provide support.

The adapted scales, too, have considerable construct validity. All three correlated as would be theoretically predicted with measures of team development and outcomes of team performance. The adapted scales–Quality of Communication, Quality of External Relations, and Team Effectiveness–were negatively correlated with a Team Anomie Scale, an indicator of team development that measures lack of mission and role clarity in the team; correlations were -.72, -.42 and -.55, respectively; $p < .001$. They were positively correlated with a Cohesion Subscale, an outcome measure indicating members' commitment to the team and to each other; correlations were .61, .32 and .60, respectively; $p < .001$ (unpublished data from Schmitt, Heinemann, & Farrell's NIA funded study of geriatric health care teams in the VA system).

Predictive/Discriminant

No data are available for these types of validity.

Evaluation

The relatively short, adapted scales are easy to administer in a survey format; respondents had no difficulty understanding or completing them. Both the original and adapted scales are conceptually sound and have strong theoretical underpinnings. Shortell and associates provide a wide range of reliability and validity data for the original scales. The adapted ones also have considerable psychometric data. They provide good outcome data in four areas of team performance and are most appropriate for large-scale survey research studies. Other original scales from the ICU Study also could be adapted for use with health care teams.

Status/Availability

The original instrument and adapted subscales are copyrighted and can be utilized with the developers' permission. There is no charge for using the instrument. For information about the ICU Nurse/Physician instrument, contact S.M. Shortell, Kellogg Graduate School of Management, 2001 Sheridan Road, Donald P. Jacobs Center, Evanston, IL 60208-2001; (847) 491-3300. For information about the adapted subscales, contact Madeline H. Schmitt, School of Nursing, University of Rochester, Elmwood Avenue, Box SON, Rochester, NY 14623; (716) 275-8889; e-mail, madeline_schmitt@urmc.rochester.edu.

Relevant Publications

Shortell, S.M., Rousseau, D. Gilles, R. Devers, K., & Simons, T. (1991). Organizational assessment in intensive care units (ICUs): Construct development, reliability and validity of the ICU Nurse-Physician Questionnaire. *Medical Care, 29*, 709-726.

Shortell, S.M., Zimmerman, J., Rousseau, D., Gilles, R., Wagner, D., Draper, E., Knaus, W., & Duffy, J. (1994). The performance of intensive care units: Does good management make a difference? *Medical Care 32*, 508-525.

Schmitt, M.H., Heinemann, G.D., & Farrell, M.P. (1992). Unpublished questionnaire and data from the NIA-funded Quality of Geriatric Team Functioning Study.

TEAM SKILLS QUESTIONNAIRE

Developed by Ruth Ann Tsukuda and A.J. Stahelski, 1990
Reviewed by Kathryn Hyer and Ruth Ann Tsukuda

The Team Skills Questionnaire is a 49-item measure of team skills necessary in providing quality geriatric care. It focuses on collaboration, participation, communication, formal decision-making interaction, and maintaining team process. Although long, it is easy to complete and score. No psychometric testing has been conducted to determine reliability and validity to date. It can be used to measure baseline, self-reported skills of trainees and clinicians and to help educators tailor training based on the self-perceived needs of team members. Its use to monitor performance over time is uncertain at this time.

Conceptual Framework

The skills of health care clinicians on teams must be well developed if they are to represent their respective disciplines appropriately during collaborative patient care. The process of care planning involves effective identification of the patient's needs and health problems and the negotiation of priorities for intervention. In addition, the patient's and his/her family members' perceptions and preferences must be considered and included in the plan of care. This complex, interactive process requires quality communication among clinicians and between clinicians and the patient and/or family. The final, individualized care plan should represent a consensus of opinion and be agreeable to all members of the team, the patient, and his/her family.

The team is a group of health care clinicians or professionals whose goal is to create and implement interdisciplinary health care plans for geriatric patients. The quality of teamwork and the quality of care and treatment to patients increase when clinicians are skilled in team processes.

Description of Measure

Tsukuda and Stahelski developed this instrument to assess the use of team process skills among members and/or trainees of geriatric health care teams. It is best suited to assess entry-level skills of new team members, establish their baseline skill levels, and determine their educational needs. A guide for team skills accompanies the instrument; it provides definitions and explanations for each skill identified in the instrument; it also provides descriptions of optimal team performance behaviors in a collaborative environment. The guide is useful for team training after the actual assessment of skills.

Components of Team Performance Measured

The instrument measures the skills of teamwork in five areas–collaboration, participation, communication, decision-making, interaction, and maintaining team process. Communication includes both listening and speaking. Goal setting, problem solving, and conflict resolution make up the area of formal decision-making interaction. Maintaining team process includes task production and orientation/reorientation of team members as well as showing interest in the work activities of other team members.

The instrument addresses all four domains and five of the eight dimensions (team structure, team context, interdependence, growth and development, and strategies for productivity) of our team performance model.

Formatting and Scoring

The instrument includes 49 Likert-formatted items. Respondents answer each item by circling answer codes from 0 to 5. Each item represents a skill behavior; respondents rate their ability to consistently perform this task from almost never to almost always. Zero on this scale means no experience with this skill. Other labels for answer choices appear in the item formatted below:

No experience with this skill	Almost Never	Rarely	Occasionally	Frequently	Almost Always
0	1	2	3	4	5

COLLABORATION
As a geriatric team member, I . . .

3. Work for consensus	0	1	2	3	4	5

Reprinted by permission of developers.

Developers recommend an item analysis to examine skill levels in each of the specific areas. Baseline scores and post educational intervention scores are compared. Individual scores also can be compared to a team average item by item.

Psychometric Testing

The developers used an iterative process in designing the instrument. They identified team competencies and worked with clinical team members and an adult educator to refine them. Desired team skills were defined and broken down into specific behaviors related to collaboration and working together. The developers made several refinements before individual items were deemed appropriate for inclusion in the instrument. No psychometric data are available.

Evaluation

The second reviewer, one of the developers, has used the instrument with health professions trainees in conjunction with team training in a VA geriatric setting. She also has used it with clinical geriatric teams interested in improving the skills of team members.

The questionnaire is clearly worded and easy to administer. Its length makes item analysis scoring cumbersome, however. It is geared specifically for health care professionals and trainees providing geriatric care. Verbal anchors for the answer choices could be clarified; for example, there is little difference between almost never and rarely and between frequently and almost always. A five point, rather than a six point, scale might be more effective with 0 = no experience with skill, 1 = almost never, 2 = occasionally, 3 = sometimes, and 4 = almost always. No psychometric testing has been conducted to date to determine if items can be scaled or if the instrument is reliable over time or as a pre-/posttest measure.

Status/Availability

The instrument and accompanying guide are available from Ruth Ann Tsukuda, Portland VA Medical Center (P3MIRECC), 3710 Southwest U.S. Veterans Hospital Road, Portland, OR 97207; (503) 273-5227; e-mail, ruthann.tsukuda@med.va.gov.

Relevant Publications

Tsukuda, R.A., & Stahelski, A.J. (1990). *Team Skills Questionnaire*. Unpublished instrument.
Tsukuda, R.A., & Stahelski, A.J. (1990). *Guide to Team Skills*. Unpublished guide.

ANALYZING TEAM EFFECTIVENESS

Developed by Glenn Varney, 1991
Reviewed by Julia Kasl-Godley and Antonette M. Zeiss

Analyzing Team Effectiveness is a relatively short, 12-item educational instrument designed to yield information about task accomplishment and team process (i.e., how the team performs its tasks). It has theoretical underpinnings and is easy to read, complete, and score. No psychometric testing has been conducted. Using an item analysis, teams can identify their problem areas and begin to plan for improvement.

Conceptual Framework

Varney uses a model of productive teams, developed by Rubin, Fry, and Plovich (1978), as the conceptual underpinnings for all three of his instruments included in this volume. (See also the critiques of the Teamwork Survey in this chapter and the Team Profile Survey in Chapter 10). Team productivity is a function of clearly defined and accepted roles and goals, well-defined processes and procedures, effective leadership, and positive relationships. It also is a direct consequence of how well team members work together (i.e., open communication; cooperation; responsibility; and minimal conflict, complaints, or mistake). Quality teamwork results in capitalizing on opportunities, good decision-making, achieved goals, decreased costs, effective use of time, and innovative, effective problem solving.

Teams are work groups within complex organizations. They are living entities that come to life, grow, develop, mature, and eventually die.

Description of Measure

Varney developed the instrument to identify problems or barriers to quality team performance. Team members, then, agree upon a plan for improving team performance. Team members complete the instrument individually. The instrument provides information about the team as a whole.

Components of Team Performance Measured

The instrument measures five components of task performance and seven components of team process. The components of task performance are planning and organizing, problem definition and solution, control, goals and objectives, and follow-up. The components of team process are listening, communication, conflict management, involvement and participation, commitment, mutual support, and flexibility.

The instrument measures all four domains and five of the eight dimensions (team structure and context, interdependence, growth and development, and accomplishments) of our model of team performance, displayed in Chapter 3.

Formatting and Scoring

The instrument includes 12-items; each item has a descriptive label indicating the concept being measured. Respondents circle one answer choice for each item along a five-point continuum. A score of 1 indicates minimal teamwork conditions, and a score of 5 indicates ideal teamwork conditions.

2. *Communications*
   Guarded, cautious   Open, authentic
   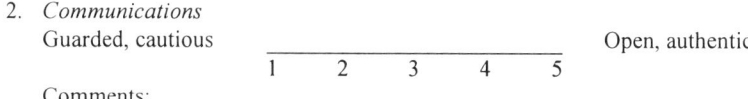
   Comments:

In Varney, G.H. *Building productive teams: An action guide and resource book* ©1991. Reprinted by permission of Jossey-Bass, Inc., a subsidiary of John Wiley & Sons, Inc.

The first five items measure different components of task performance. Respondents choose from 1 = Team does not meet task requirements, 2 = Team meets some task requirements, 3 = Team meets the major task requirements, 4 = Team meets all task requirements, and 5 = Team consistently exceeds expectations. For the seven items measuring team process, verbal anchors are given for each of the extreme scores only.

Each item is analyzed separately. Varney recommends using visual graphics such as bar charts or percentage distributions to summarize the data and present it to the team. Mean scores for each item also can be generated. The reviewers suggest that items on which the majority of team members score lower than two or items with an average team score lower than two should be examined closely as potential problem areas.

Psychometric Testing

No reliability or validity data are available.

Evaluation

The instrument addresses both process and task in its measurement of team performance. It is easy to complete and score and has good readability. It has theoretical underpinnings and face validity; no psychometric testing has been completed, in part, because the developer recommends an item analysis of results and does not scale the items. The descriptive label, Attitudes toward differences within group, for item three in the process section (Section II) is misleading given that the item is not an attitude item, but asks about conflict management. Additionally, some of the items attempt to measure more than one concept. Completion of this instrument and analysis of findings can facilitate discussion of problem areas and guide action planning.

Status/Availability

The instrument is copyrighted and presented in Varney (1991) below. For permission to reproduce it, contact Jossey-Bass, 350 Sansome Street, San Francisco, CA 94104; (415) 433-1740.

Relevant Publications

Rubin, I., Fry, R., & Plovich, M. (1978). *Managing human resources in health organizations*. Reston, VA: Reston Books.

Varney, G.H. (1991). *Building productive teams: An action guide and resource book* (pp. 31-32). San Francisco: Jossey-Bass.

TEAMWORK SURVEY (TWS)

Developed by Glenn H. Varney, 1991, 1999
Reviewed by Alice M. DeFrise, Carole Morrell, and Gloria D. Heinemann

The 1999 version of the TWS includes 33 items and five subscales–Interpersonal, Task/Process, Team Leadership, Reward/Feedback, and Perceived Productivity. Varney designed it to assess teams working within a complex organization. He has conducted reliability testing and revised the instrument to improve its conceptual soundness and internal consistency. No validity testing has been conducted to date. Expanding the subscales, Reward/Feedback and Perceived Productivity would strengthen the instrument as would precoding the answer choices.

Conceptual Framework

Varney uses Rubin, Fry, and Plovich's (1978) model as a conceptual framework for the TWS. Team productivity is the result of both indicators (i.e., effective team processes) and causes (i.e., a well-defined team structure). Indicators include open communication, minimal mistakes, low levels of conflict, cooperation, responsibility, and minimal complaints. Causes include clear and accepted team roles, clear and agreed upon goals, positive relationships, well-defined processes and procedures as well as effective leadership. Results of indicators and causes include capitalizing on opportunities, correct decisions, deadlines met, decreased costs, effective use of time, and innovative and effective problems solving. Rubin and associates view teamwork as a dynamic process in which team members and leaders continually assess, analyze, and improve indicators and causes in order to maximize results.

Teams are work groups within complex organizations. They are living entities that come to life, grow, develop, mature, and eventually die.

Description of Measure

Varney developed the TWS to assess team effectiveness within organizations. Results can help formulate a team's action plan for improving its effectiveness. Team members complete the instrument anonymously; they and the team as a whole are targets of assessment.

Components of Team Performance Measured

The 1999 version of the TWS includes five subscales: Interpersonal (a 13-item subscale that includes items 4, 7, 9, 13, 15, 16, 18, 24 26, 27, 31, 32, 33); Task/Process (a nine-item subscale that includes items 1, 2, 5, 6, 10, 12, 14, 17, 28); Team Leadership (a five-item subscale that includes items 8, 11, 19, 21, 22); Reward/Feedback (a four-item subscale that includes items 3, 25, 29, 30); and Perceived Productivity (a two-item subscale that includes items 20 and 23).

The instrument measures all four domains and six of the eight dimensions (organization and team structure, team context, interdependence, growth and development, and accomplishments) of our model of team performance.

Formatting and Scoring

For each of the 33 items in the 1999 version of the instrument, the verbal anchor statement on the left is the opposite of the statement on the right.

Between the two statements there are five answer choices or Xs. The middle X is intended to reflect neutral feelings toward the statement. The two Xs on the left of the middle answer choice indicate degrees of agreement with the statement on the left. The two to the right of the middle answer choice indicate degrees of agreement with the statement on the right. The Xs closest to each statement indicate strong agreement. For each item, the respondent circles the X that most closely approximately his/her perception (see item example below).

Each of the five answer choices is converted to a numeric score. Responses to items 1, 2, 4-12, 14, 16, 17, 21-24, 26-29, and 31-33, should be scored, from left to right, 1 through 5. Responses to items 3, 13, 15, 18-20, 25, and 30, should be scored, from left to right, 5 through 1 so that 1 = most negative and 5 = most positive. Scores for each of the five subscales are summed. Subscale scores can be averaged across team members to analyze items within each subscale.
In the 1991b version of the instrument, respondents fill in the appropriate circle for each item rather than circling the appropriate X.

	X	X	X	X	X	
	I strongly agree with the statement on the left				I strongly agree with the statement on the right	
33. The team does not have a clear sense of direction.	X	X	X	X	X	The team has a clear sense a clear sense of direction.

Reprinted by permission of the developer.

Psychometric Testing

Internal Consistency Reliability

The Cronbach's alphas are .91 for Interpersonal Subscale, .87 for the Task/Process Subscale, .75 for the Team Leadership Subscale, .61 for the Rewards/Feedback Subscale, and .71 for the Perceived Productivity Subscale.

Test-Retest Reliability

The 1999 version of the instrument has not been subjected to test-retest reliability. Test-retest reliability was examined for the earlier 1989 version of the instrument. The instrument was administered on two occasions two to three weeks apart. Seven of the 43 items had strong test-retest reliability, $r = .75$ or above.

Inter-Rater Reliability

Inter-rater reliability is not appropriate since this instrument is self-administered.

Validity

No validity data are available.

Evaluation

This instrument has been through several iterations. The 1991b version includes 43 items. It differs from earlier versions in that it has a verbal anchor for each of the five answer choices, and some of the items have been reworded for purposes of clarity. Psychometric testing reduced the number of items to 33 in the 1999 version; additional item rewording occurred as well. We recommend using the 1999 version of the instrument, but prefer the verbal anchors for each of the five answer choices in the 1991b version. We also recommend precoding the answer choices on the instrument as opposed to filling in a circle or circling an "X" and attaching numeric codes at a later time. Some minor rewording of items would improve clarity.

Revisions based on the results of a factor analysis improved the instruments reliability and better defined the subscales. The subscales, Interpersonal and Task/Process have strong internal consistency. The subscales, Reward/Feedback and Perceived Productivity are short–four items and two items respectively. Reviewers suggest additional work to develop other relevant items that measure these concepts. The Team Leadership Subscale is misnamed in that none of its items are directly related to leadership within the team. A subscale measuring power sharing in the team or empowerment of team members might be a positive addition to the instrument. We suggest further psychometric testing given that no validity has been established.

Status/Availability

Early versions of the TWS are reproduced in Varney (1991a, 1991b). For the 1991a publication, contact Jossey-Bass, 350 Sansome Street, San Francisco, CA 94104; (415) 433-1740. To purchase the University Associates publication (1991b), contact University Associates at (619) 578-5900). The 1999 version can be obtained from Dr. Varney: P.O. Box 703, Bowling Green, OH 43402; (419) 352-7782; e-mail, gvarney@bgnet.bgsu.edu.

Relevant Publications

Rubin, I., Fry, R., & Plovich, M. (1978). *Managing human resources in health organizations.* Reston, VA: Reston Books.

Varney, G.H. (1991a). *Building productive teams: An action guide and resource book* (pp. 33-36). San Francisco: Jossey-Bass.

Varney, G.H. (1991b). *Teamwork Survey (adapted).* In J.W. Pfeiffer (Ed.), *The encyclopedia of team-development activities* (pp. 251-258). San Diego, CA: University Associates.

Varney, G.H. (1999). *Team Work Survey,* 1999 revised version. Faxed communication.

TEAM COMMUNICATION, COOPERATION, AND CONTRIBUTION SURVEYS

Developed by Suzanne Willis Zoglio, 1993
Reviewed by Ruth Ann Tsukuda and Patricia L. Evans

These three surveys assess team members' perceptions of the quality of communication within the team, cooperation among members of the team, and contributions or functioning of the team. Zoglio recommends an item analysis to ascertain positive, negative, and mixed perceptions of team members. After a discussion, members should develop a plan to improve negatively perceived behaviors. The surveys are short and easy to complete and score; items are clearly and simply stated. The strength of the surveys is their ability to focus the team discussion on areas for improvement. Limitations include the lack of psychometric testing to determine the robustness of the concepts being measured. The three surveys included in this review represent only a portion of group activities described in Zoglio's *50 Activities for Teams at Work.*

Conceptual Framework

Zoglio based the surveys on a seven-key model of team performance. The keys or factors that influence team effectiveness are commitment, contribution, communication, cooperation, conflict management, change management, and connections. When team members are committed to the same goals and their energies are directed toward achieving them, the team develops a synergy that increases cohesion and improves functioning. In high performing teams, members contribute their diverse ideas, talents, and skills. They communicate effectively with one another in an open and friendly manner. As members become more cooperative, the team's flexibility, responsiveness, and efficiency improve. In effective teams, conflict is accepted as a normal part of team dynamics and is managed well in order for members to be productive and satisfied with their jobs. Managing change well ensures that teams keep up with technological changes, customer demands, and shifts in expectations. Finally, connections among team members, other teams, and other facets of the organization are strong. When these seven factors are maximized, team members become more cohesive and respect one another's time; improve their work processes, especially their ability to problem solve; take more initiative and more risks; meet their commitments; and improve their productivity.

A team produces better quality outcomes than do any of its individual members. Well performing teams contribute to the success of an organization.

Description of Measures

The three surveys attempt to ascertain the quality of communication, level of cooperation among tea, members, and the contribution a team makes (i.e., how well it functions). Team members discuss results, identify strengths and weaknesses, and develop an action plan to improve the team. Team members, leaders, organizational managers, trainers, and consultants can use the surveys. Individuals complete them. The focus of assessment is the team itself.

Components of Team Performance Measured

The Team Communication Survey (15 items) focuses on quality communication in the team (i.e., clear goals, clear roles, provide feedback on performance, show respect, hear friendly exchanges, high level of participation, disagree with ideas rather than individuals, compliments given, little prolonged griping, listen to new ideas with an open mind, concise when speaking, listen well, say what's on their minds, little talking behind one another's backs, and solution-oriented). The Team Cooperation Survey (10 items) addresses timeliness for meetings and returning phone calls, consideration of members' schedules in planning, completing assignments, helping one another, conflict, decision-making by consensus, creative problem solving, celebrating together, and cooperation level. The Team Contribution Survey (10 items) measures members' perceptions of the level of contribution on the team or how effectively their team functions (i.e., clarity of roles and responsibilities, use of members' talents, willingness to "pitch in" and get the job done, attendance at meetings, participation at meetings, willingness to take the lead, importance of continual learning, keeping commitments, confidence in team's potential, and benefits to contributing to the team).

The surveys include items in all four domains and six of the eight dimensions (organizational and team structure, team context, interdependence and growth/development, and strategies for productivity) of our team performance model.

Formatting and Scoring

For each survey, there are four Likert-formatted answer choices; code 4 is the most positive and code 1, the most negative. The Team Communication and the Team Cooperation Surveys have the same answer choices–1 = strongly disagree, 2 = disagree, 3 = agree, and 4 = strongly agree. For the Team Cooperation Survey, blanks are included for teams to add items also measuring facets of cooperation. For the team Contribution Survey, 1= not very, 2 = somewhat, 3 = quite a bit, and 4 = extremely. Respondents write the number that corresponds closest to their perceptions of the team to the left of each item. An example from the Cooperation Survey follows:

4 = strongly agree 3 = agree 2 = disagree 1 = strongly disagree

[ ] 1. We are on time for meetings.

Reproduced from "Teams at Work" 7 Keys to Success" ©1993, 1997 by Suzanne W. Zoglio, Ph.D. Used by permission, Tower Hill Press, Doylestown, PA.

Zoglio does not scale the surveys, but recommends an item analysis for each. Responses are transferred to the cells of a tally sheet (i.e., number of items multiplied by four, the number of answer choices) on a flip chart for discussion with team members. Items of special interest are those rated positive (4 or 3) by 75% of team members, those rated negative (1 or 2) by 25% of members, and those with a wide range of responses (i.e., on which there was no consensus). These three sets of items should be discussed among team members. In the discussion, members give examples of the team's successes when discussing the positive items, attempt to understand why they did not come to consensus on the variable response items, and determine which of the negative items include behaviors the team should attempt to improve.

Psychometric Testing

No data reliability or validity data are available.

Evaluation

Each of the surveys offers a quick and simply written approach to gathering information about team functioning. The surveys are easy to read, understand, and complete without the assistance of a trainer or facilitator. Instructions for completing and scoring them are clear and concise. They are especially appropriate for natural work groups that include members with less than a college education and/or unfamiliar with test taking.

No psychometric testing has been conducted on the surveys, and some of the items across surveys are similar; this calls into question the adequacy of the concepts being measured. For example, both the communication and contribution surveys include an item about clear roles within the team. Despite directions indicating that information be shared through discussion, the amount of time suggested for group dialogue is insufficient. Finally, these surveys are probably best used as part of the developer's companion book, *Teams at Work: 7 Keys to Success*, which describes a multi-step program for team improvement.

Status/Availability

The developer holds the copyright. The three surveys appear in the references below. To purchase the publications, contact Tower Hill Press, P.O. Box 1605, Doylestown PA 18901; (888) 370-8807.

Relevant Publications

Zoglio, S.W. (1993). *50 Activities for Teams at Work*. Doylestown, PA: Tower Hill Press.
Zoglio, S.W. (1993). *Teams at Work: 7 Keys to Success*. Doylestown, PA: Tower Hill Press.

CHAPTER 12
FULL-SPECTRUM INSTRUMENTS

Glenda F. Brown, Ed.D.
VA Central Arkansas Health Care System, Little Rock, AR, VISN 16

Evelyn P. Mahairas, Ph.D.
VA Medical Center, Coatesville, PA, VISN 4

Each of the 16 full spectrum instruments critiqued in this chapter covers all four of the domains and seven or eight dimensions of team performance (see Chapter 3). They differ from the other instruments in their broad coverage of team performance, their measurement of team performance within complex organizations, and the number of instruments that are proprietary and must be purchased as part of a consulting package of services or have some other cost associated with their use. Table 12.1 summarizes relevant information about these instruments. Instruments in bold face print in the table and with an asterisk after their respective titles at the beginning of the critiques are designated as "best measures."

OVERVIEW

The full-spectrum instruments vary in length and ease of completion and scoring. Some have good readability; others contain complex wording and, as a result, are inappropriate for front-line employees. The number of items per instrument ranges from a low of 20 to a high of 108. Most instruments are generic in nature. All instruments are self-administered or have a self-administered component.

With regard to purpose, most developers designed their respective instruments for general assessment, consultation, education, and to stimulate discussion for improvement. Two of the 16 also are research instruments (Glaser and Glaser's TEP and Wheelan and Hochberger's GDQ). Ten instruments were based on an identifiable theoretical framework; however, three of these were critiqued as being weak or limited in this regard. Six had no apparent theoretical framework. Instrument formatting does not differ significantly from instruments discussed in Chapters 9 through 11.

Instruments designated as "best measures" from the full-spectrum group include Campbell and Hallam's TDS, Glaser and Glaser's TEP, McClane's Team Assessment Worksheets, and Wheelan and Hochberger's GDQ. For further information about them, see Chapter 14.

Unique Features of the Instruments

Several of the instruments contain unique features. Campbell and Hallam's TDS uses both team members and outside observers to collect data. Harper and Harper's Team Building Assessment is flexible given that it encourages teams to add their own items to the survey. Richard and Smyth and Tercon, Inc. both include action planning as part of their training packages. Glaser and Glaser's TEP and Wheelan and Hochberger's GDQ identify a team's stage of development. Another unique feature of the GDQ is the requirement that individuals attend training to become certified as trainers prior to using the instrument. Finally, McClane's instrument is the only one designed specifically for health care teams.

Proportion with Psychometric Testing

Six of the sixteen instruments have undergone some psychometric testing. One, Wheelan and Hochberger's GDQ, has especially strong psychometric support. Campbell and Hallam report good reliability and validity for their instrument. Campion, Medsker and Higgs report good reliability and good preliminary validity for their instrument. The other three instruments have only preliminary psychometric data at this time. Most of the instruments would benefit from more extensive testing.

Implications for Use

A number of these instruments are proprietary and require a significant financial or time investment to administer, score, and interpret. For some teams, issues of time, staffing considerations, and dollar investment impact the choice of an instrument. Nevertheless, because of the breath of dimensions measured, the full-spectrum measures offer a good "snapshot in time" of the team and factors, throughout the organization, impacting its productivity. These instruments are especially appropriate for educating and consulting with teams in complex organizations, especially those that have undergone major change such as those in the VA system. They hold promise for establishing a baseline for performance post restructuring and prior to educational interventions. With the exception of the two research instruments mentioned above, most are not recommended for research purposes due to insufficient psychometric testing. A summary of the full-spectrum instruments is presented in Table 12.1.

Table 12.1 Summary of Full-Spectrum Instruments

Instrument	Developer(s)	# Items	Purpose	Target Group	Psychometrics
Individual-Team-Organization (ITO) Survey	Anderson	52	Assess & help improve functioning	Generic work groups/teams	None
Team Development Survey (TDS)	Campbell & Hallam	72; 22 observer	Assess, monitor & help improve functioning	Generic work groups/teams	Good reliability & validity
Work Group Characteristics Measure	Campion, Medsker & Higgs	54	Assess & help improve functioning	Generic work groups/teams	Good reliability & good preliminary validity
Team Assessment Inventory (TAI)	Elledge & Phillips	36	Assess & help improve functioning	Generic professional teams	None
Team-Review Survey	Francis & Young	108	Assess & help improve functioning; determine readiness for team building program	Generic work groups/teams	None
Team Effectiveness Profile (TEP)	Glaser & Glaser	50	Assess & help improve functioning; identify stage of development; research	Generic work groups/teams	Good preliminary reliability & validity
Team-Building Assessment	Harper & Harper	71	Assess & help improve functioning	Generic work groups/teams	None
Team Character Inventory	Jamieson	37	Assess & help improve functioning	Generic work groups/teams	None

Instrument	Developer(s)	# Items	Purpose	Target Group	Psychometrics
Team Effectiveness Checklist	Lewis	25	Assess & help improve functioning	Generic work groups/teams	None
Team Assessment Worksheets	McClane	24	Assess & help improve functioning	Clinical rehabilitation teams	Preliminary reliability; no validity
Team Effectiveness Dimensions (TED) Survey	Parry	20	Assess & help improve functioning	Generic work groups/teams	None
Team Well-Being Assessment	Richards & Smyth	28	Assess & help improve functioning	Generic work groups/teams	Preliminary reliability & validity
Team Effectiveness Rating Scale	Rothermich & Saunders	35	Assess & help improve functioning	Generic work groups/teams, (esp. new teams)	None
Team Strength Survey	Tercon, Inc.	35	Assess & help improve functioning	Generic work groups/teams	None
Group Development Questionnaire (GDQ)	Wheelan & Hochberger	60	Assess, monitor & help improve functioning; identify stage of development; research	Generic work groups/teams	Strong reliability & validity
Team Performance Profile	Wilson Learning Corporation	65	Assess & help improve functioning	Generic work groups/teams	None

INDIVIDUAL-TEAM-ORGANIZATION (ITO) SURVEY

Developed by Will Anderson, 1987
Reviewed by Sara A. Brallier and Glenda F. Brown

The Individual-Team-Organization (ITO) Survey is a 52-item, three subscale measure designed to provide a broad organizational analysis by comparing employees' perceptions about their jobs, their experiences on teams, and the organization in which they work. The instrument's strengths include the breadth of dimensions of performance covered and its well-constructed items. It would benefit from reliability and validity testing as well as clarification of answer choices. Each section or subscale could be administered separately given the length of the instrument. It is appropriate for identifying components of employee, team, and organizational performance that require improvement.

Conceptual Framework

Anderson conceptualizes the team in a symbiotic relationship with both the individual employee and the organization. Productivity depends upon the free flow of energy, communication, and resources between employee and team and between team and organization. Effective exchanges require clarity and conscious agreement about desired outcomes as well as the methods and resources needed for achieving them. The greater the congruence between the employee/team and the team/organization, the greater the team's productivity.

The team is the bridge or link between individual employees and the larger organization. The team exists in a give-and-take relationship with both employees and the organization. It must support employees, who do the work of the team. It also must meet the needs of the organization that, in turn, provides the overall framework and resources that enable it to accomplish its tasks.

Description of Measure

The purpose of this measure is threefold: (a) to provide individuals with an opportunity to assess and influence their work environment; (b) to provide teams with means to assess their own functioning and identify areas of strength and weakness; and (c) to provide management with information useful for designing future training to improve the work environment and productivity.

Individual team members complete the instrument, which can be used to make comparisons between (a) members of the same team, (b) team members and the team itself, (c) teams responsible for similar work, and (d) teams and the organizational norms. These comparisons can identify important differences in perceptions of team or organizational characteristics. Dimensions of individual, team, and organizational behaviors (e.g., individual role clarity, team leadership, or organizational climate) can be examined independently to identify specific areas needing improvement.

Components of Team Performance Measured

The ITO Survey measures employees' perceptions of three aspects of work-life: (a) personal and coworker behaviors and working conditions (20 items); (b) team functioning (16 items); and (c) the framework and resources provided by the organization (16 items). The first aspect or subscale includes role clarity, job satisfaction, rewards, communication, collaboration, time management, risks, employee assistance, influence, and purpose. The second aspect, team functioning, addresses the quality of leadership, meeting effectiveness, conflict management, problem solving, productivity, time management, influence, and the clarity of the team's purpose. The third aspect includes items measuring planning, structure, procedures, climate, stress, time management, influence, and organizational mission and goals in the overall organization.

This instrument includes items in all four domains and all eight dimensions of team performance outlined in our model. The majority of the items are concentrated in the dimensions of organizational structure and context and interdependence. Unique elements include risk-taking, time management, employee assistance, and productivity.

Formatting and Scoring

The items are Likert formatted. For each item, there are six answer choices ranging from "almost always" = 5 to "almost never" = 0. Respondents circle the response that most closely represents how often that statement is true for them (see item example below).

	How Often Statement Is True					
	Almost Always	Usually	Frequently	Occasionally	Seldom	Almost Never
Role Clarity						
1. I know what my job is	5	4	3	2	1	0

In J.W. Pfeiffer (Ed.), *The 1987 annual: Developing human resources* ©1987. Reprinted by permission of Jossey-Bass, Inc., a subsidiary of John Wiley & Sons, Inc.

Item responses are summed for each subscale. The individual subscale ranges from 0 to 100. The team and organizational subscales both range from 0 to 80. A high score indicates a positive perception for each of the three subscales.

Psychometric Testing

No reliability or validity data are available.

Evaluation

The ITO Survey is unique in that it attempts to measure not only team functioning, but also perceptions of individual employees and organizational behaviors and performance. It covers a broad range of team performance dimensions, including several unique elements–risk-taking, time management, and the availability of employee assistance. The items are well constructed; they are clear, concise, and measure the appropriate underlying concepts.

Some minor modifications would strengthen the instrument. First, some items ask the respondent to rate the frequency of a behavior or condition occurring "here" (e.g., "I believe that rewards are given fairly here."). It may be difficult for respondents to remember which section of the instrument they are completing (e.g., team or organizational) when answering these questions. We suggest that the term "here" be clarified in each item. Second, the answer choice labels are not distinct from one another (e.g., the answer choices "usually" and "frequently" are very similar in meaning). The instrument would be stronger if the "usually" choice were omitted. Third, all items are positively worded, which creates the potential for response bias. Finally, the instrument is long and, thus, may be inappropriate for busy clinicians or front line workers unfamiliar with test taking. When used with these respondents, we suggest administering each of the three sections at different times. The instrument would benefit from psychometric testing, especially since the developer scales the items.

Status/Availability

The instrument is copyrighted. For large-scale use of the instrument, written permission must be obtained from the developer. The instrument appears in the 1987 publication below. Contact University Associates at (619) 578-5900.

Relevant Publications

Anderson, W. (1987). The Individual-Team-Organization (ITO) Survey: Conscious change for the organization. In J. William Pfeiffer (Ed.), *The 1987 annual: Developing human resources* (pp. 135-148). San Diego, CA: University Associates.

TEAM DEVELOPMENT SURVEY (TDS)*

Developed by David Campbell and Glenn L. Hallam, 1997
Reviewed by Glenda F. Brown and Sara A. Brallier

The Team Development Survey (TDS) provides teams with feedback regarding their effectiveness. It is theoretically based, has good readability, and is relatively easy to complete. A unique feature is that key outside observers complete a shorter survey and its results are included in the overall analysis. The member survey includes 72 items; the observer survey includes 22 items. All completed surveys are returned to National Computer Systems for scoring and analysis. They provide reports from both surveys along with practical recommendations designed to impact positively on team morale, communication, and productivity. This version has good reliability and good preliminary validity; it would benefit from further psychometric testing.

Conceptual Framework

Campbell and Hallam's team success model serves as the theoretical underpinnings for this instrument. This model presumes that all teams have tangible (e.g., a budget) and intangible (e.g., knowledge, time) resources that can help them accomplish their work. A team can increase its effectiveness by assessing its resources and looking for ways to build, expand, or improve them. The team also can improve its performance by using its resources more efficiently. Finally, to maximize its performance the team must evaluate it and seek continuous improvement. Leadership is a primary force in helping the team improve. Teams that build on their resources, use them effectively, and attend to their processes will be high performing and will have members who are satisfied and happy to be part of it.

The team consists of individuals working together in departmental or project-based work groups to accomplish mutual tasks within a complex organization.

Description of Measure

Developers designed the TDS to assess a team's strengths and weaknesses and identify ways to improve upon the weaknesses. Work groups can use the findings to stimulate discussion about the team's performance, facilitate action planning, assess how well the team is meeting the needs of its internal and external customers, and benchmark team progress. The developers also suggest that this information can be used to improve team morale, productivity, and communication; assist the team in self-management efforts; and support total quality management and continuous improvement programs. Using the respective forms, team members and selected outside observers, who are familiar with the team's work, assess its performance.

Components of Team Performance Measured

The survey includes 72-items grouped into 18 subscales and an overall Index of Performance. The Index and the subscales are categorized into four themes–efficiency, resources, improvement, and team success. Subscales included in the efficiency theme are Mission Clarity, Individual Goals, Team Coordination, Empowerment, and Team Unity. Subscales included in the resources theme are Time and Staffing, Organizational Support, Information, Skills, Material Resources, and Commitment. The improvement theme includes the subscales, Team Assessment, Rewards, Innovation, Leadership, and Feedback. Subscales within the team success theme are Satisfaction, Performance, and the overall Index of Performance.

Because developers believe that some teams are overly insulated and would benefit from feedback outside the team, they designed a companion, observer survey to be completed by three to eight outside observers. Key observers can include suppliers, customers, or coworkers who are not members of the team. The observer survey includes 22 items measuring perceptions of the team's functioning and performance. Components of this survey include resources and organizational support provided to the team, the effectiveness of the team's leadership, the clarity of its mission and goals, team members' skills and commitment to the team, and how well the members work together. It also measures the extent to which the team is organized, innovative, plans well, and meets its objectives; the overall quality of the team's work; and the observers' satisfaction with the team's work.

It measures all four domains and all eight dimensions of our model of team performance. A unique feature is its measurement of time management.

Formatting and Scoring

The member survey is composed of 72 Likert formatted items. For each statement, respondents indicate their perceptions by filling the appropriate circle with a number two pencil. Answer choices are strongly agree = **A**, agree = A, slightly agree = a, slightly disagree = d, disagree = D, and strongly disagree = **D**. Each of the 18 subscales includes three to six items. Ten of the items appear on more than one subscale, and four of the items do not appear on any of the subscales. The response format for the 22-item observer survey is the same as the member survey. It also includes items about the observer's familiarity with the team's effectiveness, relationship to the team, and gender.

The company scores the instrument. Items and subscales are standardized so that the mean is always 50 and the standard deviation, 10. On each of the standardized subscales, two-thirds of the population scores between 40 and 60.

Teams receive a team member report and a team report. Each team member receives a copy of the member report, which describes how his/her item and subscale scores compare to the team's scores. It includes suggestions for improvement in the areas that the member perceived such a need. The team report includes descriptive statistics and graphic presentations depicting the team's scores on the overall index and the subscales as well as a summary of the team members' responses to each item.

Psychometric Testing

Internal Consistency Reliability

For 1,881 team members who completed the third version of the TDS, the Cronbach's alpha scores ranged from .61 to .95. The mean of the alphas was .73, and the median, .69. The inter-item correlations ranged from .16 to .68; item-to-scale correlations ranged from .30 to .76.

Test-Retest Reliability

Developers administered the TDS twice, 17 days apart, to 11 teams and 88 individuals. Test-retest correlations ranged from .69 to .90 with a median of .80.

Inter-Rater Reliability

No data are available.

Content or Face Validity

Developers identified the components of team performance through an extensive literature review. They selected those frequently mentioned as relevant to team effectiveness, applicable to a wide variety of teams, and measurable by asking team members for their attitudes, opinions, and perceptions. The final version is a result of three iterations. Refinements were based on psychometric testing and feedback from respondents.

Concurrent Validity

For 1,881 team members who completed the third version of the survey, statistical tests were performed to determine whether the subscale scores on the survey correlated with the corresponding items in the observer survey. Correlations between the average subscale scores for the team and observers' scores ranged from .26 to .70 with a .66 correlation between the observers' overall rating of the team and the team's score on the overall Index.

The average subscale scores for the team were correlated with performance assessed by the observers (N =107 teams), the Team Leader (N = 162 teams), and the members who were not team leaders (N =194 teams). The Skills Subscale (r = .66, .50, and .66, respectively), the Commitment Subscale (r = .58, .43, and .66, respectively), the Innovation Subscale (r = .56, .41, and .61, respectively), and the Leadership Subscale (r = .58, .36, and .60, respectively) correlated highest with the three performance measures. The Materials Resources Subscale (r = .12, .19, and .16, respectively) and the Time and Staffing Subscale (r = .18, .29, and .39, respectively) correlated lowest with the performance measures. Although almost all of these correlations are significant due to the large sample size, the absolute size of these relationships is small.

Construct/Predictive Validity

No data are available.

Discriminant Validity

Correlations between average subscale scores for the team and team members' demographic characteristics indicate that the subscale scores are unrelated to extraneous demographic factors, such as gender, race, or age.

Evaluation

This instrument is based on a theoretical framework, has good readability, is relatively easy to complete despite its length, and has good initial psychometric data. It also is based on a thorough review of the literature and has undergone numerous iterations. The instrument is unique in that it includes an observer survey, which enables team members' perceptions to be corroborated by persons outside the team. Additionally, it permits flexibility to meet specific needs of a team in that up to 13 additional items can be added to it.

The final version would benefit from further psychometric testing since a number of the items are included in more than one subscale and several items are not included in any of the subscales. The integrity of the subscales could be improved by factor analyses.

Developers recommend a trained outside facilitator be responsible for guiding the administration and feedback process. Completed instruments must be sent back to National Computer Systems for scoring and analysis. The reports, sent back to the participants, include practical suggestions for improvement.

Status/Availability

The instrument and accompanying manuals/guides are copyrighted and may be purchased from National Computer Systems, Inc., 9701 West Higgins Road, Rosemont, IL 60018; (800) 221-8378 or http://asessments.ncs.com.

Relevant Publications

Campbell, D., & Hallam, G.L. (1997). *Team Development Survey*. Rosemont, IL: National Computer Systems, Inc.

Campbell, D. (1994). *Manual for the Campbell-Hallam Team Development Survey.* Minneapolis, MN: National Computer Systems, Inc.

WORK GROUP CHARACTERISTICS MEASURE

Developed by Michael A. Campion, Gina J. Medsker, and A. Catherine Higgs, 1993
Reviewed by Linda O. Nichols and Martha S. Waite

The Work Group Characteristics Measure is self-administered and includes 54-items assessing team effectiveness related to five themes (i.e., job design, interdependence, composition, context, and process) and 19 group characteristics. It has a strong theoretical basis, good reliability data, and good preliminary validity data. It has considerable breadth and depth with regard to the concept of team effectiveness and includes some unique elements often omitted from other team assessments. Reviewers suggest revisions of a number of items to improve clarity, reduce redundancy, and adapt the instrument for health care settings. Additional reliability and validity testing with larger and more diverse employee populations would strengthen the instrument as well. It is appropriate for organizational assessment and to indicate when managers should intervene in work groups to improve their effectiveness.

Conceptual Framework

The theoretical framework results from a number of perspectives (i.e., social psychology, sociotechnical theory, industrial engineering, and organizational psychology). Increasingly work in organizations is being organized around groups or teams of employees. Such a work design is risky in that work groups have the potential for both positive and negative outcomes. Thus, it is important to identify the characteristics of work groups that are positively related to or have the potential to increase productivity and employee satisfaction. Developers identified job design, interdependence, composition, context, and process as themes related to effectiveness (i.e., productivity and employee satisfaction).

Developers view the team as a work group whose members function interdependently and cooperate with other work groups in the organization.

Description of Measure

Developers designed the instrument to measure effectiveness in work groups and to help managers learn to create and maintain effective groups within their respective organizations and to know when and how to intervene in the groups (e.g., alter size or composition, train, appraise, and reward groups). Members complete the instrument individually. Average scores provide team profiles.

Components of Team Performance Measured

Developers identify five themes and 19 group characteristics of effectiveness. Job design, includes five characteristics–self-management, participation, task variety, task significance, and task identity (i.e., the degree to which the group is responsible for all aspects of a product). Interdependence includes three characteristics–task interdependence, goal interdependence, and interdependent feedback and rewards. Four characteristics make up composition–heterogeneity, flexibility, relative size, and preference for group work. Organizational context includes three characteristics–training, managerial support, and communication/cooperation between groups. Four characteristics make up process–potency or team spirit, social support, workload sharing, and communication/cooperation within the work group.

The instrument includes items in all four domains and seven of the eight dimensions of our team performance model. There are no items measuring strategies for productivity. Items are concentrated in the domain of interdependence; there is good representation of items measuring organizational structure and team context as well. Unique elements include fit between team and individual goals, self-management, individual rewards for teamwork, team size, provision of education/training, and managerial support.

Formatting and Scoring

The 54-item instrument is self-administered. All items are scored using a five-point Likert format with 5 = strongly agree and 1 = strongly disagree. The items measure the 19 characteristics identified above under description of the measure. Seventeen of the characteristics or subscales consist of three items each; Relative Size is measured by one item, and Managerial Support is measured by two items. Respondents write the appropriate answer choice on the blank provided for each item. Answer choices are depicted at the top of the page.

$$\begin{aligned}
\text{Strongly agree} &= 5 \\
\text{Agree} &= 4 \\
\text{Neither agree nor disagree} &= 3 \\
\text{Disagree} &= 2 \\
\text{Strongly disagree} &= 1
\end{aligned}$$

Goal Interdependence (Goals)
_____ 19. My work goals come directly from the goals of my team.

In Campion, M.A., Medsker, G.J., & Higgs, A.C. Relations between work group characteristics and effectiveness: Implications for designing effective work groups ©1993. Reprinted by permission of *Personnel Psychology*.

The items for each of the 19 characteristics are summed to create 19 subscales; the size item is reverse-coded. The subscales can be divided by the team size to obtain team averages.

Psychometric Testing

Internal Consistency Reliability

Developers forced a 19-factor solution to ensure that the 19 characteristics are distinct from one another; they explained 73% of the total variance. Intercorrelations among the characteristics were low (average r using z transformation = .22). Internal consistency reliabilities showed only communication/cooperation between groups was below .60 (actually .47). Items within each subscale were not intercorrelated.

Test-Retest Reliability

No data are available.

Inter-Rater Reliability

Intraclass correlations assessed the reliability of the aggregate responses across members (N = 5) of the teams (N = 78) for the 19 characteristics. Fourteen were significant. None of the items in the interdependence theme (i.e., task interdependence, goal interdependence, and interdependent feedback and rewards) were significant, nor were heterogeneity or managerial support. Inter-rater agreement was moderate (.50) to high with the exception of flexibility, relative size, and workload sharing. When managers' ratings were correlated with employees' ratings, only 11 of 19 were significant, and most correlations were low. In summary, all scales showed reliability in at least one analysis and 15 showed reliability in two or more analyses.

Content or Face Validity

Developers do not present data regarding this type of validity. Items resulted from an extensive literature review. They are consistent with the respective underlying concepts being measured; however, there is not much depth to the measurement of each concept.

Concurrent and Construct Validity

Developers correlated the 19 characteristics and a composite score for each of the five themes with three other measures of effectiveness–another productivity measure completed by employees and managers, employee satisfaction from an organizational opinion survey, and managers' judgements of effectiveness. Six of the 19 characteristics (self-management within the job design theme; relative size within the composition theme; and all of the characteristics within the process theme–potency, social support, workload sharing, and within group communication/cooperation) correlated significantly ($p < .05$) with the other measure of productivity. Eight characteristics (participation, task variety, and task significance within the job design theme; interdependent feedback and rewards within the interdependence theme; relative size within the composition theme; training and managerial support within the context theme; and potency within the process theme) correlated significantly with the measure of employee satisfaction. Eight characteristics (self-management, task variety, and task significance within the job design theme; flexibility and relative size within the composition theme; training within the context theme; and potency and workload sharing within the process theme) correlated significantly with managers' judgements of effectiveness.

Several of the characteristics (task identity, task interdependence, goal interdependence, heterogeneity, and communication/cooperation between work groups) were unrelated to any of the other measures of effectiveness. Developers partially addressed this by revising the heterogeneity items. Items measuring these characteristics require more validity testing in other employee populations.

For four of the five themes, employees' composite scores correlated significantly ($p < .05$) with the other productivity measure and managers' judgements of effectiveness; organizational context was not significantly related to either of these measures. Again employees' composite scores on four of the five themes correlated significantly with employee satisfaction; process was not significantly related to employee satisfaction.

Predictive/Discriminant Validity

No data are available.

Evaluation

This instrument is comprehensive with strong theoretical underpinnings. It includes items measuring fit between team and individual goals, self-management, individual rewards for teamwork, team size, provision of education/training, and managerial support, which are sometimes missing from other measures. It also has good reliability and good preliminary validity data. The instrument should be tested on larger and more diverse samples of employees. It is relatively easy to score, but somewhat lengthy.

Too often two or three items are worded so much alike that they are measuring the same thing rather than different facets of the same concept (e.g., items measuring participation, task interdependence, goal interdependence, preference for group work, potency, and workload sharing). Additionally, some of the items would benefit from minor revision to improve clarity (e.g., items measuring social support) and for more appropriate use in health care settings (e.g., items measuring task identity and flexibility). Team size includes only one item about the negative effects of teams that are too small. This does not take into account that too large a team or inappropriate professionals on the team also can negatively affect team effectiveness.

Status/Availability

The copyrighted instrument is reprinted in the Campion, Medsker, and Higgs (1993) publication below. Note that items measuring heterogeneity have been revised post psychometric testing since the original items were not related to the measures of effectiveness used to establish validity.

Relevant Publications

Campion, M.A., Medsker, G.J., & Higgs, A.C. (1993). Relations between work group characteristics and effectiveness: Implications for designing effective work groups. *Personnel Psychology, 46*, 823-850.

TEAM-ASSESSMENT INVENTORY (TAI)

Developed by Robin L. Elledge and Steven L. Phillips, 1994
Reviewed by Antonette M. Zeiss and Steven Lovett

The TAI is a 36-item measure of team effectiveness. Developers designed it for use in team development and to identify components of team performance needing improvement. It is based on a theoretical framework that includes the five components of team effectiveness–team goals, team roles, team processes and procedures, team relationships, and team leadership. Developers also included a sixth component of effectiveness, general productivity and climate. The instrument's theoretical underpinnings are strong, and it is relatively easy to complete and score. Weaknesses include lack of psychometric testing, redundancy in the measurement of several components, and items that attempt to measure more than one concept. Due to wording complexity, it is recommended for professional and managerial teams only.

Conceptual Framework

The theoretical model, developed by Beckhard (1972) and Starchevich and Stonell (1990), identifies five interrelated components of team effectiveness–goals, roles, processes and procedures, relationships, and leadership. Goals provide purpose and direction for the team's actions. Commitment and ownership of goals keep the energy within the team focused. Designing roles (i.e., structuring work, designing jobs, and allocating responsibilities) helps ensure that the team's goals will be accomplished. Processes and procedures refer to how the team conducts its business. Relationships among members involve the development of trust and cohesiveness, and leadership refers to the qualities of the supervisor or team leader and the capacity of all team members to assume a leadership role when necessary.

Developers view the team as a rope. "Each strand of the rope must be strong, but the strands also must be woven together in such a way that the individual strands support and add strength to the whole" (Elledge & Phillips, 1994, pp. 22).

Description of Measure

Developers designed the instrument to assess how well or poorly a team is functioning and to identify its strengths and weaknesses. Team members complete the instrument individually; their perceptions can be summarized for specific items. Problem solving sessions can help with action planning.

Components of Team Performance Measured

The instrument measures the five components in the model of team effectiveness–goals (items 7-12), roles (items 13-18), processes and procedures (items 19-24), relationships (items 25-30), and leadership (items 31-36) described above. In addition, developers added a sixth component, general productivity and climate (items 1-6). This component measures how the team perceives its performance and any environmental issues that might affect it.

The instrument measures all four domains and all eight dimensions of our team performance model. It is heavily biased toward measurement of elements of performance within the team.

Formatting and Scoring

Respondents rate their perceptions of the team along a continuum from 5 = most effective to 1 = least effective. Two opposing statements of behavior anchor the answer choices. In all instances, the positive item appears on the left side of the instrument (see item example below).

28. Different points of view are encouraged; varied behavior is accepted; diversity is fostered.	5 4 3 2 1	The team narrowly defines what is acceptable behavior and speech; diversity is discouraged.

In Elledge, R.L., & Phillips, S.L. *Team building for the future: Beyond the basics* ©1994. Reprinted by permission of Jossey-Bass, Inc., a subsidiary of John Wiley & Sons, Inc.

Developers recommend three scoring methods. The first is an item analysis in which team members' responses are averaged for each item. The nine items with the highest average scores represent the team's strengths; the nine items with the lowest average scores represent the team's weaknesses. The second method is a component analysis that involves average scores for each of the six components. The third method is an overall average score of responses for all 36 items. Developers note that average scores above 3.5 represent strong effectiveness and those below 2.5 require development and improvement.

Psychometric Testing

No reliability or validity data are available.

Evaluation

The instrument has good theoretical underpinnings and is easy to complete and score. Scoring instructions are clear. For the goals, roles, and leadership components, items measure the underlying concepts, respectively, but are not exhaustive with regard to the concepts. The components–general productivity and climate, relationship, and processes and procedures–are not distinct from one another in that some of the items across these components are measuring the same underlying concept. The instrument would benefit from psychometric testing; a factor analysis would help determine which items "hang together" with regard to concept measurement. Given that all positively worded items appear along the left side of the instrument and the instrument is relatively long, there is the possibility of response bias. Additionally, many of the items attempt to measure more than one concept. Revision of items would improve conceptual soundness and clarity. Finally, for such a broad measure, it does not adequately tap the role of the team within the organization. The wording of items is complex; thus, the instrument is inappropriate for nonprofessional employees.

Status/Availability

The copyrighted instrument appears in the 1994 publication by Elledge and Phillips (see below). Prior written permission is necessary to reproduce more than 100 copies or for any electronic reproductions. To purchase the publication, contact Pfeiffer & Company at (800) 274-4434.

Relevant Publications

Beckhard, R. (1972). Optimizing team building efforts. *Journal of Contemporary Business, 1,* 23-32.

Elledge, R.L., & Phillips, S.L. (1994). *Team building for the future: Beyond the basics* (pp. 10-31). San Diego, CA: Pfeiffer & Company.

Starchevich, M., & Stonell, S. (1990). *Teamwork: We have met the enemy and they are us.* Bartlesville, OK: The Center for Management and Organizational Effectiveness.

TEAM-REVIEW SURVEY

Developed by Dave Francis and Don Young, 1979, 1992
Reviewed by Thomas F. Miller and Linda O. Nichols

The Team Review Survey consists of 108 forced-choice questions that identify 12 potential problems or blockages to team effectiveness. The instrument is broad based and addresses the team within an organizational context; it is useful in identifying the team's strengths and weaknesses. The weaknesses identified can be addressed through discussion and team development activities. No psychometric testing has been conducted, and it would benefit from additional revision of some items to improve conceptual clarity of the subscales. It comes with a facilitator's guide and scoring template. It is best suited for consultation and training and is inappropriate for research.

Conceptual Framework

Francis and Young base their approach to teams and the Survey on an investigation of teams in industry, commerce, education, social welfare, shipping, media production, and military organizations. They utilize the stages of small group development as a theoretical framework; they view team building as "a series of steps toward maturity," achieved through nurturing and systematic planning. As the team matures, it addresses a variety of problems. Unresolved problems become obstacles or "blockages."

There are several metaphors that Francis and Young use to describe teams. One is the team as small group that develops and matures (i.e., becomes more effective over time and with the help of consultation/training). Another is the team as "energy," characteristics or facets of effectiveness (e.g., leadership, membership, etc.) as "generators," and problems within these facets as "blockages." A third metaphor is the team as "family" that provides identity, support, love, and protection. Finally, the team is perceived as a "crystal" in which its many facets appear differently depending on the viewing angle.

Description of Measure

The purpose of this instrument is to help team members explore the team's strengths and weaknesses, to determine whether they have the desire and energy to begin a team building program, and to help team members define and understand the characteristics of effective teamwork. The original scale was modified to improve clarity of items in 1992. Team members complete the instrument individually. It can be used to compare members' responses with one another or with the team average. It also can be used to describe the team as a whole. The revised version comes with a facilitator's guide and scoring template.

Components of Team Performance Measured

The developers identified 12 components of teamwork–leadership, membership, commitment, climate, achievement orientation, role development, effectiveness of work methods, team organization, critiquing, individual development, creative capacity, and intergroup relations.

This instrument measures all four domains and all eight dimensions of team performance outlined in our model of team performance. It focuses on the dimensions of team structure, interdependence, and growth and development. Unique features of the instrument are its measurement of leadership, evaluation, intergroup relations, and individual development.

Formatting and Scoring

The instrument consists of 108 forced choice items in 12 dimensions or blockages of teamwork. The items are phrased as negative statements about the team. Each team member rates the statements as "A," generally true for this team, "B," sometimes true for this team, or "Blank," generally untrue for this team (see example below). There are nine statements placed throughout the instrument for each of the 12 dimensions or blockages.

> A = Generally true for this team
> B = Sometimes true for this team
> Blank = Generally untrue for this team

_____ 49. The leader is not willing to have his or her ideas challenged.

In Francis, D., & Young, D. *The Team-Review Survey* ©1992. Reprinted by permission of Jossey-Bass, Inc., a subsidiary of John Wiley & Sons, Inc.

For each blockage, the individual's total score is calculated by multiplying the number of "A" responses by three, multiplying the number of "B" responses by one, and then summing the products. Each individual ranks his or her total score, from 1 = most problematic to 12 = least problematic, for each blockage. This determines the individual team member's perception of the team's strengths and weaknesses. From the individual scores, an average team score is calculated for each blockage. The average team scores also are ranked from 1 through 12, with the highest average score given a score of one, the problem or blockage most in need of attention.

Psychometric Testing

No reliability or validity data are available.

Evaluation

The instrument measures considerable breadth and depth with regard to team effectiveness. It is long (requires 20 minutes to complete), yet relatively easy to score. In the revised version, wording clarity of some items is improved.

There are some conceptual and methodological problems with the instrument. Negatively worded items and negatively labeled subscales create the potential for response bias. Some redundancy exists among items in several of the subscales (i.e., soft critiquing and stunted individual development), and some of the subscales' names do not clearly reflect the concept measured by the items. For example, the Ineffective Work Methods Subscale deals exclusively with team meetings, and some of the items in the lack of Role Clarity Subscale seem to be measuring goals and objectives not roles and responsibilities. Some subscales attempt to measure overly general concepts, and reviewers question the internal consistency reliability of their items (i.e., Unqualified Membership, Unconstructive Climate, and Low Achievement Orientation).

The revised instrument is appropriate for team development and identifying strengths and weaknesses for discussion in team consultations. It would benefit by further revision to improve the measurement of concepts. Given the lack of reliability and validity data, it is inappropriate for research.

Status/Availability

The instrument is copyrighted. The original instrument appears in the 1979 publication below. The revised version can be purchased from the publisher. In the manual, developers discuss team building and include a copy of the revised instrument. Contact Pfeiffer & Company at (800) 274-4434.

Relevant Publications

Francis, D., & Young, D. (1992). *The Team-Review Survey.* San Diego, CA: Pfeiffer & Company.
Francis, D., & Young, D. (1992). *Improving work groups: A practical manual for team building (revised): Professional edition.* San Diego, CA: Pfeiffer & Company.
Francis, D., & Young, D. (1979) *Improving work groups: A practical manual for team building.* San Diego, CA: University Associates.

TEAM EFFECTIVENESS PROFILE (TEP)*

Developed by Rollin Glaser and Christine Glaser, 1980, 1995
Reviewed by Theresa J.K. Drinka and Steven Lovett

The 1995 version of the Team Effectiveness Profile is a 50-item, diagnostic instrument designed to identify blockages to team effectiveness. The instrument has good theoretical underpinnings, good readability, and although long, it is relatively easy to complete and score. The 1995 TEP is the result of several revisions of earlier instruments. It comes with a facilitator's guide and scoring forms and templates. The TEP has credible internal consistency, face validity, and some construct validity; however, it would benefit from further psychometric testing. It is appropriate for work groups at any level of an organization. Its findings help stimulate discussion for improving team effectiveness. It has some potential, pending further psychometric testing, as a research evaluation instrument that measures the impact of education/training interventions.

Conceptual Framework

The instrument is based on Beckhard's (1969) five categories of group issues/blockages that can inhibit team effectiveness. These categories include group mission, planning and goal setting, roles, operating processes, interpersonal relationships, and intergroup relations. Groups or teams can function effectively or ineffectively in each of these areas. The ineffective behaviors represent blockages that the group needs to identify, confront, and remove to become a well performing team. Blockages are most likely to occur in new groups, traditional work groups, and groups that have not developed over time. Once members work together as a team, they find ways to reduce and eliminate blockages.

The team includes people who share work goals and must coordinate their efforts to achieve them. The developers suggest that work groups move through five stages of development from immature group to synergistic team.

Description of Measure

The TEP's purpose is to identify members' perceptions of blockages to their group's performance. Once identified, the group should begin to eliminate these blockages in order to improve output and group members' satisfaction. It also can be used to identify a team's the current stage of development. Group/team members complete the instrument individually. It is intended for intact groups, including their respective manager or supervisor; it also can be useful to groups where members do not report to the same manager. It can be used to compare members' responses with one another or with the group average, to describe one team, or to compare teams. The measure has been used with utility companies, pharmaceutical companies, schools, waste disposal companies, banks, insurance companies, hotels, and oil companies; it also has been used in research.

Components of Team Performance Measured

The 50-item instrument measures five facets of group effectiveness/performance–group mission, planning and goal setting, group roles, group operating processes, interpersonal relationships, and intergroup relations. Each of the five concepts is measured by 10 items. A summation of all of the 50 items provides a measure of overall team effectiveness.

The instrument is a broad measure of all four domains and all eight dimensions of our team performance model.

Formatting and Scoring

The 1995 version of the TEP has 50 items that are both positively and negatively worded. The five answer choices for each item are 1 = completely uncharacteristic, 2 = usually uncharacteristic, 3 = somewhat characteristic, 4 = usually characteristic, and 5 = completely characteristic of my group or team. The 50 items are listed together on the inventory pages. Respondents circle the appropriate answer choice on the Response Form. Their answers are transferred to the Scoring Form via pressure sensitive paper, where numeric answer choices are assigned to responses.

Individual scores are summed in each of the five areas/categories of team effectiveness on the Scoring Form. Category scores of each member are summed to achieve his/her team effectiveness score. The individual team effectiveness scores of all members can be summed and averaged for an overall team effectiveness score. Each of the five scores range from a low of 10 to a high of 50, and the overall effectiveness score ranges from a low of 50 to a high of 250. Negatively worded items are reverse coded on the Scoring Sheet so the higher the scores the more effective the team. Individual scores and team scores can be plotted for each category to create a team profile, which can be compared to normative data. Normative mean scores are provided for each category of teamwork. These scores were developed from a combined sample of 550 respondents from several organizations.

Developers suggest the following cut off points for interpreting scores. For the five category scores, scores between 43 and 50 indicate "very effective;" scores between 37 and 43, "effective;" scores between 32 and 37, "somewhat effective;" scores between 26 and 32, "ineffective;" and scores between 10 and 26, "very ineffective." For overall effectiveness, scores of 216-250 indicate a highly developed and interdependent, synergistic team. Scores of 189-215 indicate an effective group that has developed both task and process skills and where members work well together, but there is room for improvement. Scores of 161-188 indicate a cohesive group with strong interpersonal relationships and allegiances. Scores of 134-160 indicate a fragmented group in conflict on a number of issues, and scores of 50-133 indicate an immature group in which individuals have not begun to develop their tasks and process skills and are dependent on a leader for direction and support.

Psychometric Testing

Internal Consistency Reliability

The original, 28-item TEP was administered to many groups of various sizes and compositions. Split half reliability on all groups showed consistency of responses within groups. Developers used Cronbach's alpha to measure the internal consistency of the 1995 version and each of its five categories. In a study of 140 nursing team leaders, the alpha coefficient was .98. In a combined sample of 139, drawn from various organizations, the instrument achieved a reliability coefficient of .96. For this same combined sample, the alphas for each of the five categories of team effectiveness were: group mission, .76; group roles, .80; group operating processes, .83; group interpersonal relationships, .89; and intergroup relations, .85. Developers chose not to conduct a factor analysis of each of the five categories because they regard them as related facets of team effectiveness and not as separate scales.

Test-Retest/Inter-Rater Reliability

No data are available regarding test-retest reliability, and testing for inter-rater reliability is inappropriate since the measure is self-administered.

Content or Face Validity

In preparing the 1995 version, 60 items were assessed by a panel of reviewers familiar with the team effectiveness literature. On the basis of their assessment, items were dropped, reworded, and new items added that better measure the five categories or areas of team effectiveness.

Concurrent Validity

No data are available.

Construct Validity

One would expect team effectiveness to be positively related to quality and quantity of work. In one study, the five categories/areas of team effectiveness and the total team effectiveness score were correlated with measures of the quality and quantity of simulated work in both U.S. and Malaysian workshop teams. All 24 of the possible correlation coefficients between team effectiveness and work quality and quantity were expected to be positive. Results were mixed in that 19 coefficients were positive and five were negative. Six coefficients were significant at the .05 level. For U.S. teams, group roles and group interpersonal relationships were correlated significantly with quality of work, and intergroup relations was correlated significantly with quantity of work. For Malaysian teams, group-operating processes, group interpersonal relationships, and total team effectiveness were correlated significantly with quality of work.

Predictive/Discriminant Validity

No data are available for these types of validity.

Evaluation

Considerable time and expertise went into developing the current or third edition of the TEP. It is based on a sound theoretical framework, and the categories and items are reasonable representations of their respective underlying concepts. Although long, it is easy to read, complete, and score. Scoring directions and templates accompanying the instrument are clear and easy to use. Normative data have been established and scores can be easily interpreted. The preliminary psychometric testing suggests that the instrument is reliable and valid; however, further testing is recommended, especially given that some of the initial testing used workshop teams rather than actual work teams. It also is unclear to what degree the five category scores are interrelated. The utility of creating a profile score cannot be assessed without such data. This instrument is useful for teams interested in identifying areas of team performance for improvement and for stimulating action planning.

Status/Availability

The TEP is copyrighted by and available commercially from HRDQ, 2002 Renaissance Boulevard #100, King of Prussia, PA 19406-2756; (800) 633-4533.

Relevant Publications

Beckhard, R. (1969). *Organization development: Strategies and models*. Reading, MA: Addison-Wesley.

Glaser, R., & Glaser, C. (1995). *Team Effectiveness Profile: How is your team working?* (3rd ed.). King of Prussia, PA: Organization Design and Development, Inc.

Glaser, R., & Glaser, C. (1995). *Team Effectiveness Profile: Facilitator guide*. (3rd ed.). King of Prussia, PA: Organization Design and Development, Inc.

TEAM-BUILDING ASSESSMENT

Developed by Ann Harper and Bob Harper
Reviewed by Gloria D. Heinemann and Thomas F. Miller

The Team-Building Assessment is a 71-item measure of team or work group performance within a complex organization. Developers designed it as a learning tool to help teams identify their strengths and weaknesses and plan for improving their performance. Its covers a broad range of team performance dimensions, and its use of simple, clear language makes it appropriate for work groups at any level of the organization. Given that no psychometric data exist for the measure, it should not be used for other purposes. It is especially appropriate for organizations undergoing restructuring and change.

Conceptual Framework

The instrument is based on an informal framework that outlines the characteristics of successful teams. Such teams have a shared mission to which all members agree and are committed, a climate of trust and openness, open and honest communication, a sense of belonging, diversity valued as an asset, creativity and risk-taking, ability to self-correct, interdependence of members, consensus decision-making, and shared leadership.

The team is a self-directed work group within a complex organization. It reacts to change quickly, delivers high quality products/services to customers, and continuously attempts to improve.

Description of Measure

The instrument's purpose is to help teams identify and come to consensus about their strengths and weaknesses. Team members discuss results to generate and prioritize a list of actions to facilitate team development. Team members complete the instrument individually.

Components of Team Performance Measured

The instrument addresses components of team performance within the team and between the team and organizational management. Components measured within the team include team mission, team and individual goals, trust among team members/between leader and members, leadership and influence, and relationships among team members (e.g., cooperating, competing, helping, supporting, feelings of closeness). Also measured are feelings toward the team, communication and listening, feedback, decision-making and problem solving, responsibility for follow through, the role of conflict, effectiveness of team meetings, ideas and risk-taking, opportunities for growth and development, customer priority, and productivity. Components linking the team to management and the organization include: feelings toward one's job (e.g., committed, motivated, loyalty); communication with and support from management; career opportunities; time given for development and problem solving; job security; individual productivity; and recognition/rewards for teams and individuals.

Several components include more than one item (e.g., the team meetings component includes 10 items, role of team leader and team members each include three items, ability to influence includes four items). Developers encourage team members to add additional components that are specific to their respective teams.

The instrument measures all four domains and seven of the eight dimensions of our team performance model. Only the dimension, strategies for productivity, is not measured. It is unique in that it measures "groupthink," participation of team members, and learning and improving among members. It also measures team leadership, relations between leader and members, and team effectiveness in considerable depth.

Formatting and Scoring

The instrument includes 71 positively worded items, whose Likert formatted answer choices include 0 = never, 1 = some of the time, 2 = most of the time, and 3 = always (see item example below).

	Never	Some of the Time	Most of the Time	Always
11. Team receives the technical training it needs.	0	1	2	3

In Harper, A., & Harper B. *Skill-building for self-directed team members* ©1992. Reprinted by permission of MW Corporation.

Developers suggest using item and total score analyses. Total scores can range from 0 to 213; the higher the score, the better developed is the team.

Psychometric Testing

No reliability or validity data are available. The instrument appears to have good face validity in that it includes a broad range of items found in the literature about team performance and used in other measures of it.

Evaluation

Strengths of this instrument are its broad coverage of team performance, clear wording, easy readability, and use of results for discussion and action planning. Its weaknesses include lack of psychometric testing, a possibility of response bias since all items are positively worded, and poor verbal anchors for the answer choices (i.e., "never" and "always" for the extreme choices, which are superlatives and rarely selected). Better answer choices would be "almost never," "some of the time," "much of the time," and "almost always." The developers sum the items for a total score without knowing if the items have any internal consistency. Additionally, for a number of items, the reference is unclear (i.e., reference to the team/work group or the organization).

The instrument is appropriate as a learning tool for teams and natural work groups at all levels of an organization. It facilitates members' reflecting on their respective team or work group's performance level and attempting to improve it. With psychometric testing, the instrument might be appropriate for other uses. The reviewers believe some of its items might form interesting subscales; however, it is doubtful that all items form a unidimensional scale.

Status/Availability

The instrument appears in Chapter 3 of the publication below. MW Corporation, a full-service consulting firm, holds the copyright. To order the publication or other books and videos on teams, call (914) 962-2933.

Relevant Publications

Harper, A., & Harper B. (1992). *Skill-building for self-directed team members: A complete course.* New York: MW Corporation.

TEAM CHARACTER INVENTORY

Developed by David W. Jamieson, 1989
Reviewed by Antonette M. Zeiss and Gloria D. Heinemann

The purpose of this 37-item instrument is to identify strengths, weaknesses, and overall effectiveness of a team during a consultation. It includes six item clusters related to team effectiveness, but lacks theoretical underpinnings and psychometric testing. Administration is relatively straightforward, and several scoring options are explained in the scoring instructions accompanying the instrument. It would benefit from some psychometric testing and refinement.

It has potential for use as a pre/post-test to measure the impact of an educational intervention once test-retest reliability is established.

Conceptual Framework

Jamieson does not present a theoretical framework for the instrument. He views the team as an organizationally based work group.

Description of Measure

The instrument's purpose is to assess a team's strengths, weaknesses, and overall effectiveness. It is most appropriate for consulting and planning interventions. Individual team members complete it. The team as a whole is the primary target of assessment based upon members' average scores for overall effectiveness and average team scores for each item and each item cluster.

Components of Teamwork Measured

The instrument includes 37 items and six item clusters–plans and goals (four items), roles (six items), operating procedures (12 items), interpersonal relationships (nine items), individual strengths (two items), and general effectiveness (four items).

The measure covers all four domains and all eight dimensions in our model of team performance. Most items, however, are concentrated in the process domain and the interdependence dimension.

Formatting and Scoring

Items are presented as verbal descriptors at opposing ends of and below a continuum; the continuum includes five answer choices. The descriptor are on the far left side is always negative (answer code 1); the descriptor on the far right is always positive (answer code 5). Respondents circle the number that they feel is most descriptive of their team.

Handling conflicts within team

	1	2	3	4	5	
21. Deny, avoid, or suppress conflicts.						Accept conflicts and "work them through."

In Phillips, S.L., & Elledge, R.L. *The team-building source book* ©1989. Reprinted by permission of Jossey-Bass, Inc., a subsidiary of John Wiley & Sons, Inc.

The developer suggests three scoring options and provides a scoring template with instructions. The first option is to calculate an overall average score by summing the responses and dividing by 37, the total number of items. This average score is calculated for each team member. The score ranges from 1 to 5 with higher scores indicating greater overall perceived team effectiveness. The second scoring option is to sum all team members' responses for each item cluster and divide by the number of items in the respective cluster; this number is then divided by the number of team members. These average scores can be compared to see where the team performs well (i.e., scores above 3) and where it needs to improve (i.e., scores below 3). The third scoring option is to calculate the average scores for each item across team members; sum all responses for each item and divide by the number of team members. Items with mean scores of four or five represent team strengths, while items with mean scores of one or two indicate problem areas within the team.

Psychometric Testing

No reliability or validity data are available.

Evaluation

The instrument's major strengths are its broad coverage of the team performance domains and the variety of scoring options. The response format is simple and straightforward; however, the wording of items is general and vague in many instances. Some "verbal descriptors" are worded as declarative sentences containing more than one concept; others are phrases or sentence fragments. This inconsistency could confuse respondents and negatively affect data quality.

With regard to content or face validity, inspection of the instrument suggests both strengths and limitations. While the six dimensions measured do have a good fit with our conceptual model of team performance, the items often do not have an obvious connection to one another within item clusters. For example, "roles" includes items about control, cooperation, and interdependence as well as items about expectations of team members. A second weakness is that the developer provides no rationale for the clustering. Some items do not fit well within their respective clusters, in part, because they attempt to measure more than one concept. Third, the items are not equally distributed across the clusters; for example, "individual strengths" includes only two items, while "operating procedures" includes 12. Very few items address the team within the organization. Finally, because all of the positively worded items are along the right side of the instrument and the instrument is relatively long, there is the potential for response bias. The measure would benefit from some refinements and psychometric testing.

Status/Availability

The copyrighted instrument appears in the publication below. To order, contact the publisher at (619) 578-5900.

Relevant Publications

Phillips, S.L., & Elledge, R.L. (1989). *The team-building source book* (pp. 22-29). San Diego, CA University Associates, Inc.

TEAM EFFECTIVENESS CHECKLIST

Developed by Ralph Lewis, 1994
Reviewed by Steven Lovett and Antonette M. Zeiss

The Team Effectiveness Checklist is a 25-item instrument designed to assess overall team effectiveness. It is based on a theoretical framework that takes account of both the internal and external environment of the team and both the people and tasks related to the team. It is easy to read and complete. Item wording is clear and appropriate for individuals working on a wide variety of teams. No scoring instructions accompany the instrument. No psychometric data are available for it. Its results can be used as a discussion aid for teams wishing to improve their functioning.

Conceptual Framework

According to Lewis, internal and external factors, as well as the people factors (e.g., methods of communicating and motivating members) and task factors (e.g., clarity of goals and objectives) affect team functioning. Internal and external factors intersect with the people and task factors to form four quadrants: (a) external-people; (b) external-tasks; (c) internal-people; and (c) internal-tasks. The "external-people" quadrant includes the needs of the team's customers and other people within the organization. The "external-tasks" quadrant includes organizational constraints on team activity and resources made available to the team. The "internal-people" quadrant contains the needs, motivations, and commitment of team members. The "internal-tasks" quadrant considers the communication among team members and the organization of team activities.

The team is a small, task-focused group within a complex organization. It matures over time, and its members work together for a common purpose.

Description of Measure

The instrument assesses perceptions of the team's effectiveness. Results can be used to stimulate discussion regarding the team's strengths and weaknesses and how to plan for improving its functioning. Team members complete it anonymously.

Components of Team Performance Measured

The instrument measures the extent to which team members effectively address the four quadrants of team functioning. These quadrants are external-people, external-task, internal-people, and internal-task.

The instrument also measures eight components of the problem solving and planning processes needed to achieve the team's objectives. These include: (a) making linkages with the wider organization and considering the diversity among team members; (b) setting shared team goals; (c) analyzing factors affecting work; (d) considering options; (e) planning; (f) communicating openly/addressing disagreements; (g) coordinating efforts and completing tasks in a timely fashion; and (h) carrying out performance reviews and rewarding team members for their efforts. These eight components are not mentioned in the theoretical framework for this instrument; thus, it is not clear why they were selected for inclusion or how they might interact with one another.

The instrument includes items in all four domains and seven of the eight dimensions of our model of team performance; only the dimension of growth and development within the process domain is omitted.

Formatting and Scoring

The instrument contains 25 positively worded items with answer choices along a continuum from 1 = very low to 7 = very high. Verbal anchors are given for the extreme answer choices only. There are two items for each of the four quadrants and two items for each of the eight components of the problem solving/planning process. A final item measures overall team effectiveness (see item example below).

No scoring instructions accompany the instrument. Reviewers recommend an item analysis. Average scores for team members also can be calculated for each of the four quadrants and for each of the eight problem solving/planning components.

		Low	High
1.	**External–People** The team manages its relationships with others well.		1 2 3 4 5 6 7

In Lewis, R. *Team-building skills–Participants' guide* ©1994. Reprinted by permission of McGraw-Hill, Inc.

Psychometric Testing

No reliability or validity data are available. The majority of items appear to have a high degree of face validity. The items have less face validity when grouped within the quadrants and problem solving/planning components.

Evaluation

The instrument covers a broad range of issues relevant to team effectiveness, and results from it provide a good stimulus for discussing a team's strengths and weaknesses. It is based on a theoretical framework that takes account of both the internal and external environment of the team and both the people and tasks related to the team and its activities. It is easy to read and can be completed in approximately 15 minutes. All items are positively worded which could lead to a response bias. There is no evidence of reliability and validity testing; thus, it is impossible to know whether the items can be scaled or whether several subscales exist within the instrument. The lack of reliability data makes it difficult to determine the instrument's sensitivity to change in teams over time. It is probably best employed as an instructional aid in a team training workshop and to stimulate discussion for improving team functioning.

Status/Availability

Harbridge Consulting Group, Ltd. holds the instrument's copyright. It appears in the reference below as part of a one-day workshop series published by McGraw-Hill, Inc. To order, contact the publisher at (800) 2-MCGRAW.

Relevant Publications

Lewis, R. (1994). *Team-building skills–Participants' guide*. New York: McGraw-Hill, Inc.

TEAM ASSESSMENT WORKSHEETS*

Developed by William E. McClane, 1992
Reviewed by Martha S. Waite and Glenda F. Brown

This 24-item instrument measures team performance in clinical rehabilitation teams. It addresses organizational and team context, team processes, and outputs of the team. It has theoretical underpinnings, good readability for a professional group of respondents, and is relatively easy to complete and score. The developer designed the instrument as a learning device to help members identify strengths and weaknesses in their team, discuss and come to consensus about them, and develop a plan of action to improve the team's functioning level. Developers have not conducted psychometric testing; the first reviewer did some initial testing to confirm internal consistency among the five potential subscales. It includes some unique items–timeliness, benefits to team members of working on a highly functional team, external relationships, acceptability of recommendations, and functional recovery of patients. Although designed for a specific type of clinical team, it has potential for use among other clinical health care teams.

Conceptual Framework

The developer addresses both external and internal facets of team performance in three broad areas. First are factors in the hospital environment (i.e., its policies and processes) and the environment of the team itself. Second are the processes within the team (i.e., team membership, team roles, and problem solving/decision-making). Third are the team's outputs or the degree to which it achieves its objectives.

The therapeutic rehabilitation team works within the hospital to provide treatment to patients and to improve their level of physical functioning.

Description of Measure

The developer designed the instrument to assess the team's current level of functioning and initiate the team's change process through discussion, developing a priority list, and action planning to improve its performance. The instrument is part of an educational package; an overview of team evaluation and accountability with learning objectives and supplemental workshop materials come with it. Team members complete the instrument anonymously.

Components of Team Performance Measured

The developer identifies three components of team performance, context, processes, and output. Organizational context refers to policies and procedures of the health care setting that are external to the team, but directly affect team process and output. It includes organizational culture, team rewards, external relationships, goals and objectives, and performance feedback (five items).

Process includes team membership, team roles, and problem solving/decision-making. Team membership refers to the degree to which the team is functioning collaboratively rather than as a collection of individuals. It includes clarity of membership, quality of the exchange among members, team size, level of cohesiveness, and clarity of leadership (five items). The concept, team roles, refers to the way members bring their knowledge into the team and the degree of autonomy they have in utilizing their expertise. This facet of performance includes team members' roles, knowledge and skill, and autonomy (three items). The concept, problem solving/decision-making, refers to how team members bring their skills to bear in solving therapeutic problems and providing solutions. Included here are agreement management, conflict management, meeting effectiveness, and participation in decision-making (four items).

Outputs refer to the team's accountability and recommendations to its customers (e.g., patients, families, other teams, and service lines). Outputs include timeliness, capacity for future interaction with other teams, innovation, clarity, workability, acceptability of team recommendations, and patients' functional recovery (seven items).

The instrument measures all four domains and seven of the eight dimensions of our team performance model. The dimension, strategies for productivity, is not measured.

Formatting and Scoring

The measure has a total of 24 positively worded items that make up five subscales. For each item, the respondent rates "the degree to which this describes our team." The answer choices are Likert formatted and range 1 to 5 such that 1 = not at all, 2 = very little, 3 = somewhat, 4 = to a large degree, and 5 = fully (see item example below).

Team output dimensions	Rating degree to which this describes our team	Comments
Timeliness: The team is able to complete its work in a timely manner.	(1) Not at all (2) Very little (3) Somewhat (4) To a large degree (5) Fully	

In McClane, W.E. Evaluation and accountability. In *Guide to interdisciplinary practice in rehabilitation settings* ©1992. Reprinted by permission of author and American Congress of Rehabilitation Medicine.

A Team Rating Form accompanies the instrument to facilitate summing individual responses across the items for an item analysis. For each item, the higher the score, the more positive the perception of the team.

Psychometric Testing

Internal Consistency Reliability

The first reviewer undertook limited reliability testing for internal consistency by administering the instrument to a rehabilitation team of 28 members. Cronbach's alpha was .85 for Organizational Context, .90 for Team Membership, .85 for Problem Solving/Decision-Making, and .95 for Team Output. Although this sample size is small, alpha scores ranging from .85 to .95 indicate high internal consistency for each area and suggest the appropriateness of scaling items in each of the five areas.

Test-Retest/Inter-Rater Reliability

No data are available regarding test-retest reliability, and testing for inter-rater reliability is inappropriate since the measure is self-administered.

Validity

No validity data are available.

Evaluation

The instrument's strengths are its measurement of both external and internal elements of team performance and its concise and efficient measurement of a considerable number of dimensions of team performance. It also measures some unique facets of team performance.

The first reviewer used the instrument in a workshop with a large, 28-member rehabilitation team. She found that for a large team, it was difficult to tally members' responses during the workshop. Additionally, nonprofessional members of the team (e.g., nursing aides) took much longer to complete the instrument in comparison to their professional counterparts. When used specifically with health professionals, the instrument has good readability and is easy to administer and score. Additional psychometric testing would help determine whether the items are scalable. Given that all items are positively worded, there is the potential for response bias.

The instrument and its accompanying materials provide a team consultant with a nice package for team assessment and planning for improvement. It also serves as a good example of how facets of our model of team performance can be customized for a specific type of clinical health care team.

Status/Availability

The copyrighted instrument appears in the publication below. For information, contact the American Congress of Rehabilitation Medicine, 5987 East 71st Street, Suite 111, Indianapolis, IN 46220; (317) 915-2250; e-mail, acrm@acrm.org.

Relevant Publications

McClane, W.E. (1992). Evaluation and accountability. In American Congress of Rehabilitation Medicine, *Guide to interdisciplinary practice in rehabilitation settings* (pp. 158-172). Skokie, IL: Author.

TEAM EFFECTIVENESS DIMENSIONS (TED) SURVEY

Developed by Scott Parry, 1987, 1998
Reviewed by Glenda F. Brown and Sara A. Brallier

The Team Effectiveness Dimensions (TED) Survey is a 20-item, self-administered instrument designed to assess team effectiveness and identify strengths and areas for improvement. The instrument includes two subscales–organizational issues and interpersonal issues. Its strengths are ease of administration and the measurement of two different types of issues affecting team effectiveness. However, it lacks reliability and validity data and has several conceptual and methodological problems, the most serious being the lack of clear distinction between the two subscales. Designed for consultation with teams, it is not recommended as a research instrument.

Conceptual Framework

Parry provides only a limited conceptual framework for the TED. For teams to be effective, they must address both organizational and interpersonal issues. Organizational issues include both those within the organization and within the team itself. Interpersonal issues focus on team dynamics and processes within the team and the team's relationship to other teams.

The developer views the team as a work group within a large, complex organization.

Description of Measure

This measure's purpose is to identify perceived strengths and areas for improvement in the team. Team members are the targets of assessment. The 1998 version for teams is a revision of the 1987 version for work groups.

Components of Team Performance Measured

The TED includes two subscales–organizational and interpersonal issues. Each subscale includes 10 items related to effectiveness. The Organizational Issues Subscale includes items measuring team mission, goals, and standards; problem solving effectiveness; organizational barriers to effectiveness; ability to stay focused on tasks; meeting effectiveness; effective membership mix; effective team leadership; feedback from management; balance between task and process goals; and pride in the team. The Interpersonal Issues Subscale includes items measuring cooperation, dealing with differences/conflict, decision-making, communication, respect from outside the team, ability to listen, improving performance, personal growth, productivity, and job satisfaction.

The items cover elements in all four domains and all eight dimensions of our model of team performance. The items are relatively well balanced across the dimensions with a slight concentration within interdependence. Unique items are those addressing organizational barriers to team effectiveness and balance between task and process goals.

Formatting and Scoring

Each item of the 20-item instrument includes a pair of opposing statements–one positively describing a facet of team functioning and the other negatively describing it. There are five boxes separating the statements, and the respondent marks the box that best reflects his/her perception of the team (see below).

17. We're so busy with work (task) that we've neglected improving our teamwork (process).   We've got a good balance between getting the work done (task) and improving our teamwork (process).

☐ ☐ ☐ ☐ ☐

In Parry, S.B. *Group Effectiveness Dimensions (GED)* ©1993. Reprinted by permission of Training House.

Scale and subscale scores are calculated by assigning numerical values to the answer choices for each item. Item scores range from 1 (total agreement with the negative descriptor of team performance) to 5 (total agreement with the positive descriptor). Scores of the odd-numbered items are summed to create the

Organizational Issues Subscale; the even-numbered items are summed to create the Interpersonal Issues Subscale. Subscale scores range from 10 to 50. The two subscales are summed for a team effectiveness score ranging from 10 to 100. High scores indicate positive perceptions of team effectiveness.

Psychometric Testing

No reliability or validity data are available.

Evaluation

The instrument's strengths are its broad measurement of team performance, inclusion of organizational support as a dimension of team effectiveness, and ease of administration. Analyzing the items individually can assist teams in identifying their strengths and weaknesses, and results serve as a "spring board" for discussion about how to improve functioning.

Several conceptual and methodological problems do exist. First, the Organizational Issues Subscale includes items addressing structural issues both within the organization and within the team. If analyzed statistically, it is doubtful that these items would load on one subscale. Additionally, several of the items within this subscale could be conceptualized as "interpersonal issues" (e.g., problem solving). Thus, the distinction between the two subscales is not well delineated. Second, three of the items attempt to measure more than one concept (e.g., decision-making and commitment to the group appear in the same item). Psychometric testing would help resolve some of these problems. Finally, the instrument would be easier to use and score if the items were precoded (i.e., the respondent circled a number, instead of marking a box which is later assigned a number during the scoring process).

Status/Availability

The instrument is copyrighted. It appears in the publications below. Contact HRD Press at (800) 822-2801 or http://www.traininghouse.com. For the revised, 1998 version for teams, contact McGraw-Hill at (800) 2-MCGRAW.

Relevant Publications

Parry, S.B. (1998). How Effective Is Your Work Team? In M. Silberman (Ed.), *Team and organization development sourcebook* (pp. 127-135). New York: McGraw-Hill.

Parry, S.B. (1993). *Group Effectiveness Dimensions (GED)*. Princeton, NJ: Training House.

TEAM WELL-BEING ASSESSMENT

Developed by Dick Richards and Susan Smyth, 1994
Reviewed by Martha S. Waite and Amy L. Noe

This 28-item measure of team well-being includes seven areas key to team success or effectiveness–purpose, role, strategy, processes, people, feedback, and interfaces. The measure combines team members' scores into one team score, which is then compared with the team profile percentiles indicating the level of team well-being. The instrument is well grounded in a conceptual framework; however, several of the areas of well-being are not distinct from one another. While developers provide preliminary reliability and validity data, the measure would benefit from more extensive testing. It is appropriate for developing teams and helping them improve their functioning.

Conceptual Framework

Members of healthy, effective teams have a shared sense of purpose, emotional commitment to it, shared responsibility, and a willingness to monitor how well they work together. The developers identify seven aspects of well-being that teams need to address in order to become effective. These areas–purpose, role, strategy, processes, people, feedback, and interfaces–are connected and dependent upon one another. According to the model, a team's purpose is central to the quality of its work; however, becoming a healthy, effective team is a complex task and is not accomplished in a linear fashion.

Developers view the team as a bundle of energy that members must harness and direct. The team's energy is powerful and potentially chaotic if not managed. When managed, the team becomes a well functioning system.

Description of Measure

Developers designed the instrument to assess aspects of a team's well-being in order to determine how effective or healthy it is and where it should focus attempts to improve its functioning. Members of a team complete the instrument individually. Scores are averaged to arrive at the team scores in each of the seven areas of well-being. The instrument comes with a team leader's or educator's manual that includes a scoring form and a team well-being profile form (i.e., a percentile ranking that shows where a specific team ranks compared to other teams). A manual for team members provides guidelines and references to help improve the team's well-being and effectiveness.

Components of Team Performance Measured

The instrument measures seven areas–purpose, role, strategy, process, people, feedback and interfaces. Purpose refers to a vision statement, a mission statement, or a contract. Team members are clear in their understanding and commit energy toward achieving that purpose. The concept, role, is used differently in this instrument than in most other instruments. Instead of defining professional roles or formal roles such as leader, the term is used to describe the team's enactment of planning, problem solving, communicating, decision-making, etc. to achieve its purpose. Strategy is what teams need to continue doing or discontinue doing to achieve their goals. Processes are how things get done in the team (e.g., how decisions are made, how members communicate with one another, how conflict is managed). The concept, people, refers to whether members feel well utilized and valued. Feedback is the mechanism by which stakeholders convey information the team can use to improve its work. Finally the concept, interfaces, refers to building and maintaining critical relationships with those outside the team.

This instrument measures facets of all four domains and all eight dimensions in our model of team performance. Items are concentrated in the dimensions of interdependence and strategies for productivity. Unique features include its measurement of feedback and strategies for productivity, including action plans.

Formatting and Scoring

There are four items in each of the seven areas of well-being. A paragraph defining each area precedes the items. Items are Likert formatted from strongly disagree = 1 to strongly agree = 6. Respondents write the appropriate answer code on the blank to the left of each item.

Team averages are calculated for each of the seven areas of well-being from the scoring sheets. Scores range from 1 (low well-being) to 6 (high well-being). A team's scores are compared with team percentile scores in the attached Team Well-Being Profile in order to determine its degree of well-being.

Psychometric Testing

Internal Consistency Reliability

Information obtained from a study of 173 members from 25 teams yielded a high score (.96) on a split-half reliability test. A rank test was performed to determine whether significant differences exist between the seven area averages measured on the assessment. Differences were significant at the .01 level; thus, the seven areas of well-being are distinct from one another.

Test-Retest/Inter-Rater Reliability

No data are available regarding test-retest reliability, and testing for inter-rater reliability is inappropriate since the measure is self-administered.

Content or Face Validity

Developers state that the instrument makes sense to experts in teamwork and that it is consistent with the model of team well-being.

Concurrent Validity

Independent raters, who were non-team members, but familiar with the 25 teams' work, evaluated the teams on three criteria–their ability to meet their commitments, how well members worked together, and their ability to produce quality work to the satisfaction of those who depend on them. The sum of the seven averages from the instrument correlated with the raters' overall evaluations at the .025 significance level and at the .05, .025, and .10 levels, on the three criteria, respectively.

Construct/Predicative/Discriminant Validity

No data are available for these types of validity.

Evaluation

The instrument is unique in that it takes into account the measurement of strategies for becoming productive. The "purpose," "feedback," and "interfaces" areas of well-being are well conceptualized and measured. Problems are apparent with the conceptualization of several of the other areas of well-being. "Role" is not defined in the sociological sense of the term. The "role," "strategy," and "processes" areas are not well delineated from one another. Additionally, the items within the "people" area do not seem to be on the same conceptual level. One item addresses competence; two are related to climate within the team, and the fourth reflects interdependence among team members.

Most items are clearly written; however, a five rather than a six point range of answer choices might be more appropriate since the verbal anchors are somewhat confusing (e.g., the difference between mostly and strongly is not clear). The positive wording of items and of the descriptive paragraphs preceding them may contribute to positive response bias. When reporting reliability and validity data, the developers report significance of tests without providing their method of analysis or the actual statistical values.

This instrument is appropriate for educating and consulting with teams, especially those in complex organizations. The reviewers recommend revisions to the "role," "strategy," "processes," and "people" areas and the answer choices.

Status/Availability

The copyrighted instrument appears in the publication below. To purchase it, contact the publisher, Pfeiffer & Company, at (800) 274-4434.

Relevant Publications

Richards, D., & Smyth, S. (1994). *Assessing your team: 7 measures of team success.* San Diego, CA: Pfeiffer & Company.

TEAM EFFECTIVENESS RATING SCALE

Developed by A.E. Rothermich and J.M. Saunders, 1977
Reviewed by Stephen K. Harmon and Gloria D. Heinemann

The instrument includes 35 items, grouped into four conceptual areas related to team effectiveness–goals, roles, decisions/problem solving, and interaction. It assesses members' perceptions of team effectiveness and identifies the team's strengths and weaknesses. It can determine congruence between the leader's and members' perceptions and the degree to which the team is functioning according to defined goals and expectations. Especially appropriate for newly developing teams, it is easy to complete although a number of items contain sophisticated wording. No guidelines for scoring or interpreting results accompany the instrument. Items grouped in the "interaction" conceptual area do not measure one concept as well as those in the other three areas. With appropriate psychometric testing, it has potential for tracking team effectiveness over time.

Conceptual Framework

This instrument is based on McGregor's Theory Y (1960), in which he proposed that employees have creative potential not utilized fully in the work situation. When their personal and work goals coincide, they can become highly committed to the goals of the organization and will work collaboratively with other employees in their work group to achieve these goals. Team development is almost always necessary since managers often are unfamiliar with skills and requirements (e.g., clear goals and roles, shared decision-making and problem solving, and positive interpersonal relationships) of an effective team approach.

The developers view the team as a work group having the capacity to develop over time and contribute to the overall goals of the organization.

Description of Measure

Developers designed the instrument as an educational/consultation tool to help teams develop and improve their effectiveness. It can establish baseline data on team effectiveness and provide insights for improving it.

Components of Team Performance Measured

The instrument includes four conceptual areas–goals (four items), roles (four items), decisions/problem-solving (10 items) and interactions (17 items). Respondents rated the team's goals on their degree of clarity, feasibility, priority for the team, and the extent to which they correspond with personal goals. They rate team members' roles on their degree of clarity, the extent expertise among members is known/unknown and utilized/not utilized, and the extent to which members are stereotypical/rigid or changing/expanding.

Ratings for decisions/problem solving include the extent to which the team makes effective decisions as needed, members share decision-making, decisions are carried out, and members have the authority to carry out tasks. Also rated as part of this concept area are clarity of power distribution, the exploration of problems, the generation of multiple problem solutions or options, and the examination of possible consequences of solutions. Additionally, this concept area includes the degree of clarity of feedback, timelines, and assignments as well as the frequency of evaluation of effectiveness of solutions.

The interactions area includes the degree to which there is open expression in discussions, all members are listened to, members are interrupted, and messages are clear. Additionally, enthusiasm/energy for group work, verbal expression of feelings, revealing thinking and feelings, open expression of criticism, and expression of emotions also are measured. Finally, this concept area takes into account taking responsibility for meeting one's own needs, giving feedback to one another, the usefulness of feedback, openly raised conflict, positive or negative perception of conflict, mutual gain from conflict, flexible leadership, shared leadership, and good group production.

The instrument includes all four domains and seven of the eight dimensions of our model of team performance; only organizational context is not measured. Unique elements include fit between individual and team goals and productivity.

Formatting and Scoring

Developers use a five-point rating format for each of the items with 1 as most negative and 5 as most positive score. The five answer choices form a continuum between two opposing statements; the negative statement is on the left, and the positive statement is on the right for each item (see item example below).

	Decisions/Problem Solving	
9. Group hesitates to make decisions.	1 2 3 4 5	Group makes decisions as needed.

Reprinted by permission of developers.

No guidelines for scoring or interpreting results accompany the instrument. The number of items is lengthy for an item analysis; yet, no psychometric data are available to support the scalability of items. Often items within each conceptual area are summed to obtain four subscale scores. The Goals and Roles Subscales each range from 4 to 20; the Decisions/Problem Solving Subscale ranges from 10 to 50; and the Interactions Subscale ranges from 17 to 85. In all instances, the higher the score, the more effective is the team. An item analysis can be used to identify strongly or weakly perceived items.

Psychometric Testing

No reliability or validity data are available. With regard to content or face validity, the developers' experience educating and consulting with teams influenced the development, final selection, and grouping of items for this measure. They also used relevant literature and other measurement instruments in construction of the instrument; however, there are no formal face validity data reported. The developers believe the instrument can be used to measure team effectiveness over time. Again, psychometric data are not presently available to support this assertion or the scalability of items.

Evaluation

The instrument has merit for education and consultation, especially with regard to newly formed teams, whose members need to learn how to establish goals, clarify their roles, and develop skills related to group process and interpersonal relations. It is easy to administer and score. The first reviewer has used it for team training and consultation activities with clinical health care teams and found it to be a useful tool. Information obtained from it permits the consultant and team members to explore the team's strengths and weaknesses.

Limitations of the measure include the potential for response bias, lack of guidelines for scoring and interpreting results, and lack of psychometric testing. Items making up the goals, roles, and decisions/problem solving conceptual areas appear to be measuring important facets of these respective concepts. Items making up the interaction area are more varied and seem to include a wide variety of team process issues from shared participation, communication skills, to conflict and leadership. Several of the items dealing with feelings and emotions seem redundant. It is questionable whether these items make up a single subscale. It would be premature to use the instrument to monitor team performance over time or for research purposes given no psychometric data.

Status/Availability

This instrument is unpublished; there is no charge for its use. For a copy of it, contact the first reviewer at e-mail, stephen.harmon@med.va.gov.

Relevant Publications

McGregor, D. (1960). *The human side of enterprise.* New York: McGraw-Hill, Inc.
Rothermich, A.E., & Saunders, J.M. (1977). *Team Effectiveness Rating Scale.* Unpublished instrument

TEAM STRENGTH SURVEY

Developed by Tercon, Inc., 1986, 1996
Reviewed by Steven Lovett and Gloria D. Heinemann

The Team Strength Survey (1996) is a 35-item instrument developed as an instructional and assessment tool. It yields scores on seven subscales measuring characteristics of "high involvement" teams (i.e., teams whose members work collaboratively to achieve goals). It is easy to read, complete, and score. There is potential for response bias since all items are positively worded. While it has been extensively used with teams in a variety of settings, reliability and validity data are not available for the 1996 version. It is part of a package that includes collecting, scoring, and interpreting the data as part of a consulting contract.

Conceptual Framework

Organizations are changing from a control-oriented to an involvement-oriented culture. In the control-oriented culture, results are obtained by controlling the work of others, maintaining order, and prescribing solutions to problems. In contrast, an involvement-oriented culture empowers employees to become involved and contribute to the work; it creates an atmosphere for open, honest communication and shared decision-making. In this new culture, employees making decisions are those closest to the actual work; other characteristics of this culture include shared responsibility for accomplishing goals, a commitment to teamwork, reasonable risk-taking, and a sense of ownership and direct involvement of employees in the organization's activities. In order for this new culture to have positive results for the organization, work groups must be developed into well performing teams.

The developer views teams as work units within organizations; they produce quality results and accomplish organizational goals. "High involvement" teams are empowered and encouraged to function as self-managed work teams.

Description of Measure

The instrument assesses factors that affect team productivity and relations among members and provides information about their effectiveness. The developer emphasizes the use of the instrument for identifying weaknesses in the team's current functioning and as a means of tracking functioning or performance over time. A re-evaluation is recommended every six months for new teams and yearly for established teams. Individual team members complete the instrument; averaged subscale scores provide information about the team.

Components of Team Performance Measured

The 1996 version of the instrument measures seven components of team performance. These include purpose/direction, roles and responsibilities, commitment to the team, quality of team meetings, quality of team decisions, dealing with conflict, and mutual support. Each subscale includes five items.

The instrument addresses all four domains and seven of the eight dimensions of our team performance model. It excludes the dimension of organizational context. Unique elements include consistency between goals and activities, action planning, and effectiveness with other groups in the organization.

Formatting and Scoring

The instrument consists of 35 positively worded items. The answer choices for each statement range from 1 to 5; anchors for rating include 1 = We never do this; 2 = We seldom do this; 3 = We occasionally do this; 4 = We frequently do this; and 5 = We always do this.

Tercon scores the instrument as part of its consulting services. Items for each of the seven subscales are summed and averaged for the team as a whole. Each subscale has a potential range from 5, low performance, to 25, high performance.

Psychometric Testing

Internal Consistency Reliability

The instrument has been used with over 2,000 teams since its initial development in 1986. The data from an early, 90-item version with four answer choices per item (N = 1,145) were factor analyzed and nine factors or potential subscales were identified. The subscales were correlated, and findings showed that several of them were measuring similar facets of team performance. These findings may have influenced the reduction of subscales from nine to seven and the number of items from 90 to 35. There is no evidence of reliability testing on the 1996 version of the instrument.

Test-Retest/Inter-Rater Reliability

No data are available regarding test-retest reliability, and testing for inter-rater reliability is inappropriate since the measure is self-administered.

Validity

There is no evidence of validity testing. The items do seem to have face validity with regard to the measurement of team performance.

Evaluation

The instrument is based on a model of team functioning that is very similar to the interdisciplinary model used in health care settings. Its items are free of business terms and seem applicable to a wide array of team settings, including health care. It can be completed easily in approximately 10-15 minutes. Statements are clearly worded and have a relatively high degree of face validity. Scoring is straightforward; scores provide feedback about the team as a whole. All items are positively worded, which could result in response bias. The instrument would benefit considerably from additional psychometric testing to determine its reliability over time and its potential use in research.

Status/Availability

Tercon, Inc. holds the copyright for this instrument. The company sells it as part of a consulting service package to teams and organizations. Fees for a consulting package are tailored to specific customers. Contact the company at 12920 Metcalf Avenue, Suite 120, Overland Park, KS 66213; (800) 877-4776; http://www.tercon.com; e-mail, consultants@tercon.com.

Relevant Publications

Tercon, Inc. (1996). *Module 11: The Team Strength Survey leader's guide.* Overland Park, KS: Author.

GROUP DEVELOPMENT QUESTIONNAIRE (GDQ)*

Developed by Susan Wheelan and Judith M. Hochberger, 1993
Reviewed by Julia Kasl-Godley and Antonette M. Zeiss

The Group Development Questionnaire (GDQ) is a 60-item self-report instrument designed to measure a group's stage of development, stage one through four, from dependency/inclusion, to work/productivity. It provides the group with a profile to facilitate improving its performance and productivity. The GDQ also can be used to determine the impact of an intervention on a group. It is grounded in an integrative theory of group development that is empirically supported. It is relatively easy to read and complete, has strong reliability and validity data, and is a broad measure of team performance. Somewhat problematic are the answer choices that use the extremes of "always" and "never." A factor analysis revealed two subscales rather than four; however, this may be a result of some similarity between the first two and last two stages of development. The accompanying manual is well written and clearly presents information about the instrument, how to use it, and how it has been used to date. It has been used in health care settings and is appropriate for such teams and work groups. Individuals must be trained to use the instrument.

Conceptual Framework

An integrative theory of group development serves as the underpinnings for this instrument. The model describes five nonlinear stages of group development: (a) dependency and inclusion, stage one; (b) counterdependence and fight, stage two; (c) trust and structure, stage three; (d) work and productivity, stage four; and (e) termination for groups convened around a short-term goal, stage five. According to the model, the first stage of group development is characterized by members' dependency on the designated leader (i.e., members relying on the leader for direction and support). Interpersonal relationships are tentative and polite, and members tend to avoid work tasks for fear of creating conflict. Conflict among members and between members and leader(s) characterize the second stage. Members struggle with developing group structure and goals and defining roles; they often experience conflict in the process. Work tasks continue to be avoided. Stage two must be successfully negotiated to progress to the third stage, trust and structure.

In stage three, increased trust and collaboration among group members and among members and leader(s) become evident. The group's structure, goals and norms, and members' roles are clearly delineated, and members work more effectively and productively as a result. Members give focused attention to their work at this stage. In stage four, work is more effective as members communicate freely about ideas and information, have an awareness of time constraints, and use available resources to accomplish their tasks. They discuss their processes, evaluate their work together, and give feedback to one another. The final stage, termination, is characterized by approaching and reaching end points. According to the model, progression through the stages of development is not automatic. Groups can get stuck at a particular stage or regress to earlier stages at any point as a function of factors such as external demands, changes in group membership, and multiple changes impacting the team simultaneously. The developers conducted validation studies of the integrated model using systematic observation and content analysis of audiotapes of numerous groups' discussions. Results lend support to the model.

Developers view the team as a small group that matures across four or five stages from newly forming to well functioning, and for some teams, terminating.

Description of Measure

The GDQ's purpose is to facilitate groups' efforts to be supportive environments for members and to achieve shared goals. The developers designed it as both an assessment and research instrument to be used by qualified trainers and consultants. It is effective in evaluating the impact of interventions/ consultations with teams to help them improve their functioning. The developers also believe it has potential usefulness in organizational consultation.

The instrument should not be used as an individual diagnostic instrument since it was not designed for this purpose. Neither is it intended for use in evaluating groups for the purpose of reprimanding them or their members since it cannot identify the reasons for a particular group profile, and some barriers to high performance are outside the group and beyond its control. Group or team members complete the instrument; their responses are averaged to provide information about the group as a whole.

Components of Team Performance Measured

The instrument measures the four stages of group development; the fifth stage, termination, is omitted. The four, 15-item subscales correspond to the four stages of development. Subscale I measures characteristics of the first stage of development such as inclusion and safety issues, dependency, and lack of structure. Subscale II addresses the issues in the second stage of development (e.g., conflict, counterdependence, and signs of an emerging structure). Subscale III identifies characteristics of the third stage of development such as structure (e.g., clarity of goals, planning, and developing strategies for goal achievement); trust, cooperation, and positive emotions; and using the leader as a resource. Subscale IV measures characteristics of stage four including effective organization; culture, norms, and values; and external relations.

The instrument measures all four domains and all eight dimensions of our model of team performance.

Formatting and Scoring

Using a five-point Likert response format, respondents rate how accurately each statement describes their group at the present time. Anchors for answer choices are 1 = never true of this group, 2 = rarely true of this group, 3 = sometimes true of this group, 4 = frequently true of this group, and 5 = always true of this group.

Responses are summed across the subscale items; scores for each subscale range from 15 to 75. The higher a subscale score, the greater the perceptions of members that their group is functioning at this particular stage of development. Each subscale score is averaged for a group score. A group profile is developed using the group's grand total, effectiveness ratio, percentage of group energy focused on each GDQ subscale, and range of responses to each GDQ subscale. A subscale analysis addresses the items on which group members scored three or above. Demographic information about respondents also is collected and analyzed in conjunction with the GDQ to examine potential subgroup differences. The manual accompanying the instrument provides instructions and examples for scoring, developing the group profile, and conducting the item analysis.

The instrument's developers caution that profile interpretation requires significant skill and experience given that identical GDQ results can have different implications for groups depending on the environmental context in which the group is operating, type of tasks accomplished, group size, and length of time as a group. Thus, only certified GDQ trainers/consultants are permitted to purchase, administer, and score the instrument.

Finally, norms for subscale scores are provided in the manual. The manual also provides average scale score norms for select types of groups (i.e., hospital, other health care/social service, finance, and engineering).

Psychometric Testing

Internal Consistency Reliability

To establish internal consistency, 164 individuals completed the instrument. Cronbach's alpha for the four subscales, respectively, were .69, .88, .74, and .88. The subscales intercorrelated as expected. Subscales I and II correlated .37; Subscale II correlated with Subscales III and IV -.37 and -.39, respectively. Subscales III and IV correlated .83, which suggests that there is considerable overlap between the third and fourth stages of group development.

Results from the GDQ were factor analyzed; this analysis yielded two factors. Twenty-five of the 30 items from Subscales III and IV loaded on the first factor, and 20 of the 30 items from Subscales I and II loaded on the second factor. No factor loading was below .39. These factors are consistent with the earlier correlations between Subscales I and II and between Subscales III and IV. Cronbach's alpha scores for the two factors were .90 and .88, respectively. The items that did not load as expected on either factor were reworked and submitted to further psychometric testing.

Test-Retest Reliability

Forty-five individuals completed the instrument twice within a two-week period. Test-retest correlations for Subscales I through IV, respectively, were .74, .89, .69, and .82; all were significant. Test-retest correlations for the total score were not reported.

Inter-Rater Reliability

This type of reliability testing is not appropriate since the instrument is self-administered.

Content or Face Validity

The GDQ is based on an extensive review of research, theory, and other measures of group development. Group development experts critiqued the first draft of the GDQ; their comments led to a second draft, which underwent psychometric testing. The current instrument resulted from this process.

Concurrent Validity

Comparing the GDQ with the Group Attitude Scale (Evans & Jarvis, 1986 as cited by Wheelan, 1993), which measures members' attraction to the group, assessed concurrent validity. The scores of 20 individuals on the GDQ were correlated with their scores on the Group Attitude Scale (GAS). Correlations with the GAS ranged from .18 (Subscale I) to .67 (Subscale III); all except Subscale I were significant above $p < .05$. The total score GDQ correlated with the total score on the GAS .48; these correlations indicate moderate concurrent validity. The developers note that, as expected, Subscale III, an indicator of trust and teamwork among members, was most highly correlated with the GAS and Subscale I, an indicator of dependency and inclusion issues was not significantly correlated with the GAS.

The developers and their colleagues compared results on the GDQ with actual behavior of group members in two studies. Actual behavior of members in meetings was ascertained by categorizing verbal statements of members from audiotaped meetings using the Group Development Observation System (Verdi & Wheelan, 1992; Wheelan & McKeage, 1993; Wheelan & Verdi, 1992). Statements were categorized as dependency, counterdependency, fight, flight, pairing, counterpairing, and work statements; categories were collapsed to correspond to the GDQ subscales. Correlations between the verbal categories and the GDQ subscales for three work teams (study one) were .68, $p < .001$; .91, $p < .001$; and .99, $p < .001$. In the second study of seven groups, members' responses to the GDQ subscales correlated with four of the eight uncollapsed verbal categories. Two additional verbal categories, expected to correlate with Subscale I, had higher correlations with Subscale II. This supports the factor analysis findings that there is considerable overlap between Subscales I and II.

Construct Validity

According to theory, new groups should have higher dependency/inclusion scores than groups that have been in existence for some time. Findings showed new groups have significantly higher scores on Subscales I and II than long-term groups. Other research showed that large groups are more likely than small ones to express disagreement. Additionally, findings indicated that large groups have significantly higher scores on Subscales I and II and significantly lower scores on Subscales III and IV in comparison to small groups.

Predictive Validity

The previously cited studies comparing the GDQ to actual behavior might have provided evidence of predictive validity had data from both measures not been collected simultaneously (i.e., during the same group meeting). The developers described these studies as examples of predictive validity; however, these reviewers view it as additional evidence of concurrent validity.

Discriminant Validity

Discriminant validity has been tested in several studies. The GDQ subscales were correlated with demographic variables (i.e., age, education level, years of employment, gender, and ethnicity). The only significant correlation was level of education; it correlated $-.24$, $p < .01$ with GDQ Subscale I and $-.31$, $p < .001$ with Subscale II. Thus, the higher a respondent's education, the lower they score on Subscale I, dependency and inclusion, and Subscale II, conflict and counterdependence. Respondents of different ages, years of work experience, gender, and ethnicity (i.e., Caucasian versus minority group member) do not respond to the instrument in any systematically different ways (i.e., they do not perceive the group differently based on these characteristics). One study's results showed a status difference in that low status group members were significantly more likely than high status ones to view their groups as dependent.

The developers noted a relationship between high education level, high status, and leadership among group members. High status members or group leaders tend to view the group more positively than other members. They tend to overrate the functional level of their group to avoid the feeling of personal failure. Trainers/consultants using the GDQ should be aware that the scores for Subscales I and II may be underestimates for highly educated and high status group members or group leaders.

Evaluation

Developers have put much thought and effort into the design of the GDQ. The instrument is theoretically driven, based upon an extensive review of the literature and measurement instruments, and has strong reliability and validity. The theoretical framework is strong and empirically supported. The instrument can be completed in approximately 30 minutes and is relatively easy to read and complete. It has been translated into multiple languages, and the Spanish version has undergone psychometric testing. Developers have demonstrated the instrument's usefulness in determining the level of a group's functioning and in evaluating the impact of interventions on groups. The manual accompanying the instrument is thorough and well written. It provides numerous examples of the GDQ's use with a variety of groups, explains how to use results to conduct interventions with groups, and discusses ethical issues related to its use. The instrument has been used in health care settings and has applicability for clinical health care teams and natural work groups. While the training required to use the instrument might create time and cost problems for some groups, it ensures that qualified persons administer the instrument.

One weakness in the instrument is the use of "extremes" (i.e., always and never) in the answer choices given respondents hesitate to select them.

Status/Availability

The GDQ is copyrighted; only certified GDQ trainers/consultants are permitted to use it. Costs of the training and materials are undisclosed; materials are offered at reduced cost for organizations with limited finances. Information about the instrument and certification training can be obtained by contacting GDQ Associates, 144 N. Bread Street, Philadelphia, PA, 19106; (215) 568-1338.

Relevant Publications

Verdi, A.F., & Wheelan, S.A. (1992). Developmental patterns in same-sex and mixed-sex groups. *Small Group Research, 23*, 256-278.

Wheelan, S.A. (1993). *The Group Development Questionnaire: A manual for professionals.* Philadelphia: GDQ Associates.

Wheelan, S.A., & Hochberger, J.M. (1993). *The Group Development Questionnaire.* Philadelphia: GDQ Associates.

Wheelan, S.A., & Hochberger, J.M. (1996). Validation studies of the Group Development Questionnaire. *Small Group Research, 27*, 143-170.

Wheelan, S.A., & McKeage, R. (1993). Developmental patterns in small and large groups. *Small Group Research, 24*, 60-83.

Wheelan, S.A., & Verdi, A.F. (1992). Differences in male and female patterns of communication: A methodological artifact? *Sex Roles: A Journal of Research, 27*, 1-15.

TEAM PERFORMANCE PROFILE

Developed by Wilson Learning Corporation, 1982
Reviewed by Antonette M. Zeiss and Martha S. Waite

The Team Performance Profile provides a broad measurement of team performance for teams working in large, complex organizations. It includes 65 items that make up 10 subscales and one item that is a global measure of team performance. It is somewhat lengthy, and a few of the items contain words that may require definition for respondents. The instrument could be strengthened considerably by psychometric testing to assess its reliability and validity. It was not developed specifically for health care settings, but seems readily applicable to them.

Conceptual Framework

The developers do not present a theoretical framework for the instrument. They recognize the impact of the organization on team performance as well as the multidimensional nature of such performance.

The team is a work group within a complex organization. Within any organization, a variety of teams exist. Some teams are functional work groups within a specific department; others are short-term or long-term cross-functional teams, and still others are made up of supervisors or managers (i.e., the management team).

Description of Measure

The 65 items, making up the 10 components of team performance, and item 66, the global measure, are part of a consultation questionnaire that includes at total of 78 items. Wilson Learning Corporation provides brief guidelines for scoring and using the instrument (Leimbach, 1982). The instrument provides a broad assessment of team performance/effectiveness. Developers designed it for use among teams located in large, complex organizations. Team members complete the instrument individually. Average subscale scores provide an assessment of performance at the level of the team.

Components of Team Performance Measured

The developer identifies 10 components of team performance. Functional diversity (five items) measures breadth and appropriateness of expertise among team members. Alignment on purpose (six items) refers to having a shared goal or vision. The component, rational processes (four items), addresses effective use of meetings. Creative diversity (five items) focuses on the team's creativity and encouragement of new ideas from team members. The component, shared norms (seven items), includes the team's ground rules and shared values. The component, communication processes (five items), measures openness of communication and ability to express and resolve disagreement. Team performance (six items) includes having effective meetings, achieving work objectives, staying task focused, creating innovative solutions, and producing quality results and decisions. Team fulfillment (five items) relates to team members' feelings of cohesiveness, respect, and feeling valued in the team. Individual satisfaction (six items) refers to satisfaction with the work of each team member and the way the team is managed. Team satisfaction (six items) addresses satisfaction with teamwork and performance. Finally, there is one item that serves as a global measure of team performance. Leimbach (1982) indicates that the first six components of performance can be grouped into three overarching categories, collaboration (functional diversity, rational process, and creative diversity), commitment (alignment on purpose and shared norms), and communication (communication processes).

This instrument is a broad based measure in that it includes items in all four domains and all eight dimensions of our model of team performance. A unique feature of this instrument is its measurement of information management.

Formatting and Scoring

There are six Likert formatted answer choices for each of the 65 items making up the 10 subscales. For the first 53 positively worded items, the answer choices are 1 = almost never, 2 = rarely, 3 = seldom, 4 = sometimes, 5 = usually, and 6 = almost always. For items 54 through 65, respondents are asked how satisfied they are. The answer choices range from 1 = not satisfied to 6 = very satisfied; answer choices 2 through 5 do not have verbal anchors. For item 66, the global measure of team effectiveness, respondents rate their team on a scale from 1 = not at all effective to 10 = completely effective.

Wilson Learning Corporation provides detailed instructions for calculating standardized subscale scores for each of the 10 components of performance. Each of the subscales is standardized such that their scores range from 0 to 100.

Psychometric Testing

No reliability or validity data are available. Face validity seems apparent although no formal testing has been conducted.

Evaluation

The instrument has considerable breadth with regard to its coverage of team performance. There are clear guidelines for completing and scoring it; however, the large number of items makes completing it somewhat time-consuming. The instrument lacks theoretical basis and psychometric testing. Verbal anchors across the subscales are inconsistent. Unlike the other eight subscales, the Satisfaction Subscales have verbal anchors for only the extreme answer choices. The language used in several of the items might need some clarification for team members having never received team training as they may not understand such concepts as "team norms" and "ground rules."

Status/Availability

Wilson Learning Corporation holds the copyright. Contact the company at Wilson Learning Research and Development, 7500 Flying Cloud Drive, Eden Prairie, MN 55344; (612) 828-8645.

Relevant Publications

Leimbach, M. (1982). *Research use of the Team Performance Profile* (Available from Wilson Learning Research and Development, 7500 Flying Cloud Drive, Eden Prairie, MN 55344).

Wilson Learning Corporation. (1982). *Team Performance Profile*. Eden Prairie, MN: Author.

CHAPTER 13
INSTRUMENTS FOR HEALTH CARE TEAMS

Glenda F. Brown, Ed.D.
VA Central Arkansas Health Care System, Little Rock, AR, VISN 16

Martha S. Waite, M.S.W.
VA Greater Los Angeles Healthcare System, Sepulveda, CA, VISN 22

A team performance instrument should be sensitive to the culture of the group it targets for assessment. Thus, it is logical to ask how health care teams differ from other types of teams and whether or not these differences are reflected in the instruments developed or adapted for them. As we mentioned in Chapters 1 and 2, two unique characteristics set health care teams apart from other types of teams–their products and the types of team members serving on clinical or treatment teams. Unlike teams in business and industry, health care teams do not produce a single, tangible product. Natural work groups set goals and perform services and activities that directly and indirectly affect patients, their families, and visitors to the hospital or health care facility. Performance improvement teams problem solve and take actions to improve the health care organization and how it operates, and clinical teams provide direct treatment, care, and services to patients and their family members and caregivers. Readers adapting an instrument, whose origin is business and industry, need to consider how the products and outcomes measured in the instrument must be altered to reflect the complex, interpersonal, and more amorphous nature of the products of health care teams.

With regard to types of members, the members of the clinical team differ from other work group members in that each represents a health profession with its own knowledge base, attitudes and values, status, and set of skills. Each profession or discipline has its own roles and responsibilities that evolve through negotiation and agreement in educational institutions, clinical practice settings, courts, and communities. These varied professionals have different perceived levels of importance within the health care system and the clinical team. Thus, when an instrument refers to a given profession (e.g., physician, nurse, social worker, etc.), it "calls to mind" certain expectations of persons in that profession as well as the names and faces of specific members of one's own team. The elements of performance measured and the language used in the instruments designed or adapted for health care teams should take these differences into account.

In this chapter, we discuss 22 of the 66 instruments in this volume. These 22 instruments fall into four categories. The first two categories comprise instruments for clinical or treatment teams (i.e., three or more team members from different professions working together). The first category includes instruments developed specifically for use with these teams; the second category includes instruments adapted for use with them. Seven instruments were developed specifically for use with clinical teams, and five were adapted for such use.

The last two categories encompass generic instruments with a history of use in health care settings and supplemental instruments having the potential for adaptation and use in health care settings. Five generic instruments have been used consistently with teams in health care settings, and five supplemental instruments have potential for adaptation or use in conjunction with team performance instruments. We present the critiques of the first three categories of instruments in Chapters 9 through 12; the critiques of the fourth category of instruments appear at the end of this chapter.

The team performance measures appearing in bold face print in the tables of this chapter have been selected as "best measures" and are discussed further in Chapter 14.

Instruments Developed for Health Care Teams

Several assumptions underlie the development of instruments for clinical teams. These assumptions include: (a) the team has regular team meetings; (b) the team works within a hospital or other type of health care organization; (c) members of the team represent different health professions; and (d) the team develops formal care plans for each patient. These instruments are distinct from the more generic measures in that they include items about patients' and family caregivers' needs and preferences, goals for patients, treatment planning, patient care delivery, and patient outcomes. Additionally, they also include items about how well team members understand one another's roles, how well they work together, and whether members experience role overload or inappropriate role overlap (i.e., overstepping the boundaries of one's professional role). Some instruments include wording specific to a particular type of team. For example, two instruments include references to geriatric teams, and a third (a rehabilitation instrument) includes questions about patients' functional abilities. None would be difficult to adapt, with developers' permission, for use with other types of health care teams.

All seven instruments target specific types of health care teams; four target geriatric teams; and one each targets developmentally disabled, psychiatric, and rehabilitation teams. Six of the seven are self-administered–completed anonymously by team members. Bailey and Helsel-DeWert's duel purpose instrument also has an observational component. The Team Anomie Scale, the Attitudes Scale, and the Team Integration Measure are large-scale research instruments. The Attitudes Scale also has a duel purpose in that Hyer and colleagues (2000) used a version of it successfully to determine the impact of a large educational intervention. Hepburn and colleagues' Team Skills Scale assesses the impact of an educational intervention in geriatrics, and Tsukuda & Stahelski's instrument assesses baseline knowledge and skills of geriatric team members and trainees. McClane's instrument identifies strengths and weaknesses of the rehabilitation team for purposes of improving its performance (see Table 13.1).

Table 13.1. Instruments Developed for Health Care Teams

Instrument	Developer(s)	Type	Purpose	Target
Rating Individual Participation in Teams	Bailey & Helsel-DeWert	Focused Ch. 9	Assess & help improve functioning; research	Developmentally disabled direct care teams
Team Anomie Scale	Farrell, Schmitt & Heinemann	Focused Ch. 9	Research	Geriatric clinical teams
Attitudes Toward Health Care Teams	Heinemann, Schmitt & Farrell	Focused Ch. 9	Research; evaluate educational intervention	Geriatric clinical teams
Team Skills Scale	Hepburn, Tsukuda & Fasser	Focused Ch. 9	Evaluate educational intervention	Geriatric clinical teams
Team Integration Measure	Lichtenstein, Alexander, Jinnett & Ullman	Middle-Range Ch. 10	Research	Psychiatric treatment teams
Team Assessment Worksheets	McClane	Full-Spectrum Ch. 12	Assess & help improve functioning	Rehab. treatment teams
Team Skills Questionnaire	Tsukuda & Stahelski	Broad-Spectrum Ch. 11	Assess skill levels of members & trainees	Geriatric clinical teams

Instruments developed specifically for health care teams have a number of common characteristics. For most of them, the language used in the items specifically relates to health care settings. Some use sophisticated language and are appropriate for well-educated professionals only. Most are based on a sound theoretical framework with an emphasis on brevity; clarity; and ease of completing, scoring, and interpreting results to allow for busy health professionals' time and the space-saving needs of large-scale research projects. Most have been subjected to some psychometric testing.

Instruments Adapted for Health Care Teams

Of the five instruments adapted for clinical teams, two original versions target nurses and physicians specifically. The other three original instruments target generic teams and organizational work groups, multiple types of groups, and/or families (see Table 13.2).

Table 13.2. Instruments Adapted for Health Care Teams

Instrument	Original Developer(s); Adapter(s)	Type	Purpose	Targets
Collaboration & Satisfaction about Care Decisions	Baggs; Schmitt, Heinemann & Farrell	Focused Ch. 9	Research	Nurses & physicians in ICUs; geriatric clinical teams
Modified FAD for Teams (MFADT)	Epstein, Baldwin & Bishop; Waite &Harker	Broad-Spectrum Ch. 11	Assess & help improve functioning	Families; geriatric clinical teams
Factors Influencing Productivity & Excellence of Team Work	Lazar; Brown	Broad-Spectrum Ch. 11	Assess & help improve functioning	Organizational work groups; clinical teams
Group Environment Scale (GES); subscales adapted–Cohesion, Leader Support & Expressiveness	Moos & Humphrey; Schmitt, Heinemann & Farrell	Broad-Spectrum Ch. 11	Research	Multiple types of groups; geriatric clinical teams
ICU Nurse/Physician Instrument; subscales adapted-Communication, External Relations & Effectiveness	Shortell & Rousseau.; Schmitt, Heinemann & Farrell	Broad-Spectrum Ch. 11	Research	Nurses, physicians & ward clerks in ICUs; geriatric clinical teams

Instruments are adapted for health care teams for a number of reasons. The original instrument often includes content relevant to assessing the performance of such teams. It may be exceptionally well constructed (i.e., conceptually and methodologically sound with strong psychometric data), or it may capture unique information relevant to the assessment of performance (e.g., actual and expected perceptions). One benefit of adapting instruments is that much of the work has been completed already. Thus, adapting rather than designing a team performance instrument can save considerable time and prevent duplication of effort in the field. Schmitt and colleagues chose to adapt Baggs' collaboration instrument, the GES, and the ICU Nurse/Physician Instrument because they are well established, research-tested instruments with strong reliability and validity data. Brown adapted two of Lazar's instruments to expand the number of dimensions of team performance measured in one instrument (i.e., to include organizational as well as team elements). She also chose these instruments because they assess both actual and expected perceptions of performance and facilitate the ability of a consultant to assist a team to improve its functioning. Waite and Harker selected the FAD for adaptation because it is a well-established, reliable and valid instrument. Its assessment of the health of the family system paralleled their interest in the team as a functioning system whose processes bear some resemblance to those of families.

Instruments developed for use in health care settings usually require minimal changes when adapting them for clinical or treatment teams. Two of these instruments assess nurse/physician collaboration and decision-making in the intensive care unit. Baggs' instrument measures collaboration between physicians and nurses in the ICU. When this instrument was adapted, an additional discipline, social work, was included and the specific language changed to reflect the "core team" of physician, nurse, and social worker. Since the setting changed from the ICU to geriatrics, the task around which collaboration was measured changed from "patient transfer" to "patient discharge," and the term, unit, was changed to team. Schmitt and colleagues made similar changes in their 1992 adaptation of subscales from Shortell and Rousseau's ICU Questionnaire for geriatric clinical teams.

When instruments from business and industry or other settings outside of health care are adapted for health care teams, they sometimes require more extensive changes. For clinical teams, the definition of team often must be modified to reflect the relationship among health professionals who create and implement care plans for a given set of patients. In addition, the language must be appropriate for the settings, processes, and tasks of teams or work groups in health care. Finally, questions about leadership and organizational issues need to be reviewed carefully for relevance.

In some instances, subscales or specific items of an original instrument are not appropriate for health care teams. The adaptations of the GES and the FAD provide examples. The Anger and Aggression Subscale from the GES works well in assessing therapy groups and support groups where an important goal for members is to express anger and aggression openly. Items in this subscale were confusing to members of geriatric clinical teams since they viewed anger and aggression in their respective teams as a barrier to quality care for patients and, therefore, inappropriate. While it is important to express feelings in the health care team, this subscale did not translate well as a measure of appropriate expression. The FAD includes items appropriate for assessing family dynamics; some of its items and subscales translate well to health care teams (e.g., measurement of affective involvement and emotional connection to others in the group). Other items are inappropriate and were excluded from the adapted MFADT (e.g., an item about hitting one another).

Generic Instruments Used in Health Care Settings

Five generic instruments have a history of use with teams and work groups in health care settings (see Table 13.3). The TCI is a reliable and valid research instrument that measures four facets of a team's climate related to innovation.

Table 13.3. Generic Instruments Used in Health Care Settings

Instrument	Developer(s)	Type	Purpose	Target
Team Climate Inventory (TCI)	Anderson & West	Broad-Spectrum Ch. 11	Research	Clinical & management teams
Team Development Scale	Dyer	Focused Ch. 9	Assess & help improve functioning	All types of health care teams
Analyzing Team Effectiveness	McGregor	Broad-Spectrum Ch. 11	Assess & help improve functioning	All types of health care teams
Team Effectiveness Rating Scale	Rothermich & Saunders	Full-Spectrum Ch. 12	Assess & help improve functioning	Clinical teams, especially new teams
Group Development Questionnaire (GDQ)	Wheelan & Hochberger	Full-Spectrum Ch. 12	Research; evaluate educational intervention; assess & help team develop & mature	All types of health care teams with a team leader

They are vision, participative safety, task orientation, and support for innovation. The Team Development Scale and Analyzing Team Effectiveness are well-established instruments for assessing team functioning and facilitating its improvement. They are short and easy to complete. The former instrument has some psychometric data; the latter one uses an item analysis for summary and interpretation of results. The latter instrument also has been used successfully in educational workshops. The Team Effectiveness Rating Scale, too, is an assessment and improvement measure. In comparison to the previous two instruments, it is considerably longer and is most appropriate for newly developing clinical teams. No psychometric testing has been conducted to determine its reliability and validity. The GDQ is a relatively long, multipurpose instrument measuring team performance in considerable depth; it is appropriate for professional teams and natural work groups; however, it assumes a leader within the team. It is based on a strong theoretical framework and has strong reliability and validity data.

Supplemental Instruments with Potential for Adaptation

We identified five instruments with potential for adaptation for teams in health care settings (see Table 13.4). Four of the five measure facets of organizational performance. They address the setting (structure and context) in which teams are located and function. Each examines the interface between individual and organization and how this interaction impacts employees' work effectiveness and interrelationships with others. Adapting them would provide

Table 13.4. Supplemental Instruments with Potential for Adaptation

Instrument	Developer(s)	# Items	Purpose	Target
Organizational System Survey (OSS), versions for health care & nursing employees	Baehr & associates	104, 108	Assess & help improve performance	Health care organizations
Organizational Climate Questionnaire (OCQ)	Furnham & Goodstein	108	Assess & help improve performance	Organization
Jefferson Survey of Attitudes Toward Nurse-Physician Collaboration	Hojat et al.	15	Evaluate educational intervention	Nurses, physicians, & trainees
Work Environment Scale (WES)	Moos & Insel	90	Research; evaluate educational intervention; assess & help improve performance	Organization
Organizational Performance Survey	Tercon, Inc.	80	Assess & help improve performance	Organization

broad measures of team performance for teams and work groups in hospitals, nursing homes, and other health care facilities. Instruments such as these, measuring the impact of the organization on team performance, are especially important for assessing today and tomorrow's health care teams. Given the tremendous changes in health care, teams cannot function without an understanding of the team approach and support for it at all levels of the organization including management (Ilgen, 1999).

The OSS offers versions specific to health care employees and nursing staff based on morale theory. Additional items that apply to a specific organization can be added from several categories, including diversity, change and stress management, and managed care. The Organizational Climate Questionnaire measures 14 facets of organizational climate and includes two subscales, Agreement and Importance, for each facet. The WES evaluates employees' perceptions of the organization from real, expected, and ideal perspectives. The Organizational Performance Survey determines how closely employees feel their organization matches the developer's model of a high performance organization (i.e., involvement-oriented versus the traditional, control-oriented).

The Attitudes Toward Nurse-Physician Collaboration Survey also has potential for adaptation. It assesses the effectiveness of collaborative education in medical schools and nursing programs. Minor wording changes in items would make it amenable to clinical teams.

Health care teams are being asked increasingly to demonstrate their effectiveness through outcome measures–cost savings, functional improvement, shorter waiting time, higher patient satisfaction ratings, shorter lengths of inpatient stays, and reduced staff turnover. Instruments designed from business and organizational perspectives tend to focus on outcome measurement. Additionally, the need for interprofessional education is becoming greater, and determining its impact is becoming increasingly important as complexity and change in health care require collaboration among health professionals and health care workers. As a result, these instruments hold tremendous potential for measuring team performance in health care settings; however, psychometric testing will need to be conducted on any adapted versions since their unit of analysis changes from the organization to the team. These instruments also can be used in conjunction with other team performance measures.

REFERENCES

Hyer, K., Fairchild, S., Abraham, I., Mezey, M., & Fulmer, T. (2000). Measuring attitudes related to interdisciplinary training: Revisiting the Heinemann, Schmitt and Farrell 'attitudes toward health care teams' Scale. *Journal of Interprofessional Care, 14*, 249-258.

Ilgen, D.R. (1999). Teams embedded in organizations: Some implications. *American Psychologist, 54*, 129-139.

ORGANIZATIONAL SYSTEM SURVEY (OSS)

Developed by M.E. Baehr and The Human Resource Center, University of Chicago, 1962; updated 1985
Reviewed by Steven Lovett and Gloria D. Heinemann

The developers designed the OSS for business/industry (four versions) and health care (five versions). Each version targets a different type of employee. Although long, it has a sound theoretical framework and is relatively easy to complete. The two versions (i.e., health care employees and nursing staff) critiqued by these reviewers ranged from 104 to 108 positively and negatively worded items, respectively. No scoring instructions are available since National Computer Systems, (NCS), Inc. does all scoring, data processing, and report preparation. The survey provides flexibility in that additional items can be added that are specific to a particular organization. The three answer choices for items limit variability of responses and permit an "uncertain" option for respondents. No psychometric data are available for review. The NCS services package must be purchased to use the survey.

Conceptual Framework

All OSS instruments in the survey are based on a theory of employee morale developed by psychologists at the Human Resource Center, The University of Chicago. Morale includes three types of satisfaction–intrinsic (i.e., identification with the organization and job satisfaction), extrinsic (i.e., satisfaction with compensation/pay and benefit program), and social (i.e., satisfaction with supervisory leadership practices and relationships among employees and groups of employees). Other, more general items have their basis in the organizational management literature, and the developers have used them to assess facets of organizational effectiveness. Developers view teams and teamwork as parts of organizational life that have the potential to improve the organization's productivity.

Description of Measure

The instrument elicits employees' perceptions of how well the overall organization functions and how satisfied they are with it. The developers designed the instrument for use with employees working in health care and business/industry settings. It can be used to assess the impact of organizational change on systems and procedures. Results can guide decision-making related to employee hiring, employee relations, administrative strategies, and promotion decisions. The instrument also can be used to improve cooperation among various groups of employees and to help identify problems negatively affecting employees' morale and productivity. Results can establish a baseline for evaluating organizational progress and improvement over time. Finally, the developers believe findings can help improve the performance of teams, leaders, and organizations and identify their training needs.

Nine occupation-specific versions are available–four for business and industry (i.e., organization, sales, managerial, and professional) and five for health care (i.e., physicians, nursing staff, paraprofessionals, non-medical professionals, and health care workers). Individual employees complete the instrument.

Dimensions of Organizational Performance Measured

In addition to the morale factors, each version of the survey includes the following effectiveness categories: general administrative effectiveness; interdepartmental coordination; communication effectiveness; supervisory administrative practices; performance and personal development; management effectiveness; customer service; work organization; work efficiency; and reactions to the survey. Demographic data also are elicited.

The survey can be modified to meet the needs of specific organizations. Up to 36 additional items can be added from the categories of teamwork, diversity management, gender fairness, change management, visionary leadership, quality initiatives, stress management, project management, and managed care.

Formatting and Scoring

The nursing staff version includes 108 items; the health employee version includes 104 items. Items are positively and negatively worded. For each item, respondents choose among three answer choices A = agree, ? = uncertain, and D = disagree. Using a number 2 pencil, they darken the appropriate circle for each item. General and demographic questions appear on a separate page of each version of the instrument.

The developers designed the instrument so a scanner can score answers. Scoring and processing of information is carried out by NCS. The company sends a comprehensive report back to the client along with an interpretation guide and workbook. The report includes "percent favorable" responses for each dimension of organizational performance assessed and for individual items within a dimension. These scores are compared to those of a normative group. NCS uses bar graphs and percentage tables to present feedback.

Psychometric Testing

No reliability or validity data are available.

Evaluation

The instrument is long, but relatively easy to complete. The accompanying instructions are clear and explicit. Flexibility permits the inclusion of additional questions about employees' perceptions of their teams and natural work groups. Answer choices do not permit much variability in responses, and respondents can avoid a straightforward answer by selecting the "uncertain" choice. These reviewers are unaware of any psychometric data evaluating the survey's reliability and validity. Additionally, the group used to determine normative data is not clear. NCS reports of results are clear and descriptive with good use of graphs and charts; little interpretation of findings is provided, however.

Status/Availability

Melany E. Baehr, Ph.D. holds the copyright to the OSS. The survey, scoring, and report must be purchased from National Computer Systems (NSC), Inc., P.O. Box 1416, Minneapolis, MN 55440; (800)-221-8378.

Relevant Publications

Baehr, M.E. (1985). *Organizational Survey System Health Care Employee Survey*. Minneapolis, MN: National Computer Systems, Inc.

Baehr, M.E. (1985). *Organizational Survey System Health Care Nursing Staff Survey*. Minneapolis, MN: National Computer Systems, Inc.

Baehr, M.E. (1999). *Organizational Survey System (OSS) sample report for health care: Nursing staff*. Minneapolis, MN: National Computer Systems, Inc.

ORGANIZATIONAL CLIMATE QUESTIONNAIRE (OCQ)

Developed by A. Furnham and L.G. Goodstein, 1997
Reviewed by D. Erik Everhart and Sara A. Brallier

The Organizational Climate Questionnaire (OCQ) assesses organizational structure and context as it relates to job satisfaction and productivity. This 108-item instrument measures 14 facets of organizational climate. It is unique in that it measures both agreement (i.e., employee satisfaction with how things are done) and importance for each facet. The developers provide materials to guide efforts for improvement. Although it takes considerable time to complete and score, the instrument is broad-based, conceptually sound, and easy to read. There are several methodological problems with it, and additional psychometric testing would be beneficial. It provides an organizational analysis and requires adaptation for teams unless used in conjunction with a team performance measure.

Conceptual Framework

The developers view organizational climate as multidimensional, transitory, and malleable. Climate is influenced by changes in systems, structures, and managerial behavior and stabilized by enduring group values and norms. It directly affects job satisfaction, which impacts both individual and organizational productivity. Assessment of the various facets of organizational climate provides important diagnostic indicators of organizational functioning. Teamwork/collaboration is one of the 14 facets of organizational climate.

Description of Measure

The developers designed the OCQ to provide a psychometrically sound instrument applicable to a broad international population to evaluate the current climate and the impact of organizational change initiatives. Employees complete the instrument anonymously. Team and/or departmental averages can be compared across the organization.

Components of Organizational Performance Measured

The OCQ measures 14 facets of organizational climate–role clarity, respect, communication, reward system, career development, planning and decision-making, innovation, relationships, teamwork and support, quality of service, conflict management, commitment and morale, training/learning, and direction.

Formatting and Scoring

Developers use a seven-point Likert rating format for each of the 108 items such that 1 is the lowest score (i.e., strongly disagree or quite unimportant), and 7, the highest score (i.e., strongly agree or essential). Respondents provide two answers to each item–how much they agree with the item, an indication of their satisfaction, and how important they perceive the item to be.

Two subscales measure each of the 14 facets of organizational climate. The first is the Agreement Subscale (employee satisfaction with how things are done), and the second is the Importance Subscale (the degree to which employees believe that the items are significant aspects of the way work is performed in the organization). Subscale scores are averaged for team profiles.

Alternatively, for each of the 108 items, team or departmental averages can be calculated for Agreement and Importance. Developers note that mean agreement scores of 4.0 or above are considered high, and mean agreement scores of 2.5 or below are considered low. Mean importance scores of 5.0 or above are high, and mean importance scores of 2.0 are low. Users of the instrument should inspect their own distributions of agreement and importance scores to be sure the cut-off-points recommended by the developers are appropriate for their respective samples. Once items that yield high and low scores have been determined, they are entered into a two by two matrix. The process assigns items to one of four descriptive categories–fix, (low performance and high importance), ignore (low performance and low importance), consider (high performance and low importance), and celebrate (high performance and high importance). Developers suggest a course of action for each of the four descriptive categories.

Psychometric Testing

Internal Consistency Reliability

Developers calculated Cronbach's alpha coefficients for each of the 14 OCQ facets of agreement and importance for two different samples. Alphas for the agreement ratings ranged from .60 to .85 with a mean of .77 (first sample) and from .63 to .85 with a mean of .78 (second sample). For importance ratings, alphas ranged from .70 to .88 with a mean of .78 (first sample) from .73 to .87 with a mean of .81 (second sample).

Intercorrelations between facets ranged from .22 to .70 with an average of .51. Commitment and morale correlated with virtually all other facets. Correlations between ratings of agreement and importance ranged from -.08 to .24 with an average of .06; these data support the independence of the subscales (i.e., each is measuring a different concept).

Test-Retest/Inter-Rater reliability

No data are available regarding test-retest reliability, and testing for inter-rater reliability is inappropriate since the measure is self-administered.

Content or Face Validity

According to the developers, test items were "reviewed by several directors of human resources in a large number of both large and small organizations as well as a number of management consultants and teachers of organizational behavior and management." The mean importance ratings on each facet exceeded 5.0 (using a seven-point answer choice format) for each of the two samples; this suggests that the respondents believed the facets are important.

Concurrent Validity

No data are available.

Construct Validity

Using ANOVA, significant differences in agreement scores as a function of seniority were found for both samples. These differences in seniority were systematic, substantial, and similar across both samples. Specifically, the more senior the employee, the higher the rating they gave across all 14 facets. These findings indicate that employees who have positive perceptions of the organization are more apt to remain employed by the organization or that seniority may lead to greater positive perceptions of the organization. Both explanations are conceptually sound; thus, the relationship between seniority and perception of organizational climate is an indicator of the instrument's construct validity.

Predictive/Discriminant Validity

No data are available for these types of validity.

Evaluation

This instrument is a broad-based measure of organizational effectiveness and the impact of change on the organization. It is conceptually sound, and items are easy to read. It is unique in that it addresses agreement and importance for each facet of organizational climate. The two by two table helps identify priorities for taking action and facilitates the development of more accurate and precise intervention. Some evidence supports the reliability and validity of the instrument; however, correlation matrices, means and standard deviations, $\underline{F}$ values, and $\underline{p}$ values are unavailable. Thus, it is difficult to evaluate the developers' conclusions and statements regarding the instrument's reliability and validity.

The instrument takes considerable time to complete and score. Several methodological problems also exist. First, some of the items require reverse coding, though no directions are available for doing so. Second, the use of seven answer choices per item may be overly detailed and confusing to respondents; a five-point range might be more appropriate. For example, the difference between "essential, 7" and "important, 6," with regard to degree of importance, is not easily distinguishable. Third, in using the two-by-two matrix, relevant information is lost since only high and low scores appear in the matrix. Finally, several of the items are redundant, and several almost identical items are presented as though they measure different facets of organizational climate.

Because the instrument does not focus specifically on measuring team performance, the reviewers recommend using it in conjunction with such a measure to provide insight regarding the relationship between organizational structure and context and team performance. Alternatively, it could be adapted, with permission, to measure team performance within the organization.

Status/Availability

This instrument is in the public domain and appears in the 1997 article by the developers (see relevant publications). To purchase this publication, contact Pfeiffer & Company at (800) 274-4434.

Relevant Publications

Furnham, A., & Goodstein, L.D. (1997). The Organizational Climate Questionnaire (OCQ). In *The 1997 annual: Volume 2, consulting* (pp. 163-181). San Francisco: Pfeiffer, An Imprint of Jossey-Bass, Inc.

JEFFERSON SURVEY OF ATTITUDES TOWARD PHYSICIAN-NURSE COLLOABORATION

Developed by M. Hojat, S.K. Fields, J.J. Veloski, M. Griffiths, M.J.M. Cohen, and J.D. Plumb, 1985, 1997, 1999
Reviewed by Carrie L. Hill and Theresa J.K. Drinka

The 1999, third version of the instrument includes 15 items, designed to measure attitudes of physicians and nurses toward mutual collaboration. The instrument's purpose is to evaluate interdisciplinary educational programs. The survey is easy to understand, administer, and complete. Although the authors have conducted preliminary psychometric testing, additional testing is warranted. It could be useful for health care teams that include physicians and nurses as members. It also has potential for measuring collaboration among professionally diverse team members.

Conceptual Framework

The instrument does not have a strong theoretical basis. Developers do support a team approach to health care delivery that involves collaboration, problem solving, and working toward common goals among professionals. They note that despite the benefits of a team approach, relationships among team members often are strained due to disparities in attitudes about the roles and responsibilities of different health professionals. Attitudes of physicians and nurses about their professional collaboration are the focus of this instrument.

Description of Measure

Developers designed the original, 1985 instrument to measure attitudes toward nurses. A second, 1997 version focused on attitudes toward the physician-nurse alliance in the areas of authority, dependence/independence, mutual decision-making, and role expectations. A slight revision from the second version, the 1999 version measures, via pretest and post-test, the effectiveness of collaborative education in medical schools and nursing programs. Developers believe it also has potential to evaluate attitudes among physicians and nurses who are currently in practice. The 1999 version is the focus of this review.

Components of Performance Measured

The instrument measures attitudes toward physician-nurse collaboration in four areas–shared education and collaborative relationships, caring versus curing, nurses' autonomy, and physicians' authority.

Formatting and Scoring

The third version of the instrument has 15 positively and negatively worded items. Developers use a four-point Likert format for each item such that 4 = strongly agree, 3 = agree, 2 = disagree, 1 = strongly disagree; the last two items (14 and 15) must be reverse scored prior to summing. They score the instrument as if it were a unidimensional scale, which is not supported by their factor analysis. The unidimensional scale has a potential range of 15-60. The higher the score, the more positive is the attitude toward physician-nurse collaboration.

Psychometric Testing

Internal Consistency Reliability

Factor analysis showed that the instrument measures four underlying factors that are consistent with conceptual discussions about physician-nurse collaboration. They include shared education and collaborative relationships (factor one), caring as opposed to curing (factor two), nurse's autonomy (factor three), and physician's authority (factor four). Seven items loaded above .40 on factor one, and it explained 27% of the total variance. Three items each loaded on factors two and three, and each explained 7% of the variance. Only two items loaded on factor four; it explained 6% of the variance. The developers report an alpha reliability estimate of .85 for the combined groups of nursing and medical students, which is in the acceptable range. Item-to-total score correlations ranged from .40 to .65.

Test-Retest/Inter-Rater Reliability

No data are available regarding test-retest reliability, and testing for inter-rater reliability is inappropriate since the measure is self-administered.

Content or Face Validity

The Shared Educational and Collaborative Relationships Subscale has the most face validity. The second, third, and fourth subscales probably omit important facets of their respective concepts given that they include only two to three items.

Construct Validity

If one can hypothesize that women are more amenable to collaboration than men, than data support this type of validity given that first year female medical students held significantly more positive attitudes toward physician-nurse collaboration than their male counterparts.

Concurrent/Predictive/Discriminant Validity

No data are available for these types of validity.

Evaluation

The instrument is easy to understand, administer, and complete; however, it requires additional psychometric testing to fully establish its reliability and validity. Once this is accomplished, it has potential use as a pre/post-test measure. It also could be useful for health care teams that include physicians and nurses. Ascertaining similarities and differences of team members' attitudes about collaboration between physicians and nurses or among team members generally could provide a starting point for team growth and development. The instrument also has potential as a cross-cultural measure given its translation into other languages (see section below).

It is premature to adapt this instrument until all psychometric data are collected, and developers are still in the process of collecting it. Three weaknesses should be addressed in any future adaptations. First, the items in the 1999 version over emphasize nurses and their attitudes. The wording of the items and the absence of parallel physician-oriented items contribute to this bias. Second, the concepts, autonomy and authority, could be defined better. Autonomy can be construed as merely being self-directed, whereas authority can connote either supremacy over others or appropriate leadership. For relevance as a team measure, the factors of autonomy and authority should be defined and perhaps combined under a heading of collaborative leadership. Autonomy and authority each has a place on an interdisciplinary health care team, and practitioners must learn when and where to use them. Finally, factor analysis does not support one unidimensional scale. More attention should be given to the development of conceptually sound subscales.

Status/Availability

Information about this instrument and its development appears in the 1999 publication below. Spanish (Mexican and Cuban) and Japanese versions of the instrument also are available.

Relevant Publications

Hojat, M., Fields, S.K., Veloski, J.J., Griffiths, M., Cohen, M.J.M., & Plumb, J.D. (1999). Psychometric properties of an attitude scale measuring physician-nurse collaboration. *Evaluation & The Health Professions, 22*, 208-220.

Hojat, M., Fields, S.K., Rattner, S.L., Griffiths, M., Cohen, M.J.M., & Plumb, J.M. (1997). Attitudes toward physician-nurse alliance: Comparisons of medical and nursing students. *Academic Medicine, 72*, S1-S3.

Hojat, M., & Herman, M.W. (1985). Developing an instrument to measure attitudes toward nurses: Preliminary psychometric findings. *Psychological Reports, 56*, 571-579.

WORK ENVIRONMENT SCALE (WES)

Developed by Rudolf H. Moos and Paul M. Insel, 1974, 1994
Reviewed by Kimberly D. Kalish, Sara A. Brallier, and Antonette M. Zeiss

The Work Environment Scale (WES) is a 90-item, self-administered instrument consisting of three forms. It measures employees' and managers' perceptions of their current work environment (Real Form), their expectations of a work environment (Expectations Form), and their conceptions of an ideal environment (Ideal Form). The WES is based on a conceptual framework and is relatively easy to administer and score. It has good reliability and validity and is appropriate for consultation and research purposes. The WES does not measure team performance; however, it could be adapted to do so with the developers' permission.

Conceptual Framework

The conceptual framework for this instrument integrates three major workplace perspectives–the human relations approach, the sociotechnical perspective, and the social information processing orientation. According to developers, employee outcomes (i.e., morale and performance) and organizational outcomes (i.e., quality of services and client outcomes) are directly and indirectly affected by the organizational system and the characteristics of individual employees. The organizational system comprises the physical features of the workplace, organizational structure and policies, work task factors, and work climate. Relevant individual characteristics include job position, level of experience, sociodemographic background, personal resources, and expectations and preferences about the workplace. Work stressors and employees' abilities to cope with the stressors can mediate the impact of the organizational system and individual characteristics on outcomes.

Description of Measure

Developers designed the instrument as a consultation and research tool. The Real Form measures employees' perceptions of their current work environment. It is used to target areas of the work environment in need of improvement or to determine the impact of an intervention via pre/post-test. It also is used to determine how changes in the work environment (e.g., reorganization, layoffs, or expansions) impact employees' perceptions of their workplace.

The Expectations Form is used to determine an employee's expectations of a workplace. This form is intended for use before employment begins or when one is returning to the work environment after an extended absence. Discrepancies found between results from the Real and Expectations Forms indicate the need to educate individuals to develop more realistic expectations. The Ideal Form is used to determine employees' and managers' preferred work environment. When this form is used in conjunction with the Real Form, one can isolate specific areas in which the actual work environment differs from the ideal. Individual employees complete the instrument; averaged work group scores permit comparison of groups or comparisons over time.

Components of Organizational Performance Measured

The 10 subscales measure three broad facets of the workplace environment–relationships, personal growth, and systems maintenance and change. The Involvement Subscale is the extent to which individuals within work groups are invested in their jobs. The Coworker Cohesion Subscale is the degree to which employees are friendly and supportive of one another. The Supervisor Support Subscale measures the extent to which management supports employees and encourages them to support one another, and the Autonomy Subscale measures the extent to which employees are encouraged to be independent. The Task Orientation Subscale measures the amount of energy used in planning and completing tasks. Other subscales include: Work Pressure, the extent to which the work environment is dominated by high work demands and time pressure; Clarity, the degree to which employees can anticipate their daily routine and are knowledgeable about rules and regulations; and Managerial Control, the degree to which management uses rules and procedures to control employee behavior. Finally, the Innovation Subscale is the extent to which variety, change, and new approaches are encouraged, and the Physical Comfort Subscale is the extent to which the physical surroundings influence the work environment.

Formatting and Scoring

Each of the 10 subscales includes nine items. For each of the 90 items, respondents indicate whether the statement is "true or mostly true" or "false or mostly false" by marking an "X" in the appropriate box.

A template for reverse coding items and scoring the answer sheet comes with the WES. Subscale scores range from 0 to 9; the higher the score is, the stronger the perception of the construct being measured. Subscale scores are averaged to obtain work group scores. Tables are provided for converting individual and work-group scores into standard scores. A profile form is available for graphic presentation of scores. Results can be sent to the publisher for interpretation and a narrative report if desired.

Psychometric Testing

Internal Consistency Reliability

Based on a sample of 1,045 nurses, the internal consistencies are as follows: involvement, .84; coworker cohesion, .69; supervisor support, .77; autonomy, .73; task orientation, .76; work pressure, .80; clarity, .79; managerial control, .76; innovation, .86; and physical comfort, .81 (Constable, 1984 as cited by Moos, 1994). Very similar internal consistencies were reported for a sample of 742 teachers (Fisher & Fraser, 1983 as cited by Moos, 1994).

Based on data collected from the 1,045 nurses, the corrected average item-to-subscale correlations are: involvement, .52; coworker cohesion, .36; supervisor support, .44; autonomy, .39; task orientation, .42; work pressure, .47; clarity .45; managerial control, .41; innovation, .53; and physical comfort, .49 (Constable, 1984 as cited by Moos, 1994).

Test-Retest Reliability

In order to assess the test-retest reliability of the WES, 75 respondents completed the instrument twice, with an interval of one month between administrations. The test-retest correlations for each subscale are as follows: involvement, .83; coworker cohesion, .71; supervisor support, .82; autonomy, .77; task orientation, .73; work pressure, .76; clarity, .69; managerial control, .79; innovation, .75; and physical comfort, .78 (Moos, 1994).

Inter-Rater Reliability

Testing for inter-rater reliability is not applicable since the instrument is self-administered.

Content or Face Validity

The items were developed from structured interviews with employees and managers (Moos & Billings, 1991 as cited by Moos, 1994). Developers used Moos' other social climate scales as sources for items. The 90-item scale is the result of two earlier versions of the instrument.

Concurrent Validity

No data available.

Construct Validity

Evidence supports the WES subscales' ability to distinguish between two groups that are theoretically anticipated to be different. For example, nurses working the day and night shift, respectively, differed as expected. Day shift nurses reported higher levels of supervisor support, autonomy, involvement, task orientation, work demands, and lower levels of managerial control (Buccheri, 1985; Turnipseed, 1990 as cited by Moos, 1994). The WES also demonstrated theoretically anticipated differences between primary nurses and team or functional nurses. Primary nurses scored higher on the Involvement, Cohesion, Managerial Support, and Autonomy Subscales; they scored lower on the Managerial Control Subscale compared to team or functional nurses (Thomas, 1992 as cited by Moos, 1994). The WES distinguished between nurses working in non-specialized and specialized hospital services. As anticipated, nurses in specialized services reported higher levels of involvement, cohesion, task-orientation, and work demands than did nurses working on less-specialized units.

Several of the WES subscales related as theoretically anticipated to elements of organizational structure and climate in a comparison of two social service agencies. The agency that emphasized the team approach to delivery of services, supported team training, and encouraged the formation of employee support groups had higher levels of involvement, cohesion, task-orientation, clarity, managerial control, and innovation than the agency that emphasized individual case management and did not actively promote employee development.

As expected, the Involvement, Cohesion, Supervisor Support, and Task-Orientation Subscales were positively correlated with a measure of staff morale in two health care clinics. Among nurses, high levels of work pressure and low levels of autonomy and innovation were associated with high rates of illness and absenteeism.

Predictive/Discriminant Validity

No data are available.

Evaluation

Although each of the three forms of the WES consists of 90 items, the developers note that it only takes about 15 minutes to complete each form. The instrument has considerable breadth and depth and is based on a conceptual framework. Although long, it is relatively easy to administer and score; its readability permits administration with both professionals and front-line employees. The WES has been used extensively in a wide variety of work settings and has been subjected to rigorous psychometric testing.

Status/Availability

The instrument and manual are available for purchase from Consulting Psychologists Press, Inc., 3803 E. Bayshore Road, Palo Alto, CA 94303; (650) 969-8901.

Relevant Publications

Moos, R.H., & Insel, P.M. (1974). *Work Environment Scale, Forms R, I, & E*. Palo Alto, CA: Consulting Psychologists Press, Inc.

Moos, R.H. (1994). *Work Environment Scale manual: Development, applications, research*. Palo Alto, CA: Consulting Psychologists Press, Inc.

Moos, R.H. (1993). *Work Environment Scale annotated bibliography*. Palo Alto, CA: Center for Health Care Evaluation, Stanford University and Department of Veterans Affairs Medical Centers.

ORGANIZATIONAL PERFORMANCE SURVEY

Developed by Tercon, Inc., 1995
Reviewed by Steven Lovett and Antonette M. Zeiss

Designed to measure respondents' perceptions of how closely their organization matches the characteristics of a "high performance" organization, the instrument includes 80-items and is self-administered. It includes eight components of high performance: (a) leadership; (b) organizational structure; (c) technical systems; (d) information; (e) rewards and recognition; (f) decision-making; (g) staffing and development; and (h) roles and expectations. While the developers provide average subscale scores for each of the eight components, their factor analysis supports a unidimensional scale. The instrument is easy to complete, has good internal reliability and face validity, but is prone to response bias; it would benefit from additional psychometric testing.

Conceptual Framework

The developers differentiate organizations as having either a traditional (control-oriented) or high performance (involvement-oriented) culture. Traditional cultures emphasize enforcement of rules and top down specification of activities that tend to restrict employee initiative. High performance cultures emphasize involvement and expect managers to lead by providing guidance role modeling. The developers subscribe strongly to the high performance culture. The instrument helps determine how closely employees feel their organization matches the developers' ideal of a high performance organization.

Description of Measure

Developers designed the instrument for consultation and educational purposes. It facilitates the identification of areas in which the organizational structure could be modified to resemble more closely a high performance organization. They recommend administering the instrument on at least a yearly basis to assess changes. Employees complete the instrument anonymously. It taps their perceptions of the organization as a whole. Results indicate the degree to which employees perceive their organization reflecting the values and practices identified as those of high performance organizations. Tercon recommends using this instrument in conjunction with their Team Strength Survey (see critique in Chapter 12).

Components of Organizational Performance Measured

Developers designed the instrument to include eight components of organizational climate–leadership, organizational structures, technical systems, information, rewards and recognition, decision-making, staffing and development, and roles and expectations. Leadership refers to how well management empowers individuals, teams, and departments. It measures how well leadership challenges the present state, creates a vision for the future, and models future-oriented, collaborative activities. The organizational structure component reflects the overall flow of work and decision-making in the organization. Effective organizational structure is defined as team-based, flexible and adaptive, and driven by performance rather than politics.

The technical systems component refers to effective use of technology, which occurs when it is used as a tool to meet goals rather than as an end in itself, when it creates a competitive advantage, and when it is carefully integrated with the organization's social system. Information refers to how information is exchanged within the organization. The goal is to maintain an open and informal flow of information and encourage performance feedback. The rewards and recognition component is the degree to which rewards and recognition are associated with performance reflecting the organization's values, and rewards are commensurate with the results achieved. Decision-making is the degree to which decision-making is done cooperatively and where constructive conflict is expected.

The staffing and development component reflects the degree to which the organization values its employees, maximizes the use of their talents, and invests in the development of new skills. It also measures the degree to which organizational policies and procedures reflect trust in employees. The roles and expectations component assesses the degree to which employees' roles are flexible and adaptive, performance goals are specified clearly and well understood, and cooperation is encouraged.

Formatting and Scoring

The instrument includes 80-items. The answer choices range from 5 = strongly agree to 1 = strongly disagree; these verbal anchors appear at each extremes of the extreme responses. Respondents also can indicate a "not applicable" response by circling "0." All items are worded such that the higher the rating, the greater the perception of high performance traits within the organization.

Formal scoring instructions are not provided in the documentation accompanying the measure. From a sample report provided, it appears that Tercon examines both average item scores and average subscale scores for each of the eight components. Both average item scores and average subscale scores range from one to five, where five indicates the greatest correspondence to the ideals of a high performance organization. Tercon appears to use the instrument solely to characterize the organization as a whole and not as a means of characterizing individual respondents.

Psychometric Testing

Internal Consistency Reliability

Cronbach's alpha ranges from .83 to .87 for the eight subscales; these alphas indicate a high level of internal consistency for all subscales. A principal components factor analysis on a sample of over 800 respondents produced one strong factor for the measure, another indicator of strong internal consistency. The factor ascertains respondents' general perceptions of the organization's overall fit with the characteristics of high performance organizations as defined by the instrument's developers.

Test-Retest/Inter-Rater Reliability

No data are available regarding test-retest reliability, and testing for inter-rater reliability is inappropriate since the measure is self-administered.

Content or Face Validity

The face validity of the instrument is good. Items are well constructed and have a logical connection to the concepts they measure.

Concurrent/Construct/Predictive/Discriminant Validity

No data are available for these types of validity.

Evaluation

The instrument is easy to understand and complete. It is comprehensive and covers numerous facets of organizational structure and processes. It has a high degree of face validity and is likely to be accepted by respondents as meaningful.

A weakness of the instrument is the potential for response bias as all of the items are positively worded. Moreover, the wording of the items makes it clear that higher ratings are more desirable, which may influence respondents' answers if they feel pressure not to be critical of their organization.

The identification of one general factor in the factor analysis reported above fails to support the developer's expectation that individuals' perception of organizational performance is a function of eight relatively independent components. The results of the factor analysis indicate that respondents with the highest scores on any one subscale tend to have the highest scores on all other subscales. This lack of discrimination is not a critical flaw, however, since the instrument appears to be used primarily to profile organizations and determine where specific improvements need to be made. Finally, the reviewers believe the instrument requires more extensive psychometric testing, especially if it is to be used to monitor or track perceptions of performance over time.

Status/Availability

Tercon, Inc. holds the instrument's copyright. The company does not market the instrument as an independent product. The administration, scoring, and interpretation of results are provided as part of consulting services offered by the company. Tercon, Inc. can be contacted at 12920 Metcalf Avenue, Suite 120, Overland Park, KS 66213-2625; (800) 877-4776; website, www.tercon.com.

Relevant Publications

Tercon, Inc. (1995). *Organizational Performance Survey.* Overland Park, KS: Author.
Tercon, Inc. (1998). *Organizational Performance Survey results: Company A International OPS report.* Overland Park, KS: Author.

CHAPTER 14
ASSESSMENT AND DEVELOPMENT: NOW AND IN THE FUTURE

Steven Lovett, Ph.D.
VA Palo Alto Health Care System, Palo Alto, CA, VISN 21

Antonette M. Zeiss, Ph.D.
VA Palo Alto Health Care System, Palo Alto, CA, VISN 21

Gloria D. Heinemann, Ph.D.
VA Western New York Healthcare System, Buffalo, NY, VISN 2

In this final chapter, we address the state of the field of team performance with respect to assessment, theory, and education/consultation. Initially, we identify the "best measures" from the instruments we have critiqued in Chapters 9 though 12 along with the criteria and rationale for their selection. Instruments critiqued in Chapter 13 that do not currently measure team performance were not included in the selection of "best measures." Next, we address future measurement of team performance with particular emphasis on what needs to be measured as health care organizations, teams, and technology change and evolve. Changes in measurement include both the development of new instruments and the improvement of current ones. Finally, we discuss how the instruments and the data they provide and our model of team performance can be used to facilitate education and consultation with teams and help them better monitor and evaluate their own development, effectiveness, and performance.

Criteria for Determining "Best Measures"

In designating instruments as state-of-the-art, we considered both their conceptual and methodological soundness. We identified instruments with a clearly articulated underlying conceptual model or theory. Additionally, we searched for instruments measuring relevant and unique elements of team performance and instruments with adequate breadth and depth of concept coverage. We also expected clear and unambiguous items and response options, readability appropriate for the target group, and clear, practical scoring and interpretation procedures. We considered evidence of reliability and validity, although the level of psychometric support we accepted was related to the instrument's purpose. Finally, we looked favorably on instruments whose developers used more than one method of data collection and had developed normative data for interpreting scores.

A standardized application of the criteria above was difficult to apply across instruments due to differences in the complexity of concepts measured, populations assessed, and ways in which results are used. For example, validity is easier to establish for instruments measuring a single aspect of team performance than for those measuring multiple facets of it. An expedient instrument designed as an educational aid to stimulate team discussion does not need to demonstrate the same high level of reliability and validity as one designed for research and evaluation. An instrument that requires a high level of reading proficiency can be considered well designed for a target audience of professionals, but not when recommended for use with all types of health care workers.

We found quality measures among all four categories of instruments critiqued in Chapters 9 through 12 of this volume. Our choices were not influenced by comprehensiveness with regard to measuring the team performance concept per se. Such comprehensive instruments almost always target teams within complex organizations and tend to be lengthy. Thus, they are not appropriate for all types of teams or for all measurement purposes (e.g., large-scale research projects or self-monitoring by team members themselves).

Some of the instruments have exceptional or unique features, but lack a sufficient number of the factors mentioned above for us to designate them as state-of-the-art. These we labeled honorable mention instruments. In many instances, they would qualify as state-of-the-art with minor revisions or psychometric testing.

"Best Measures"

We selected 15 instruments as "best measures," nine state-of-the-art and six honorable mention. Critiques of these instruments appear in Chapters 9 through 12, Focused, Middle-Range, Broad-Spectrum, and Full-Spectrum Instruments, respectively. In these chapters, we identified "best measures" by an asterisk next to their respective names in the critique titles and by bold face print in the summary tables in part two of this volume. Our intent in this chapter is to highlight features of the instruments that resulted in their selection as "best measures."

We believe the instruments presented in Tables 14.1 and 14.2 are sound instruments worthy of "best measures" status and first consideration by readers searching for a measure of team performance. The designation as state-of-the-art does not mean we believe they are flawless measures. Some would benefit from additional psychometric testing, and many have minor problems noted in the critiques by reviewers. Additionally, a state-of-the-art instrument will not always be the best choice for a specific situation. Readers attempting to measure team performance need to balance numerous factors prior to selecting an instrument, such as the target audience, the time available for completion, and the ultimate use of the information obtained. Each of the instruments reviewed in this book is likely to be a good choice for specific needs and circumstances. Lastly, our decision not to designate a measure as state-of-the-art does not imply that it has serious flaws. There are many promising instruments among those reviewed for which there is simply not enough information about their psychometric properties or general usability to determine overall utility at this time.

State-of-the-Art

Three focused instruments were selected as state-of-the-art–the adaptation of Baggs' Collaboration and Satisfaction about Care Decisions by Schmitt, Heinemann, and Farrell; Bailey and Helsel-DeWert's Rating Individual Participation in Teams; and Heinemann, Schmitt, and Farrell's Attitudes Toward Health Care Teams. All three instruments have sound conceptual/theoretical bases, and each is a strong, comprehensive measure of its respective underlying concept(s). Baggs' instrument (in both original and adapted forms) is unique in its measurement of collaboration related to a specific decision-making situation. Heinemann and colleagues' Attitudes Scale includes a measure of physician centrality, a concept infrequently measured in team performance instruments. Bailey and Helsel-DeWert's instrument is unique because it employs two forms of data collection and has test-retest reliability data, making it a legitimate "tracker" of meeting effectiveness over time. All three are research instruments with psychometric data attesting to their reliability and validity. The latter two are dual-purpose measures as well. Bailey and Helsel-DeWert's instrument can help teams assess, monitor and improve their meeting effectiveness, and Heinemann, Schmitt, and Farrell's instrument has been used successfully to evaluate the impact of a large-scale educational intervention (Hyer et al., 2000).

One middle-range instrument, Lichtenstein and colleagues' Team Integration Measure, meets state-of-the-art criteria. Based on a strong theoretical framework, it is a short, concise research tool measuring within team integration. It is unique in its measurement of accomplishments and has good preliminary reliability and validity data.

Table 14.1. State-of-the-Art Instruments

Instrument	Original Developer(s); Adapters	Type	Rationale for Selection
Team Climate Inventory (TCI)	Anderson & West	Broad-Spectrum/ Health Teams Ch. 11 & 13	Measures facets of team climate that predict innovation; good preliminary reliability & good validity data
Collaboration Satisfaction about Care Decisions	Baggs; Schmitt, Heinemann & Farrell	Focused/ Health Teams Ch. 9 & 13	Strong theoretical framework; good measurement of collaboration; unique in its measurement of collaboration related to a specific decision-making situation; good reliability & strong validity data; short, concise research instrument appropriate for busy professionals
Rating Individual Participation in Teams	Bailey & Helsel-DeWert	Focused/ Health Teams Ch. 9 & 13	Good measurement of meeting effectiveness; unique in its collection of data from team members & observers; dual purpose–assess, monitor & help improve team meeting effectiveness & research; strong reliability & validity
Team Development Survey (TDS)	Campbell & Hallam	Full-Spectrum Ch. 12	Broad measurement of team performance, data collected via self-administered & observer forms; good reliability & validity data; can be used legitimately to monitor performance over time
Team Effectiveness Profile (TEP)	Glaser & Glaser	Full-Spectrum Ch 12	Multi-purpose–assess & help improve functioning, identify stage of development, research; good preliminary reliability & validity data; normative data established

Two broad-spectrum instruments–Anderson and West's Team Climate Inventory and Schmitt and colleagues' adaptation of Shortell and Rousseau's ICU Nurse/Physician Instrument–are included as state-of-the-art. Both are well-constructed research measures. The former assesses support for innovation within the team, and developers have demonstrated its utility in a wide variety of settings. It is unique in its measurement of strategies for productivity; it has good preliminary reliability and strong validity data. The latter instrument and its adaptation both have strong reliability and validity data. The brevity of Heinemann and colleagues' adaptation makes it appropriate for large-scale research with busy health professionals.

Table 14.1. State-of-the-Art Instruments (continued)

Instrument	Original Developer(s); Adapters	Type	Rationale for Selection
Attitudes Toward Health Care Teams	Heinemann, Schmitt & Farrell	Focused/ Health Teams Ch. 9 & 13	Good conceptual framework; dual purpose–research & evaluate educational intervention; strong reliability & validity data
Team Integration Measure	Lichtenstein, Alexander, Jinnett & Ullman	Middle-Range/Health Teams Ch. 10 & 13	Strong theoretical framework; short, concise research instrument appropriate for busy professionals; good preliminary reliability & validity data
ICU Nurse/Physician Instrument	Shortell & Rousseau; Schmitt, Heinemann & Farrell	Broad-Spectrum/ Health Teams Ch. 11 & 13	Strong reliability & validity data; adaptation is short, concise research instrument appropriate for busy health professionals
Group Development Questionnaire (GDQ)	Wheelan & Hochberger	Full-Spectrum/ Health Teams Ch. 12 & 13	Strong, validated theoretical framework; multi-purpose–assess, monitor & help improve functioning, identify stage of development, research; training required for use; strong reliability & validity data; normative data established

Three instruments meet the criteria for state-of-the-art from the full-spectrum category, Campbell and Hallam's Team Development Survey, Glaser and Glaser's Team Effectiveness Survey, and Wheelan and Hochberger's Group Development Questionnaire. All three are proprietary measures with broad coverage of the team performance concept. Each of these instruments measures all eight dimensions of our team performance model. The first instrument's purpose is to assess and facilitate the improvement of team functioning. It is unique in its collection of data from both team members and observers, and it has good reliability and validity data. The second and third instruments are both multi-purpose measures; both assess and facilitate the improvement of team functioning, identify a team's stage of development, and are strong research tools. Glaser and Glaser's instrument has good preliminary reliability and validity data and normative data established. Wheelan and Hochberger's instrument has a strong theoretical framework, strong reliability and validity data, and has normative data established. Both Campbell and Hallam's and Wheelan and

Hochberger's instruments have adequate test-retest reliability that supports their use as monitors of team performance over time. These state-of-the-art instruments are summarized in Table 14.1.

Honorable Mention Instruments

Two instruments in the focused category deserve honorable mention, Aram and colleagues' Team Collaboration Index and Farrell and colleagues' Team Anomie Scale. The first instrument is based on an organizational model that emphasizes collaboration and consensus for promoting the goals of both individual employees and the organization in which they are located. It is short, easy to administer and score, and has good reliability and preliminary validity data. The second instrument is dual-purpose in that it can be used to assess and help improve team functioning and in research. It has good theoretical underpinnings and strong reliability and validity data. It is most appropriate for assessing new teams.

One middle-range instrument, Kormanski and Mozenter's Team-Development Rating Scale, received honorable mention status. It identifies a team's stage of development and the task and relationship outcomes related to each stage. This short, duel purpose measure has a strong theoretical basis that links leadership style with stage of development; it also has preliminary reliability and validity data. Additional psychometric support and some rewording of items and answer choices, suggested in its critique, would make it an even stronger measure.

Two broad-spectrum instruments are worthy of honorable mention, Jones and Bearley's Group Development Assessment and McGregor's Analyzing Team Effectiveness. Jones and Bearley's instrument has a strong theoretical framework that expands the traditional developmental stages beyond the four or five usually identified. The instrument identifies the current stage of development along the dimensions of task behaviors and process behaviors. Although there are numerous steps to scoring, instructions are clearly presented. Scoring sheets and guidelines for action planning accompany the instrument. McGregor's instrument is one of the earliest developed to assess managerial and work groups in organizations. It is based on a strong theoretical framework, McGregor's own Theory Y. Both his instrument and his theory have influenced the development of numerous other measures. Although it is short, it covers a relatively large number of team performance dimensions. Its brevity makes it easy to use for self-monitoring, in workshop settings, and for short consultations. There are no psychometric data to support its reliability or validity; an item analysis is useful to summarize and present results.

Table 14.2. Honorable Mention Instruments

Instrument	Original Developer(s); Adapters	Type	Rationale for Selection
Team Collaboration Index	Aram, Morgan & Esbeck	Focused Ch. 9	Good theoretical framework; good reliability & preliminary validity
Team Anomie Scale	Farrell, Schmitt & Heinemann	Focused/ Health Teams Ch. 9 & 13	Good theoretical framework; dual-purpose–research & assess/help improve functioning; strong reliability & validity
Group Development Assessment (GDA)	Jones & Bearley	Broad-Spectrum Ch. 11	Strong theoretical framework; identifies stage of development along two dimensions (task behaviors and process behaviors); scoring sheets and clearly written action planning guides accompany the instrument
Team-Development Rating Scale	Kormanski & Mozenter	Middle-Range Ch. 10	Strong theoretical framework; dual purpose–research & assess/help improve functioning; identifies stage of development & the task and relationship outcomes associated with each stage; preliminary reliability & validity data; short, concise instrument appropriate for busy professionals
Analyzing Team Effectiveness	McGregor	Broad-Spectrum Ch. 11	Strong theoretical framework; major influence on the development of other assessment instruments; good coverage of team performance for a short instrument
Team Assessment Worksheets	McClane	Full-Spectrum/ Health Teams Ch 12 & 13	Broad, yet concise measurement instrument; includes unique facets of team performance in the areas of external and internal context, team process, and outputs of the team (e.g., team accomplishments including patients' outcomes); serves as an excellent example of how to customize facets of the team performance model for a specific type of health care team

McClane's Team Assessment Worksheets, a full-spectrum measure, is included in the honorable mention group. It was designed to be part of a team assessment and education package. Insufficient psychometric data are available to determine the measure's utility as a stand-alone assessment of team performance. It is a shorter measure than others in the full-spectrum category, but still includes seven of the eight dimensions in our team performance model. It was developed for clinical rehabilitation teams, a group not frequently targeted by other instruments. The honorable mention instruments are summarized in Table 14.2.

FUTURE DIRECTIONS IN MEASUREMENT

The instruments summarized above as state-of-the-art and honorable mention are excellent tools for assessing team performance in many situations. However, there are still important gaps in the measurement of the team performance concept and its many facets. In this section, we consider issues at three levels with regard to future measurement. First, how can a more integrative, widely shared model of team performance unify thinking and provide an impetus to research and practice in interprofessional care? Second, what areas of team performance, omitted from or not adequately assessed in current instruments, require inclusion in future instruments? And, third, what methodological research efforts might reduce or eliminate the limitations and expand the usefulness of some of the current instruments?

Using the Team Performance Model to Guide Measurement

Our efforts to critique instruments and identify the current "best practice" measures were guided by our model of team performance, presented in Chapter 3 and expanded upon in Chapters 4 through 7. We believe that instrument development is highly dependent upon theory, so our goals have been both to develop a model to help understand and organize the current instruments measuring facets of team performance and to help guide the development of future ones.

Using our model can facilitate unification of a field that has been characterized, to date, by fragmentation. Currently, most team educators and researchers develop and use theory based upon their own idiosyncratic challenges and experiences rather than building on the integrative efforts of many professionals. Although micro-level, setting-specific models can be useful in looking at local issues, efforts based upon such work are not powerful in advancing the field of interdisciplinary or interprofessional teamwork. We advocate for the use of an integrative approach and our model of team performance in future educational, research, and practice efforts. We welcome further development and refinement of the model. We believe the elements identified to date are essential, and elimination of any of them would weaken it. We are aware that continuing changes in the health care system could reduce the relevance of some of the elements in measuring team performance, however.

While our efforts have been broad and integrative, additional efforts are necessary. Many theories applicable to team performance describe similar constructs and relationships among them using discipline-specific jargon. Thus, translating terms and developing a common language remains a goal yet to be accomplished. More work also is needed to integrate the organizational and management literatures within a team performance framework. This effort would facilitate the assessment of relationships between teams and the organizations in which many are embedded and function.

In addition, work integrating basic science into practical models of team performance would be fruitful. For example, Bandura (2000) has expanded his work on self-efficacy to consider a new concept of "collective efficacy." He has argued that individuals' beliefs in their ability to produce desired outcomes and prevent undesired outcomes are the major underlying elements in determining whether people become motivated to act and persist in difficult courses of action. He has extended this notion to consider how a shared, "collective" sense of efficacy "fosters groups' motivational commitment to their missions, resilience to adversity, and performance accomplishments" (Bandura, 2000, p. 75). Although he does not explicitly link the concept of collective efficacy to interdisciplinary team performance, the relevance of his ideas to the field is obvious. Future efforts to incorporate this approach and other concepts coming out of basic research in human motivation and performance can provide fresh, innovative perspectives that will help to further elucidate a truly comprehensive model of team performance.

Finally, as the health care system continues to change, our model will require modification to reflect the impact of such changes on team performance. For example, members of a virtual clinical team are dispersed geographically although they share one population of patients and need to coordinate their treatment and care activities. Virtual teams add new issues to the measurement of performance with regard to how commitment, cohesion, and team identity are developed and nurtured and how technology is used for effective communication. In addition, health professionals and health workers are becoming members of multiple teams. These employees must learn to manage the complexities of conflicting loyalties and expectations across teams. They must learn to shift easily among teams in different stages of development and with different norms, values, and cultures. Such complexities are not included and measured in current theory and assessment.

Long-term, our model of team performance will require continuing review and development as organizational and management theories, basic science, and a continuously changing health care system push the boundaries of what is currently known about team performance and what needs to be included in its measurement. Short-term, the domains, dimensions, and elements of our model of team performance require additional measurement and refinement since current instruments do not capture its full complexity. This state of affairs can be remedied by developing new instruments and strengthening those currently available and in use.

Developing New Instruments

Challenges confronting the developers of future instruments measuring team performance are threefold. The first is to develop more comprehensive instruments that measure more of the domains, dimensions, and elements of our team performance model than do current instruments. The second is to develop more focused instruments that measure elements of performance that are changing and emerging as the health care system changes. Because of their changing nature, they are not adequately covered in current instruments. The third is to develop instruments that collect data about a team's performance from respondents and/or observers outside the team as well as from team members themselves.

Need for Comprehensive Measures

Current instruments are multidimensional, but many are not truly comprehensive. Several important dimensions of our model of team performance are omitted or not measured in much depth. The most underrepresented dimensions of the model in current instruments are organizational structure and context and both dimensions of productivity–strategies for productivity and accomplishments (see Table 14.3). Given that more and more health care teams function within complex organizations, organizational structure and context influence the functioning and productivity levels of teams. These dimensions of performance must be addressed more precisely in future measurement instruments. Many current measures address teams apart from their organizational settings, as if they were freestanding entities that control their own missions, goals, and resources. Although teams, especially high-performing ones, do have some autonomy and control, it is increasingly important to understand the team embedded within a complex organization both for purposes of research, evaluation, and education designed to facilitate team development.

Today strong support for health care teams requires them to be accountable and provide evidence of their productivity. Thus, future measures of team performance must address strategies for productivity as well as actual accomplishments. While instrument developers are beginning to address teams' outcomes due to pressure to be cost-effective in a high cost health care environment, less effort has been given to identifying and measuring the strategies teams use to be productive and provide quality products, services, and outcomes. Developing comprehensive assessment instruments that capture these dimensions is an important agenda item for the future. Some of the instruments critiqued in Chapters 12 and 13 can stimulate ideas with regard to such measurement.

Measuring New and Expanding Concepts

While we advocate for the development of more comprehensive, full-spectrum instruments, more focused instruments that concisely measure a few, new and important elements of performance also are needed. For many research, evaluation, and educational/self-assessment purposes, the overall performance of the team is not the relevant issue. Instead, team members often want to focus on a particular problematic area, understand it better, and set goals for improvement. Instruments that measure facets of performance among virtual teams need to be developed; such instruments could expand the measurement of communication to include the use of new technology (e.g., phone mail, e-mail, audio and teleconferences, the Internet, and the use of palm pilots or small, hand-held computers). Future instruments might also expand the concept of meeting effectiveness to include the use of technology in preparing for and conducting meetings. And finally, instruments that assess employees' experiences as members of multiple teams need to be developed, which would expand the concept of team member flexibility. Additional work also is required with regard to assessing the level of success teams have training future health professionals to work in teams, often with a specific patient population.

Expanding Respondent and Data Collection Options

Most current instruments rely only on individual team members' self-reports. While members' perceptions of themselves as team members, their perceptions of other team members, and their perceptions of the team, itself, are important, more objective measures of performance need to be developed as well. Future instruments should collect team performance data from all relevant customers of a team both inside and outside the organization,

Table 14.3. Team Performance Instruments by Dimensions of Performance Measured

Developer(s); Adapters	OS	TS	OC	TC	I	G&D	SP	A
Alexander		X		X	X	X	X	
Anderson	X	X	X	X	X	X	X	X
Anderson & West		X		X	X	X	X	
Aram, Morgan & Esbeck				X	X	X		
Bader, Bloom & Chang		X		X	X	X	X	X
Baggs; Schmitt, Heinemann & Farrell				X	X			
Bailey & Helsel-DeWert				X	X	X		
Burns & Gragg (Meeting Evaluation)		X		X	X			X
Burns & Gragg (Work Group Effectiveness)		X			X	X	X	
Campbell & Hallam	X	X	X	X	X	X	X	X
Campion, Medsker & Higgs	X	X	X	X	X	X		X
Carew, Parisi-Carew, Stoner & Blanchard		X		X	X	X	X	X
Chartier	X	X		X	X			
Dimock (Team Development)				X	X	X		
Dimock (Post Meeting Reaction)		X		X	X			X
Dyer (Team Development)		X		X	X			
Dyer (Team Maturity)	X	X		X	X	X	X	
Elledge & Phillips	X	X	X	X	X	X	X	X
Epstein, Baldwin & Bishop; Waite & Harker		X		X	X	X		X
Farrell, Schmitt & Heinemann		X		X	X			
Francis & Young	X		X	X	X	X	X	X
Gibb		X		X	X	X		X
Glaser & Glaser	X	X	X	X	X	X	X	X
Goodstein, Cooke & Goodstein		X		X	X			
Hall	X	X		X	X			
Harper & Harper (Team Meeting)		X		X	X			
Harper & Harper (Team Building)	X	X	X	X	X	X		X
Heinemann, Schmitt & Farrell		X		X				
Hepburn, Tsukuda, & Fasser						X		
Hoevemeyer	X	X	X	X	X	X	X	
Jamieson	X	X	X	X	X	X	X	X

Developer(s); Adapters	OS	TS	OC	TC	I	G&D	SP	A
Kormanski & Mozenter		X		X	X		X	
Lawler, Cammann, Nadler & Jenkins	X	X		X	X	X		
Lazar		X		X	X	X		X
Lazar; Brown	X	X	X	X	X	X		
Lewis	X	X	X	X	X		X	X
Lichtenstein, Alexander, Jinnett & Ullman		X		X	X			X
McClane	X	X	X	X	X	X		X
McGregor		X	X	X	X			X
Moos & Humphrey; Schmitt et al.		X		X	X	X	X	X
Parker (Cross Functional Teams)	X	X	X		X	X	X	
Parker (Team Development)		X	X	X	X	X	X	
Parry	X	X	X	X	X	X	X	X
Pfeiffer & Jones (Group Growth)		X		X	X	X		
Pfeiffer & Jones (PostMeeting Evaluation)				X	X			
Preziosi		X		X	X	X	X	
Reagan	X	X	X		X	X		
Richards & Smyth	X	X	X	X	X	X	X	X
Rothermich & Saunders	X	X		X	X	X	X	X
Schein		X		X	X	X		
Shortell & Rousseau; Schmitt et al.			X		X	X	X	X
Tercon, Inc.	X	X		X	X	X	X	X
Tsukuda & Stahelski		X		X	X	X	X	
Varney (Team Effectiveness)		X		X	X	X		X
Varney (Team Profile)		X		X	X	X		
Varney (TWS)	X	X		X	X			X
Weisbord		X		X	X			
Wheelan & Hochberger	X	X	X	X	X	X	X	X
Wilson Learning Corporation	X	X	X	X	X	X	X	X
Zoglio	X	X		X	X	X	X	

NOTE: The abbreviations used as column headings represent the eight dimensions of our model of team performance; OS = Organizational Structure; TS = Team Structure; OC = Organizational Context; TC = Team Context; I = Interdependence; G&D = Growth & Development; SP = Strategies for Productivity; A = Accomplishments.

including patients and their family members for clinical teams. Customers are identified in more detail in Chapter 7. New instruments should ascertain customers' perceptions of the team and how well or effectively it functions and accomplishes its goals as well as their satisfaction with its performance. Observational measures that capture the actual behavior of team members as they meet and work together should be developed as well. Data from such instruments provide corroboration for the subjective experiences reported by team members and the reports of others in contact with the team.

Improving Current Instruments

As we mentioned previously, a number of the team performance instruments might rival those selected as "best measures" if they had psychometric data to support their reliability and validity. Methodological research is needed to strengthen current instruments and determine whether or not they are reliable and valid measures of facets of team performance. Such psychometric testing would make an excellent project in graduate or undergraduate research or statistics courses or could be undertaken by team researchers, educators, and/or consultants who have easy access to teams in health care settings. A natural starting point for such efforts would be to determine whether items in a particular instrument can be scaled or whether they are independent of one another and should be analyzed separately. Another starting point would be to establish the test-retest reliability for instruments purporting to track changes in team performance over time or to determine the appropriateness of an instrument's use in evaluating the impact of an educational intervention as a pre/post-test measure. Demonstrating that particular instruments are sensitive to change would be a major contribution to the field.

Psychometric testing, too, can improve the wording and clarity of an instrument's items and eliminate any items unrelated to the concepts being measured. Pilot testing current instruments with a team also can improve item wording, item and answer choice formatting, and instructions to respondents. Pilot testing also permits team members to provide feedback about the face validity of concepts being measured. For example, are they mutually exclusive and exhaustive? Do they contain extraneous items?

Finally, developing norms for some of the current team performance instruments would be beneficial. At the present time, we can compare the scores of particular teams against theoretically defined "ideal" performance, which may be an unrealistic benchmark. Teams might be better served by knowing how they are doing compared to other teams in similar settings or other teams at comparable stages of development. Developing such norms is not a simple matter since locating large numbers of team members in any local setting is challenging. Collaborative efforts among team researchers using an integrative model of team performance and combining data sets would be one way to establish normative data. Developing national data sets from team performance research, which could be utilized by networks of researchers, also would facilitate this effort.

FUTURE DIRECTIONS IN EDUCATION AND CONSULTATION

Using the model of team performance and an assessment instrument in an educational program or consultation with teams can enhance members' understanding of the team performance concept and improve their ability to self-monitor such performance. We have some experience using the model for training in workshops and consultations with specific teams. Heinemann recently used the model and an assessment instrument in an educational consultation with six teams–five nursing home teams and a home based primary care team in one VA medical center. Team members completed an assessment form and returned it to her prior to her consultation visit. The form included McGregor's 10-item instrument (Analyzing Team Effectiveness), a question about satisfaction with the team, and open-ended questions asking team members to list two strengths and one weakness of their respective teams. For each team, she prepared an item analysis showing the average team score and the range of responses for each item of McGregor's instrument. Average scores ascertained whether perceptions of the team were positive, negative, or neutral for each facet of team effectiveness measured; the range served as an indicator of consensus among members. She also created a summary list of perceived strengths and weaknesses of the team from the perspective of its members. These she grouped under the appropriate domains and dimensions of the team performance model. She used the model to guide the discussion about what the team does well and where it needs to improve. Strengths and weaknesses also were compared to the data from McGregor's instrument.

Heinemann found that using the team performance model as an organizing framework for presenting and discussing a team's strengths and weaknesses stimulated team members to think in broader terms about their team. Given an exposure to the eight dimensions of team performance, they were able to identify additional strengths and weakness that had not come to mind earlier when they completed the assessment form. Comparing their list of strengths and weaknesses with their quantitative results also helped them elaborate on, clarify, and come to consensus about what the team does well and where it needs to continue to develop and improve.

Similar positive impact resulted when we used the model to organize educational presentations about team theory and team functioning. Bringing together the domains, dimensions, and elements of team performance, this model facilitates the integration of other information and experiences. As a result, it is a powerful tool for evaluating team performance instruments and for educating and consulting with teams. It provides a framework for analyzing and interpreting assessment data to gain a comprehensive overview of teams' strengths, weaknesses, and areas where additional educational efforts should be focused.

REFERENCES

Bandura, A. (2000). Exercise of human agency through collective efficacy *Current Directions in Psychological Science. 9*, 75-78.

Hyer, K., Fairchild, S., Abraham, I., Mezey, M., & Fulmer, T. (2000). Measuring attitudes related to interdisciplinary training: Revisiting the Heinemann, Schmitt and Farrell 'attitudes toward health care teams' scale. *Journal of Interprofessional Care, 14*, 249-258.

INDEX

accomplishments, 15, 21, 30, 33, 39-41, 43, 47, 65, 67, 68, 71, 73, 89, 97, 99, 100, 101, 108, 289, 334; *see also* outcomes

accountability, 24, 39, 44, 55, 49, 82, 94, 218, 395

action plan, 13, 51, 90, 98, 100, 163, 215

Alderfer's Imbedded Intergroup Relations Theory, 195

analysis of variance (ANOVA), 121

attitudes, 47, 50, 53, 63, 102, 106, 155, 179, 195, 246, 355, 373

authority, 35, 37, 39, 46, 77, 140, 155, 191, 196, 258, 268, 277, 371, 372

Bandura's Self/Collective Efficacy Theory, 393

Beckhard, 316, 322

Blansfield's Team Effectiveness Theory, 165,166

boundaries, 22, 50, 54, 55, 277, 356
  insulation, 62, 78, 83, 84
  permeability, 54, 196

career development, 36, 58, 59

climate/environemnt, 13, 36-38, 53, 57, 60, 62-65, 68, 77, 98, 100, 103, 106, 140, 148, 163, 179, 184, 202, 218, 246, 253, 261, 272, 326, 334, 370; *see also* context

cohesion, 8, 13, 39, 61-64, 66-68, 79, 140, 295, 316, 326; *see also* stages of development

collaboration, 5, 13, 21, 31, 37, 38, 46, 53, 54, 61, 75, 79, 92, 93, 103, 106, 107, 127, 131, 136, 144, 258, 350, 366, 370, 373

commitment, 13, 36-38, 43, 44, 46, 49-51, 57-59, 61-63, 66-68, 76, 77, 95, 99, 107, 155, 176, 184, 188, 200, 225, 258, 295, 296, 316, 331, 340, 347

communication, 13, 34, 38, 48, 49, 61, 63, 65, 66, 73-75, 79, 82, 93-95, 102, 104, 160, 163, 165, 174, 176, 179, 202, 205, 215, 236, 272, 286, 295, 304, 326, 331, 347; *see also* feedback, group processes, and technologies

competence/competencies, 44, 47, 58, 72, 76, 82

concurrent validity, 26, 27, 118; *see also* psychometric testing

confidence/self-esteem, 11, 53, 57, 61, 62, 64, 67, 77, 78, 102, 103

conflict, 8, 13, 35, 37, 38, 51, 52, 54, 59, 65, 76-80, 98, 166, 195, 196, 205, 277, 295, 350; *see also* group processes and stages of development
  disagreement, 64, 65, 78, 94, 272, 277
  management/resolution, 72, 78, 79, 80, 107, 215, 295

consistency, 13, 46, 47, 51, 53, 91

construct validity, 26, 27, 118; *see also* psychometric testing

consultation to teams, 14, 15, 19, 22, 23, 38, 39, 48, 76, 90, 98, 117, 119, 136, 250, 253, 258, 319, 399, 400

content or face validity, 26, 27, 118; *see also* psychometric testing

context, 12, 30, 32, 36, 37, 57, 58, 63, 68, 71, 231, 312, 394; *see also* climate

contribution, 13, 46, 72, 188, 253, 295, 347

cooperation, 52, 76, 90, 131, 205, 295, 312
  of respondents, 22, 23

coordination/organization, 61, 68, 76, 77, 97, 102, 104, 322, 331

correlation coefficient, 120

cost-effectiveness, 19, 24, 61, 76, 93, 94, 96 101, 104, 108, 289

creativity, 58, 64, 72, 77, 83, 85, 86, 97, 215, 326

Cronbach's alpha, 120

cross-training, 84, 85

customer relations/service, 40, 80, 103, 240, 331; *see also* satisfaction

data quality, 22, 23, 119, 199, 211, 330

decision-making, 44, 49, 61, 62, 64, 65, 72, 78, 80, 83, 85, 93, 100, 107, 131, 179, 195, 205, 218, 236, 289, 326, 344, 347, 378; *see also* groupthink
  compromise, 13
  consensus, 8, 13, 78, 80, 127, 239, 272, 286, 326; *see also* stages of development

dependency, 8, 31, 351; *see also* stages of development

discriminant validity, 27, 118; *see also* psychometric testing

diversity, 72, 86, 107, 195, 236, 272, 277, 326

education/training, 3, 14, 16, 17, 22, 24, 38, 39, 48, 59, 60, 66, 72, 76, 82, 89, 92, 94, 98, 99, 101, 107, 136, 141, 144, 160, 181, 191, 200, 250, 253, 258, 319, 343, 366, 399, 400
  of students/trainees, 3, 4, 40, 75, 91, 106, 107

efficiency, 6, 7, 19, 40, 46-49, 52-54, 60, 63, 65, 67, 71, 76, 81, 84, 89, 92-95, 102, 280, 295, 307

effective/well functioning teams, 6-8, 13, 38-40, 43, 46, 47, 50-53, 58, 60, 64, 65, 66, 73, 75, 76, 81, 83, 86, 91, 92, 96-98 101, 102, 136, 140, 144, 155, 160, 165, 166, 176, 179, 183, 191, 196, 202, 236, 239, 240, 272, 295, 316, 340, 344, 394; *see also* interdependence, interdisciplinary team, self-managed team, and stages of development
  barriers/blockages to, 13, 27, 31, 37, 74, 75, 100, 136, 155, 140, 195, 319, 322

employee assistance, 58, 59

401

energy/enthusiasm, 37, 59, 65, 67, 79, 99, 101, 104, 304, 316, 340
expectations, 19, 36, 37, 44, 50, 52-54, 57, 58, 60, 61, 64, 77, 83, 89, 96, 97, 99, 100, 356
factor analysis, 120, 121
feedback, 39, 49, 58, 74, 75, 83, 84, 166, 176, 203, 218, 231, 236, 350; *see also* communication
feedback system, 13, 14, 83, 155, 355
flexibility, 36, 37, 39, 45, 60, 84, 85, 202, 218, 236, 295
geographic proximity, 35, 36, 46, 54
goals, 5, 7-10, 29, 36, 37, 40, 43, 44, 47, 50-53, 55, 59, 63, 64, 67, 72, 81, 84, 85, 90-93, 100, 127, 136, 148, 163, 166, 176, 187, 188, 195, 200, 202, 205, 215, 218, 231, 236, 268, 289, 292, 295, 316, 322, 331, 343, 344, 350, 355, 356, 373; *see also* stages of development
  individual/personal, 52, 66, 343
  task-oriented/process, 8, 9, 13, 40, 81, 90
group processes/process or maintenance behaviors, 8, 14, 30, 33, 36, 38, 39, 51, 54, 57, 58, 61, 67, 71, 73, 80, 81, 86, 89, 97, 100, 104, 183, 195, 202, 205 222, 242, 280, 281, 289, 292, 307, 312, 316, 319, 322, 334, 337, 340
groupthink, 62, 69, 72, 78, 84; *see also* decision-making
growth/development/maturation, 6, 8, 14, 29, 36, 38, 39, 48, 58-60, 54, 65, 76, 78, 81-83, 86, 90, 98, 101, 136, 140, 148, 141, 181, 184, 191, 200, 203, 205, 215, 227, 236, 242, 349, 272, 319; *see also* stages of development
individual development plan, 40, 90, 92
informal learning, 83, 93, 98, 101, 202, 203
information management, 94-96
innovation, 37, 58, 60, 83, 85, 86, 218
instrument evaluation, 116, 118, 119
instrument selection and use 124, 125, 170, 171, 211, 299-301, 361, 362, 364, 365, 386-389, 91, 396, 397
instruments, types of
  best measures, 116, 122, 126, 127, 131, 135, 148, 155, 173, 191, 195, 212-214, 217, 242 257, 280, 302, 303, 307, 321, 334, 349, 361, 362, 364, 386-392
  broad-spectrum, 115, 209-214, 388-391
  focused, 115, 123-126, 383, 387, 390
  full-spectrum, 115, 299-303, 389-392
  middle-range, 115, 169-173, 388, 390
  observational, 23, 26, 135, 140, 215, 307, 361, 387, 389
interdependence, 5, 8, 33, 36, 38-40, 46, 47, 61, 65, 68, 72, 86, 144, 236, 240 312, 326; *see also* effective teams
interdisciplinary/interprofessional team, 5, 8, 9, 38, 47, 75, 86, 102, 104, 105; *see also* effective teams
internal consistency reliability, 25, 118, 120; *see also* psychometric testing
inter-rater reliability, 26, 118; *see also* psychometric testing
leadership, 9, 10, 13, 35, 36, 38, 47, 64, 66, 68, 76-78, 82, 83, 94, 101, 102, 107, 184, 188, 205, 227, 280, 289, 292, 307, 316; *see also* power and responsibility
  effectiveness, 47, 77, 78, 101
  sharing, 8, 10, 47, 53, 76, 77, 86, 101, 140, 215, 225, 236, 272, 316, 326
  skills, 36, 37, 47, 77, 78, 83, 98, 100, 101, 106, 107
  style, 10, 11, 36, 38, 39, 57, 63, 77, 85, 101, 191
McMaster Model of Family Functioning, 230, 231
marketing, 40, 41, 51, 89, 96, 97
meetings, 13, 14, 21, 40, 54, 82, 93, 94, 97, 100, 101, 104, 136, 152, 163, 174, 181, 356
metaphor, 116, 117
mission/purpose, 8, 35-37, 40, 43-45, 50, 51, 54, 55, 61, 63, 66, 67, 81, 85, 99, 101, 102, 148, 187, 191, 202, 225, 253, 272, 322, 326, 340
morale, 37, 58-62, 65, 67, 68, 78, 99, 224, 225, 239
motivation, 49, 58, 60-62, 66, 67, 222, 331
multidisciplinary team, 8, 56, 104-106
Nahavandi & Aranda, 277
negotiation, 80
norms/values, 35, 36, 44, 50, 53, 58, 60, 66, 74, 79, 82, 94, 107, 183, 184, 187, 188, 202, 350, 370
normative/standardized data, 118, 119, 388-390, 398
outcomes, 14, 39, 41, 47, 53, 59, 62, 66, 71, 78, 86, 89, 95, 97, 99-101, 104-108, 131, 165, 191, 195, 205, 222, 231, 280, 292, 296, 304, 312, 334, 377 393, 395; *see also* accomplishments
participation/involvement/sharing, 8, 35, 36, 38, 53, 72, 73, 77, 78, 100, 104, 136, 140, 163, 178, 195, 236, 268, 272, 381
patient care plan, 3, 13, 91, 95, 160, 284, 286
planning, 40, 45, 49, 51, 55, 61, 75, 77, 80, 90-93, 97, 100, 131, 160, 319, 322
  priorities, 50-55, 60, 85, 160
power, 35, 36, 47, 60, 76, 86, 163, 165; *see also* leadership
predictive validity, 26, 27, 118; *see also* psychometric testing
problem solving, 8, 13, 38, 49, 54, 64, 65, 72, 78, 85, 100, 102, 195, 205, 289, 344, 373
productivity, 19, 21, 30, 33, 39, 40, 43, 46, 47, 52, 53, 58-62, 65, 67, 68, 71, 72, 76, 82, 84,

86, 89, 92, 98, 101, 102, 106-108, 140, 141, 181, 205, 222, 224, 225, 236, 239, 253, 275, 289, 292, 296, 304, 312, 394, 395
psychometric testing, 24-27, 118, 120, 121, 125, 126, 170-173, 210, 212-214, 300, 302, 303, 398; *see also* types of reliability and validity
purpose of instruments, 23, 117-121, 126, 172, 173, 212-214, 302, 303, 361, 362, 364, 365, 388, 389, 391
regulations/rules/procedures, 8, 13, 35, 36, 44, 45, 49, 51-53, 55, 85, 98, 141, 148, 166, 176, 181, 188, 202, 205, 215, 289, 292, 316; *see also* stages of development
relationships/interactions, 10, 64, 67, 80-82, 85, 205, 231, 280, 289, 292, 304, 316, 373
  across organization, 19, 40, 41, 46, 58, 62, 63, 67, 99, 102, 103, 268, 272, 322, 331, 337
  interpersonal, 9, 19, 36, 58, 59, 63, 81, 127, 183, 184, 322, 350
reliability, 24, 25; *see also* internal consistency, inter-rater, and test-retest reliability
resources, 13, 31, 38, 41, 44, 46, 54, 55, 57, 59-62, 68, 72, 73, 75, 77, 84, 85, 202, 304, 307, 331, 350
respect/value/care about, 13, 58, 59, 61, 64, 65, 67, 71, 82, 96, 103, 107, 165, 176, 183, 188, 240, 296
responsibility, 6, 11, 36, 37, 40, 46, 61, 64, 73, 75, 76, 78, 83, 98, 99, 101, 131, 196, 205, 340, 347, 373; *see also* leadership
rewards/recognition, 13, 15, 31, 34, 40, 41, 49, 50, 55, 59, 61, 68, 77, 89, 96, 99, 103, 106, 188, 222, 268
risk-taking, 83, 85, 179, 236, 296, 326, 340, 347
roles, 11, 12, 35, 37, 38, 46, 48, 50, 52, 53, 64, 68, 79, 83, 91, 98, 107, 140, 148, 166, 174, 176, 188, 195, 205, 215, 236, 272, 289, 292, 316, 322, 334, 344, 350; *see also* stages of development
  role bending, 84; *see also* informal learning
Rubin, Fry, & Plovich, 205, 289, 292
satisfaction, 14, 37, 38, 41, 48, 49, 59, 61-63, 67, 68, 78, 96, 103, 127, 131, 188, 307, 312, 367, 370, 394; *see also* customer relations
Sherif & Sherif's basic/minimal conditions for teamness, 187
skills, 14, 38, 47-49, 53, 54, 64, 67, 72, 74, 76-79, 82, 83, 91, 98, 100, 101, 106, 107, 152, 160, 163, 165, 176, 183, 184, 195, 258, 268, 286, 295, 343; *see also* leadership skills
space, 46, 50, 54
stages of development, 7-12, 29, 35, 37-39, 59, 63, 65, 76, 98, 99 101, 102, 116, 136, 140, 148, 155, 191, 203, 215, 224, 225, 236, 242, 319, 349, 350; *see also* growth/development/maturation

Jones' Model of Group Development, 242
Lacoursiere's Group Development Stage Theory, 224, 225
Tuckman/& Jensen, 148, 242, 272
standards, 13, 39, 44, 50, 53, 77, 81, 187, 188
statistical significance, 121
Starchevich & Stonell, 316
strategies for productivity, 33, 39, 40, 41, 89, 97, 98, 100, 108
stress/pressures, 52, 59, 62, 65, 66, 73, 97, 102, 148, 377
structure, 12, 30-32, 34-36, 43, 44, 48, 50, 54, 55, 71, 141, 148, 165, 181, 187, 188, 205, 292, 350, 394
results driven, 13, 53, 100
support/encouragement, 8, 10, 39, 64, 66, 74, 75, 77, 82, 83, 85, 86, 140, 236, 272, 304, 350
  of organization/management. 13, 31, 34, 36, 37, 41, 43, 46, 48, 50, 57, 58, 61, 62, 68, 82, 85, 100, 102, 218, 268, 277, 381
systems thinking, 19, 99, 107
Tajfel's Social Identification Theory, 195
task orientation/behaviors/effectiveness, 8, 10, 37, 38, 47, 48, 50, 51, 53, 61, 64, 67, 72, 81, 82, 85, 97, 100, 183, 200, 218, 242, 360
team approach, 3-5, 7, 13, 31, 44, 46, 57, 58, 68, 97, 99, 104, 107
team identity/unity, 37, 39, 62-64, 66-68, 101, 148, 187, 188, 195, 196, 347
team performance assessment/evaluation, 13-15, 22-24, 89, 96-98, 101, 102, 106, 108, 181, 222, 225, 258, 307, 350
  self-monitoring of, 13-15, 97, 98, 200, 205, 215, 272, 326, 340
team performance measurement, 19-24, 108, 115, 117, 119, 121, 123-125, 169, 170, 209, 210, 299, 300, 385, 392-395, 398, 399
  in health care, 14, 359, 360, 366
  instrument adaptation, 362-364, 366
team performance model, 29, 30, 32, 33, 41, 71, 86, 100, 102, 108, 115, 117, 121, 122, 392-394, 399, 400
teams, types of
  clinical or treatment, 4, 5, 9, 13, 14, 35, 40, 41, 47, 51, 54, 62, 73, 84, 90, 93-96, 103, 104, 117, 170, 196, 359, 362
  natural work groups, 5, 6, 9, 35, 36, 57, 84, 90, 96, 359
  performance improvement, 4, 6, 8, 9, 90, 99, 107, 359
  self-directed, self-managed, 6, 9, 76, 100-102, 152, 239, 326, 347
  virtual, 34, 93, 95, 393
team size, 47, 85, 102
team spirit, 63, 67
team within organization (framework), 29, 116, 144, 184, 191, 222, 253, 268, 280, 304, 311,

312, 331, 337, 343, 346, 347, 356, 367, 377, 381
 Hackman & Oldham, 246
 McGregor's Theory Y, 200, 258, 343
 morale theory, 367
 Shepard, 127
technology, 34, 41, 49, 60, 81, 82, 85, 92-94
test-retest reliability, 25, 26, 120, 211, 387, 390, 398; *see also* psychometric testing
Thomas' Collaboration Model, 80, 131

time/cost constraints, 58, 60, 61, 71, 73, 78, 80, 104, 166, 174, 350
time management, 41, 89, 97, 205, 289, 292
trust, 37, 39, 57, 58, 61, 64, 65, 67, 68, 75, 77, 79, 98, 103, 107, 103, 127, 141, 179, 215, 236, 316, 326, 350
validity, 24, 25-27, 121; *see also* content, concurrent, construct, discriminant, and predictive validity
Veterans Affairs, 3-5, 34, 95, 100, 107